Postcolonial Criticism

LONGMAN CRITICAL READERS

General Editor:

STAN SMITH, Professor of English, University of Dundee
Published titles:
K.M. NEWTON, *George Eliot*
MARY EAGLETON, *Feminist Literary Criticism*
GARY WALLER, *Shakespeare's Comedies*
JOHN DRAKAKIS, *Shakespearean Tragedy*
RICHARD WILSON AND RICHARD DUTTON, *New Historicism and Renaissance Drama*
PETER BROOKER, *Modernism/Postmodernism*
PETER WIDDOWSON, *D.H. Lawrence*
RACHEL BOWLBY, *Virginia Woolf*
FRANCIS MULHERN, *Contemporary Marxist Literary Criticism*
ANNABEL PATTERSON, *John Milton*
CYNTHIA CHASE, *Romanticism*
MICHAEL O'NEILL, *Shelley*
STEPHANIE TRIGG, *Medieval English Poetry*
ANTONY EASTHOPE, *Contemporary Film Theory*
TERRY EAGLETON, *Ideology*
MAUD ELLMANN, *Psychoanalytic Literary Criticism*
ANDREW BENNETT, *Readers and Reading*
MARK CURRIE, *Metafiction*
BREAN HAMMOND, *Pope*
GRAHAM HOLDERNESS, BRYAN LOUGHREY, ANDREW MURPHY, *Shakespeare's Roman Plays*
LYNN PYKETT, *Reading* Fin de Siècle *Fictions*
REBECCA STOTT, *Tennyson*
STEVEN CONNOR, *Charles Dickens*
ANDREW HADFIELD, *Spenser*
TESS COSSLETT, *Victorian Women Poets*
BART MOORE-GILBERT, GARETH STANTON AND WILLY MALEY, *Postcolonial Criticism*

Postcolonial Criticism

Edited and Introduced by

BART MOORE-GILBERT,
GARETH STANTON AND WILLY MALEY

Longman
London and New York

Addison Wesley Longman
Edinburgh Gate
Harlow
Essex CM20 2JE
England
and Associated Companies throughout the world.

Published in the United States of America
by Addison Wesley Longman Inc., New York.

First published 1997

ISBN 0 582 23797 1 CSD
ISBN 0 582 23798 X PPR

British Library Cataloguing-in-Publication Data

A catalogue record of this book is available
from the British Library

Library of Congress Cataloging-in-Publication Data

A catalog entry for this title is available
from the Library of Congress

Set by 35 in 9/11.5pt Palatino
Produced by Longman Singapore Publishers (Pte) Ltd.
Printed in Singapore

i 137 65590

Contents

General Editors' Preface

The outlines of contemporary critical theory are now often taught as a standard feature of a degree in literary studies. The development of particular theories has seen a thorough transformation of literary criticism. For example, Marxist and Foucauldian theories have revolutionized Shakespeare studies, and 'deconstruction' has led to a complete reassessment of Romantic poetry. Feminist criticism has left scarcely any period of literature unaffected by its searching critiques. Teachers of literary studies can no longer fall back on a standardized, received, methodology.

Lecturers and teachers are now urgently looking for guidance in a rapidly changing critical environment. They need help in understanding the latest revisions in literary theory, and especially in grasping the practical effects of the new theories in the form of theoretically sensitized new readings. A number of volumes in the series anthologize important essays on particular theories. However, in order to grasp the full implications and possible uses of particular theories it is essential to see them put to work. This series provides substantial volumes of new readings, presented in an accessible form and with a significant amount of editorial guidance.

Each volume includes a substantial introduction which explores the theoretical issues and conflicts embodied in the essays selected and locates the areas of disagreement between positions. The pluralism of theories has to be put on the agenda of literary studies. We can no longer pretend that we all tacitly accept the same practices in literary studies. Neither is a *laissez-faire* attitude any longer tenable. Literature departments need to go beyond the mere toleration of theoretical differences: it is not enough merely to agree to differ; they need actually to 'stage' the differences openly. The volumes in this series all attempt to dramatize the differences, not necessarily with a view to resolving them but in order to foreground the choices presented by different theories or to argue for a particular route through the impasses the differences present.

The theory 'revolution' has had real effects. It has loosened the grip of traditional empiricist and romantic assumptions about language and literature. It is not always clear what is being proposed as the new agenda for literary studies, and indeed the very notion of 'literature' is questioned by the post-structuralist strain in theory. However, the uncertainties and obscurities of contemporary theories appear much less worrying when we see what the best critics have been able to do with them in practice. This series aims to disseminate the best of recent criticism and to show that it is possible to re-read the canonical texts of literature in new and challenging ways.

RAMAN SELDEN AND STAN SMITH

The Publishers and fellow Series Editor regret to record that Raman Selden died after a short illness in May 1991 at the age of fifty-three. Ray Selden was a fine scholar and a lovely man. All those he has worked with will remember him with much affection and respect.

Acknowledgements

We are grateful to the following for permission to reproduce copyright material:

The author's agents for an extract from 'An Image of Africa: racism in Conrad's *Heart of Darkness*' by Chinua Achebe in *Hopes and Impediments: Selected Essays 1967–87* (published Heinemann); Harper Collins Publishers/Grove Weidenfeld for the article 'On National Culture' by Frantz Fanon in *The Wretched of the Earth* (originally published by McGibbon & Kee, 1955); Monthly Review Foundation for an extract from *Discourse on Colonialism* by Aime Césaire, trans. John Pinkham. © 1972 by Monthly Review Press (originally published as *Discours sur le Colonialisme* (Paris, Editions Presence Africaine, 1955)); the Editor, Oxford Literary Review, for '"Race", Time and the Revision of Modernity' by Homi K. Bhabha, from *Neocolonialism* ed. Robert Young in *Oxford Literary Review* 13 (1991) © 1991 Oxford Literary Review; Oxford University Press for the article 'Toward a Theory of Minority Discourse: What is to be done?' by Abdul R. JanMohamed and David Lloyd in *The Nature and Context of Minority Discourse/Cultural Critique Nos 6 and 7* (1992); the author's agents for 'Orientalism Reconsidered' being a speech by Edward Said reprinted in *The Proceedings of the Essex Conference on the Sociology of Literature,* July 1985. © 1985 by Edward Said (originally published in the Autumn 1985 edition of *Race and Class.* Reprinted by permission of The Wylie Agency Inc); the author, Prof. Gayatri Chakravorty Spivak for her article 'Three Women's Texts and a Critique of Imperialism' in *'Race', Writing and Difference* ed. H.L. Gates (1986, Columbia University Press); Turnaround Press Ltd for 'Revolutionary Black Women: Making Ourselves Subject' by bell hooks in *Black Looks: Race and Representation*; Verso/New Left Books Ltd for excerpts from *In Theory: Classes, Nations, Literatures* by Ahjaz Ahmad. © Verso/New Left Books 1992;

Postcolonial Criticism

We have been unable to trace the copyright holder of 'West Indian Literature and the Australian Comparison' by Diana Brydon and Helen Tiffin from *Decolonising Fictions* (Dangaroo Press, 1993) nor the whereabouts of Homi K. Bhabha, and would appreciate any information which would enable us to do so.

The authors would also like to acknowledge the assistance of Maria MacDonald in the preparation of their text.

Introduction

Orientations

Postcolonialism is one of the most fruitful and rapidly expanding fields in current academic study. It is interdisciplinary, appealing across a range of subjects, with a particularly strong base in literary and cultural studies. Yet despite, or perhaps because it has inspired some of the most challenging academic work in recent years, postcolonialism remains an elusive and contested term. It designates at one and the same time a chronological moment, a political movement, and an intellectual activity, and it is this multiple status that makes exact definition difficult. It is significant that much of postcolonial criticism is concerned with self-definition, with circumscribing a space – academic, geographical, political – within which something called postcolonialism can occur. Every new movement or school sooner or later breaks down, through internal division or under external pressure. In the case of postcolonialism, this process of dissolution has marked it from its inception. Most essays that begin by asking what postcolonialism is soon turn into diagnoses of what is wrong with it. It is difficult to think of a modern intellectual practice that has been subject to more self-criticism. Questions of the type 'What is . . . ?', that is, questions of definition, are both crucial and difficult, crucial because in a sense postcolonialism is about difference, but difficult because to try to fix the meaning of the term, and, by extension, the terms of the debate, is to engage in the politics of identity and exclusion. We have therefore chosen in this introduction to display oppositions as much as to define positions. In fact, many of the essays that seek to define postcolonialism circle around the themes mapped out below. What we want to do in this Introduction is to raise a few questions of a more specific nature, and to signpost some relevant texts and contexts. Precisely what postcolonialism is remains a fraught question, and it may be more profitable to begin this discussion by asking, not what, but when,

1

where, who, and why. Rather than ask 'What is it?', let us go and make our visit.

When is 'the postcolonial'? Does 'post' mean 'after', 'semi', 'late', 'ex' or 'neo'? There is a tendency for critics to focus on the modern, post-enlightenment period as the definitive epoch of imperialism, ignoring classical and renaissance precedents. Postcolonial critics work in the modern period, and therefore colonialism is of the modern period. This simple tautology is rarely questioned. Postcolonialism possesses a 'problematic temporality'. One of the things that postcolonialism does is to undo neat chronologies. Clearly an entrenched periodization is as dangerous as the claim that postcolonialism represents nothing, but culture, by virtue of its fragmentation and repetition, is anachronistic. The time of postcolonialism is out of joint. As academics, we are often slaves to our own periods, and it comes as no surprise that we find the origins of capitalism or colonialism at the threshold of our special subject areas. The 'post' in postcolonial can imply an end, actual or imminent, to apartheid, partition and occupation. It hints at withdrawal, liberation and reunification. But decolonization is a slow and uneven process. Postcolonialism, if it is a period, had to be, by its very nature, a period that is characterized by a suspicion of progress. After all, it was in a period of so-called progress for the West that the rest of the world had its development arrested, its resources exploited, and its people enslaved. What was done in the name of progress, of historical advance, can be seen now as backward, degrading, reactionary.

A new generation of academics have responded to postcolonialism as a rallying point for a fresh assessment of the interaction of class, race and gender. There is a growing constituency of diasporic critics working in Western universities. This can be seen as a process of infiltration, an overturning from within. There is a division within postcolonialism between those who are happy with the emphasis on culture and literature and theory, and those who – though they may themselves be academics – see real politics as taking place outside the teaching machine. Clearly this approach is to some extent gendered, and reflects on one level a 'masculine', but also a 'Leftist' discomfort with reading and writing as insufficiently revolutionary activities: an old anxiety that underestimates the power of education as a force for change. Postcolonialism occupies the space between the ivory tower of a cloistered academic world – one which is always less insular than it sometimes imagines itself to be – and a larger cultural community. It is not a question of choosing, but of negotiation and transgression. If postcolonialism is interdisciplinary, it is not immune to disciplinary critique. As our conclusion indicates, the charge of 'appropriation' underlies many of the criticisms of postcolonialism, but even here attitudes differ.

One way to orient postcolonialism would be to place it between Marxism and existentialism, because many of its practitioners fuse political radicalism with a fundamental reconception of the self, in what Fanon called a stretching of Marxism, and others have termed a new humanism or a revolutionary psychology. Another approach would be to situate it in the space between literary and cultural studies. The advent of postcolonialism heralds the end of consensus in higher education in two ways. On the one hand, the growing presence of Third World intellectuals within Western academe has foregrounded and concretized the issue of cultural difference. On the other hand, as the humanist project, in its Western manifestations, has become exhausted, and as its teachers become disenfranchised and cynical, a new humanism has taken hold, championed by these new critics. It is only proper that a domain of study that is preoccupied with ambivalence, hybridity and migrancy, should itself be marked by such in-betweenness – between theory and practice, between literary and cultural studies, between Marxism and existentialism, between localism and universalism, between personal and public, between self and state.

In terms of political orientation, postcolonialism is a site of radical contestation and contestatory radicalism. Postcolonialism's relation with Marxism is complex. In 1913 Lenin wrote of 'backward Europe and advanced Asia', predicting revolutionary storms in the East, in a move away from an earlier Marxist position that had looked to the advanced capitalist countries to lead the struggle for socialism. Henceforth the colonies would hold the key to world revolution. While Arif Dirlik accuses postcolonial critics of lacking a critique of global capitalism, much postcolonial theory has acted as a focal point for socialist criticism. In an important sense, postcolonial theory marks not only the return of the repressed, or the return of the native, but the return of class as a marker of difference. A concern with social class and revolution is evident in the work of Fanon, Ahmad and hooks, all of whom, together with Cedric Robinson, Cornel West and others, share a profound concern with the interface between race and class.[1] At a time when theory, and literary theory in particular, was moving away from class-based criticism, these critics have brought it back into the reckoning. Postcolonialism has come up against classical Marxism, taking issue with Marx's famous formulation on the 'Asiatic mode of production'. Moreover, the concept of class itself – never fully elaborated by Marx – is reoriented. One can detect in Gayatri Spivak's use of 'subaltern' the echo of a term Marx recovered from history for his own purposes – 'proletarian'. Conversely, there are those who see in postcolonialism not the return of the repressed, but the return of the Same in the guise of the Other. The language of race, class and nation is commuted into a universal crisis of 'identity' that makes these vexed issues more palatable within the academy/Thus, from this perspective, postcolonialism would not be a radicalization of postmodernism or Marxism, but a domestication of anti-colonialism and anti-racism.

The question of language is crucial, and not simply at the level of a national language, but in terms of idiom, since many of the arguments within postcolonial theory turn on exactly how critics should discuss their subject, with a sharp divide between what the editors of *Fanon: A Critical Reader* (1996) attack as 'theoretical decadence', and what Henry Louis Gates, Jr calls, after Paul de Man, the 'resistance to theory'.[2] The work of Spivak, with its sophisticated vocabulary, might suggest that theory is not intrinsically masculine, while the writings of bell hooks manage to combine a passionate commitment to theory with an insistence on a polyphonic critical discourse. Paradoxically, hooks is frequently charged with being insufficiently theoretical.

Postcolonialism can be used to provide alternative understandings of 'cultural' production, for example, opening up the question of the relationship between 'orature' and literature. Literature is dominant, from the title of Achebe's novel, *Things Fall Apart*, drawn from Yeats's 'The Second Coming', to the influence of Shakespeare evident in Aimé Césaire's *Une Tempête* (1969), and Octave Mannoni's *Prospero and Caliban* (1950). Another pair of quotations from the same canonical texts might serve here as reminders of two issues central to postcolonialism: namely the reversal or displacement of the core-periphery model of development, indeed the questioning of 'development' itself, and the issue of whether the colonial subject comprises both colonizers and colonized. 'The centre cannot hold', and 'This thing of darkness I acknowledge mine', aptly summarize much recent debate.[3] The subtitle of hooks's *Feminist Theory: From Margin to Center* signals the decentring or recentring of what was hitherto deemed liminal, while Prospero's owning of, and owning up to Caliban, can be read alongside arguments around the colonial subject between Bhabha and JanMohamed, for example, and the accusations of appropriation, and what or who is properly postcolonial.[4]

Postcolonialism impinges upon questions of nationalism. Aijaz Ahmad is one of a number of critics who point out that while some in the West herald the end of the nation-state, that formation remains dominant, both in the West and in the rest of the world.[5] Postcolonial critics often have a stake in postcolonialism as a political process in the context of specific national struggles. One thinks here of Fanon and Algeria, and Said and Palestine. It is common for postcolonial critics to be exiles. As exiles, their relationship with the colony in the act of becoming 'post' is complex. A common criticism of postcolonial critics working in the West is that they cannot properly appreciate or understand the places they have left behind, or those to which they have never belonged. The issue of location is a key theme. It is the whole question of belonging, and the status of the insider/outsider, that postcolonialism serves to dislocate. It is a contested fact of postcolonial criticism that no simple oppositional model can capture the relationship between colonizer and colonized. Assimilation, integration and collaboration prolong the colonial experience. The existence of a national bourgeoisie immediately complicates any simplistic oppositional model.

In the spirit of Arif Dirlik, the glib answer to the question 'Where is postcolonialism?' would be 'in the academy'. Another response, equally appropriate and equally problematic is that, like Foucault's conception of power, postcolonialism is everywhere. Both responses will worry those who resist universality and insist that the University is a privileged site removed from political struggle, and who maintain that the true sphere of postcolonial activity should be the former colonies, and not the colonizing countries. But Europe and the West are not coterminous, nor are they homogeneous/ One of the features of postcolonialism that can be seen as enabling or appropriative depending on one's standpoint is that the binarism that placed 'Europe' or 'the West' in opposition to an 'East' or an 'Orient' or a 'Third World' is no longer tenable or easily accepted. To see Europe and the West as self-evident and self-contained entities is to repeat the imperialist and colonialist mythologies that one is supposed to be deconstructing.

Following on from this undoing of the opposition between East and West, the second aspect of the location of postcolonialism is its geographical remit. This raises the problem of 'internal colonialism' within the British Isles, and of the status of indigenous peoples in America, Australia and New Zealand, and touches on issues of allegiance and place within the international community. 'Including America', as Peter Hulme has argued, is both imperative and controversial.[6] The work of David Lloyd on Ireland, and Said's treatment of Yeats's nationalism in terms of 'negritude' in *Culture and Imperialism*, together with the essays by Terry Eagleton, Fredric Jameson and Edward Said collected in *Nationalism, Colonialism and Literature* offer a series of approaches to this problematic. Following Said, Lloyd links 'the celebratory nationalism of "Celtic Twilight" or "Negritude" formations which reverse the stereotype but thereby preserve predominant social relations as the given'.[7] Of course, once we accept the idea of 'internal colonialism' then we might have to acknowledge that, as a Pole, Joseph Conrad was himself a colonial subject. This inclusiveness, seen by some as liberating, is viewed by others as a dilution of the specificity of the colonial experience.

Another way in which postcolonialism can be approached, turning back to the question of theory, is by way of its relations with other 'postisms', such as post-structuralism, post-Marxism, post-communism, post-realism or post-industrialism. Postcolonialism is seen to entail on one level a political critique of postmodernism around questions of race and Empire. It raises questions too about the role of the intellectual, the way in which postmodernism as a category may be seen to be in some ways bound up with the university, especially in 'the West'. Certainly the place of intellectuals, their responsibility to a culture, community and country, has been a key feature of postcolonialism. It also asks specifically about the place of English literature within postmodernism. Thus one might think of the postcolonial not as a phase or a space but as an individual, an intellectual, so that where one previously spoke of the humanist, or the New Critic, or the deconstructivist, one now speaks of the postcolonial.[8] Sara Suleri has complained of being treated as an 'otherness machine', while Kwame Anthony Appiah speaks of the pressure on postcolonial intellectuals 'with the manufacture of alterity as our principal role'.[9] This is the plight of the postcolonial intellectual, being called upon or brought out as an example of difference: the subaltern, the native informant. This raises once more the question of authenticity, local knowledge, and the insider/outsider dichotomy. Post-structuralism is another term often juxtaposed with postcolonialism. The post-structuralist 'critique of the subject' has come under fire from postcolonial critics who see in it an attempt to ward off new, oppositional subjectivities. Anti-essentialism, implicit in the critique of 'negritude', for example, can become a way of attacking other people's essences.[10]

In *Beyond Ethnicity: Consent and Descent in American Culture*, Werner Sollers distinguishes between identity as determined – descent – and as autonomous – consent.[11] What postcolonialism provides is a way of deconstructing, or negotiating the difference between consent and descent. It is not a question of securing assent or consensus. Cornel West, one of those who are unhappy about the dominance of literature in postcolonialism, speaks of 'dissensus'.[12] It is to the maintenance of this productive dissensus, rather than its resolution, that the most challenging work in this field is dedicated. If this is disorientating, if it makes some critics lose the place, if it entails a change of position and perspective, as well as a possible transformation of places – the world turned upside down – then perhaps this is to be celebrated rather than lamented. Postcolonialism, notwithstanding the pedagogical necessity of a Reader like this to present a unified, coherent view of what is debatable terrain, is also about dissent from the canon and the conservative cultural consensus that nurtures it. Dissent is the one thing all postcolonial critics, and critics of postcolonialism, agree on, and it is dissent that marks the essays that follow as both representative and exemplary, not all-encompassing, but compass readings of a map whose co-ordinates are constantly shifting.

Nonetheless, it was Senghor's championing of negritude which gave the concept such currency and enabled a range of positions to be included under the rubric. In sum, negritude can be regarded as both the historical movement of French-speaking black intellectuals, and the statement that there is something intrinsic to the black world. In respect of this latter sense we can refer to Senghor himself: 'Negritude is simply the totality of civilising values of the Negro world. It is not racism, but culture; it is a situation understood and overcome in order integrate and harmonise with the cosmos.'[24] In fact, Senghor defined negritude in a variety of different ways in his writings. 'Feeling', he once wrote, 'is negro.'[25] Much of his own verse celebrates Africa, its distinctive rhythms, colours and smells, whereas that of Césaire, the other key figure in the movement, concentrates chiefly on the myths spun by the colonialists. Césaire's famous poem, *Return to my Native Land*, reveals another side to the romantic images of the Caribbean promulgated by the French – lives led in poverty, under the imperial gaze: 'At the end of the wee hours burgeoning with frail coves, the hungry Antilles, the Antilles pitted with smallpox, stranded in the mud of this bay, in the dust of this town sinisterly stranded.'[26] The aggressive rejection of assimilation comes across clearly in the lines of another of the founders of the movement, Leon Damas, here taken from his poem 'Solde' ('Sell-out'):

I feel ridiculous
among them
like an accomplice
among them
like a pimp
like a murderer among them
my hands hideously red
with the blood of their
ci-vi-li-za-tion.[27]

It can be seen then that negritude is a movement which grew up in opposition to the values and codes of European civilization as they were conceived within the colonial context, a civilization with its roots in ancient Greece and Rome and its pinnacle in the colonial powers of the nineteenth and twentieth centuries; an arrogant cultural formation which denied that there was anything of any interest or worth in the other cultures encountered in the process of colonial expansion. Indeed it was part of the same series of historical expansions which saw the development of the Atlantic slave trade and the attempts at the radical erasure of cultural identity, sense of self and rootedness. Movements such as the Harlem Renaissance or negritude both push against the flow of such denials, attempt to negate the refusals and non-recognitions of

9

the oppressive 'Other' by giving substance and shape to cultural forms which have been simply ignored, or worse, denigrated by the world of the West. No longer would a black poet feel forced to write in the following tones of despair: 'It's no joke: a Latin among the Celts and with the features of a Celt – I say this with no wish to mock. And this is what I am: imperiously, violently, naturally, a Latin among the Melanians. And with the latter's features.'[28] This is the voice of the Malagasy poet Jean-Joseph Rabearivelo, as recorded in his personal journal. Rabearivelo was seen by Senghor as both 'a precursor and an emblem'[29] of the negritude movement, and his poetry was anthologized in Senghor's 1948 collection.

While negritude was embraced with some fervour, it has always had its critics. Probably the best known among these is the French philosopher and writer Jean-Paul Sartre, who contributed the introduction to Senghor's celebrated anthology. While applauding the collection itself, Sartre went on in the piece, which he entitled 'Black Orpheus', to suggest that this was only the first step. In a well-known paragraph the philosopher commented as follows:

> Negritude is the low ebb in a dialectical progression. The theoretical and practical assertion of white supremacy is the thesis; negritude's role as an antithetical value is the negative stage. But this negative stage will not satisfy the Negroes who are using it, and they are well aware of this. They know that they are aiming for human synthesis or fulfilment in a raceless society. Negritude is destined to destroy itself; it is the path and not the goal, the means but not the end.[30]

Whether negritude should eventually cede priority to 'class' in line with the progress of the Marxian dialectic is a question which still influences contemporary debate. Indeed, Fanon's refusal to follow Sartre here is one of the reasons which Homi Bhabha gives to underline Fanon's importance for postcolonial critics.[31] Without evoking class, however, other critics have challenged the abiding power of an ideology of 'blackness' to generate lasting unity in those diverse parts of the world where the black diaspora finds itself. Stanislas Adotevi invokes the experiences of the American, Richard Wright, and the South African, Peter Abrahams, in their own travels in Africa. Their failure to feel at one with the Africans themselves, Adotevi suggests, is evidence for the assertion that there can be no shared negritude in the modern world.[32] Under such conditions Adotevi argued, negritude was no more than an 'artificial quest for tradition', or 'a cheap search for the exotic'.[33] Some critics have drawn attention to the differences between Césaire and Senghor and singled out the latter, in particular, for criticism. Marcien Towa argues that 'the contrasting of negro emotivity and white rationality' effectively ensures the subordination of one to the other.[34]

A younger generation of writers has been even more outspoken in their criticisms, seeing in a number of proponents of negritude a form of collaboration with and capitulation to French culture. This has been partially a result of the political careers which writers such as Senghor have subsequently followed, but also reflects a critique of some of the early sources of inspiration for many of the pioneers of negritude. In a controversial novel, *Bound to Violence* (1971), the Malian novelist Yambo Ouologuem produced an outspoken denunciation of negritude which is described as a 'magico-religious, cosmological, and mythical symbolism'[35] based on the teachings of 'Shrobenius', a drooling fraud and charlatan. Shrobenius is a thinly veiled portrait of the German anthropologist Frobenius whose ethnographic work had a deep influence on the early protagonists of negritude. These critiques are analysed in Christopher Miller's *Theories of Africans* (1990).

Some Francophone critics have fiercely debated the scope and value of negritude but others remain unmoved. Sembene Ousmane, the Senegalese novelist and film-maker stated that 'to me it is like the sex of the angels'.[36] While criticism of negritude has been voiced within the Francophone world, Sembene's response resembles more closely those of Anglophone Africa which has always proved more resistant to its blandishments. The South African critic Ezekiel Mphahlele has suggested that this is no surprise and can be accounted for in part by the different administrative strategies employed by the British in Africa, so-called 'indirect rule'. That is not to say that Mphahlele rejects the historical relevance of negritude for its pioneers; rather, he suggests, 'as an artistic program' negritude 'is unworkable for modern Africa'.[37]

Despite all these disputed positions (and this is only a selection of the numerous authors who have written on the subject), the negritude movement must be acknowledged as an important development in the critique of Western imperialism. The later positions of some of the founder members of the movement may seem increasingly naïve and self-serving in the eyes of some commentators, but work such as that of Césaire retains its original power and his *Discourse on Colonialism* (1955) is still a rich source of insight for students of empire and colonialism. One recent critic, Abdulrazak Gurnah, suggests that 'At the heart of the discourse of negritude is an Africanness in direct and precise defiance of the imperial metaphors of African savagery, ugliness and stupidity.'[38] Its significance, Gurnah suggests, is that it represents an attempt to engage Europe's representations of Africa in a critical fashion. This engagement continued over the years in the shape of *Présence Africaine*, the journal which grew out of the negritude movement in Paris, and which, as V.Y. Mudimbe suggests, had as its central project a rigorous questioning of the imperial ambition of Western civilisation.[39]

11

Frantz Fanon

Frantz Fanon is a figure around whom the arguments about how the postcolonial struggle is to be waged in terms of theory and practice continue to circulate. If critics are divided between those who see humanism and modernity as incomplete projects that can be improved and extended, and those who take up vehemently anti-enlightenment and anti-humanist positions, then it is not surprising that Fanon should be a 'battlefield' for such debates, since his combination of a militant anti-imperialism and a reconstructed and reoriented humanism make him a strong ally for either side. Indeed, the fact that Fanon is constantly enlisted in order to support competing causes is itself a source of conflict. Some readers are opposed to Western appropriations of Fanon. Yet others see him as a fundamentally Western figure, and detect in his adoption of Algeria another form of appropriation.

Fanon is a transgressive figure in that he manages to combine opposition to cultural imperialism with a vigorous defence of culture as a strategy of resistance and a locus of national identity. Because it is bound up with language and race, culture, whether imperialist or liberatory, shapes the mind as well as the map. Thus Fanon's early work is situated at the interface between radical psychology and colonial critique, and his linking of mental disorders with imperialist domination is one of his most important contributions to contemporary debates around postcolonialism. In *Black Skin, White Masks*, Fanon arguably laid the groundwork for a modern black existentialism that continues to resonate, and nowhere more so than in the African–American context, where it fuses with his humanism to form a radical cultural politics preoccupied with the realities and fantasies of daily living.

There are those who want to detach Fanon the revolutionary from Fanon the psychiatrist, a split which the genealogy and chronology of Fanon's work might be seen to invite. The problem with this split is that it assumes a development or a deformation, or at least an incoherence. Just as Marx's early work is often opposed or juxtaposed to his later writings, so Fanon is seen either to have matured into a more revolutionary position, or to have abandoned a youthful humanism for a more strident – and cynical – rhetoric of confrontation. Yet when we read *Black Skin, White Masks* alongside *The Wretched of the Earth* what is most striking is the way in which Fanon constantly exposes the interplay of psychological and political factors, showing time and again that colonialism affects individuals as well as societies. In this respect, Fanon's work forces us to take psychoanalysis seriously, and to attend to the pervasive influence of empire in fantasy, fiction and ideology.

Fanon's theorizing of the relationship between colonialism and psychology is the most significant feature of his early work. Indeed, while it would be tempting to see this initial phase of Fanon's theoretical development as part of a process of political maturation, a move from psychology to revolution, we ought to regard such a developmental account of his work with some suspicion. The notion that Fanon's thought followed a progressive trajectory from his training as a psychiatrist to his active participation in the Algerian Revolution is, in any case, flawed in so far as Fanon's psychiatric practice can be viewed as a decisive intervention in that wider political struggle. To try to choose between Fanon the psychologist and Fanon the revolutionary is to compartmentalize a thinker whose greatest gift was an ability to splice a politics of self-emancipation with an ideology of national liberation. Whether we celebrate or decry the resultant radical mix of humanism, culturalism, nationalism and existentialism depends upon our appreciation of each and our attitude to their transformation in Fanon's discourse.

Another crucial aspect of Fanon's work is his refiguring of the concept of the nation. As Edward Said observes: 'Fanon was the first major theorist of anti-imperialism to realize that orthodox nationalism followed along the same track hewn out by imperialism, which while it appeared to be conceding authority to the nationalist bourgeoisie was really extending its hegemony. To tell a simple national story therefore is to repeat, extend, and also to engender new forms of imperialism.'[40] Fanon, though he challenges the modern orthodoxy that nationalism is 'a phase that humanity has left behind', and warns against those who desire to 'skip the national period', remains sceptical about the narrow national interests of the native bourgeoisie.

If one strategy of containment enacted by critics is contextualism or historicism, then another is universalism, the inclination to make of Fanon a type, an example. The will to particularity goes hand-in-hand with an urge to universalize. Henry Louis Gates, wary of Edward Said's efforts to make Fanon global, insists that remembering Fanon

> means *reading* him, with an acknowledgement of his own historical particularity, as an actor whose own search for self-transcendence scarcely exempts him from the heterogeneous and conflictual structures that we have taken to be characteristic of colonial discourse. It means not to elevate him above his localities of discourse as a transcultural, transhistorical Global Theorist, nor simply to cast him into battle, but to recognize him as a battlefield in himself.[41]

Derek Wright, on the other hand, claims that Fanon is almost irrelevant from an African perspective, being chiefly a European figure. Fanon himself – at least in one of his guises – argued that: 'The responsibility of the native man of culture is . . . a global responsibility with regard to the totality of the nation, whose culture merely, after all, represents one aspect of that nation.'[42]

Fanon's humanism also presents a problem for critics, especially in view of the fact that many anti-colonial figures see humanism – and the humanities – as part of the problem rather than part of the solution. There is no doubt that Fanon saw himself as expounding a new philosophy of 'Man' through a critique of colonialism, arguing that 'in the specific case of the North African who has emigrated to France, a theory of inhumanity is in a fair way to finding its laws and its corollaries'.[43] Fanon's militant humanism harbours a powerful critique of colonialism. His conception of the interconnectedness, interdependence and implicatedness of global relations led him to declare that: 'The future of every man today has a relation of close dependency on the rest of the universe. That is why the colonial peoples must redouble their vigilance and their vigor. A new humanism can be achieved only at this price.'[44]

Fanon's influences, and his influence, his sphere of influence, continues to be the subject of much debate. Those who wish to preserve Fanon as an example of the active, committed, political intellectual, tend to overlook the fact that Fanon's strength was his knitting together of theory and practice, and that to use him as an antidote to theoreticism is inappropriate. Fanon's work tends to undo the distinction between theoretical reflection and political action. The list of figures who informed Fanon's work includes Marx, Nietzsche, Freud, Sartre and Lacan. Marxism, psychoanalysis, phenomenology, and existentialism all feed into Fanon's approach to questions of race, culture and colonialism. Some critics see this eclecticism as both enabling and ennobling, but for others the dependence upon Western theory is an obstacle to a more radical ethos. Derek Wright sees Fanon's immersion in European culture as limiting, and maintains that 'the social and political analysis of postcolonial Africa on which Fanon based his own recommendations was severely flawed by inaccuracy and simplification'.[45] Wright, in a familiar complaint, portrays Fanon as an outsider who never quite comprehended his subject. But of course Fanon is no more a final authority on Algeria and Africa than is Wright, and rootlessness is arguably the lot of every postcolonial intellectual, rather than a particular ailment of some. Given his charged advocacy of violent resistance to colonial rule, it may be surprising that Fanon has been well-received in the West, and not simply, as Wright would have it, for guerrillas and terrorists. Yet Wright's view of Fanon as an outsider is shared by other critics who have addressed the vexed issue of his representativeness, his right to be cited as a source of local knowledge. Irene Gendzier concludes:

'For him to have understood the arabization problem would have required a greater familiarity not only with Algerian and Arab culture, but with the complicated relations of that culture and the West.'[46] Gates elaborates thus: 'As Fanon's biographers remind us, most Algerian revolutionaries scant his role and remain irritated by the attention paid to him in the West as a figure in Algerian decolonization: to them – and how ironic this is to his Western admirers – he remained a European interloper.'[47] It is ironic, too, that Fanon, such a determined transgressor of boundaries, should in the end fall victim to a discourse of purity and exclusivity.

If culture, humanism, Marxism and nationalism are all stretched by Fanon in order to accommodate the colonial situation, then his conception of colonialism appears at first glance to be restrictive. Thus Fanon maintains that 'Colonialism is not a type of individual relations but the conquest of a national territory and the oppression of a people: that is all.' Or, again: 'Colonialism is the organization of the domination of a nation after military conquest.'[48] It may be that Fanon's devotion to culture and his faith in the humanist project prevented him from seeing a deeper complicity between that universalism and the colonial enterprise itself.

Some of the most challenging recent work on Fanon revolves around questions of gender and sexuality. Perhaps the most vigorous and incisive of these is Gwen Bergner's 'Who is that Masked Woman? or, The Role of Gender in Fanon's *Black Skin, White Masks*'.[49] Bergner takes Homi Bhabha to task for glossing over Fanon's treatment of sexual difference in his foreword to that work. Perhaps the greatest strength of Bergner's intervention is her recuperation of *Black Skin, White Masks* as a political, rather than merely an autobiographical text. Bergner thus unsettles the tendency within a certain masculinist tradition of privileging Fanon's later revolutionary writings over his earlier psychoanalytic texts. In doing so, she not only reinstates one of Fanon's crucial contributions to postcolonial theory, namely his critique of the psychological effects of colonialism, but, in the best Fanonian tradition, she stretches his insights to include a critique of the misogyny implicit in some of his formulations.

Fanon's direct style and avoidance of essentialism mark him out as a powerful example of engagement and accessibility. Joy Anne James puts it succinctly in the 'Afterword' to the Fanon Reader: 'Perhaps the affinity that progressives, blacks, or Third World peoples feel toward Fanon is that he neither argued for sophisticated critiques as a surrogate for activism nor romanticized black or mass culture as inherently revolutionary. Instead, Fanon set high standards reflecting the even higher stakes for the native intellectual engaged in social change.'[50] This is an apt characterization of a writer whose work still sets standards and raises stakes.

Anglophone criticism of Africa and the Caribbean

The world of the negritude writers was the creation of French colonialism, even if the sentiments which they expressed were opposed to the hypocrisies of the imperial world. In the British colonies in the twentieth century, cultural criticism has taken a rather different path. In general, the educational models provided by the British appear to have militated against a poetic movement such as negritude. Local modes of expression were careful imitations of English literary norms long after Césaire denounced the idyllic French view of the Caribbean, and many writers have commented upon the alienating sense of composing lines addressed to unknown realities such as snow. The cold abstractions of Britain and the rigid English language needed to thaw out before they could address a Caribbean reality. Nowhere is this process better explored than in the autobiographical writings of Trinidadian writer C.L.R. James.[51] James was an extraordinary man whose life encompassed Britain, America and the Caribbean.[52] His novel *Minty Alley*[53] was among the earliest black Anglophone novels of the Caribbean, but his extensive political writings and social analysis and his literary critical writings[54] have been woefully ignored. He, in a very real sense, gave voice to a whole new movement within Anglophone literary production. In the Caribbean we can view his work as a precursor to that of Barbados-born George Lamming or the Guyanese novelist Wilson Harris.[55] Like James, Harris adopts a sophisticated attitude towards questions of colonialism and language, and his work actually prefigures aspects of postcolonial theory in very important ways. He rejects any binary models of the colonial or postcolonial condition because he considers that 'indigenous' and 'European' systems of being are locked together. Cross-culturalism, he suggests, 'can no longer be evaded because the whole world has been built on it for centuries'.[56] He writes of the need to transcend oppositions and arrive at what he describes as a perverse cross-culturalism. This position is akin to the theoretical elaborations of Barbadian poet and critic Edward Brathwaite who in the 1970s attempted to outline a complex theory of Caribbean 'creolization'.[57] In more recent work, however, he has developed in an altogether different direction, but one which links him back to C.L.R. James. Brathwaite has attempted to sketch what he describes as the 'history of the voice'[58] in the Caribbean, suggesting that literary expression there has its roots in slavery and the African past rather than in a sense of writing back to Empire. For James it was the game of cricket that enabled the peoples of the Caribbean to express themselves in relation to the British and he argued that that game in many respects reflected the class and ethnic divisions within Caribbean society. For Brathwaite too, cricket marked an important turning point. It was when the Hampshire burr of commentator John Arlott first made itself heard on Caribbean radios that the shackles of the classical English education began to fall away and the people of the Caribbean were suddenly able to value their own forms of oral expression and creativity and clear the way for a more general appreciation of spoken language from calypso to reggae and through to the dub poetry of artists such as the late Michael Smith.

In the context of Africa similar concerns emerged, notably in Nigeria which, of all the British African colonies, has been the most fecund of literary sources.[59] Any divisions we might wish to make, however, between black writings of various provenances are no more than initial guides to the complex range of influences and interactions which have produced black writing in Africa, the Caribbean and the New World. The appearance of such work reflects the complex flux of black history, the multiple trails, trials and tribulations which make up what Paul Gilroy[60] has called the 'black Atlantic'. We have seen already how the negritude tradition was inspired to a certain extent by the writings of African-Americans in the United States, writers such as W.E.B. Du Bois and the loosely affiliated group which was given the title the Harlem Renaissance. One strand of their writings was to rediscover the African past and explore its legacy in the ex-slave communities, to attempt to rebuild a specific black identity in the so-called New World using elements of this and features of the dominant white culture which at that time were considered in a positive light, Du Bois' famous 'double consciousness'.[61] In this respect black writing conforming to European models, by and large, begins in the New World of the Americas. Most commentators stress the point that the 'original' African situation was one of orature, where tradition was recorded not in writing, but rather was lodged in the memories of griot singers, and other members of society whose role it was to preserve 'tradition'. Oral traditions and oral skills were something which individuals acquired with adulthood and initiation. It is this emphasis on the oral which has come to be incorporated into recent attempts to define an African–American literary theory, most notably in the work of Henry Louis Gates, Jr.[62]

This is, of course, a simplified line of argument, and the postcolonial critic would be quick to point out that this characterization of an entire continent solely on the basis of a concept such as 'oral tradition' is in itself a gross misrepresentation; another facet of what philosopher and novelist V.Y. Mudimbe has called the 'invention of *Africa*'.[63] Nonetheless, that very invented entity, the 'Africa' of European discourse has itself become part of the process of re-invention which has gone on at various levels, amongst diverse groups at different times. Indeed, it could be said to have assumed its own ghostly reality. One point that the 'Africa' presented here ignores is the complex history of Africa itself. As is common in many Western discourses of the 'other', the historicity of

Africa is denied. It is 'imagined' as a timeless place, without history or social change. Its very 'coevalness' is even denied.[64] In fact it is certain that Africa south of the Sahara has been the home of complex civilizations, such as Great Zimbabwe, which in nineteenth-century Western eyes were by definition deemed impossible. Moreover, Martin Bernal[65] has put a very strong argument forward for regarding Egypt and its ancient civilization as the root of Graeco-Roman civilization; his work comes on the heels of scholars such as Cheikh Anta Diop[66] who for decades have been trying to recast the historical relationship between Africa and the rest of the world. In short, Africa has its own dynamics, a range of historical trajectories and a complex social existence which cannot be subsumed under the European category 'Africa'. As Nobel prize-winning Nigerian author Wole Soyinka suggests, his own work has been an effort to overcome such limited and limiting views of Africa. He has attempted to apprehend his 'own world in its full complexity'.[67] This is to escape from a certain trick which has historically been played on Africa: 'Africa minus the Sahara North is still a very large continent, populated by myriad races and cultures. With its millions of inhabitants it must be the largest metaphysical vacuum ever conjured up for the purpose of racist propaganda.'[68]

The way in which European critics have approached black literary production has been through such an initial misunderstanding. In some cases, in fact, all black literary production has been seen as the outcome of a specious concept of the 'African'. Perhaps, one of the earliest efforts to systematize black literature is that of Janheinz Jahn who developed his notion of 'neo-African' writing in the 1950s and 1960s. Jahn's interpretation of this literature was based on his own reading of African religion, which he saw as a universe consisting of a structure of living forces, organized hierarchically.[69] While his work at least treated its subject matter seriously, it remains at the time a totalizing vision of Africa. Recently it has been described as: 'the now fossilized anthropological scholarship of the sort associated with Janheinz Jahn, Ulli Beier and others. . . . In this totalizing fixation with Africa as a vast homeland of the exotic, the linguistic, ethnic and class heterogeneity of Africa is conveniently forgotten.'[70]

Essentially, then, Jahn's approach posited something equating to the black essence identified by some adherents of the negritude movement. As we have already hinted in our discussion of negritude, Wole Soyinka feels that the movement itself became involved in the West's projections of what Africa represented:

> In attempting to refute the evaluation to which black reality had been subjected, Negritude adopted the Manichaean tradition of European thought and inflicted it on a culture which is most radically anti-Manichaean. It not only accepted the dialectical structure of European

ideological confrontations but borrowed from the very components of its racist syllogism.[71]

More recently, Soyinka too has been accused of just this category mistake by fellow-Nigerian Chinweizu. Much of the work dealing with African literature has placed a great deal of weight on the fact that we are dealing with artistic traditions rooted in the spoken rather than the written word. It is with this opposition of spoken and written that critics have commonly approached the study of the *novel tradition* in Africa. Back in the mid 1970s, for example, the prolific Guyanese scholar and novelist O.R. Dathorne pointed out the dilemma faced by the African writer, a writer still unable to 'draw the world, still sounding it'.[72] The African writer in the twentieth century is, he argues, a cultural entrepreneur who manipulates 'the apparatus of culture for export'.[73] In this sense there is often an attempt to convey elements of orality in the written form. One of the earliest West African novels to be published in English, Amos Tutuola's *The Palm-Wine Drinkard*[74] (1952), is often cited in this context. From the book's opening lines, Tutuola draws on a sense of difference and distorts the syntax to try and convey another way of telling: 'I was a palm-wine drinkard since I was a boy of ten years of age. I had no other work than to drink palm-wine in my life. In those days we did not know other money, except COWRIES, so that everything was very cheap, and my father was the richest man in our town.'[75]

As with the Caribbean critics it is language in another sense which is at the heart of a number of contentious debates engaged in by African writers. Why should the African writer need to write in what is essentially a foreign tongue? We shall return to this issue, because it represents an interesting point of departure from the attitudes of the negritude writers. But first it is worth mentioning briefly the history of vernacular literature in Africa. Dathorne points out that this was to be found mainly in the former English-speaking areas of Africa where, in the nineteenth century at least, pressure was not as intense to produce Africans who expressed themselves in the language of the colonists. In the early stages vernacular literature generally arose under mission influence. The first mission press was established in southern Africa at Lovedale in 1823, publishing in Xhosa. As the nineteenth century progressed such printing houses developed in a variety of places, some publishing newspapers and even translations of Shakespeare. Such literatures, Dathorne argues, evolved over time, 'beginning as didactic sermonizing . . . the literature developed to such an extent that many vernacular works can stand side by side with any of the writings in European languages'.[76] While these works have not often been considered within the confines of postcolonial criticism, the debates sparked by the Kenyan novelist, Ngugi wa Thiong'o,[77] when he famously denounced the use of the English language as a vehicle for

African literary production and his own championing of African languages, demonstrate how an older literary tradition is merging with more recent developments in critical debate.[78]

As we can see, the situation is complex and here we are only considering those areas of Africa under British colonial influence. Indeed, Ngugi's stance is at odds with another author who, in other regards, has taken a highly critical view of the relationship between literary production and the ravages of colonialism, the Nigerian novelist, Chinua Achebe. His work marks a new phase in the development of the African novel published in English outside South Africa. He also represents a watershed in his role as founding editor of the Heinemann African Writers series, which has been an important outlet for many of the best-known African writers.

Achebe's celebrated first novel, *Things Fall Apart*,[79] was written in rebuttal of the views of Africa portrayed in the fiction of writers such as Joyce Cary. Achebe searched hard for a representation of the Africa that he knew and grew up in. Finding none, he set out to produce his own. *Things Fall Apart* tells the story of the colonial encounter from the African perspective, recounting the changes which took place in a small Igbo village. In the novels the critical intent is embedded in the text and the unfolding of the narrative, but in his non-fictional writings Achebe has been explicitly critical about several assumptions taken for granted in the West, while at the same time arguing for the right of the African writer to express him or herself[80] in English. For reasons of space we will only highlight two of his particular attacks here.[81]

In his influential essay 'Colonialist Criticism', Achebe attacked those critics who argued that African writing in effect had to transcend its setting and aspire to the universal before it could truly be considered great art. Indeed, Achebe called for a rejection of the term universal as applied to African literature, arguing that the term simply masked 'the narrow, self-serving parochialism of Europe', and in this respect he mirrors much of the criticism of the writers associated with negritude. A similar sentiment is expressed in his notorious denunciation of an English classic, Joseph Conrad's *Heart of Darkness*.[82] In 'An Image of Africa: Racism in Conrad's *Heart of Darkness*', Achebe condemns Conrad's novel for its stereotyped projections of Africa and its general refusal to grant the African characters in the novel real humanity on their own terms. He also points out that the creative impetus of what was to become modernist art was inspired by masks produced by 'savages' such as those which appear in parodied form in Conrad's work.

In the 1970s and 1980s a group of Nigerian critics took it upon themselves to continue this process of 'decolonizing' African literature. The cultural task, they argued, was to end all foreign domination of

African culture and 'to systematically destroy all encrustations of colonial and slave mentality'.[83] Chinweizu, who describes himself as an 'occidentalist', and his colleagues, Onwuchekwa Jemie and Ihechukwu Madubuike, have made it clear that they regard themselves as engaged in what they call *bolekaja* criticism. This term, meaning 'Come down let's fight!', is used to describe the behaviour of the touts for passenger lorries in parts of Nigeria.

Their objective has been to challenge what they perceive to be an official perception of African literature as 'a new and fledgeling product of the twentieth century; it is written in European languages, by and for a Western-educated African elite'.[84] This work they castigate as 'Euro-assimilationist', masquerading as 'universalist' (along the lines of Achebe's criticisms over a decade before). Because of its adherence to 'Euromodernist' aesthetics, this work embodies 'the anti-African, and even the racist, prejudices of the West'.[85]

One prime target of *bolekaja* has been Wole Soyinka. His work, in their opinion, is Euromodernist jargon, and epitomizes all that is wrong with so-called 'African literature'. Not only is it obscurantist, but it gives 'Eurocentric' critics the opportunity to regiment African literary production in line with critical standards developed to judge the European canon. Naturally, they consider that this is unjustified. Their solution is to broaden the definition of 'African literature' so that it includes contributions from oral and written parts of more 'traditional' and folkloric works, and those from both African and non-African languages (as long as the authors show no signs of the prejudices of non-African audiences). Soyinka has not been slow to defend himself, accusing the trio of indulging in 'neo-tarzanism'.[86]

Ashcroft, Griffiths and Tiffin[87] have suggested that there is less disagreement between the parties than the vicious rhetoric might have suggested. But that has not eased matters. When Soyinka was awarded the Nobel prize, Chinweizu announced that it was a case of the undesirable honouring the unreadable.[88] Even more recently, Chinweizu has suggested that the poetry of Soyinka would flatter Hitler, such are its colonialist suppositions.[89] In critical terms it might well seem that the whole debate has come full circle. Anthony Appiah has dubbed the *bolekaja* critics 'nativists', and suggested that their criticism has simply generated a reverse discourse, 'Railing against the cultural domination of the West, the nativists are of its party without knowing it.'[90]

Edward Said

It is easy to form the impression that postcolonial criticism begins with Said's *Orientalism* (1978). Homi Bhabha, for instance, argues that the text 'inaugurated the postcolonial field' and Gayatri Spivak describes it as 'the source book in our discipline'.[91] Important, even critical, though Said's intervention in the field has been, such praise risks devaluing, or marginalizing, the earlier work described in preceding sections of this introduction, as well as other kinds of postcolonial criticism contemporary with Said but grounded in different methodological presuppositions, histories or social experience. While *Orientalism* may itself have been partly responsible for creating such an impression, by failing to sufficiently acknowledge this prior work, what Said indisputably inaugurates, nonetheless, is the application of certain kinds of contemporary 'high' theory to the study of the relationships between (neo-)colonialism and cultural production. In particular, he adapts to this field of analysis Foucault's argument about the intimate relationship between power and knowledge. Consequently, as Said puts it, 'ideas, cultures and histories cannot seriously be understood or studied without their force, or more precisely their considerations of power, also being studied.'[92] The enormous impact which the text has had on the Western academy, especially, relates to the striking contrast that such assumptions represent to the traditional Western liberal humanist perspective which conceives of the aesthetic sphere as 'beyond' political affiliations or commitments and scholarship, in the humanities at least, as organized by the 'disinterested' pursuit of 'pure' knowledge. Said's Foucauldian method is grafted onto an older Marxist tradition of cultural analysis in the form of Gramsci's theory of hegemony, which seeks to demonstrate the role that culture plays in soliciting the consent of subordinate (or 'subaltern') social constituencies in the rule of the dominant order. By contrast, Said is equally important for inaugurating the critique of contemporary Western 'high' theory by bringing to bear upon it issues of race, empire and ethnicity. Said suggests that despite its overt aim of destabilizing the authority of the West, its habitual blind-spots in these respects reveal 'high' theory's characteristic Eurocentrism.

The most immediate concern of *Orientalism* is analysis of the degree to which the West's systems of scholarship, and its canons of aesthetic representation, have been implicated in the long history of the West's material and political domination of the non-Western world. More specifically, Said is interested in the relationship between the West and the East and the particular discourse which mediated that relationship, which he calls Orientalism. In using this term, Said appropriates and redefines a label which had hitherto been used to describe Western scholars such as Sir William Jones, who worked in India in the period 1780–1830. For Said, what is at issue is not so much the question of whether identification with Eastern culture in such scholarship was sympathetic or not, but the fact that (as he sees it) all Western discourse about the East is determined in the last instance by the will to domination over Oriental territories and peoples. For Said, the pursuit of knowledge in the colonial domain cannot be 'disinterested' because the relationship between cultures on which it depends is an unequal one, and such knowledge, whether of the language, customs or religions of the colonized, is consistently put at the service of the colonial administration. This point is reinforced by the fact that many of the scholars and writers whom Said addresses in *Orientalism* were also formally part of the imperial structure of government.

In Said's view, Orientalism (in the new sense in which he uses the term) operates in the service of the West's hegemony over the East principally by producing the East discursively as the West's inferior 'Other', a manoeuvre which strengthens – indeed, even partially constructs – the West's self-image as a superior civilization. It does this primarily by distinguishing and then essentializing the identities of East and West through a dichotomizing system of representations most evident in the regime of stereotype, with the aim of making rigid the sense of difference between the European and Asiatic parts of the world. As a consequence, the East is characteristically coded negatively in Orientalist discourse as – variously – voiceless, sensual, female, despotic, irrational, backward. By contrast, the West is characteristically represented in positive terms, as masculine, democratic, rational, moral, dynamic and progressive.

Such binary oppositions – and the power relations they inscribe – are illustrated with reference to an enormous diversity of Western representations and kinds of knowledge. While centred primarily on the West's relations with the Islamic world of the Middle East, *Orientalism* ranges over much of the rest of the Eastern world and at times suggests that its arguments bear on the imperialized world as a whole. Said's analysis is also ambitious in terms of the range of fields of knowledge which he analyses: 'I set out to examine not only scholarly works but also works of literature, political tracts, journalistic texts, travel books, religious and philological studies.'[93] *Orientalism* addresses these fields principally in the context of the imperial histories of Britain and France before moving on to explore the influence of such histories on the contemporary neocolonial global order supervised by the United States. The historical range of Said's enquiry is even more comprehensive than this might suggest, however, stretching as it does from American interventions in Islamic regions in the 1970s (and in more recent writings he takes this history up to the Gulf War) right back to the era of classical Greece and the conflict between Athens and Persia. It is Said's demonstration of the apparent consistency of Western regimes of knowledge and their associated will to power, across very diverse historical periods, cultures of origin and disciplinary and aesthetic

domains which, more than anything else, gives *Orientalism* its
extraordinary power.

The subsequent critiques of *Orientalism* can be divided, albeit
schematically, into two kinds. The first concentrates on the
inconsistencies of Said's method. For a number of critics, there is
a fundamental incompatibility between Foucault and Gramsci as
methodological sources. In so far as Said follows Foucault, he argues
that the 'Orient' is a discursive construct which has at best a tangential
relationship to the 'real' East which Marxist theory, by contrast, would
assume to exist independently of the observer and to be, in theory at
least, available for 'true' knowledge. This leads Said into a whole series
of conflicting arguments. For instance, it is unclear whether Orientalism
is the cause, or consequence, of imperialism. It is equally unclear
whether Orientalism can be seen as a misrepresentation or ideological
distortion of the East if 'reality' is itself, in fact, constructed by
discourse. Nor is it easy to see how any alternative to Orientalism is
possible if 'truth' is always a fictive construct authorized by relations
of power.

A second pattern of methodological inconsistency can be detected in
Said's attempt to reconcile the anti-humanism of discourse theory and
Marxism with a reconstituted humanism which derives from an older
tradition of western scholarship. The difficulties this involves can be
illustrated in two ways. On the one hand, Orientalism is represented as
a totalizing system, the determinations of which no one can escape, so
that at one point Said argues that Westerners are ontologically incapable
of representing the East in true or sympathetic ways. Yet Said himself,
despite being part of the Western academic system which has historically
been responsible for the production of so much of Orientalism, is
nonetheless able to somehow get beyond its gravitational pull to
provide an 'objective' and 'true' account of it, principally by virtue of
a traditional humanist (and New Left) appeal to the special privileges
conferred by his own 'lived experience'. Secondly, in so far as Said
envisages a way forward out of Orientalism (and he is contradictory
over whether this is, in fact, possible), it is through an appeal to a
transnational, transcultural and transethnic, even transcendental, notion
of 'human experience'.

The second main kind of critique of *Orientalism* centres on the
inconsistencies in Said's representations of Orientalism itself. There
is continual conflict over the degree to which the 'latent', 'deep' or
'archival' structures of Orientalism determine its 'manifest', 'surface'
or individual particulars, a conflict which recalls similar problems in
the base–superstructure models employed in traditional Marxism,
Freudian psychoanalysis and Saussurean linguistics. Consequently, Said
prevaricates damagingly over the degree to which Orientalism varies

over historical periods, between different national cultures (for instance, France and the United States), across disciplines and between individual writers and scholars. At times, as in his treatment of literature and of gender issues in Orientalism, Said's analysis is undoubtedly homogenizing in precisely the way he accuses Orientalism itself of being. Said's accounts of resistance to Orientalism are equally conflictual. On the one hand he concedes the existence of 'good' Orientalists (and there are a surprising number in *Orientalism*) who challenge the totalizing 'vision' of the discourse. On the other he suggests that no resistance from within the dominant formation was possible, so that even Marx is represented as just one more Orientalist. (The text has also been much criticized for a 'failure' to attend to opposition to Orientalism from amongst the subordinate peoples.)

In more recent work, especially the essays collected in *Culture and Imperialism*, Said has in certain respects developed in strikingly different directions, especially in terms of his political vision. While *Orientalism* sees current and future global relations as inevitably soured by the histories of colonialism, and the current era as one in which colonialism has simply reconstituted itself as neocolonialism, the latter has a much more optimistic vision of the possibilities of reconciliation and an end to domination and confrontation between West and non-West. Said's new thinking in this respect is partly signalled by an abandonment of what he increasingly sees as the totalizing and deterministic conception of power in Foucault. Indeed a growing disenchantment with 'high' theory more generally is a marked feature of the intervening text, *The World, the Text, and the Critic* (1983). *Culture and Imperialism* instead emphasizes the method of 'counterpoint', bringing together apparently quite discrete kinds of cultural production, periods and regions, as in the comparison of Yeats with Césaire, or of Camus with indigenous Algerian writers, in order to reveal the unexpected kinds of interconnectedness which now make global co-operation imperative.

As this might suggest, *Culture and Imperialism* is in some ways more ambitious than *Orientalism*, addressing a wider range of cultural histories and cultural forms (including opera). In particular, the later Said pays much more attention to anti-colonial and postcolonial cultural production, an area almost wholly ignored in *Orientalism*, which tends (like Orientalism itself) to conceive of the colonized as 'the silent interlocutor' of the dominant discourse. In the later volume, there is discussion of the African novel, of West Indian criticism, and the material struggle for liberation from imperialism. (Having said this, however, the longest section of the chapter entitled 'Resistance and Opposition' is devoted to the work of the Anglo-Irish Ascendancy poet W.B. Yeats.) Equally striking is the shift of emphasis from non-literary to literary forms of colonial discourse and an engagement with the

canonical figures of metropolitan culture, such as Jane Austen or
Conrad, rather than comparatively marginal work like the travel writing
which preoccupies *Orientalism*, as part of Said's ambitious analysis of
the widespread, even structural, connections between Western culture
and imperialism.

While Said certainly charts new territory in *Culture and Imperialism*,
producing some dazzlingly innovative readings, the text is also to be
understood as a 'sequel' to *Orientalism*.[94] Ironically, the continuities are
nowhere so apparent as in the recurrence of methodological problems
which plagued the earlier volume. Thus while *Culture and Imperialism*
often promises a more flexible model of the relationship between base
and superstructure, it all too often accords the former term the same
privileged status generally assigned to it in *Orientalism*. The readings of
Austen, Verdi and, above all, Said's interpretations of the origins of the
novel, all depend on a somewhat simplistic vision of the determining
influence of imperialism on Western cultural production. Similarly,
while the later text demonstrates a greater interest in resistance to the
dominant order from within the colonizing and colonized societies
alike, Said's problems with the relationship between hegemony and
resistance continue to be widely and damagingly evident, whether in
his unconvincing discriminations between different kinds of postcolonial
intellectual according to their location, or in his attempted defence of
writers like Conrad and Kipling against the kind of arguments mounted
by a 'nationalist' critic like Achebe. Consequently, there is considerable
justice in the criticism made by Abdul JanMohamed that, despite his
apparently profound rethinking of the Foucauldian problematics of
agency and power after *Orientalism*, 'Said's equivocation about the
relations between a subject and the determining socio-political situation
has reached an infinitely periphrastic refusal to come to terms with the
issue.'[95]

Despite these problems, it is still difficult to overestimate the
importance of Said's contribution to postcolonial criticism, especially
as practised in the Western academy. Said's work has provided a
springboard for many of those who come after him, from Spivak and
Bhabha to JanMohamed and Robert Young. While such work is often
contestatory and revisionary, of course, it is Said who so often sets up
the terms for subsequent debate. Indeed, Said has been influential to an
extent matched by only a handful of other contemporary cultural critics.
In English literature, history, comparative literature, anthropology,
sociology, area studies and political science, Said's ideas have engendered
widespread interest and excitement, and enabled a very considerable
amount of subsequent work. As Michael Sprinker comments: 'Specialists
in these fields have often been critical of his interventions, but they
have not on the whole been able to ignore or dismiss him out of hand.'[96]

This attests to the continuing vital importance of many of the questions which Said has asked in his long and distinguished career. Amongst the most important of these is whether it is possible to conceive of cultural difference without resorting to essentialist models of identity or reducing different cultures to the status of neutral and exchangeable terms in a system of more or less arbitrary equivalences. Just as pressingly, Said's work asks whether 'true' knowledge – or even non-coercive and non-reductive representations of the Other – are indeed possible. Behind these enquiries lies another, deeper, preoccupation which Said expresses as follows: 'Can one divide human reality, as indeed human reality seems to be genuinely divided, into clearly different cultures, histories, traditions, societies, even races, and survive the consequences humanly?'[97] It is for raising some of the most pressing issues of our time, in the terms he does, and for ensuring that they have remained in the forefront of contemporary cultural analysis, that Said's reputation remains secure – whatever criticism (as well as praise) he has since received for the particular answers he himself has given them.

Gayatri Chakravorty Spivak

Gayatri Spivak is the second member of what Robert Young's *Colonial Desire* (1995) describes as 'the Holy Trinity' of postcolonial critics (the others being Said and Bhabha) who bring to bear contemporary Western 'high' theory upon postcolonial issues (and, equally importantly, vice versa). The exciting, if often formidable, challenge of Spivak's work derives in part from her refusal to be contained within the horizon of any one particular critical theory (or the political values it implies). Thus she draws effortlessly and eclectically on discourses as diverse as feminism, psychoanalysis, deconstruction and neo-Marxist versions of political economy. Such fluency led Colin McCabe to describe her, in the foreword to Spivak's *In Other Worlds* (1987), as 'a feminist Marxist deconstructivist'. Apt though this label is, it should not be taken to imply a desire on Spivak's part to synthesize these discourses into a new form of cultural critique which one might describe in any simple fashion as 'postcolonial theory'. Indeed, an important characteristic of Spivak's work is the manner in which these various kinds of critical theory are brought together in order to demonstrate their respective limits and incompatibilities.

Spivak's methodological affiliations point to instructive differences and continuities between her work and that of other postcolonial critics. Whereas Said is generally dismissive about deconstruction and sceptical about Marxism, and Bhabha is sympathetic to the former but hostile to the latter, Spivak embraces both in a largely affirmative manner. In so far as she insists upon the continuing importance of Marxism (while recognizing that its classical formulations must be modified by the specific experiences and histories of the Third World), she can be linked back to an older strand of postcolonial criticism represented by figures like Césaire, Fanon and Cabral. Even more important, however, is the fact that Spivak is the first figure in the field to consistently inflect postcolonial criticism with a feminist agenda. While focusing primarily on the colonized female and her heirs in the neocolonial era, Spivak also recognizes the agency of white women in colonialism, as in 'Three Women's Texts and a Critique of Imperialism' (1985) and addresses the symbolic roles they perform in colonial discourse, as 'Imperialism and Sexual Difference' (1986) illustrates. In all these respects she remedies serious gaps not only in the work of Said and Bhabha, but in a great deal of earlier postcolonial criticism.

The early work of both Said and Bhabha can be schematically described as focusing mainly upon the colonizer and the discourses of the dominant orders of Western society. Their later criticism also has parallels by virtue of a shared engagement with the predicament and discourses of the Third World migrant to the Western metropolis. In so far as this figure is characteristically a critic or artist of some kind, s/he is relatively empowered – at least by comparison with the vast majority of those who have been (usually voluntarily) left behind in such migrants' countries of origin. By contrast, Spivak is concerned more than anything else throughout her career with the less privileged constituencies which have no choice but to remain located in the Third World. To describe these social formations, Spivak adapts the term 'subaltern' from Gramsci (to whom Said – as has been seen – is also indebted), in whose writing it signifies subordinate or marginalized social groups in European society, most characteristically designating the proletariat, or rural labour. In 'Can the Subaltern Speak?' (1988), her longest and arguably most important essay, Spivak extends the scope of the term within a Third World (and particularly Indian) context to signify 'subsistence farmers, unorganized peasant labour, the tribals and communities of zero workers on the street or in the countryside',[98] extending this definition in her later work to disadvantaged sectors within the metropolis, particularly those involuntary economic migrants represented by the 'urban home-worker'. Spivak's analysis is directed especially at the predicament of the female subaltern whom she represents as doubly marginalized, no matter where she is located, by virtue of both relative economic disadvantage and gender subordination.

A principal concern of Spivak's is whether the subaltern can speak for him- or her-self, or whether the subaltern is condemned only to be known, represented and spoken for in distorted or 'interested' fashion by others. In reaching the unequivocal conclusion that 'There is no space from which the sexed subaltern can speak'[99] (i.e. make her experience known to others in her own voice), there is some convergence with *Orientalism*'s conception of the colonized as the 'silent interlocutor' of the dominant order. However, whereas Said ascribes this state of affairs to the all-powerful nature of the colonizer, Spivak's particular target is the contemporary Western 'radical' intellectual who, ostensibly at least, is the champion of the oppressed. Spivak's objections are partly methodological. In this respect, the essential problem is that while such figures ('Can the Subaltern Speak?' identifies Foucault and Deleuze as examples) announce the 'death of the (Western, liberal, bourgeois, sovereign, male) subject' in the postmodern episteme, they retain a conception of the self-knowing, unified subject in respect of marginalized groups, such as prisoners or women, who allegedly can 'speak for themselves'. By implication at least, according to Spivak, the Third World subaltern is included in this analysis (though, like Bhabha, she repeats Said's complaints about Foucault's failure to pay sufficient attention both to the contemporary international division of labour and the historical experience of empire.)

This methodological critique underpins a more important political objection to the apparent 'benevolence' of some Western 'high' theory. On the one hand, Spivak accuses figures like Deleuze and Foucault of believing that they are 'transparent' *vis-à-vis* the objects of their attention. In other words they assume that they are able to escape the determinations of the general system of exploitation of the Third World – in which Western modes and institutions of knowledge (such as 'high' theory and universities themselves) are deeply implicated – in order to intervene in the struggle of the subaltern for greater recognition and rights. Moreover, in ascribing a subject-position to the subaltern which the latter is then presumed to be capable of speaking from, such Western intellectuals in fact themselves come to represent (in the sense, particularly, of speaking for, or standing in for) the subaltern. Spivak sees this gesture as continuous with the history of the construction of subject-positions for the colonized, and the articulation of their voice, in the era of formal Western imperialism, a process illustrated with great force in both 'The Rani of Sirmur' (1985) and 'Can the Subaltern Speak?'.

Spivak advances her argument in the latter essay by interposing in her analysis of Foucault and Deleuze an account of how British colonialists assumed the prerogative to speak for the colonized woman in the discourse surrounding the prohibition of *sati* (the immolation of Hindu widows) in early nineteenth-century India. The key manoeuvre was to construct an assenting subaltern female which justified the imposition of the 'modernizing', 'liberating' and 'progressive' regime of empire.

The claim to speak for the subaltern woman in this way consolidated imperial Britain's self-image as 'civilized' in comparison with both the 'degraded' subaltern and her 'barbaric' local oppressors, the Indian men who enforced the custom of *sati*. Central to this competition to represent the colonized female's 'best interests' between both British colonialists and indigenous male defenders of the practice was the ascription of a 'voice' – representing free will and agency – to the Indian woman. In the case of British discourse, this voice supposedly cried out for liberation; to the native male, by contrast, the voice assented voluntarily to *sati*. In both interpretations of *sati*, the voice of the subaltern is ventriloquized; 'spoken for' as she is, Spivak suggests, one 'never encounters the testimony of the women's voice-consciousness'.[100] Spivak demonstrates a similar process of 'benevolent' subject-constitution on behalf of the colonized woman a century later in the work of Edward Thompson, missionary campaigner and at times fierce critic of colonialism, who in her view also appropriates the Hindu woman as his to save against the 'system'. Thompson provides a link between classical colonialist 'benevolence' and that of some radical Western intellectuals in the contemporary phase of the international division of labour. Thus between (neo-)colonialism and patriarchy, 'the figure of the woman disappears, not into a pristine nothingness, but into a violent shuttling which is the displaced figuration of the "third-world woman" caught between tradition and modernization'.[101]

On the evidence of this kind of argument, Spivak's affiliations to feminism are clear. Yet, one of the most striking themes of her work is a persistent criticism of Western feminism for its failure to 'dehegemonize', even decolonize, its own guiding presuppositions. Pre-eminent among these is that 'Woman' is implicitly understood as being white, heterosexual and middle-class, to the same extent that in humanism, 'Man' is constructed in practice in similarly narrow and ethnocentric terms. Indeed, Spivak's critique of Western radical theory is extended in essays such as 'French Feminism in an International Frame' (1981) and 'Three Women's Texts and a Critique of Imperialism' to consideration of the 'transparency' of some strands of Western feminism, especially its (self-)interested intervention on behalf of the subaltern woman. In such essays, Spivak explores the way in which some kinds of Western feminism are in fact complicit in the dominant discourses of the world's privileged societies.

For Spivak, Julia Kristeva's work provides a striking instance of this process, with *About Chinese Women* (1977) arousing her particular antagonism. Kristeva's interest in the subaltern Chinese woman is, for Spivak, an example *par excellence* of the manner in which 'benevolent' First World feminists exploit the Third World in the process of *self*-constitution; she locates Kristeva's research within the long history of the West's attempt to appropriate Chinese culture for its own ends. For Spivak, Kristeva's work expresses above all the disillusioned turn of Western radicals, after the failure of the May 1968 Paris *événements*, to 'the individualistic avant-garde rather than anything that might call itself a revolutionary collectivity'.[102] This suggests the essential irrelevance of Kristeva's work to a genuinely international feminism: 'The question of how to speak to the "faceless" women of China cannot be asked within such a partisan conflict.'[103] Kristeva's shortcomings are repeated not just in a lot of other French feminism, according to Spivak, but in Anglo-American versions as well, as 'Three Women's Texts and a Critique of Imperialism' argues forcefully. Spivak concludes: 'The academic [Western] feminist must learn to learn from [Third World women], to speak to them, to suspect that their access to the political and sexual scene is not merely to be *corrected* by our superior theory and enlightened compassion.'[104]

For all Spivak's strictures about the failures of Western radical theory in terms of its actual treatment of the (neo-)colonial domain, there is (ostensibly) no question of her supporting 'the tired nationalist claim' that only the native can know the native. She argues that contemporary Western 'elite' theory, especially Derrida, is necessary to postcolonial criticism, because it encourages both scrupulous vigilance in those who would engage in any serious way with the non-Western Other and undermines all foundational models of identity which might lead to a reverse ethnocentrism. Thus despite her collaboration in and sympathy with certain aspects of the work of the counter-hegemonic historiography of the Indian Subaltern Studies group, Spivak argues in 'Subaltern Studies: Deconstructing Historiography' (1985) that the project is flawed by an attempt to restore the historical subaltern to voice. In her view, the Subaltern Studies historians mistakenly assume that there is a 'pure' or 'essential' form of subaltern consciousness, the 'truth' of which can be retrieved independently of the determinations of the colonial discourses and practices which have historically constructed the subject-position and even identity of that social formation. These have in fact precipitated an 'epistemic fracture' which makes impossible the recovery of an original, or originary, subaltern consciousness which is anterior to, or independent of, the intervening history of colonialism. For Spivak, the failure of the Subaltern Studies group to take into account this 'fracture' leads to a reinscription of bourgeois/humanist models of both identity and agency. Spivak concludes that one must see in such practices a repetition of as well as a rupture with colonial epistemology.

This concept of 'repetition-in-rupture' might well be used to organize a critique of Spivak's own work. Perhaps the most striking instance of this is that in so far as Spivak asserts that the subaltern cannot speak, she is, of course, repeating the gesture of constituting and speaking for, or in place of, the subaltern – the very manœuvre for which she criticizes Foucault and Deleuze. As Bruce Robbins observes in a different context: 'The critic who accuses another of speaking for the subaltern by denying that subalterns can speak for themselves, for example, is of course also claiming to speak for them.'[105] Indeed, the greatest irony of an essay like 'Can the Subaltern Speak?' is that if Spivak's account of subaltern muteness were true, then there would be nothing but the West (and the native elite, perhaps) to write about. Consequently, there is an inescapable sense that Spivak in fact herself primarily addresses the West rather than the subaltern, and focuses thematically not so much on the subaltern, but the Western intellectual, as her privileged object of investigation. Her polemics on the importance of 'unlearning one's privilege' are clearly directed at Western colleagues and the prescriptions of 'French Feminism in an International Frame', for example, function just as much as Kristeva's *About Chinese Women* as 'a set of directives for class- and race-privileged literary women'.[106] Moreover, the 'benevolent' Western would-be ally of the subaltern is left with the seemingly impossible task of opening up to the Other's ethic and identity without in any way 'assimilating' that Other to his/ her own ethic and identity. Finally, while Spivak is excellent on 'the itinerary of silencing' endured by the subaltern, there is little attention to the process by which the subaltern's 'coming to voice' could be achieved. In this respect, Spivak might justifiably be considered to be both deterministic and politically pessimistic.

Arguably, however, Spivak's work does exemplify her concept of the 'success-in-failure' that often accompanies deconstruction which, despite what she describes as its inevitable 'cognitive failure', nonetheless produces 'constructive questions, corrective doubts'.[107] The feminist framework she elaborates in texts such as 'Three Women's Texts and a Critique of Imperialism' has been particularly fruitful for subsequent workers in the field.[108] Above all, perhaps, Spivak forces all who work in postcolonial criticism, whatever their origin or location, to consider scrupulously their political positional and affiliations as well as the 'interests' of their critical assumptions and approaches. After Spivak there can be no question of 'innocent', transparent, or intrinsically politically correct readings of (neo-)colonial problematics, grounded in an assumed but unexamined identification with, or 'benevolence' towards, the oppressed.

Homi Bhabha

Homi Bhabha's career can be roughly divided into two phases (though the discontinuities between them should not be exaggerated). The first (from approximately 1980–88) is distinctive for its attempt to move beyond the analysis of colonial relations in terms of the systems of binary oppositions which underwrite both Said's *Orientalism* and the later, better known work of Fanon, such as *The Wretched of the Earth* (1961). While Bhabha recognizes that Said 'hints continually at a polarity or division at the very centre of Orientalism', his description of Said's analysis in this respect as 'underdeveloped',[109] expresses a belief that such tensions, contradictions and polarities as *Orientalism* does note in colonial relations are finally but illegitimately resolved and unified by Said's conviction of the unidirectionality and intentionality of colonial knowledge as will to power. For Bhabha, this ironically reinforces the very division between colonizer and colonized which Said deplores in colonial discourse itself. Bhabha meanwhile suggests that, under the increasing pressure of political exigencies (particularly the Algerian war of independence), Fanon's later work offers models of colonial identity as psychically and phenomenologically fixed in the same way as *Orientalism*.

More specifically, Bhabha's first phase can be understood as an attempt to shift the attention of these earlier versions of colonial discourse analysis to the way in which the subjectivities of both colonizer and colonized are constituted, and fragmented, by reconsideration of questions of identity-formation, psychic affect and the operation of the unconscious in the imperial context. For Bhabha the relationship between colonizer and colonized is more complex, nuanced and politically ambiguous than early Said and late Fanon suggest, chiefly because the contradictory patterns of psychic affect and identification in colonial relations (desire for, as well as fear of the Other, for example), undermine the argument that the identities of colonizer and colonized exist in fixed and unitary terms which are at once absolutely distinct and necessarily in conflict. In this respect, Bhabha's main methodological debts are to Freud and Lacan, whose radical revisions of Freudian models of identity-formation underlie Bhabha's principal theoretical premise in his treatment of colonial relations. This is that 'identity is only ever possible in the *negation* of any sense of originality or plenitude, through the principle of displacement and differentiation . . . that always renders it a liminal reality'.[110] This adaptation of Lacanian theory to analysis of colonial relations was anticipated in Fanon's *Black Skin, White Masks* (1952), which for Bhabha offers a much more enabling starting point than a work like *The Wretched of the Earth*. Fanon's earlier text is praised above all for its focus on intersubjective realities (rather than privileging the 'public sphere' of law, economic relations and the army, for instance) and for conceiving of such engagements in terms of dynamic and shifting, rather than binary and static, modes of operation: 'That

familiar alignment of colonial subjects – Black/White, Self/Other – is
disturbed . . . and the traditional grounds of racial identity are dispersed,
whenever they are found to rest in narcissistic myths of Negritude or
White cultural supremacy.'[111]

The first phase of essays, moreover, reconfigures the very category
of 'the political' as it is understood by early Said and late Fanon and,
indeed, in both traditional 'liberal' and Marxist thinking alike. By
contrast, Bhabha sites the zone of the political in this shifting, and often
unconscious, affective area 'in-between' the dominant and subordinate
cultures, across which an unstable traffic of continuously (re)negotiated
psychic identifications and political (re)positionings is in evidence: 'The
place of difference and otherness, or the space of the adversarial . . . is
never entirely on the outside or implacably oppositional. . . . The contour
of difference is agonistic, shifting, splitting.'[112] Bhabha concludes that
while psychic ambivalence on the part of both 'partners' in the colonial
relationship points to a certain complicity between the parties involved,
it also opens up unexpected and hitherto unrecognized ways in which
the operations of colonial power can be circumvented by the native
subject, through a process which might be described as psychological
guerrilla warfare. As this might suggest, concurrent with Bhabha's
reconsideration of the 'political' is an attempt to reconceptualize
resistance to colonialism in terms other than those figured by either
late Fanon or early Said. For Bhabha, the figure of the violent native
insurgent in *The Wretched of the Earth* reinscribes the Western model
of the individual as sovereign subject, by which Western modernity
itself, together with the history of colonialism which accompanied it,
is underwritten. In strong contrast to Fanon's account, but equally
unsatisfactorily in Bhabha's eyes, *Orientalism* implicitly constructs the
subaltern as an 'effect' of the dominant discourse, with no agency which
can operate oppositionally.

On the one hand, Bhabha posits an 'intransitive' model of resistance,
which recuperates the resistance which is written out in *Orientalism*,
without reinscribing the sovereign subject of Fanon's later work. For
Bhabha, colonial power is immanently liable to destabilization, or
what might be termed 'resistance from within', for three principal
reasons. Firstly, following the Foucault of *The History of Sexuality* (1976),
Bhabha suggests that, like other forms of power, colonial authority
unconsciously and 'unintentionally' incites 'refusal, blockage, and
invalidation'[113] in its attempts at surveillance. Secondly, following Lacan's
Four Fundamental Concepts of Psychoanalysis (1973), Bhabha argues that
the gaze (and integrity) of colonial authority is always troubled by the
fact that colonial identity is partly dependent for its constitution on a
colonized Other who is potentially hostile. Both these kinds of resistance
are illustrated in Bhabha's discussion of 'mimicry', a colonial strategy

which works to consolidate power by inducing its subjects to imitate the forms and values of the dominant culture. For Bhabha, this strategy can never fully succeed because it also always requires the subordinate to remain at least partially different from the dominant in order to preserve the structures of discrimination on which colonial power is based. Consequently, mimicry is 'the sign of a double articulation; a complex strategy of reform, regulation and discipline, which "appropriates" the Other'; mimicry also, however, constructs and depends upon a system of differences (or differentiations between colonizer and colonized) which 'poses an *immanent* threat to both "normalized" knowledges and disciplinary powers'.[114] Finally, following the Derrida of *Writing and Difference* (1967), Bhabha suggests that 'intransitive' resistance derives at least in part from the vicissitudes to which all language, including the language of power, is intrinsically liable, especially through the play of 'repetition' and the structure of *différance*. Thus English culture (and, indeed, 'Englishness' itself), once 'translated' into the alien context of the Indian arena, 'retains its presence, but it is no longer a representation of an essence; it is now a partial presence [in so far as it has become], a (strategic) device in a specific colonial engagement, an appurtenance of authority'.[115]

In contrast to this kind of 'intransitive' resistance, however, the first phase of Bhabha's work also explores resistance in more ostensibly conventional terms as the expression of the agency of the colonized, but in terms which are strikingly different to those proposed in the later Fanon's call for violent mobilization against colonial power. Bhabha's perception of the 'transitive' and active modes of subaltern resistance is illustrated in two particular ways. Firstly, the colonized subject is empowered to return, and consequently challenge, the colonizer's gaze: thus mimicry (and, indeed, a cognate process like hybridization) is also 'the name for the strategic reversal of the process of domination . . . that turns the gaze of the discriminated back upon the eye of power'.[116] Secondly, the subject who mimics can also refuse to return the colonizer's gaze which, Bhabha suggests, destabilizes colonial authority just as effectively in a different way. The colonizer's vulnerability is expressed partly in the 'narcissistic demand that [he] should be addressed directly, that the Other should authorize the self, recognize its priority, fulfil its outlines, replete, indeed, repeat, its references and still its fractured gaze'.[117] A refusal to satisfy the colonizer's 'narrative demand' for such recognition is, for Bhabha, always an effective act of political as well as psychic resistance.

Since the late 1980s, Bhabha has devoted himself primarily to issues generated by the legacies of colonial history, and traditional discourses of race, nation and ethnicity, and their implications for contemporary cultural relations in the neocolonial era. Bhabha is especially preoccupied by questions of cultural exchange and identification which are not overdetermined by problems of geographical distance and overt forms of political inequality, as in colonialism, but by the contiguity of cultures sharing the same (metropolitan) space and relations of ostensible, if often illusory, equality. Such issues involve Bhabha in a complex set of negotiations between the discourses of postcolonialism and postmodernism. On the one hand, he seems to suggest that in so far as colonial repression and genocide represent events as catastrophic as the Holocaust or Hiroshima, the disillusion with modernity's ideologies of reason, progress and humanism which underwrites the 'closure' of modernity in one strand of postmodernism is justified. On the other hand, like the Habermas of 'Modernity – An Incomplete Project' (1983), Bhabha suggests that the contemporary world has not yet arrived in a new (postmodern) cultural dispensation. However, whereas for Habermas modernity is incomplete because it has not yet exhausted its potential to construct a juster and more rationally organized world, despite the catastrophic events mentioned above, for Bhabha modernity cannot be considered complete because in certain crucial respects, the putatively postmodern world replicates and perpetuates certain negative aspects of modernity. This is nowhere so apparent as in the contemporary West's perpetuation, in new forms, of the social, political and economic structures (and ideological forms of Othering) which characterized the colonial history accompanying the Enlightenment and its legacies. Consequently, Bhabha proposes what he calls a 'postcolonial contramodernity' which, by reinscribing the repressed histories and social experiences of the formerly colonized, generates the same destabilizing relationship to postmodernity as colonial history represented for the West's earlier claim to modernity and Enlightenment.

While keeping modernity open (or 'unfinished') as a means through which new sites, times and kinds of enunciation are made possible for the formerly colonized in the contemporary period, however, Bhabha scrupulously avoids a reinscription of modernity as progress towards a new synthesis or resolution of historical and cultural differences and tensions. For Bhabha, this trajectory is implied in both the traditional liberal figuration of the end-point of modernity in terms of the final emergence of 'the (united and equal) family of Man' and the alternative Marxist vision of 'the end of history' which is to be effected by the triumph of the proletariat. For this reason, Bhabha's vision is strongly anti-teleological and anti-dialectical in so far as synthesis and resolution will tend to efface the cultural 'difference' of the formerly colonized within a 'higher' term. Bhabha proposes instead a conception of cultural difference which does not aspire to 'equality' with the dominant, or risk sublation within a re-articulation of these terms which preserves the former authority of the dominant, but which instead respects and preserves the peculiar and multiple histories and identities of the historically marginalized.

Cultural difference in Bhabha's sense, however, is not to be understood simply as that which remains beyond the attempt of one culture to 'integrate' or 'translate' another. While Bhabha is at pains to deny the the liberal, cultural relativist concept of 'the family of man', together with what he sees as postmodernism's 'celebration of fragmentation, *bricolage*, pastiche or the "simulacrum" ',[118] he stresses that the relationship of postcolonial or migrant experience to the dominant culture is not simply antagonistic. For this reason he opposes what he calls the doctrine of 'cultural diversity' which, like the regime of apartheid, seeks to inscribe absolute, ontological and total relations of difference between cultures. Equally, Bhabha seeks to 'revise those nationalist or "nativist" pedagogies that set up the relation of Third World and First World in a binary structure of opposition'.[119] In support of his anti-essentialist model of postcolonial identity, Bhabha cites Fanon once again: 'In destroying the "ontology of man", Fanon suggests that there is not merely one Negro, there are *Negroes*.'[120] For Bhabha, 'black nationalism', whether in the form of negritude or black separatist movements in the United States, offers a conception of culture and identity which simply reverses, but does not displace, the models of social identification in the discourses of Western racism itself.

Productive though Bhabha's intervention in the postcolonial field has undoubtedly been, both phases of his career have excited a considerable amount of criticism. In his work on colonial discourse, Bhabha has been accused of minimizing more material forms of resistance to colonial rule, and privileging instead discursive modes of resistance, with the implication that the critic who unpicks the symbolic and narrative ordering of the hegemonic order becomes the privileged locus of opposition to the dominant. This raises the question of how effective the kinds of resistance which Bhabha identifies actually were in colonial history, or could be at the present moment. Bhabha's recourse to psychoanalytic theory raises other difficult questions. Firstly, he does not really consider whether psychoanalysis may be a specifically 'First World' form of knowledge which, as such, may not be unproblematically translatable to analysis of (post)colonial problematics. Secondly, Bhabha has been accused of conflating the psychic identities of the colonizer and colonized to produce a unified model of the colonial subject which discounts the crucial material differences in their situations. A third important line of criticism has developed in turn from this objection. In so far as Bhabha unifies the colonial subject, he overlooks the problems posed to his analytic models by class and gender differentials on both sides of the colonial equation. Finally, one could argue that Bhabha fudges the question of whether the kinds of 'active' resistance he outlines are actually (self-)conscious or not, so that it remains unclear whether the agency of the colonized/postcolonial subject can be consciously purposive and programmatic.

In terms of Bhabha's more recent work, a number of criticisms suggest themselves. While he claims to be attempting to 'provide a form of the writing of cultural difference in the midst of modernity that is inimical to binary boundaries',[121] perhaps the greatest irony of this phase of his work is that his conceptualizations of the means to move beyond the binary in fact depend entirely upon the structures he is trying to undermine for their effectivity. Hybridity, perhaps the key concept throughout his career in this respect, obviously depends upon a presumption of the existence of its opposite for its force. This leads to the danger that the postcolonial or hybrid will itself become essentialized or fixed. Kristeva (an important point of reference throughout Bhabha's second phase) warns in 'Women's Time' (1979)[122] that an insistence that sexual difference is constructed in irreducibly biological terms may lead eventually to the practice of an inverted sexism. This is the same order of problem which Bhabha faces in so far as, more often than not, he presents the 'non-hybrid' alternatives to the postcolonial, notably Western neocolonialism and Third World nationalism, in unitary terms which do not do justice to their manifest internal contradictions and differential histories. Thus, in tracking the ways that (post)modernity constitutes itself as such in relation to a non-Western Other, for instance, Bhabha makes only the most token reference to the parallel processes of Othering of women and subordinate classes within the discourses of the (post)Enlightenment – as well as to (post)modernity's initial impetus, its engagement with its own (pre)modern history.

Commonwealth literary studies

The emergence of postcolonial theory needs to placed within the context of disciplinary transformations within mainstream metropolitan English studies. More specifically, it must be seen as both a reaction against and development out of what was considered to be the increasingly unsatisfactory label of 'Commonwealth' literary studies. This term was initially used to describe the writing of regions which were formally part of the British Empire. Such literature was seen to have a shared language and a common history with regards to the experience of British rule. These factors, it was argued, gave it some sense of unity. Increasingly, however, as the values and alleged benefits of the colonial period were subjected to ever fiercer critique the diversity of the literature became more apparent, while the much vaunted 'unity' seemed a mere chimera. Increasingly writers were arguing for an expansion of the field of study to include, for example, the United States. The label 'Commonwealth' slowly gave way to looser designations such as 'New Literatures in English'. The changes of direction and emphasis in the work of a representative 'Commonwealth' critic such as the Australian Helen Tiffin is indicative of these changes. In Riemenschneider's *History and Historiography of Commonwealth Literature* (1983) she defended 'Commonwealth' literary studies against claims that it was a wholly fictitious discipline based on an historical and political anachronism. The article, however, betrays a symptomatic sliding between the terms 'Commonwealth' and 'postcolonial'. In her more recent work the former expression disappears totally. This paradigm shift within 'Commonwealth' literary studies has been characterized by Gillian Whitlock as representing a transformation into postcolonial criticism, 'a practice which foregrounds the tension between the imperial centre and colonial space in a way that Commonwealth criticism did not'.[123]

Postcolonial criticism, however, makes claims to transcend the academic nexus which generated the category of 'Commonwealth' literature. As we have seen, a great deal of what has been written in the field of postcolonial criticism arises out of debates concerning the exact relationship between culture and imperialism, as traced by Edward Said. Much of our discussion, however, has focused on writers from those countries which emerged into nationhood in the latter half of this century, from countries which have tended to be described as 'Third World'.[124] We have not, though, looked at the situation in those colonies which were settled by migrants from Europe and subsequently gained independence in their own name (and often to the exclusion of indigenous peoples). The first historic sites of such developments are the Americas, both North and South, but there has been something of a reluctance to include them on the postcolonial agenda.[125] Within literary studies the definition of American literature has been largely through to those texts produced in English in the United States, written predominantly by white immigrants and their offspring. Some feel that American literature was able to establish its own literary canon which in turn could be traced to that of Western Europe and thence to the intellectual roots of 'classical civilization'. For this reason it might be thought that the postcolonial label should be avoided in reference to the United States. Ashcroft, Griffiths and Tiffin,[126] however, make a case for seeing the United States as the first postcolonial situation (in terms of English-speaking nations). Aspects of the relationship between imitation and literary expression which we witnessed in our discussions of negritude are apparent in mid-nineteenth-century North America. Theodore Parker, a theologian and writer, suggested in a speech in 1846 that 'We have no American literature which is permanent. Our scholarly books are only an imitation of a foreign type; they do not reflect our morals, manners, politics, or religion, not even our mountains, or sky. They have not the smell of our ground in their breath.'[127] The emergence of American literature reflected a concern for defining 'national character' stimulated by feeling peripheral in relation to Europe. A remark by William Carlos Williams amply demonstrates this point: 'Americans have never recognised themselves. How can they? It is impossible until someone invents the original terms. As long as we are content to be called by somebody else's terms, we are incapable of being anything but our own dupes.'[128] This is an interesting reflection on the durability of colonial values. Indeed, three years after the speech quoted above, Parker made what, potentially, is an even more controversial suggestion. In an oration on 'The American Scholar' he claimed that 'we have one series of literary productions that could be written by none but Americans, and only here: I mean the Lives of the Fugitive slaves'.[129] The other obvious point to raise here is that claims are being made about the nature of difference in America. The slave is sufficiently different to be able to relate to the new land in ways that those bound to the models on offer from the old colonizer were not. The literary products of the slaves, especially, their narratives of escape, at least in Parker's opinion, were not, however, of an order to merit serious scholarly attention, as the commonly held view was that literary production was not possible for slaves; they were deemed congenitally incapable when it came to such matters of 'high' culture.

If for our present purposes we leave the United States behind, in the English-speaking world this still leaves the remnants of Empire which retained their settlers, but gained official independence only recently; chiefly we are discussing Australia, New Zealand, Canada and South Africa (to include Ireland in this list would complicate matters considerably, but it should certainly be considered within the rubric).[130] Indeed, a number of 'postcolonial critics' have emerged from such backgrounds. Their claim is that they too have undergone the dislocations associated with imperialism and colonialism, and that the literatures generated in this environment represent an attempt to define the national, to generate a new self-identity in the face of the imperial power. The way in which this task has been approached has varied, but the basic problem is the same, that of 'establishing their indigeneity'.[131] That is, Ashcroft, Griffiths and Tiffin argue, their task is not to reclaim or reconstruct an original culture which has been superseded during the colonial period. These colonial settlers had to 'invent' the indigenous for themselves. They had to create their own historical myths and narratives. Here we must distinguish between the invention or creation of national traditions and the recourse to past 'tradition' which has been dubbed 'nativism'. Soyinka, in his critical remarks regarding both

Ireland

negritude and his disputes with Chinweizu, has argued that such reclamation is not a simple matter even for those seeking after some 'pure' version of Africa, for example. Much recent work in history[132] and, indeed, in postcolonial criticism has emphasized the flexibility of concepts such as 'national identity' and attempted to redefine national and ethnic cultures in terms of process rather than as fixed bounded units with a specified content. Ashcroft, Griffiths and Tiffin argue that in a sense the problem is again one of language; recreating a new self is difficult if the metropolitan language and usages are retained. The writer in the settler colonies is in some sense gagged and thrown into a state of silence by a lack of control over language itself.

It is increasingly difficult now to imagine the force with which the British Empire determined the ways in which people conceived of themselves and of their relations to the imperial centre. This fact applied to all those involved and it is impossible to deny that white settlers in the colonies held a great number of conflicting sentiments with regard to Britain. In the Australian context, for example, what came to be called 'cultural cringe', a slavish adherence to the norms and values of the British imperial centre was of particular importance. Cultural and literary forms, as was the case with American literature in the eighteenth and nineteenth centuries, were similarly based on models learned from Britain.

For Ashcroft, Griffiths and Tiffin[133] those in the settler colonies feel their difference from the inherited tradition and the need to assert that difference as much as, say, Nigerians such as Achebe. This talk of 'difference' perhaps occludes questions of power, but this too is a complicated issue. Again the Australian case provides an example, for here power relations were doubly felt because of Australia's historical genesis as a penal colony which became the home of wide range of people many of whom, such as the Irish, were in fact opponents of British imperial rule. It is only relatively recently that Australians have seriously come to explore the complex nature of their history. This particular aspect of imperial/colonial power has been explored in dramatic depth by Robert Hughes in his epic work *The Fatal Shore*,[134] a book which Edward Said has singled out as an exemplification of his views on the interrelation between imperialism and culture.[135] From the original sources, Hughes resurrects the silenced voices of the convict other, a very real victim of the violence of empire. He demonstrates the way in which the prison system linked up with and served the colonial order, oppressing all who stood in opposition. This would seem to give some reason to support the views of Ashcroft, Griffiths and Tiffin and those who offer similar definitions of the postcolonial.

This is not to say that there have not been voices raised against the notion that the settler colonies are in some sense akin to that axis of countries which in the past have been called 'Third World'. This was an issue raised by Vijay Mishra and Bob Hodge[136] who point out, for example, that Ashcroft, Griffiths and Tiffin conveniently forget that Indians, Africans, and West Indians occupy very different economic positions in the world order from that of an average Australian worker, as indeed do more recent migrants to the 'lucky country'. The insistence on a shared 'continuity of preoccupations', Mishra and Hodge suggest, is more a way of dropping any notion of racism from the analysis. Ann McClintock[137] has similarly pointed out that for the term postcolonial to have any specificity our actual historical analysis must be far more detailed and nuanced than the historical agenda proposed by Ashcroft, Griffiths and Tiffin. This point too has been echoed by other critics. Arif Dirlik[138] has answered Ella Shohat's question 'When exactly . . . does the "postcolonial" begin?' with the flip remark: 'When Third World Intellectuals arrived in First World Academe.'[139] This is the gist of some of Aijaz Ahmad's criticisms of both Edward Said and Salman Rushdie to which we shall turn. Dirlik's own answer to the question relates to the realm of the economic, an area often excluded in postcolonial commentary: 'Postcoloniality is the condition of the intelligentsia of global capitalism.'[140] Such an explanation admits little room for the settler colonies, but on reflection it could be argued that historically they were zones which provided raw materials of one sort or another for export and processing at the imperial centre from whence commodities flowed to be resold once again, at a profit, in the so-called periphery.

One potential blind spot when dealing with the settler colonies in the light of postcolonial theory is the inadequate treatment of the original inhabitants of these settler lands, groups who fit uncomfortably into the schema of the postcolonial. Failing to pay attention here would mean that postcolonial theory inadvertently rewrites some of the strategies of imperial subjugation. The 'empty' lands and 'native' races doomed to extinction are imperial myths which have been challenged both by demographics and by the increasingly successful insistence on land rights by a variety of indigenous social movements. Ashcroft, Griffiths and Tiffin talk about 'indigenous textuality' but, as with debates around the writing of English in other contexts, it is not clear what is to be gained from developing literatures in English; a language which has long been, in the experience of such groups, a tool for masking lies, extortion and theft.

One final complication needs to be registered in the discussion of the settler colonies, and that is the very fact that they have become increasingly the site of settlement for migrants from outside the confines of the original imperial nexus. These groups themselves are developing their own complex relationships to the English language and literary expression, and they too need to be taken into account, but to which empire are they writing back?[141]

Women's and feminist postcolonial criticism

A key issue in postcolonialism has been the search for an appropriate language in which to couch resistance and critique, whether in the sophisticated theoretical terms of Bhabha and Spivak, or in the arguably more direct, combative language of a critic like Ahmad. On one level, the debate centres upon the degree to which Western theory, by virtue of its being bound up with the academy, actually domesticates its object. Moreover, the question of language is inevitably linked to matters of power, theory and identity. In 'Talkin' that Talk', a postscript to *'Race', Writing, and Difference*, Henry Gates responded to Houston Baker, who had argued that black intellectuals should express themselves in their own idiolect. While conceding that minoritized cultures had a problematic relation to the dominant discourse of the academy, Gates insisted upon a multiplicity of styles rather than a resort to authenticity on the grounds that 'we must fight the racism of universalism in as many languages as we can utter'.[142] In postcolonial feminist criticism the issue of critical register and lexicon is especially crucial, since a rigid theoretical language can serve masculine forms of authority. In a recent exchange with Baker and Gates, Joyce A. Joyce argued that black male theorists, in adopting Western theoretical modes of criticism, were being both patriarchal and elitist.[143]

If the intersection of postcolonial criticism and feminism entails new perspectives on the body, on language, on the relationship between theory and practice, and on the complex interaction between the personal and the political, then bell hooks is an exemplary figure here precisely because she crosses the borders between what are often competing terrains in postcolonial studies. hooks is important because the questions of authenticity, representation and the status of the self that she raises are central to postcolonial theory. 'White mythology' has constructed an individual subject that excludes the Other. How can postcolonial critics conceptualize the individual within an anti-colonial discourse? Much debate around this topic has centred on the intellectual, specifically on the relations between the colonial intellectual and his or her community. One thinks here of Bhabha and Spivak. If the guerrilla and the guru constitute two competing models then the engaged, committed academic who refuses either to diminish the importance of teaching and texts, or to ignore the impact of wider political issues, offers a mediating model.

hooks foregrounds class, which places her in the camp of Ahmad; she favours theory, which puts her alongside Bhabha, Spivak and Gates; her emphasis on the voice, amply illustrated in her preference for dialogue as a critical form, breaks down the opposition between literature and orature; she speaks of revolution, and of the radical subjectivity of a reconstructed black self, which brings her close to Fanon; she writes of 'loving blackness', which locates her within debates around negritude; she traverses literature and cultural studies, writing on film, music, and fashion; and she sees politics in the classroom as well as in the culture at large, making her someone whose work effectively undoes a key opposition in postcolonialism: that which exists between those who see in it a mere 'culturalism', underestimating the transformative power of pedagogy, and those who wish it to be a political force outside of the university. She is a black woman who writes in different modes, including fictive ones, combining a passionate commitment to theory with a vigorous political style. hooks appears to negotiate the various positions taken up by Joyce, Baker and Gates, and to speak in the responsible, local speech of a larger community while also drawing heavily on the more rarefied discourse of the academy. Her approach to Western feminism resonates in important ways with the criticisms of Chandra Mohanty and Spivak.[144]

It is one of the many paradoxes of bell hooks's work that she chose a pseudonym to counter the cult of personality in feminist theory, yet her constant self-reference and regular resort to autobiography and personal experience lay her open to the charge of privileging the personal. There is of course an irony in an author using a pseudonym while opening up areas of her personal life to intense critical reflection, but it is an irony of which bell hooks is fully aware. What hooks does is to reorient the idea of the self, and she would certainly not apologize for the emphasis she places on personal experience, seeing this instead as liberating, and as a crucial cultural component of the bases of her radical female subjectivity. Indeed, it is the erasure of the body and of a history of the self in white academe that hooks is in part exposing. Teaching to transgress entails making the teacher more visible in the classroom.

For hooks, the confessional mode is an integral part of her social and cultural background. Her storytelling occupies a space between fiction and theory. 'Talking back' is a term that sums up hooks's approach: 'In the world of southern black community I grew up in "back talk" and "talking back" meant speaking as an equal to an authority figure. It meant daring to disagree and sometimes it just meant having an opinion.'[145]

hooks views the term postcolonialism with suspicion, seeing in it a premature celebration:

> Politically, we do not live in a postcolonial world, because the
> mind-set of neocolonialism shapes the underlying metaphysics of

white supremacist capitalist patriarchy. Cultural criticism can be an agent for change, educating for critical consciousness in liberatory ways, only if we start with a mind-set and a progressive politics that is fundamentally anticolonialist, that negates cultural imperialism in all its manifestations.[146]

A vigilant anticolonialist, hooks wrote her first book, *Ain't I a Woman: Black Women and Feminism*, while still an undergraduate: a text that confronted traditional feminist theory with questions of class and race. In her cross-checking and juxtaposing of racial, social and sexual difference, she is obviously working on a similar set of theoretical problems to those mapped out by Spivak in 'French Feminism in an International Frame'. From the outset, hooks has argued for a radical politics that goes beyond opposition, in a discourse that seems to respond to Edward Said's call for 'a more creative difference than mere difference'.[147] hooks does not describe herself as a 'black feminist', because she believes that 'women should think less in terms of feminism as an identity and more in terms of "advocating feminism"; to move from emphasis on personal lifestyle issues toward creating political paradigms and radical models of social change that emphasize collective as well as individual change'.[148]

For hooks, class is a key category of subjectivity, and a determinant of academic discourse, as important as race and gender in the construction of identity and difference. Defining her background as 'poor' rather than 'working-class' is just one example, however, of the urge to specify and clarify rather than opt for sweeping and inclusive categories. hooks sees postcolonialism as a way of containing the issue of race, or of talking about race under another heading, and she prefers 'feminist movement', as a description of a process or set of practices, to 'feminism'. Yet hand-in-hand with this desire to tighten up on descriptive terms goes an opposition to separatism of all kinds and a continuing call for the forging of alliances and affiliations.

hooks prefers to speak of 'white capitalist racist supremacy' than colonialism. She is as concerned with representations of whiteness and images of masculinity as she is preoccupied with hierarchies of blackness and forms of feminism. Her attentiveness to varieties of blackness drew from Sara Suleri the accusation that she was endorsing a hierarchy of colour rather than constructing a critique of that hierarchy.[149] And yet hooks is as eager to interrogate whiteness as she is to point out that the fact of blackness conceals other facts: 'What South Africa is struggling with – that myth of white supremacy – is also being played out by black Americans when we overvalue those who are light-skinned and have straight hair, while ignoring other black people.'[150] It is typical of hooks to show the local network of discriminatory discourses within larger patterns of dominance and subservience, the differences within differences.

Teaching is at the heart of hooks's work. She stresses the importance of a liberatory pedagogical practice. Influenced by the work of Paulo Freire, hooks is one of the few major theorists who constantly refers back to teaching practice, to the classroom as an exemplary site of emancipation. Paradoxically, despite her commitment to teaching, hooks has suffered from accusations of being non-academic, or not academic enough. One reason for this is her use of her own Southern black vernacular.

The question of standards of scholarship is a key element in the reception of postcolonial theory, or of any discourse that questions traditional notions of truth. If postcolonialism seeks to be inclusive, then it must experiment with voice rather than allow the language of the academy to remain exclusive. Not only humanism, but the humanities are bound up with the colonial project. In her propensity for resorting to confessional narratives, her disavowal of sources and footnotes, the absence of bibliographies and page numbers for quotes, and the general refusal of the codes of formal academic discourse, hooks does indeed stand outside of the academy, but in place of the conventional marks of scholarship we find an incredible eye for detail and an ability to argue with a level of sophistication that is simply not evident in much contemporary theory.

hooks is an anti-separatist who sees a need to link hands across a range of struggles and fronts, while recognizing the necessity of respecting differences. Her blend of styles and tendency toward informal discussion might suggest that she is more of a practitioner than a theorist, but she sees theory as both liberatory and intimately linked to issues of teaching and writing. Though generally open to theory, hooks has a highly ambivalent attitude to postmodernism. She remains suspicious of its critique of identity:

> The postmodern critique of 'identity', though relevant for renewed black liberation struggle, is often posed in ways that are problematic. Given a pervasive politics of white supremacy which seeks to prevent the formation of radical black subjectivity, we cannot cavalierly dismiss a concern with identity politics. Any critic exploring the radical potential of postmodernism as it relates to racial difference and racial domination would need to consider the implications of a critique of identity for oppressed groups.[151]

hooks's resistance to the postmodernist critique of identity is bound up with her conception of the potentially empowering nature of radical black subjectivity.

Sara Suleri, in her critique of what she perceives as the essentialism of bell hooks, warns that: 'Lived experience . . . serves as fodder for the continuation of another's epistemology, even when it is recorded in a "contestatory" position to its relationship to realism and to the overarching structure of the profession'.[152] hooks, however, maintains that 'a lot of my work views the confessional moment as a transformative moment – a moment of *performance* where you might step out of the fixed identity in which you were seen, and reveal other aspects of the self . . . as part of an overall project of *more fully becoming who you are*'.[153]

The work of bell hooks may also suggest a middle way between high theory and popular culture, and between the presumptuousness of the academic and the piety of the unrepresentable. It is one thing to say that the First World intellectual should refrain from speaking for the subaltern, as Spivak does, and another to imply that the subaltern cannot speak for herself. There may be a nostalgia or sense of longing implicit in saying that the subaltern cannot speak. A figure like Spivak, from a landowning Brahmin family, is clearly different in origin from a poor Southern black woman like hooks, but both are senior academic figures who have moved beyond their familial communities, and both can be seen to negotiate in fruitful ways the space between experience and expertise. Here, again, it is not a question of constructing hierarchies of difference but of attending to differences within groups generalized under the heading of the 'Other', something that Spivak herself can be seen to be productively engaged in. While Spivak's essay on the subaltern provided a necessary corrective to the appropriative tendencies of Western intellectuals, and to the obsession with the 'native informant', hooks can be seen to deconstruct in a different way the notions of appropriation, alienation and authenticity which continue to vex the postcolonial critic. bell hooks talks back, asks awkward questions, and insists on doing things differently. Her growing reputation as a teacher and writer speaks volumes for her commitment to theory, and to liberatory practice. In her own inimitable, back-talking, border-crossing style, bell hooks fights the racism of universalism in as many languages as she can utter.

Minority discourse and internal colonialism

Minority discourse and the discourse of internal colonialism are related in so far as each can be read as an attempt to map out the marginal within the metropolis. The focus upon dissident or minority elements within a dominant culture invites charges of a preoccupation with the West, and a blurring of the boundaries of colonial space. Ireland, for example, has long functioned as one exemplary site of such blurring, and continues to be a borderland of sorts between old and new conceptions of Empire.[154] Just as it once served as a staging-post between Europe and America, so it now functions as a halfway house between colonialism and postcolonialism.

One ethnocentric view of postcolonial theory would maintain that behind every Third World theorist is a Western intellectual tradition, often a French figure. According to this version of intellectual genealogy, behind Spivak is Derrida, behind Said is Foucault, and behind Fanon is Sartre. Of course, this approach is false for a variety of reasons. It ignores hybridity and ambivalence. It also overlooks dialectic and dialogue. Fanon, for instance, lived and worked in Paris, and imbibed existential philosophy, but he inflected and influenced it too. Moreover, Sartre was not his sole philosophical inspiration. Like Fanon, Abdul JanMohamed and David Lloyd can be seen to derive their theoretical impetus from a variety of French sources. They both adopt and adapt a notion of minority drawn from Gilles Deleuze and Félix Guattari.[155] In the move from minor to minority, what started as a way of defining a type of writing that is excluded from the canon, but which may yet aspire to canonical status, becomes a term used to refer to a whole series of marginalized groups. Indeed, 'minority', implying something lesser and younger, begins to look as though it is standing in for other terms, for example 'proletarian' and 'subaltern'. Minority discourse has its roots in a Marxist critique of a perceived tendency in post-structuralist thought to minimize the effects of class. As such, it marks the reinscription of the social as a category of difference within theoretical discourse.

'Minority' is a contested term, so it is not surprising that JanMohamed and Lloyd have had to justify their adoption of 'minority discourse' as a strategic and theoretical expression.[156] The collaborative work of the Kenyan-born founder of *Cultural Critique* and the critic who explores Irish nationalism in the wake of revisionism and postcolonialism has its origins in individual projects concerned with 'opposition' in two senses of the word. First, there was JanMohamed's insistence, in opposition to Homi Bhabha's representation of the colonial subject as comprising both colonizer and colonized, that an irreducible otherness remained which could not be incorporated into a unified colonial subject. Against syncretism and systemic analysis, JanMohamed posited a Manichaean allegory.[157] For JanMohamed, the Manichaean allegory is 'a field of diverse yet interchangeable oppositions between white and black, good and evil, superiority and inferiority, civilization and savagery, intelligence and emotion, rationality and sensuality, self and Other, subject and object'.[158] Colonial literature takes two forms, 'imaginary' and 'symbolic'. Imaginary literature is Manichaean, demonizing the native, while symbolic writers appropriate the native as a go-between. JanMohamed is opposed to the strategies of both literatures, exclusion and incorporation.

The project of minority discourse is nothing less than an alliance of the marginalized with the aim of overthrowing the canon together with the state power that produces it. It foregrounds agency, consciousness and intention. When JanMohamed and Lloyd insist that 'minority discourse is . . . the product of damage', they come dangerously close to a model of literature as therapy, as a working out of trauma. They wish to draw a line between what they call a 'pathos of hegemony', with 'its interested celebration of differences, but only of differences in the aestheticized form of recreations', and the genuine suffering of the minoritized. It is a question of wanting to distinguish between appropriation and authenticity, literature and lived experience, pathos and presence, representation and reality. Yet culture remains a central concern, since for minorities 'culture is not a mere superstructure . . . the physical survival of minority groups depends upon the recognition of its culture as viable'. Culture is not a 'mere superstructure', but it is perceived as compensatory and consolatory, that is, as a substitute for action rather than a transformative and liberatory set of practices. It is almost as though JanMohamed and Lloyd want to hold on to something outside of culture, no matter how far they stretch that category. They stress the importance of archival work 'as a form of counter-memory', underline the value of 'theoretical reflection', and foreground the role of the intellectual.

For Lloyd, minor literature does not simply seek to form an alternative canon. Rather, it is unerringly oppositional, upsetting the claims of canonical literature to represent the best that human culture can produce, by undermining such unified concepts as 'humanity'. Minority discourse alludes to a standpoint as well as a status. Minor literature, properly speaking, should be anti-canonical rather than merely non-canonical. It necessarily entails a 'questioning or destruction of the concepts of identity and identification, the rejection of representations of developing autonomy and authenticity, if not the very concept of development itself, and accordingly a profound suspicion of narratives of reconciliation and reunification'.[159] Humanism and the humanities are its twin targets. In recent postcolonial theory there is an awareness of class, but also an alertness to the liberatory capacity of teaching, writing, reading and theory, and a recognition both of the limits and the value of the traditional humanist project. Thus Lloyd argues that minority literature 'will dissolve the canonical form of Man back into the different bodies which it has sought to absorb'.[160] The critique of humanism maps on to a critique of progress and 'the developmental discourse on race'.[161]

In his contribution to *The Nature and Context of Minority Discourse*, JanMohamed takes as his starting-point Deleuze and Guattari's 'three salient characteristics of minority literature', namely 'deterritorialization', political motivation and 'collective values'.[162] The life of an individual becomes an example, a model, an instance of the generic minority. Thus in his work on Richard Wright, JanMohamed wants to insist that 'Wright's "real education" . . . had little to do with standard academic learning.'[163] While acknowledging that literature and, by extension, humanism, were instrumental in shaping Wright's consciousness, JanMohamed wants to hold on to some anterior experience, even when that experience gets mediated by a tradition and a culture which is effectively alien. Literature becomes, for Wright, a 'mode of dissemblance', providing 'the space within which one can attempt to resolve the actual contradiction of a constrained and frustrating life'.[164]

One of the difficulties with the concept of minority discourse is that it may reproduce the very inclusiveness and universalism it seeks to combat. Lloyd writes of 'the long-standing political problem of articulating the bases for solidarity between distinct groups while respecting the specificity of their own histories and projects'.[165] He distinguishes between an 'ethnic culture' that is inward-looking, and a 'minority culture' which is in 'confrontation with a dominant state formation which threatens to destroy it by direct violence or assimilation'. Minority figures are 'generic rather than individual subjects'.[166] Minority is a term, like subaltern, that establishes a centre, a *dominant* – the term JanMohamed and Lloyd most often oppose to minority. They nominate class as a major social determinant, as do other postcolonial critics such as Gates, hooks, West and Ahmad, even as Western Marxists are retreating from the concept. Lloyd and JanMohamed call for an activism that is both academic and communal.

Two contributors to the volume on minority discourse edited by JanMohamed and Lloyd provide useful cautionary notes. The key question is whether to prioritize culture and the constructedness of minority status, as Arif Dirlik and Sylvia Wynter do, or to assert the primacy of politics and experience 'in the last instance', as JanMohamed, if not Lloyd, wishes to do. Like JanMohamed, Dirlik wants to guard against 'the substitution of concepts or theory for lived experience'. The subaltern can speak. But Dirlik argues against the idea that literature is a substitute for, or even a supplement to, praxis. 'Culturalism', for Dirlik, is not the old idea of hegemony, but 'a need to insist on the necessity of recognition of some autonomy, even priority, to the question of culture in any meaningful liberating practice'.[167] Dirlik is determined to oppose culturalism as a liberating practice to both 'the West and the past'.

Sylvia Wynter argues that 'the unifying goal of *minority* discourse . . . will necessarily be to accelerate the conceptual "erasing" of the figure of Man'. But this erasure of Man is executed in the interests of a new humanism. For Wynter, minority discourse must be part of an 'opening on to new cultural forms in the context of a post-Industrial, post-Western and truly global civilization'.[168] Wynter warns that 'were we to accept *minority discourse* as a brute fact domain-in-itself, which would function as a kind of supra-*ism*, incorporating all *minorities* (as Feminism incorporates all women under the category of *gender*, Marxism, all workers under the category of *class*, Black Nationalism, all Blacks under the category of Pan-Africans) we would . . . end up with some *minorities* . . . becoming increasingly more equal than the others'. Wynter speaks of the risks implicit in trying to set up a 'dictatorship of the Minoriat'.[169]

By way of a response, JanMohamed rehearses Henry Gates's warning that mere opposition is not enough, and refers to Wynter's caution against confusing the discursive construction of a 'minority' with its existence as a 'brute fact', but still wants to retain both the idea of opposition and the possibility that minority status is a brute fact:

> If hegemonic formation is so powerfully negating that it can even control one's autonomous nervous system, one's ability to breathe, then we must face the empirical 'fact' that some, if not all, of us are indeed reduced, some, if not all, of the time, to experiencing ourselves, ideologically and physically if not ontologically, as brute, oppressed 'facts'. Thus sustained negation of the hegemony may be necessary not only for the liberation of our minds but also of our voices and bodies.[170]

We must face facts, facts that stand outside of cultural constructs. The risk implicit in such an opposition between culture and empirical reality, and in the insistence that 'facts' are something other than cultural constructs, is the familiar one of essentialism. The emphasis on experience and identity arguably undercuts the focus on culture in minority discourse, but its architects are well aware of the need to 'systematically negotiate the twin dangers of essentialism and infinite heterogeneity', a formulation that could stand as a cautionary note for this volume as a whole, if we read postcolonialism as a minority discourse, as some critics might encourage us to do.[171] Arguably a more telling caution, and a familiar refrain, is the charge of ethnocentrism. Sylvia Wynter comments that

> Bill Strickland was the first scholar to note, in a talk given at Stanford in 1980, the strategic use of the term *minority* to *contain* and defuse the *Black* challenge of the Sixties to both the founding analogic and to our present epistemic/organizations of knowledge. The term *minority*, however, is an *authentic* term for hitherto repressed Euro-American ethnic groups who, since the sixties, have made a bid to displace Anglo-American cultural dominance with a more inclusive Euro-American mode of hegemony.[172]

Once more it is a question of an oppositional outlook that always carries with it the risk of appropriation, and of an in-betweenness that can entail a majority masquerading as a minority, or, equally problematic, a minority masquerading as a majority, and of a postcolonialism that is also, in complicated ways, an internal colonialism.

Arguably one of the most important instances of minority discourse in postcolonial analysis is African–American criticism. Here, a valuable link is provided by the work of Henry Louis Gates, Jr, one of the contributors to the volume edited by Lloyd and JanMohamed, and one of the most influential cultural commentators in the United States. As editor of the Norton Anthology of African–American Literature, Gates is himself actively engaged in the process of canon-formation, while as a critic who has always drawn freely on the Western philosophical tradition he is nonetheless wary of its overweening tendencies. Committed to a culture where performance matters as much as text, Gates has recently remarked: 'I once thought it our most important gesture to *master* the canon of criticism, to *imitate* and *apply* it, but I now believe that we must turn to the black tradition itself to develop theories of criticism indigenous to our literatures.'[173] Gates represents a unique combination of infiltration and opposition, appropriating Western theory in order to question Western values. In that very process of appropriation, he is transforming the theory, and forging a new practice. As well as furnishing an exemplary case-study of minority discourse, he represents a number of different traditions which have been hinted at when we discussed both the negritude movement and Anglophone criticism of Africa and the Caribbean. Gates's work is characteristic of that of a number of intellectuals within American academe for whom the history of black expression in the New World and the emergence and definition of a black canon is of particular importance. Therefore we must give a brief outline of that tradition.

The early contributions to this literature, in the eighteenth and nineteenth centuries, are what Jahn has described as 'apprentice literature',[174] viewed as merely mimicking European models. But this charge of being derivative becomes, in Gates's hands, a claim for a productive and transformative mimicry – signifying. Gates explains that the African–American literature of the pre-1900 period is frequently described as that of the 'Mockingbird School'.[175] The black tradition was regarded as simply imitative,[176] and black writers themselves worried about their lack of novelty. Poets such as Paul Laurence Dunbar felt that they could not establish an original black voice.[177] Nonetheless, the twentieth century saw this literary tradition transform itself and flower into what became known as the Harlem Renaissance.[178] For Gates, these developments are crucial. The brand of literary theory he has evolved out of his confrontation with black literature grows out of this very fact. The black tradition is about imitation, but in very particular ways, and imitative of very particular sources.

Gates's general project has been to reinvigorate American black criticism and review the ways in which blacks have had literally to write themselves into the literary community. By doing so he has been influential in helping us to shift our appreciation of this body of work in a number of significant ways. Firstly, he believes firmly in the bringing together of Western theoretical discourse with black literature in a process which he himself describes as 'critical bricolage'.[179] Black literature, he suggests, has been resistant to theory in reaction to the elements of ethnocentrism and logocentrism which characterize much of Western aesthetic discourse. His work attempts to overcome this by using theory to actually transform itself through its encounter with black literature and thus generate a genuinely black critical tradition: 'My charged advocacy of the relevance of contemporary theory to reading Afro-American literature closely has been designed as the prelude to the definition of principles of literary criticism peculiar to the black literary tradition themselves, related to and compatible with contemporary critical theory generally, yet "indelibly black", as Robert Farris Thompson puts it.'[180] That is to say that he is working towards the creation of a black canon or 'tradition' which eschews the ideological categories implicit in such expressions as 'the Western tradition', 'American literature' or 'Commonwealth literature'. His work is an attempt to generate richer structures of meaning and in doing this, he argues, the black critic needs theory, but theory which needs to be altered for the special purposes of the black critic. Theory needs translation into the black idiom and principles of criticism need renaming; notably black principles of criticism such as signifying or 'riffing' which can then be applied to black texts. It is these latter principles which have increasingly come to predominate in his speculations as his work has drifted away from his early emphasis on using European and American literary theory to illuminate black writing.[181]

In his work he has attempted to show the difficult relationship of the black writer with the written word and outline historical white debates concerned with the possibility of black creativity. This, for example, was why the collected letters of Ignatius Sancho were published in 1783 by subscription. The publication's costs were paid for by those with an interest in the more general debate as to the actual humanity of blacks and their ability to create works of art. Sancho's work would help to prove their point. These early works, or 'slave narratives', are used by Gates as the basis for a distinct theory of black literary expression. The first key discovery here is the unearthing of what he describes as the trope of the talking book, a figure which is repeated across a number of these early black texts. He refers here to the moment of disappointment when the slave realizes that books do not speak to him. At this point he fully conceives the power that the white man holds by knowing the secret of speaking to the book. Furthermore, it is this power that determines the slave's relation to the technologies of writing and reading, i.e. one of silence.[182]

Gates wants to 'locate a metaphor for literary history that arises from within the black idiom exclusively, that is not dependent upon black–white power or racial relations, and that is essentially rhetorical'.[183] This he calls signifyin(g): 'The textual world that a black text echoes, mirrors, repeats, revives, or responds to in various formal ways. This process of intertextual relation I call Signifyin(g), the troped revision, of repetition and difference, which I take from the Afro-American idiom.'[184] This strategy he derives from the signifying monkey tales of folkloric tradition (these stories are to be found in various forms throughout the diasporic world which arose out of slavery).[185] These can often be traced back to older African cultural roots and demonstrate the importance of verbal dexterity and ingenuity which we also saw in evidence in our discussion of the Anglophone criticism of Africa and the Caribbean. It is this that comes through in the black literary canon and which is exemplified in the oral traditions and practices surrounding verbal duelling in African–American culture. Commonly called the 'dozens' these practices exist under a multitude of other names in various parts of the United States. Lawrence Levine, a folklorist, writes: 'Wherever they existed and whatever they were called, these verbal contests – referred to here collectively as the Dozens, which seems to be their oldest known name – involved symmetrical joking relationships in which two or more people were free to insult each other and each other's ancestors or relatives either directly or indirectly.'[186] The dozens is a concrete example of the process of signifyin(g) in action. Gates finds examples of the dozens documented in the black literary canon itself, showing that aspects of the black vernacular tradition were becoming absorbed into the literary canon.

The way in which signifying works within the black tradition is explained by Gates in terms of a musical metaphor: it corresponds to the way in which black musicians rework the riffs of their predecessors. In a similar fashion, Gates argues, writers themselves signify upon each other's texts and by doing so are, in effect, rewriting the received textual tradition. That tradition is the cultural archive of the Black Experience. The way in which this rhetorical strategy operates is one of the most important aspects of African–American literary history and is the central theme of Gates's full-length study *The Signifying Monkey*.[187] In an earlier work he gives a succinct definition of what he means:

'Signifyin(g) is a uniquely black theoretical concept, entirely textual or linguistic, by which a second statement or figure repeats, or tropes, or reverses the first.'[188]

While Gates's work has evidently evolved, he has always addressed himself to the black tradition. In this sense, his work continues the politically motivated attempts of the 1960s to bring a black canon into being. At that time the works were simply not available. It might be possible to trace a genealogy back through time, but the books themselves, the texts, were often only available in obscure libraries and collections. Gates has been part of a drive to change this situation, notably with the foundation of the *Schomburg Library of Nineteenth-Century Black Women*. This effort has been doubly significant because, as Gates notes: 'The birth of the Afro-American literary tradition occurred in 1773, when Phillis Wheatley published a book of poetry.'[189] In the foreword to the Schomburg series Gates recounts the story of how Wheatley, at barely eighteen years of age, came to be published. He also notes the lengths to which Phillis and her master John Wheatley had to go in order to authenticate the poems as her own, including her being quizzed by a panel of Boston's most worthy gentlemen. As writers such as Gates have suggested, since the sixteenth century Europeans had wondered whether Africans were capable of producing formal literature. The answer to this question was to provide ammunition for the debate over African enslavement, and whether or not on such grounds it was in fact justifiable (this was in large measure the topic of Gates's own doctoral dissertation). Phillis's poems were thus greeted with some interest, and widely reviewed. Thomas Jefferson, author of the Declaration of Independence, in his review stated: 'Never yet, could I find a Black that had uttered a thought above the level of plain narration; never seen even an elementary trait of painting or sculpture.'[190]

Such literary products as Wheatley's challenged conventional colonial assumptions that militated against black expression in general. Gates tells us that certainly by 1769 the spoken language of blacks was a subject of parody. In that year *The Padlock* appeared on the American stage featuring a West Indian slave called Mungo whose language was a 'caricature that signifies the difference that separated white from black'.[191] The presence that Phillis Wheatley therefore inscribed is evidently a first step in a long struggle to establish a particular black voice. In fact, her work represents the birth of two traditions: the black American literary tradition and the black women's literary tradition.[192] All black writers, Gates suggests in his numerous discussions of Wheatley, have evolved in a matrilinear line of descent. The publishing of the Schomburg library restores this fact and thus gives us deeper insight into the black literary canon. Through the signifyin(g) tradition of black composition we can trace a journey which starts with Phillis Wheatley and continues in the present day in the work of writers such as Ishmael Reed.

The British critic Paul Gilroy describes Gates as one of a number of scholars in the United States working at the interface between committed interventionist strains within cultural studies and black cultural history and theory.[193] The importance of Gilroy's own work is to point out that this is not the novelty we might consider it to be. However, as he has argued in exasperation elsewhere, the field of cultural studies has more often than not excluded the work of black radicals and cultural critics in a systematic fashion.[194] It is for this reason that the appearance of academics such as Gates is of importance for the general questions posed by the postcolonial critic. Like bell hooks and Cornell West, Gates is a first-generation academic, indeed, a first-generation professional, and one of a new school of radical humanists. Their arrival in mainstream academe coincides with the recruitment of intellectuals from other former colonies and in this respect is part of a wider problem which will be explored in more depth when we consider certain 'Dissenting Voices', who argue that it bears witness to a species of intellectual embourgeoisement.

In one of the collections of essays edited by Gates[195] he engages in an informative debate with the literary theorist Tzvetan Todorov.[196] To some extent their disagreement again echoes the critique made by Achebe of universality and humanism in relation to the African novel or, more generally, Fanon's critique of Western humanism.[197] Gates argues that readers who make claims for the universality of literature are unable to take into account the particularities of black literature, what he terms its signifying black difference. But he still argues that we must fight the racism of universalization in as many languages as possible, a comment which is directed as much against Houston Baker's demands for a specific black cultural idiom as at Todorov's insistence on the contingency and constructedness of concepts of 'race'.

Through this exchange we can see that many of the issues considered by earlier postcolonial critics remain areas of contention. This debate about black particularity can be closely compared with debates taking place within certain brands of contemporary African philosophy. Much of this debate centres on the question: Can there be a distinctive 'African philosophy'?[198] Ultimately, this particular strand of critical thinking leads in the direction of anthropology, and certainly a work such as Gates's *The Signifying Monkey* acknowledges a debt to the work of Wole Soyinka on various aspects of Igbo cosmology. Christopher Miller has demonstrated that those writing about black literary matters can turn, as earlier scholars had done, to forms of anthropology, but they must do so with a critical awareness of the development of that discipline to avoid the pitfalls of previous generations exemplified in a writer such as Senghor who rooted his vision of negritude in the dubious work of Frobenius.[199] In conclusion, Gates has been a prolific writer, one who has not only produced and edited many books, but also written a large number of important individual papers. His work continues to evolve and to find new avenues through which to convey his views on black literature and the experience of black 'difference'. His recent full-length work, *Coloured People*,[200] is an autobiographical account of growing up black in America, combining innovative theoretical perspectives with a long-standing commitment to literature of the black experience.

Dissenting voices

As the first section of this Introduction suggested, postcolonial criticism has had an enormous impact in the last two decades or so, particularly in the institutional context of the Western academy. It has transformed university syllabuses, reconsidered and extended established canons, constructed an expanding material base of journals, conferences and academic networks, stimulated new areas of both academic and non-academic publishing and changed the way that a whole range of academic disciplines have traditionally been configured and studied. Since *Orientalism*, especially, the remit of postcolonial criticism has grown remorselessly, perhaps even imperialistically, in terms of the periods, geographies, cultural predicaments and histories it addresses. Indeed, the concept 'postcolonial' has become so elastic that in recent years some commentators have begun to express anxiety that there may be a danger of it imploding as an analytic construct with any genuinely cutting edge, especially in so far as the term might be taken to imply that the problems of colonialism now belong to history. There has been increasingly heated, even bitter, contestation of the political meanings of 'the postcolonial' and of the legitimacy of seeing certain institutional locations, regions, periods and sociocultural formations as 'genuinely' postcolonial, or amenable to postcolonial analysis.[201]

Before commenting on some of these disputes in more detail, it is necessary to note the fact that postcolonial criticism has still not been fully recognized as an important or even distinct mode of cultural analysis within the Euro-American academy. It is significant, for example, that it does not always feature in recent accounts of modern literary criticism. Thus volume eight of *The Cambridge History of Literary Criticism*, subtitled *From Formalism to Post-Structuralism* (1995), which covers the twentieth century, simply ignores postcolonial criticism altogether (though Spivak is discussed in passing as a deconstructionist), as does Jeremy Hawthorn's *A Concise Glossary of Contemporary Literary Theory* (1992). By contrast, Chris Baldick's *Criticism and Literary Theory:*

1890 to the Present (1996) refers twice to postcolonial criticism, which is chiefly represented by a half-page discussion of *Orientalism*. More troubling, perhaps, than the indifference of such apparently authoritative institutional histories, is the outright hostility of traditionalists within English studies. A representative figure in this respect is Peter Conrad, of Oxford University. His *Observer* review of Said's *Culture and Imperialism* in 1993 constructs postcolonial criticism as a symptom of the 'culture of gripes and grievances' allegedly unleashed in the wake of the liberation movements of the 1960s.[202]

Critics representing other disciplines have been even harsher than Conrad. One example is Ernest Gellner (formerly Professor of Social Anthropology at Cambridge University), whose scathing review of Said's *Culture and Imperialism* in the *Times Literary Supplement* implied that Said was claiming jurisdiction over areas and issues which were beyond his competence. In the course of a bitter correspondence with Said in the *TLS*, and perhaps stung by Said's insistence on anthropology's historical complicity in techniques of colonial management, and the discourses of Orientalism more generally, Gellner dismissed not just *Culture and Imperialism* but *Orientalism*, too, as 'quite entertaining but intellectually insignificant'.[203] Similar doubts have been expressed by the historians Russell Jacoby and John MacKenzie. Jacoby once more raises the issue of the interdisciplinary competence of postcolonial critics: 'As they move out from traditional literature into political economy, sociology, history, and anthropology, do the postcolonial theorists master these fields or just poke about? Are they serious students of colonial history and culture or do they just pepper their writings with references to Gramsci and hegemony?'[204] By contrast, MacKenzie asserts that *Orientalism* deals in truisms that have long been common currency among historians, and argues that Said and his followers fail at a fundamental level to understand both imperial history and historiography. MacKenzie concludes that 'nothing better represents the *naïveté* and lack of sophistication of the left-wing literary critics'[205] than their shortcomings in these two areas.

What makes it impossible to dismiss such hostility as simply the expression of predictable disciplinary jealousies, however, is that by focusing their attacks on postcolonial studies on the work of Said, Bhabha and Spivak, MacKenzie and Jacoby reinforce a growing divide *within* the field of postcolonial analysis, which was already becoming marked as a consequence of the publication of earlier postcolonial critical texts as diverse in method, political orientation and subject matter as Stephen Slemon and Helen Tiffin's *After Europe* (1989) and Aijaz Ahmad's *In Theory* (1992). Ironically, then, politically conservative, liberal and radical critics have recently coincided in perceiving – or constructing – a deep and potentially disabling divide between what one might call postcolonial criticism on the one hand and the work of Said, Bhabha and Spivak on the other, which is characteristically described as postcolonial theory.

While other points of disagreement within the postcolonial field, for example over periodization of the 'postcolonial' and its geographies are certainly not to be discounted, perhaps the most heated current debate concerns the politics of postcolonial theory and by extension or association, at least to some degree, of postcolonial criticism more generally. In contrast to Jacoby and MacKenzie, the 'internal' doubters (who in many other respects are quite different, even mutually antipathetic), see postcolonial theory not as politically radical or even 'correct' but as deeply conservative in its ideas, operations and effects. Some, notably Aijaz Ahmad, even suggest that postcolonial theory is simply one more medium through which the authority of the West over the formerly imperialized parts of the globe is currently being reinscribed within the neocolonial 'new world order' and is, indeed, best understood as a new expression of the West's historical will to power over the rest of the world. In Ahmad's view, postcolonial theorists reproduce within the academic sphere the contemporary international division of labour authorized by global capitalism. Thus Third World cultural producers send 'primary' material (novels, for example) to the metropolis which is then turned into a 'refined' product (theory), principally for consumption by the metropolitan cultural elite. By comparison, Slemon and Tiffin's *After Europe* argues that postcolonial theory relegates other forms of postcolonial criticism, which do not rely on contemporary Western 'high theory', to an inferior category of analysis which is assumed to be both an anterior, or more 'primitive', stage in its own emergence and to be incapable of self-consciousness about its epistemological assumptions or methodological procedures.

As primary evidence of postcolonial theory's reinscription of the West's traditional cultural authority, such 'internal' opponents point to the hierarchy which organizes its choice of objects for study. The favoured field for analysis in the work of Said and his followers is identified as colonial discourse. This is deemed to privilege the Western canon over Third World culture and, moreover, represents a politically disabling shift of attention from the facts of current neocolonialism to the less contentious area of fictions produced in an era of formal imperialism now safely past. Next in the hierarchy is the work of the migrant intelligentsia of Third World origin based in the West. Said and his followers are taken to task by Ahmad in particular for assuming that writers like Salman Rushdie represent the authentic voice of their countries of origin. For Ahmad such figures belong to the politically dominant class fraction of both their country of origin and their host society, to which texts like *Shame*, like postcolonial theory itself, are in the first instance addressed. Ultimately, the detractors suggest, a lot of such work in fact needs to be placed within metropolitan discursive traditions such as 'Orientalism' itself. When Third World culture 'proper' is finally addressed, Ahmad proposes, what receives most attention are those texts which 'answer back' to imperial and neocolonial culture – for instance the fictional ripostes to *Heart of Darkness* by figures as diverse as Achebe, Harris and Salih. This attention to work that has been, in a crucial sense, interpellated by Western culture is held to reinforce the traditional relationship between centre and periphery which underlay all discourse, political and cultural, of the colonial period. In this process of critical selection, those aspects of Third World culture which are most genuinely independent of metropolitan influences and of allegiance to the Westward-looking national bourgeoisie, such as literatures written in regional languages, are either neglected or ignored. Thus the Canadian critic Diana Brydon objects to 'the narrowing of focus to the imperial/ colonial relation as if it were all that there were', and concludes: 'Deconstructing imperialism keeps us within imperialism's orbit.'[206]

Above all else, the 'internal' dissenters organize their attack on postcolonial theory around the argument that its methodological procedures derive from contemporary Euro-American critical theories which are politically regressive in a number of ways. To Ahmad, for instance, Western cultural criticism in general has become increasingly detached from popular political struggle, whether at home or abroad, since the 1960s. He then represents post-structuralism as the most striking and debilitating instance of this divorce, especially in its American versions in which, according to Ahmad, material forms of activism are replaced by a textual engagement which sees 'reading as the appropriate form of politics'.[207] The prestige of postcolonial theory is then attributed to its emergence in the wake of post-structuralist theory which flourished at a particularly conservative historical and cultural conjuncture, the period 'supervised by Thatcher and Reagan'. In an essay published the same year as *In Theory*, Helen Tiffin takes this argument even further: 'For all its potentially useful insights, post-structuralist philosophy remains the handmaiden of repression, and if I may mix metaphors, serves as the District Commissioner of the 1980s, his book title now changed from *The Pacification of the Primitive Tribes of the Lower Niger* to *Enjoying the Other: or Difference Domesticated.*'[208]

Adapting some of the perspectives and terms of Said's critique of Derrida in *The World, the Text, and the Critic* to his followers (a critique which in itself must bring into question some of the objections to the supposedly unreflective Eurocentrism of postcolonial theory), such critics attempt to recuperate a number of analytic concepts, strategies and figures which Spivak and Bhabha, in particular, deconstruct on the (supposedly mistaken) grounds that they articulate the epistemological or political values of the dominant order. For many of the contributors to *After Europe*, the centred subject, 'foundational' identities, the aesthetic sphere, the nation and nationalism, 'master'-narratives of liberation and emancipation, and authorial intention are all variously and at different times considered to be legitimate ways of conceptualizing and organizing resistance to (neo-)colonialism, whether in the spheres of politics or cultural criticism. More than anything else, *After Europe* seeks to recuperate the referential properties of language, which the volume presents as consistently sidelined by post-structuralism's characteristic attention to the fracturing of the relationship between signifier and signified, and privileging of experimental modes of writing over realism. This theoretical project is deemed to lead to an occlusion of 'the real' and defers the attempted engagement of postcolonial criticism with more pressing social and political problems. Such arguments are comparable, once more, to Ahmad's resistance to post-structuralism's 'debunking of all myths of origin, totalizing narratives, determinate and collective historical agents – even the state and political economy as key sites for historical narrativization'.[209]

Finally, the surface discourse of postcolonial theory is often no more palatable to such 'internal' critics than it is to the historians considered earlier. In contradiction of Jacoby's claim that stylistic clarity and coherence are of concern only to 'conservative' critics, Ahmad's *In Theory* laments what it sees as the inflationary rhetoric and arcane language of postcolonial theory (without, perhaps, paying sufficient attention to the cultural/political assumptions and histories underlying the use of a 'common-sense' or 'realist' discourse). For many within the broader field of postcolonial criticism, the complexity of the language of postcolonial theory is one expression of its will to power over other kinds of postcolonial analysis. Consequently many such critics insist on the importance of writing in what Ketu Katrak describes as 'a language lucid enough to inspire people to struggle and to achieve social change'.[210]

The readers of this volume must judge for themselves the merits of these various objections in the course of reading the extracts which follow. What we have attempted to do is to provide a range of significant material from different cultural locations and historical moments which illustrates the diversity, and both the convergences and incompatibilities, between the many different objects of study, political perspectives and critical procedures which might be taken to constitute the field of postcolonial criticism. The obvious danger in any such selection is that equally important material will necessarily be left out, and we recognize that there is something inescapably invidious about

our choice of what we consider to be some of the more influential
figures, essays and trends in the history of postcolonial criticism. We
aim to promote neither a canonical 'great tradition' of the milestones in
postcolonial criticism, nor a vision of the field as a kind of multicultural
critical fun-fair, where one can sample the rides as one pleases. Nor,
however, do we conceive of the field as one which is constituted by
irreducible differences which make any critical comparisons or dialogue
between its various constituent parts impossible and, consequently,
renders the concept 'postcolonial' meaningless. Perhaps a 'third space'
between these two approaches is possible, one which allows
commonality and difference to coexist in a manner which challenges
many of the assumptions of traditional 'mainstream' metropolitan
cultural configurations and their pedagogical politics. Above all we wish
to reflect the continuing excitement and challenges of postcolonial
criticism, and perhaps enhance them. As many in the field have argued,
there is always a risk that oppositional activities of the sort represented
by postcolonial criticism will be contained by incorporation within the
dominant culture, a process to which we ourselves might legitimately
be accused of contributing in the construction of a Reader like this one.
The task, then, is to maintain a sense of the destabilizing differences
of (and within) postcolonial criticism and to neither fix it, nor seek
to canonize it as a form of critique which is necessarily or safely
complementary with other kinds of contemporary cultural analysis.
For example, it is precisely because *Orientalism* has become so
monumentalized that we have decided to offer a less familiar part of
Said's work in this reader. As Patrick Williams argues: 'Whether or
not post-colonial studies are currently "dangerous", one way forward
is to make them more so, and not feel in the least mournful about it.'[211]

Notes

1. See for example AIJAZ AHMAD, *In Theory: Classes, Nations, Literatures*
   (London: Verso, 1992); BELL HOOKS and MARY CHILDERS, 'A Conversation
   about Race and Class', in Marianne Hirsch and Evelyn Fox Keller (eds),
   Conflicts in Feminism (London and New York: Routledge, 1990), pp. 60–81;
   CEDRIC ROBINSON, *Black Marxism: The Making of the Black Radical Tradition*
   (London: Zed Press, 1983).
2. See LEWIS R. GORDON, T. DENEAN SHARPLEY-WHITING, and RENEE T. WHITE,
   'Introduction: Five Stages of Fanon Studies', in *Fanon: A Critical Reader*
   (Cambridge, Mass.: Blackwell, 1996), p. 8; HENRY LOUIS GATES, JR, ' "What's
   Love Got To Do with It?"': Critical Theory, Integrity, and the Black Idiom',
   New Literary History 18: 2 (1987): 346.
3. The phrases appear in VIJAY MISHRA, 'The Centre Cannot Hold: Bailey,
   Indian Culture and the Sublime', *South Asia*, NS, 12: 1 (1989): 103–14, and in

PAUL BROWN, 'This thing of darkness I acknowledge mine': *The Tempest* and the discourse of colonialism', in Jonathan Dollimore and Alan Sinfield (eds), *Political Shakespeare: Essays in Cultural Materialism* (Manchester: Manchester University Press, 1985), pp. 48–71.

4. See HOMI BHABHA, 'The Other Question: Difference, Discrimination and the Discourse of Colonialism'; ABDUL R. JANMOHAMED, 'The Economy of Manichaean Allegory: The Function of Racial Difference in Colonialist Literature', in Henry Louis Gates, Jr (ed.), *'Race', Writing, and Difference* (Chicago: Chicago University Press, 1986), pp. 79–106.

5. See AIJAZ AHMAD, 'The Politics of Literary Postcoloniality', *Race and Class* 36: 3 (1995): 1–20; O.A. LADIMEJI, 'Nationalism, Alienation and the Crisis of Ideology', *Transition* 46 (1974): 38–43.

6. See PETER HULME, 'Including America', *Ariel* 26: 1 (1995): 117–23.

7. DAVID LLOYD, 'Ethnic Cultures, Minority Discourse and the State', in Francis Barker, Peter Hulme and Margaret Iversen (eds), *Colonial Discourse/Postcolonial Theory* (Manchester: Manchester University Press, 1994), p. 236, n. 9.

8. See ARIF DIRLIK, 'The Postcolonial Aura: Third World Criticism in the Age of Global Capitalism', *Critical Inquiry* 20 (1994): 331–48.

9. ANTHONY K. APPIAH, 'Is the Post- in Postmodernism the Post- in Postcolonial?', *Critical Inquiry* 17 (1991): 356; SARA SULERI attacks the notion of the native informant in 'Woman Skin Deep: Feminism and the Postcolonial Condition', in Patrick Williams and Laura Chrisman (eds), *Colonial Discourse and Post-Colonial Theory: A Reader* (Hemel Hempstead: Harvester/Wheatsheaf, 1994), pp. 247–52.

10. See the essays JOYCE A. JOYCE, HENRY LOUIS GATES, JR, and HOUSTON BAKER, in 'A Discussion: The Black Canon: Reconstructing Black American Literary Criticism', *New Literary History* 18: 2 (1987): 333–84. See also ARIF DIRLIK, 'Culturalism as Hegemonic Ideology and Liberating Practice', in ABDUL JANMOHAMED and DAVID LLOYD (eds), *The Nature and Context of Minority Discourse* (London and New York: Oxford University Press, 1990), pp. 394–431; SIMON DURING, 'Postmodernism or Postcolonialism Today', in Thomas Docherty (ed.), *Postmodernism: A Reader* (Hemel Hempstead: Harvester, 1993), pp. 448–62; IAN ADAM and HELEN TIFFIN (eds), *Past the Last Post: Post-colonialism and Postmodernism* (Hemel Hempstead: Harvester, 1991); BILL ASHCROFT, GARETH GRIFFITHS, and HELEN TIFFIN, *The Empire Writes Back: Theory and Practice in Post-colonial Literatures* (London: Routledge, 1989).

11. WERNER SOLLERS, *Beyond Ethnicity: Consent and Descent in American Culture* (Oxford: Oxford University Press, 1986), p. 6.

12. CORNEL WEST, 'Minority Discourse and the Pitfalls of Canon Formation', in Jessica Munns and Gita Rajan (eds), *A Cultural Studies Reader* (Harlow, Essex, and New York: Longman, 1995), p. 416.

13. C.L.R. JAMES, quoted by Julio Finn in his *The Voices of Negritude* (London: Quartet, 1987), p. i.

14. Translated into English as *Return to my Native Land* (Harmondsworth: Penguin, 1969).

15. ROBERT FRAZER, *West African Poetry: A Critical Perspective* (Cambridge: Cambridge University Press, 1986), p. 44.

16. R.N. EGUDU, *Modern African Poetry and the African Predicament* (London: Macmillan, 1978), p. 30.

17. Cliguet, quoted by EGUDU, *Modern African Poetry and the African Predicament*, p. 30.

18. AIMÉ CESAIRÉ, *Discourse on Colonialism* (1955; reprinted New York: Monthly Review Press, 1972), p. 72.

19. Quoted by LILYAN KESTELOOT, *Black Writers in French: A Literary History of Negritude* (Washington, DC: Howard University Press, 1991), p. 105.

20. Quoted by FINN, *The Voices of Negritude*, p. 33.

21. Quoted by KESTELOOT, *Black Writers in French*, p. 56.

22. Ibid., p. 57.

23. Quoted by O.R. DATHORNE, *The Black Mind: A History of African Literature* (Minneapolis: University of Minnesota Press, 1974), p. 314.

24. LEOPOLD SEDAR SENGHOR, *Pierre Teilhard de Chardin et la politique africaine* (Paris: Editions du Seuil, 1962), p. 20.

25. Quoted by EZEKIEL MPHAHLELE, *The African Image* (London: Faber & Faber, 1974), p. 86.

26. AIMÉ CESAIRÉ, *The Collected Poetry of Aimé Césaire* (Berkeley: University of California Press, 1983), p. 35.

27. Quoted by KESTELOOT, *Black Writers in French*, pp. 126–7.

28. JEAN-JOSEPH RABEARIVELO, *Translations From the Night* (London: Heinemann, 1975) p. xvi.

29. FRAZER, *West African Poetry*, p. 42.

30. Quoted by CLAUDE WAUTHIER, *The Literature and Thought of Modern Africa* (London: Heinemann, 1978), p. 278.

31. See HOMI BHABHA, 'What Does the Black Man Want?', *New Formations* 1 (1987) pp. 113–23.

32. See MINEKE SCHIPPER, *Beyond the Boundaries* (Chicago: Ivan R. Dee, 1989).

33. Quoted by WAUTHIER, *The Literature and Thought of Modern Africa*, p. 317.

34. Ibid., p. 278.

35. YAMBO OUOLOGUEM, *Bound to Violence* (London: Heinemann, 1971), p. 96.

36. Quoted by SCHIPPER, *Beyond the Boundaries*, p. 46.

37. MPHAHLELE, *The African Image*, p. 81.

38. ABDULRAZAK GURNAH, *Essays on Black Writing* (London: Heinemann, 1993), p. vi.

39. V.Y. MUDIMBE, *The Surreptitious Speech: Présence Africaine and the Politics of Otherness 1947–1987* (Chicago: University of Chicago Press, 1992).

40. EDWARD W. SAID, 'Resistance and Opposition', *Culture and Imperialism* (London: Chatto and Windus, 1993), p. 330.

41. HENRY LOUIS GATES, JR, 'Critical Fanonism', *Critical Inquiry* 17 (1991): 470.

42. FRANTZ FANON, 'On National Culture', in *The Wretched of the Earth*, trans. Constance Farrington (Penguin: Harmondsworth, 1967; 1990), p. 187.

43. FRANTZ FANON, 'The "North African Syndrome"', in *Toward the African Revolution*, trans. Haakon Chevalier (Harmondsworth: Penguin, 1967), p. 3.

44. FRANTZ FANON, 'First Truths on the Colonial Problem', in *Toward the African Revolution*, p. 126.

45. DEREK WRIGHT, 'Fanon and Africa: A Retrospect', *The Journal of Modern African Studies* 24: 4 (1986): 682.

46. IRENE L. GENDZIER, 'National Culture', in *Frantz Fanon: A Critical Study* (London: Wildwood House Ltd, 1973), p. 230.

47. GATES, 'Critical Fanonism', p. 468.

48. FANON, 'French Intellectuals and Democrats and the Algerian Revolution', *Toward the African Revolution*, pp. 81, 83.
49. GWEN BERGNER, 'Who is that Masked Woman? or, The Role of Gender in Fanon's *Black Skin, White Masks*', *Publications of the Modern Language Association* 110: 1 (1995): 75–88.
50. JOY ANN JAMES, 'Afterword: "Bread and Land": Frantz Fanon's "Native Intellectual"'', in *Fanon: A Critical Reader*, p. 310.
51. His *Beyond a Boundary* (London: Hutchinson, 1969) is a masterpiece which carefully dissects the fashion in which the British used sport and education to govern their Caribbean possessions.
52. His early work *The Black Jacobins* (London: Allison & Busby, 1980) is a brilliant example of history written against the imperial grain. He tells the story of the overthrow of the plantocracy in Haiti from the perspective of the slaves themselves and in this way rescues neglected history from obscurity.
53. C.L.R. JAMES, *Minty Alley* (London: Secker & Warburg, 1936).
54. See some of his selected writings for an idea of the scope of his work. For example *At the Rendezvous of Victory: Selected Writings* (London: Allison & Busby, 1984).
55. JAMES actually wrote an appendix to Harris's *Tradition, the Writer and Society* (London: New Beacon Publications, 1967).
56. WILSON HARRIS in A. Riach and M. Williams (eds) *The Radical Imagination* (Université de Liège: Liège, 1992), p. 41.
57. See his *Contradictory Omens: Cultural diversity and integration in the Caribbean* (Mona: Savacou Publications, 1974).
58. EDWARD BRATHWAITE, *History of the Voice: The Development of Nation Language in Anglophone Caribbean Poetry* (London: New Beacon Books, 1984).
59. See OYEKAN OWOMOYELA, *A History of Twentieth-Century African Literatures* (Lincoln and London: University of Nebraska Press, 1993), p. 4.
60. PAUL GILROY, *Black Atlantic: Modernity and Double Consciousness* (London: Verso, 1993).
61. See GILROY, *Black Atlantic*, for a discussion of Du Bois and his notion of 'double consciousness'.
62. Gates's theoretical concerns link strongly with Brathwaite's emphasis on the connections between language and music in the Caribbean and in their turn highlight the artificial nature of many of criticism's geographical divisions.
63. V.Y. MUDIMBE, *The Invention of Africa* (Bloomington: Indiana, 1988). See also ANNIE COOMBES, *Reinventing Africa: museums, material culture, and popular imagination in late Victorian and Edwardian England* (New Haven: Yale University Press, 1994).
64. JOHANNES FABIAN, *Time and the Other: How Anthropology Makes its Object* (New York: Columbia University Press, 1983). In effect, Fabian argues that the West views and describes such parts of the world as if they exist in a different time.
65. MARTIN BERNAL, *Black Athena: The Afroasiatic Roots of Classical Culture* (London: Free Association, 1987).
66. The Senegalese author has promoted his Afrocentric view of world history for several decades in books such as *The African Origin of Civilisation: Myth or Reality* (Westport: Lawrence Hill, 1974).

67. WOLE SOYINKA, *Myth, Literature and the African World* (Cambridge: Cambridge University Press, 1976), p. ix.
68. Ibid., p. 97.
69. See JANHEINZ JAHN, *Muntu: An Outline of the New African Culture* (New York: Grove Press, 1961), and *A History of Neo-African Literature* (London: Faber & Faber, 1968).
70. CHIDI AMUTU, *The Theory of African Literature: Implications for Practical Criticism* (London: Zed Books, 1989), p. 2.
71. WOLE SOYINKA, *Myth, Literature and the African World*, p. 127.
72. O.J. DATHORNE, *African Literature in the Twentieth Century* (London: Heinemann, 1976), p. xiii.
73. Ibid.
74. AMOS TUTUOLA, *The Palm-wine Drinkard, and His Dead Palm-wine Tapster in the Dead's Town* (London: Faber & Faber, 1952).
75. Ibid., p. 7.
76. O.J. DATHORNE, *African Literature in the Twentieth Century*, p. 3.
77. See especially his book *Decolonising the Mind: The Politics of Language in African Literature* (London: James Currey, 1986).
78. More detail with respect to indigenous literatures can be found in GERARD ALBERT, *African Language Literatures: An Introduction to the Literary History of Subsaharan Africa* (Washington DC: Three Continents Press, 1981).
79. CHINUA ACHEBE, *Things Fall Apart* (London: Heinemann, 1958).
80. The majority of the early novelists to find their way into print tended to be men.
81. Both essays discussed here are collected in ACHEBE's book, *Hopes and Impediments: Selected Essays 1965–1987* (London: Heinemann, 1988).
82. Despite its author being a Pole and who was himself subject to imperialism in the form of Russian occupation.
83. CHINWEIZU, ONWUCHEKWA JEMIE and IHECHUCKWU MADUBUIKE, *Towards the Decolonisation of African Literature* (Washington: Howard University Press, 1983), p. 1.
84. CHINWEIZU (ed.), *Voices from Twentieth-Century Africa: Griots and Towncriers* (London: Faber & Faber, 1988, p. xvii).
85. Ibid., p. xii.
86. WOLE SOYINKA, 'Neo-Tarzanism: The Poetics of Pseudo-Tradition', *Transition* 48 (1975).
87. ASHCROFT, GRIFFITHS and TIFFIN. *The Empire Writes Back*, p. 129.
88. See OWOMOYELA (ed.), *A History of Twentieth-Century African Literature*, p. 361.
89. CHINWEIZU, *Voices from Twentieth-Century Africa*, p. xxvi.
90. ANTHONY APPIAH, *In My Father's House* (London: Methuen, 1992).
91. HOMI K. BHABHA, 'Postcolonial Criticism' in *Redrawing the Boundaries: The Transformation of English and American Literary Studies*, ed. Stephen Greenblatt and Giles Gunn (New York: MLA, 1992), p. 465; GAYATRI CHAKRAVORTY SPIVAK, *Outside in the Teaching Machine* (London: Routledge, 1993), p. 56.
92. EDWARD W. SAID, *Orientalism* (1978; Harmondsworth: Penguin, 1991), p. 5; compare MICHEL FOUCAULT, *Discipline and Punish: The Birth of the Prison*, trans. Alan Sheridan (1975; Harmondsworth: Peregrine, 1979), pp. 27–8.
93. EDWARD W. SAID, *Orientalism*, p. 23.
94. EDWARD W. SAID, *Culture and Imperialism* (London: Chatto & Windus, 1993), p. 64.

95. ABDUL JANMOHAMED, 'Worldliness-Without-World, Homelessness-as-Home: Toward a Definition of the Specular Border Intellectual' in *Edward Said: A Critical Reader*, ed. Michael Sprinker (Oxford: Basil Blackwell, 1992), p. 100.

96. MICHAEL SPRINKER, Introduction to *Edward Said: A Critical Reader*, p. 2.

97. EDWARD W. SAID, *Orientalism*, p. 45.

98. GAYATRI C. SPIVAK, 'Can the Subaltern Speak?' (1988), in *Colonial Discourse and Post-Colonial Theory: A Reader*, ed. Patrick Williams and Laura Chrisman (Hemel Hempstead: Harvester/Wheatsheaf, 1993), p. 84.

99. Ibid., p. 103.

100. Ibid., p. 93.

101. Ibid., p. 102.

102. GAYATRI C. SPIVAK, *In Other Worlds: Essays in Cultural Politics* (London and New York: Routledge, 1988), p. 140.

103. Ibid.

104. Ibid., p. 135.

105. BRUCE ROBBINS, 'The East is a Career: Edward Said and the Logics of Professionalism' in Sprinker (ed.), *Edward Said*, p. 50.

106. GAYATRI C. SPIVAK, *In Other Worlds*, p. 136.

107. Ibid., p. 258.

108. See, for example, FIRDOUS AZIM, *The Colonial Rise of the Novel* (London: Routledge, 1993); LAURA DONALDSON, *Decolonizing Feminisms: Race, Gender, and Empire-Building* (London: Routledge, 1993); JENNY SHARPE, *Allegories of Empire: the Figure of Woman in the Colonial Text* (Minneapolis: University of Minnesota Press, 1993); JULIA V. EMBERLEY, *Thresholds of Difference: Feminist Critiques, Native Women's Writings, Postcolonial Theory* (Toronto: University of Toronto Press, 1993).

109. HOMI K. BHABHA, *The Location of Culture* (London: Routledge, 1994), p. 73.

110. HOMI K. BHABHA, 'Remembering Fanon', Foreword to FRANTZ FANON, *Black Skin, White Masks* trans. C.L. Markmann (1952; London: Pluto Press, 1986), pp. xvii–xviii. Bhabha is not, of course, the first critic to bring psychoanalytic perspectives to bear on (post)colonial problematics. Apart from FANON's *Black Skin, White Masks*, such an approach is anticipated by O. MANNONI, *Prospero and Caliban: the Psychology of Colonisation*, trans. P. Powesland (1950; London: Methuen, 1956); ALBERT MEMMI, *The Colonizer and the Colonized*, trans. H. Greenfield (London: Souvenir Press, 1965); ASHIS NANDY, *The Intimate Enemy: Loss and Recovery of Self Under Colonialism* (Delhi: Oxford University Press, 1983), L. WURGAFT, *The Imperial Imagination* (Middletown: Wesleyan University Press, 1983).

111. Ibid., p. ix.

112. HOMI K. BHABHA, *The Location of Culture*, p. 109.

113. MICHEL FOUCAULT, *The History of Sexuality*, trans. Robert Hurley, vol. 1 (1976; Harmondsworth: Penguin, 1981), p. 11.

114. HOMI K. BHABHA, *The Location of Culture*, p. 86.

115. Ibid., pp. 114–15.

116. Ibid., p. 112.

117. Ibid., p. 98.

118. Ibid., p. 238.

119. Ibid., p. 173.

120. Ibid., p. 238.

121. Ibid., p. 251.
122. JULIA KRISTEVA, 'Women's Time', in Toril Moi (ed.), *The Kristeva Reader* (Oxford: Basil Blackwell, 1984), pp. 188–211.
123. See GILLIAN WHITLOCK, 'Exiles from Tradition: Women's Life Writing' in Gillian Whitlock and Helen Tiffin (eds), *Resiting Queen's English: Text and Tradition in Post-Colonial Literatures: Essays Presented to John Pengwerne Matthews* (Amsterdam: Rodopi, 1992), p. 11.
124. Largely, that is, the countries of Asia, Africa, Latin America and the Caribbean.
125. This matter has been intelligently addressed by PETER HULME. See his 'Including America', pp. 117–23.
126. BILL ASHCROFT, GARETH GRIFFITHS and HELEN TIFFIN, *The Empire Writes Back*.
127. Quoted in C. DAVIS and HENRY LOUIS GATES JR (eds), *The Slave's Narrative* (New York: Oxford University Press, 1985), p. xxi.
128. Quoted by APPIAH, *In My Father's House*, pp. 95–6.
129. Quoted by DAVIS and GATES, *the Slave's Narrative*, p. xxi.
130. This is a much debated area. See, for example, DECLAN KIBERD, *Inventing Ireland: The Literature of the Modern Nation* (London: Jonathan Cape, 1995); DAVID LLOYD, *Anomalous States: Irish Writing and the Postcolonial Moment* (Dublin: Lilliput, 1993).
131. BILL ASHCROFT, GARETH GRIFFITHS and HELEN TIFFIN, *The Empire Writes Back*. Ironically these authors are the first to want to include Ireland within the postcolonial problematic, and yet also exclude Scotland and Wales.
132. Notably ERIC HOBSBAWM and TERENCE RANGER's, *The Invention of Tradition* (Cambridge: Cambridge University Press, 1983), but this work has generated a great deal of critical response.
133. BILL ASHCROFT, GARETH GRIFFITHS and HELEN TIFFIN, *The Empire Writes Back*, pp. 133–45.
134. ROBERT HUGHES, *The Fatal Shore* (London: Collins-Harvill, 1987).
135. See *Arena: Edward Said, the Idea of Empire*, directed Francis Hanley and Tim May (BBC, 1993).
136. VIJAY MISHRA and BOB HODGE, 'What is Post(-)Colonialism?', *Textual Practice*, 5: 3 (1991): 399–414.
137. ANNE McCLINTOCK, 'The Angel of Progress: Pitfalls of the Term "postcolonialism"', *Social Text* (Spring 1992): 1–15.
138. ARIF DIRLIK, 'The Postcolonial Aura: Third-World Criticism in the Age of Global Capitalism'.
139. Ibid., p. 329.
140. Ibid., p. 356.
141. For an attempt to address this question, albeit not in the postcolonial idiom, see MICHAEL FISCHER, 'Ethnicity and the Post-Modern Arts of Memory', in James Clifford and George Marcus (eds), *Writing Culture* (Berkeley: University of California Press), 1986.
142. HENRY LOUIS GATES, JR, 'Talkin' that talk', in Gates (ed.), *'Race', Writing, and Difference* (Chicago: Chicago University Press, 1986), p. 409.
143. See JOYCE A. JOYCE, HENRY LOUIS GATES, JR, and HOUSTON BAKER, in 'A Discussion: The Black Canon: Reconstructing Black American Literary Criticism', *New Literary History* 18: 2 (1987): 333–84.

144. See CHANDRA TALPADE MOHANTY, 'Under Western Eyes: Feminist
     Scholarship and Colonial Discourses', *Feminist Review* 30 (1988): 61–88;
     GAYATRI SPIVAK, 'French Feminism in an International Frame', *Yale French
     Studies* 62 (1981): 154–84.
145. BELL HOOKS, 'Talking Back', *Discourse: Journal for Theoretical Studies in Media
     and Culture* 8 (1986–87): 123.
146. BELL HOOKS, *Outlaw Culture: Resisting Representations* (London: Routledge,
     1994), p. 6.
147. EDWARD W. SAID, 'An Ideology of Difference', in Gates (ed.), *'Race', Writing,
     and Difference*, p. 57.
148. BELL HOOKS, *Talking Back: Thinking Feminist, Thinking Black* (Boston, Mass.:
     South End Press, 1989), p. 182.
149. SARA SULERI, 'Woman Skin Deep: Feminism and the Postcolonial Condition',
     in Patrick Williams and Laura Chrisman (eds), *Colonial Discourse and
     Post-Colonial Theory: A Reader* (Hemel Hempstead: Harvester/Wheatsheaf,
     1994), p. 251.
150. BELL HOOKS, *Outlaw Culture*, p. 45.
151. HOOKS, 'Postmodern Blackness', in *Yearning: Race, Gender, and Cultural Politics*
     (Boston, Mass.: South End Press, 1991), p. 26.
152. SARA SULERI, 'Woman Skin Deep', p. 252.
153. HOOKS, *Outlaw Culture*, p. 210.
154. See MICHAEL HECHTER, *Internal Colonialism: The Celtic Fringe in British
     National Development, 1536–1966* (London: Routledge, 1975).
155. GILLES DELEUZE and FELIX GUATTARI, *Kafka: Toward a Minor Literature*,
     trans. Dana Polan (Minneapolis: University of Minnesota Press, 1986).
     O.A. LADIMEJI has complained that Africans are more likely to be able
     to competently discuss 'Plato, Aristotle, Machiavelli, Hobbes, Locke, Mill
     and Marx' than 'Wilmot Blyden, Frederick Douglass, "Africanus" Horton,
     Booker T. Washington, Marcus Garvey, Du Bois, Padmore, Césaire and Cabral'.
     See O.A. LADIMEJI, 'Nationalism, Alienation and the Crisis of Ideology',
     Transition 46 (1974): 38–43.
156. See ABDUL R. JANMOHAMED, 'Negating the Negation as a Form of
     Affirmation in Minority Discourse: The Construction of Richard Wright as
     Subject', in Abdul R. JanMohamed and David Lloyd (eds), *The Nature and
     Context of Minority Discourse* (New York and London: Oxford University
     Press, 1990), pp. 102–23; DAVID LLOYD, 'Ethnic Cultures, Minority Discourse
     and the State', in Francis Barker, Peter Hulme and Margaret Iversen (eds),
     Colonial Discourse/Postcolonial Theory (Manchester: Manchester University
     Press, 1994), pp. 220–38.
157. ABDUL R. JANMOHAMED, 'The Economy of Manichaean Allegory: The
     Function of Racial Difference in Colonialist Literature', in Henry Louis
     Gates, Jr (ed.), *'Race', Writing, and Difference*, p. 78.
158. Ibid., p. 82.
159. DAVID LLOYD, 'Genet's Genealogy: European Minorities and the Ends
     of the Canon', in Abdul R. JanMohamed and David Lloyd (eds), *The
     Nature and Context of Minority Discourse* (Oxford: Oxford University Press,
     1990), p. 381. See also DAVID LLOYD, 'Writing in the Shit: Becket,
     Nationalism, and the Colonial Subject', *Modern Fiction Studies* 35: 1 (1989),
     special issue on *Narratives of Colonial Resistance* (ed. Timothy Brennan):
     71–86.

160. DAVID LLOYD, 'Genet's Genealogy', p. 393.
161. DAVID LLOYD, 'Race under Representation', in Robert Young (ed.), *Neocolonialism, Oxford Literary Review* 13 (1991): 69.
162. ABDUL R. JANMOHAMED, 'Negating the Negation as a Form of Affirmation in Minority Discourse', p. 103.
163. Ibid., p. 111.
164. Ibid., p. 117.
165. DAVID LLOYD, 'Ethnic Cultures, Minority Discourse and the State', p. 221.
166. Ibid., pp. 222, 234.
167. See ARIF DIRLIK, 'Culturalism as Hegemonic Ideology and Liberating Practice', in JanMohamed and Lloyd (eds), *The Nature and Context of Minority Discourse*, p. 409.
168. SYLVIA WYNTER, 'On Disenchanting Discourse: "Minority" Literary Criticism and Beyond', in JanMohamed and Lloyd (eds), *The Nature and Context of Minority Discourse*, pp. 433–34, 459.
169. SYLVIA WYNTER, 'On Disenchanting Discourse', pp. 461–2.
170. ABDUL R. JANMOHAMED, 'Negating the Negation as a Form of Affirmation in Minority Discourse', p. 123.
171. ABDUL R. JANMOHAMED, 'Worldliness-Without-World, Homelessness-as-Home', in Jessica Munns and Gita Rajan (eds), *A Cultural Studies Reader: History, Theory, Practice* (Harlow and New York: Longman, 1995), p. 457. For another nuanced critique and cautionary note, see CORNEL WEST, 'Minority Discourse and the Pitfalls of Canon Formation', in Munns and Rajan (eds), *A Cultural Studies Reader*, pp. 413–19.
172. SYLVIA WYNTER, 'On Disenchanting Discourse', p. 459, n. 53.
173. HENRY LOUIS GATES, JR, 'Authority, (White) Power, and the (Black) Critic: It's All Greek to Me', in JanMohamed and Lloyd (eds), *The Nature and Context of Minority Discourse*, p. 84.
174. JANHEINZ JAHN, *A History of Neo-African Literature*.
175. HENRY LOUIS GATES, JR, *Figures in Black: Words, Signs and the 'Racial' Self* (Oxford: Oxford University Press, 1987), p. xviii.
176. HENRY LOUIS GATES, JR, *The Signifying Monkey: a theory of African–American literary criticism* (New York: Oxford University Press, 1988), p. 113.
177. Edward Kamau Brathwaite helps us to link our discussion of the Caribbean to the developments in the New World. As he points out, one of the earliest black poets to be paid any attention in the United States was Claude McKay, who himself was Jamaican. According to Brathwaite, McKay forsook his 'nation language' in his pursuit of universality. This, of course, recalls the criticisms of Achebe. See EDWARD KAMAU BRATHWAITE, *History of the Voice: The Development of National Language in Anglophone Caribbean Poetry*, pp. 19–22.
178. This was a more diverse and complex movement than it might seem on the surface. See JARVIS ANDERSON *This was Harlem: a Cultural Portrait* (New York: Farrar Strauss Giroux, 1982); NATHAN HUGGINS *Harlem Renaissance* (Oxford: Oxford University Press, 1971); JAMES DE JONGH *Vicious Modernism: black Harlem and the literary imagination* (Cambridge: Cambridge University Press, 1990); DAVID LEWIS *When Harlem was in Vogue* (New York: Vintage, 1982).
179. GATES, *Figures in Black*, p. xviii.
180. Ibid., p. xix.

181. Exemplified, for example, in the position he adopted in the collection he edited in 1984, *Black Literature and Literary Theory* (London: Methuen).

182. The point was developed by GATES in his introduction to C. Davis and H.L. Gates (eds) *The Slave's Narrative*.

183. GATES, *Figures in Black*, p. 48.

184. Ibid., p. 2.

185. There has been intense debate over the whole question of such tales. See WILLIAM BASCOM, *African Folktales in the New World* (Bloomington: University of Indiana Press, 1992).

186. LAWRENCE LEVINE, *Black Culture and Consciousness* (New York: Oxford University Press, 1977), p. 347.

187. Published in 1988.

188. GATES, *Figures in Black*, p. 49.

189. From GATES's general foreword to the *Schomburg Library of Nineteenth-Century Black Women Writers*, p. vii.

190. GATES, *Figures in Black*, p. 5.

191. Ibid., p. 6.

192. Which GATES continues to engage with. See the collection he edited: *Reading Black, Reading Feminist: A Critical Anthology* (New York: Meridian Books, 1990).

193. PAUL GILROY, *The Black Atlantic*, p. 6.

194. PAUL GILROY, *'There Ain't No Black in the Union Jack'* (London, Hutchinson, 1987), p. 12.

195. See GATES's 'Talkin' That Talk', in the collection he edited *'Race', Writing and Difference*.

196. TODOROV was the author of the introduction to the French translation of Edward Said's *Orientalism*.

197. See ROBERT YOUNG, *White Mythologies* (London: Routledge, 1990) for a succinct account.

198. See ANDREW APTER, 'Que Faire? Reconsidering Inventions of Africa', *Critical Inquiry* 19: 1 (1992) for a summary of these debates.

199. See CHRISTOPHER MILLER, *Theories of Africans: Francophone Literature and Anthropology in Africa* (Chicago: University of Chicago Press, 1990).

200. GATES, *Coloured People* (London: Viking, 1994).

201. For examples of this debate, see the further reading pertaining to this section of the introduction.

202. PETER CONRAD, 'Empires of the Senseless', *Observer* (7 February, 1993): 55.

203. ERNEST GELLNER, Letter to the *Times Literary Supplement* (9 April 1993): 15.

204. RUSSELL JACOBY, 'Marginal Returns: The Trouble with Post-Colonial Theory', *Lingua Franca* (September/October 1995): 32.

205. JOHN MACKENZIE, *Orientalism: History, Theory and the Arts* (Manchester: Manchester University Press, 1995), p. 36.

206. DIANA BRYDON, 'New Appoaches to the New Literatures in English: Are We in Danger of Incorporating Disparity?' in *A Shaping of Connections: Commonwealth Literature – Then and Now*, ed. Hena Maes-Jelinek et al. (Mundelstrup: Dangaroo, 1989), p. 93.

207. AIJAZ AHMAD, *In Theory*, p. 3.

208. HELEN TIFFIN, 'Transformative Imageries' in *From Commonwealth to Post-Colonial*, ed. Anna Rutherford (Mundelstrup: Dangaroo, 1992), pp. 429–30.

209. AIJAZ AHMAD, *In Theory*, p. 38.
210. KETU KATRAK, 'Decolonizing Culture: Towards a Theory for Postcolonial Women's Texts', *Modern Fiction Studies* 35: 1 (Spring, 1989): 158.
211. PATRICK WILLIAMS, ' "No Direction Home": Futures for Post-Colonial Studies', *Wasafiri* 23 (Spring 1996): 6.

1 From *Discourse on Colonialism**

Aimé Césaire

Césaire was many things: poet, activist, politician, a man who was an inspiration to many – notably those from his native island of Martinique such as Frantz Fanon and Edouard Glissant. His brand of negritude had a harder edge than that of Senghor, and it is this which connects his work with that of Fanon. It is the island's history that contributes so much to Césaire's poetry, notably his *Return to my Native Land*, but it also informs his whole world-view. The nature of colonial society in Martinique was a direct reflection of this history, its class hierarchies conditioned by its economic role for the French, based largely on sugar cultivation. An élite pledged its allegience to France and French culture, but in the cane fields it was a different world, a black world of grinding poverty and ceaseless toil (powerfully evoked in Joseph Zobel's novel *Black Shack Alley*, 1980). It was this world which Césaire sought to emancipate and it was his understanding of it and its intimate links with colonialism that informed his poet's vision rather than some image of a 'pure' Africa. But Césaire's poetics were backed by a rigorous analysis of colonialism and nowhere did he state this more fully than here in his *Discourse on Colonialism* which must be viewed as a founding text for post-colonial criticism. From its very beginning we can feel the weight of Césaire's denunciation. The early almost hypnotic repetition of the word civilization prepares the ground for his contention that Western civilization, in the shape of Europe, is 'morally, spiritually indefensible'. It is the relation between this civilization and colonialism that Césaire sets out to explore and unmask. Slowly, he suggests, inexorably, this Europe proceeds towards savagery. Colonialism, in his analysis, is nothing less than the prelude to Nazism. Hitler was the logical outcome of the colonial process. A civilization which justifies colonialism and colonization is a sick civilization, one which 'calls for

*Reprinted from *Discourse on Colonialism* (1955; reprinted New York: Monthly Review Press, 1972), pp. 9–32, 57–61.

Hitler, I mean its punishment'. This is not simple assertion. Reaching back into the archive of European colonialism Césaire cites the horrors already perpetrated, the ears and heads severed, the villages and towns razed to the ground, 'the societies drained of their essence'. The purported benefits of colonization – roads laid, the 'parody of education' – are as nothing in comparison with what has been lost in the destruction of non-European civilization. In his defence of the latter Césaire comes remarkably close to the position adopted by underdevelopment theorists in the 1970s: 'The great historical tragedy of Africa has been not so much that it was too late in making contact with the rest of the world, as the manner in which that contact was brought about.' Indeed, when he talks of the disruption of natural economies we might be tempted to draw links with the representatives of modern ecology movements who, like Césaire, but using a slightly different vocabulary, suggest that if Europe refuses to change its ways it will have 'drawn up over itself the pall of mortal darkness'. This text, which was written in the 1950s, places the blame for 'Western civilization' firmly on the shoulders of the European bourgeoisie. The two major problems he sees as being the proletariat and the colonial problem and this demonstrates, in part, his allegiance to the Communist Party. But his views evolved and in 1956 he resigned his party membership. No longer, he felt, could the mission of the colonized be subsumed under the rubric of proletarian revolution. In his letter of resignation he stated his new vision which made it clear that he felt questions of race and colonialism should take central stage in any analysis of the modern world. In this way his work and thought prefigures many of the latter developments in postcolonial theory, notably Bhabha's reception of the work of Fanon.

A civilization that proves incapable of solving the problems it creates is a decadent civilization.

A civilization that chooses to close its eyes to its most crucial problems is a stricken civilization.

A civilization that uses its principles for trickery and deceit is a dying civilization.

The fact is that the so-called European civilization – 'Western' civilization – as it has been shaped by two centuries of bourgeois rule, is incapable of solving the two major problems to which its existence has given rise: the problem of the proletariat and the colonial problem; that Europe is unable to justify itself either before the bar of 'reason' or before the bar of 'conscience'; and that, increasingly, it takes refuge in a hypocrisy which is all the more odious because it is less and less likely to deceive.

Europe is indefensible.

Apparently that is what the American strategists are whispering to each other.

That in itself is not serious.

What is serious is that 'Europe' is morally, spiritually indefensible.

And today the indictment is brought against it not by the European masses alone, but on a world scale, by tens and tens of millions of men who, from the depths of slavery, set themselves up as judges.

The colonialists may kill in Indochina, torture in Madagascar, imprison in Black Africa, crack down in the West Indies. Henceforth the colonized know that they have an advantage over them. They know that their temporary 'masters' are lying.

Therefore that their masters are weak.

And since I have been asked to speak about colonization and civilization, let us go straight to the principal lie which is the source of all the others.

Colonization and civilization?

In dealing with this subject, the commonest curse is to be the dupe in good faith of a collective hypocrisy that cleverly misrepresents problems, the better to legitimize the hateful solutions provided for them.

In other words, the essential thing here is to see clearly, to think clearly – that is, dangerously – and to answer clearly the innocent first question: what, fundamentally, is colonization? To agree on what it is not: neither evangelization, nor a philanthropic enterprise, nor a desire to push back the frontiers of ignorance, disease, and tyranny, nor a project undertaken for the greater glory of God, nor an attempt to extend the rule of law. To admit once for all, without flinching at the consequences, that the decisive actors here are the adventurer and the pirate, the wholesale grocer and the ship-owner, the gold-digger and the merchant, appetite and force, and behind them, the baleful projected shadow of a form of civilization which, at a certain point in its history, finds itself obliged, for internal reasons, to extend to a world scale the competition of its antagonistic economies.

Pursuing my analysis, I find that hypocrisy is of recent date; that neither Cortez discovering Mexico from the top of the great teocalli, nor Pizzaro before Cuzco (much less Marco Polo before Cambaluc), claims that he is the harbinger of a superior order; that they kill; that they plunder; that they have helmets, lances, cupidities; that the slavering apologists came later; that the chief culprit in this domain is Christian pedantry, which laid down the dishonest equations *Christianity = civilization, paganism = savagery*, from which there could not but ensue abominable colonialist and racist consequences, whose victims were to be the Indians, the yellow peoples, and the Negroes.

That being settled, I admit that it is a good thing to place different civilizations in contact with each other; that it is an excellent thing to blend different worlds; that whatever its own particular genius may be, a civilization that withdraws into itself atrophies; that for civilizations, exchange is oxygen; that the great good fortune of Europe is to have been a crossroads, and that because it was the locus of all ideas, the receptacle of all philosophies, the meeting place of all sentiments, it was the best center for the redistribution of energy.

But then I ask the following question: has colonization really *placed civilizations in contact*? Or, if you prefer, of all the ways of *establishing contact*, was it the best?

I answer *no*.

And I say that between *colonization* and *civilization* there is an infinite distance; that out of all the colonial expeditions that have been undertaken, out of all the colonial statutes that have been drawn up, out of all the memoranda that have been despatched by all the ministries, there could not come a single human value.

First we must study how colonization works to *decivilize* the colonizer, to *brutalize* him in the true sense of the word, to degrade him, to awaken him to buried instincts, to covetousness, violence, race hatred, and moral relativism; and we must show that each time a head is cut off or an eye put out in Vietnam and in France they accept the fact, each time a little girl is raped and in France they accept the fact, each time a Madagascan is tortured and in France they accept the fact, civilization acquires another dead weight, a universal regression takes place, a gangrene sets in, a center of infection begins to spread; and that at the end of all these treaties that have been violated, all these lies that have been propagated, all these punitive expeditions that have been tolerated, all these prisoners who have been tied up and 'interrogated', all these patriots who have been tortured, at the end of all the racial pride that has been encouraged, all the boastfulness that has been displayed, a poison has been instilled·into the veins of Europe and, slowly but surely, the continent proceeds toward *savagery*.

And then one fine day the bourgeoisie is awakened by a terrific reverse shock: the gestapos are busy, the prisons fill up, the torturers around the racks invent, refine, discuss.

People are surprised, they become indignant. They say: 'How strange! But never mind – it's Nazism, it will pass!' And they wait, and they hope; and they hide the truth from themselves, that it is barbarism, but the supreme barbarism, the crowning barbarism that sums up all the daily barbarisms; that it is Nazism, yes, but that before they were its victims, they were its accomplices; that they tolerated that Nazism

before it was inflicted on them, that they absolved it, shut their eyes
to it, legitimized it, because, until then, it had been applied only to
non-European peoples; that they have cultivated that Nazism, that they
are responsible for it, and that before engulfing the whole of Western,
Christian civilization in its reddened waters, it oozes, seeps, and trickles
from every crack.

Yes, it would be worthwhile to study clinically, in detail, the steps
taken by Hitler and Hitlerism and to reveal to the very distinguished,
very humanistic, very Christian bourgeois of the twentieth century that
without his being aware of it, he has a Hitler inside him, that Hitler
inhabits him, that Hitler is his *demon*, that if he rails against him, he is
being inconsistent and that, at bottom, what he cannot forgive Hitler
for is not *crime* in itself, *the crime against man*, it is not *the humiliation of
man as such*, it is the crime against the white man, the humiliation of the
white man, and the fact that he applied to Europe colonialist procedures
which until then had been reserved exclusively for the Arabs of Algeria,
the coolies of India, and the blacks of Africa.

And that is the great thing I hold against pseudo-humanism: that for
too long it has diminished the rights of man, that its concept of those
rights has been – and still is – narrow and fragmentary, incomplete and
biased and, all things considered, sordidly racist.

I have talked a good deal about Hitler. Because he deserves it: he
makes it possible to see things on a large scale and to grasp the fact
that capitalist society, at its present stage, is incapable of establishing
a concept of the rights of all men, just as it has proved incapable of
establishing a system of individual ethics. Whether one likes it or not,
at the end of the blind alley that is Europe, I mean the Europe of
Adenauer, Schuman, Bidault, and a few others, there is Hitler. At the
end of capitalism, which is eager to outlive its day, there is Hitler. At
the end of formal humanism and philosophic renunciation, there is Hitler.

And this being so, I cannot help thinking of one of his statements:
'We aspire not to equality but to domination. The country of a foreign
race must become once again a country of serfs, of agricultural laborers,
or industrial workers. It is not a question of eliminating the inequalities
among men but of widening them and making them into a law.'

That rings clear, haughty, and brutal and plants us squarely in the
middle of howling savagery. But let us come down a step.

Who is speaking? I am ashamed to say it: it is the Western *humanist*,
the 'idealist' philosopher. That his name is Renan is an accident. That
the passage is taken from a book entitled *La Réforme intellectuelle et
morale*, that it was written in France just after a war which France had
represented as a war of right against might, tells us a great deal about
bourgeois morals.

The regeneration of the inferior or degenerate races by the superior races is part of the providential order of things for humanity. With us, the common man is nearly always a *déclassé* nobleman, his heavy hand is better suited to handling the sword than the menial tool. Rather than work, he chooses to fight, that is, he returns to his first estate. *Regere imperio populos,* that is our vocation. Pour forth this all-consuming activity onto countries which, like China, are crying aloud for foreign conquest. Turn the adventurers who disturb European society into a *ver sacrum,* a horde like those of the Franks, the Lombards, or the Normans, and every man will be in his right role. Nature has made a race of workers, the Chinese race, who have wonderful manual dexterity and almost no sense of honor; govern them with justice, levying from them, in return for the blessing of such a government, an ample allowance for the conquering race, and they will be satisfied; a race of tillers of the soil, the Negro; treat him with kindness and humanity, and all will be as it should; a race of masters and soldiers, the European race. Reduce this noble race to working in the *ergastulum* like Negroes and Chinese, and they rebel. In Europe, every rebel is, more or less, a soldier who has missed his calling, a creature made for the heroic life, before whom you are setting *a task that is contrary to his race* – a poor worker, to good a soldier. But the life at which our workers rebel would make a Chinese or a fellah happy, as they are not military creatures in the least. *Let each one do what he is made for, and all will be well.*

Hitler? Rosenberg? No, Renan.

But let us come down one step further. And it is the long-winded politician. Who protests? No one, so far as I know, when M. Albert Sarraut, the former governor-general of Indochina, holding forth to the students at the Ecole Coloniale, teaches them that it would be puerile to object to the European colonial enterprises in the name of 'an alleged right to possess the land one occupies, and some sort of right to remain in fierce isolation, which would leave unutilized resources to lie forever idle in the hands of incompetents'.

And who is roused to indignation when a certain Revd Barde assures us that if the goods of this world 'remained divided up indefinitely, as they would be without colonization, they would answer neither the purposes of God nor the just demands of the human collectivity'?

Since, as his fellow Christian, the Revd Muller, declares: 'Humanity must not, cannot allow the incompetence, negligence, and laziness of the uncivilized peoples to leave idle indefinitely the wealth which God has confided to them, charging them to make it serve the good of all.'

No one.

I mean not one established writer, not one academician, not one preacher, not one crusader for the right and for religion, not one 'defender of the human person'.

And yet, through the mouths of the Sarrauts and the Bardes, the Mullers and the Renans, through the mouths of all those who considered – and consider – it lawful to apply to non-European peoples 'a kind of expropriation for public purposes' for the benefit of nations that were stronger and better equipped, it was already Hitler speaking!

What am I driving at? At this idea: that no one colonizes innocently, that no one colonizes with impunity either; that a nation which colonizes, that a civilization which justifies colonization – and therefore force – is already a sick civilization, a civilization that is morally diseased, that irresistibly, progressing from one consequence to another, one repudiation to another, calls for its Hitler, I mean its punishment.

Colonization: bridgehead in a campaign to civilize barbarism, from which there may emerge at any moment the negation of civilization, pure and simple.

Elsewhere I have cited at length a few incidents culled from the history of colonial expeditions.

Unfortunately, this did not find favor with everyone. It seems that I was pulling old skeletons out of the closet. Indeed!

Was there no point in quoting Colonel de Montagnac, one of the conquerors of Algeria: 'In order to banish the thoughts that sometimes besiege me, I have some heads cut off, not the heads of artichokes but the heads of men.'

Would it have been more advisable to refuse the floor to Count d'Hérisson: 'It is true that we are bringing back a whole barrelful of ears collected, pair by pair, from prisoners, friendly or enemy.'

Should I have refused Saint-Arnaud the right to profess his barbarous faith: 'We lay waste, we burn, we plunder, we destroy the houses and the trees.'

Should I have prevented Marshal Bugeaud from systematizing all that in a daring theory and invoking the precedent of famous ancestors: 'We must have a great invasion of Africa, like the invasions of the Franks and the Goths.'

Lastly, should I have cast back into the shadows of oblivion the memorable feat of arms of General Gerald and kept silent about the capture of Ambike, a city which, to tell the truth, had never dreamed of defending itself: 'The native riflemen had orders to kill only the men, but no one restrained them; intoxicated by the smell of blood, they spared not one woman, not one child. . . . At the end of the afternoon, the heat caused a light mist to arise: it was the blood of the five thousand victims, the ghost of the city, evaporating in the setting sun.'

es or no, are these things true? And the sadistic pleasures, the
ameless delights that send voluptuous shivers and quivers through
Loti's carcass when he focuses his field glasses on a good massacre of
the Annamese? True or not true?[1] And if these things are true, as no
one can deny, will it be said, in order to minimize them, that these
corpses don't prove anything?

For my part, if I have recalled a few details of these hideous
butcheries, it is by no means because I take a morbid delight in them,
but because I think that these heads of men, these collections of ears,
these burned houses, these Gothic invasions, this steaming blood, these
cities that evaporate at the edge of the sword, are not to be so easily
disposed of. They prove that colonization. I repeat, dehumanizes even
the most civilized man; that colonial activity, colonial enterprise, colonial
conquest, which is based on contempt for the native and justified by
that contempt, inevitably tends to change him who undertakes it; that
the colonizer, who in order to ease his conscience gets into the habit of
seeing the other man as *an animal*, accustoms himself to treating him
like an animal, and tends objectively to transform *himself* into an animal.
It is this result, this boomerang effect of colonization, that I wanted to
point out.

Unfair? No. There was a time when these same facts were a source
of pride, and when, sure of the morrow, people did not mince words.
One last quotation; it is from a certain Carl Siger, author of an *Essai sur
la colonisation* (Paris, 1907):

> The new countries offer a vast field for individual, violent activities
> which, in the metropolitan countries, would run up against certain
> prejudices, against a sober and orderly conception of life, and which,
> in the colonies, have greater freedom to develop and, consequently,
> to affirm their worth. Thus to a certain extent the colonies can serve
> as a safety valve for modern society. Even if this were their only
> value, it would be immense.

Truly, there are stains that it is beyond the power of man to wipe out
and that can never be fully expiated.

But let us speak about the colonized.

I see clearly what colonization has destroyed: the wonderful Indian
civilizations – and neither Deterding nor Royal Dutch nor Standard Oil
will ever console me for the Aztecs and the Incas.

I see clearly the civilizations, condemned to perish at a future date,
into which it has introduced a principle of ruin: the South Sea islands,
Nigeria, Nyasaland. I see less clearly the contributions it has made.

Security? Culture? The rule of law? In the meantime, I look around
and wherever there are colonizers and colonized face to face, I see force,

brutality, cruelty, sadism, conflict, and, in a parody of education, the hasty manufacture of a few thousand subordinate functionaries, 'boys', artisans, office clerks, and interpreters necessary for the smooth operation of business.

I spoke of contact.

Between colonizer and colonized there is room only for forced labor, intimidation, pressure, the police, taxation, theft, rape, compulsory crops, contempt, mistrust, arrogance, self-complacency, swinishness; brainless elites, degraded masses.

No human contact, but relations of domination and submission which turn the colonizing man into a classroom monitor, an army sergeant, a prison guard, a slave driver, and the indigenous man into an instrument of production.

My turn to state an equation: colonization = 'thingification'.

I hear the storm. They talk to me about progress, about 'achievements', diseases cured, improved standards of living.

I am talking about societies drained of their essence, cultures trampled underfoot, institutions undermined, lands confiscated, religions smashed, magnificent artistic creations destroyed, extraordinary *possibilities* wiped out.

They throw facts at my head, statistics, mileages of roads, canals, and railroad tracks.

I am talking about thousands of men sacrificed to the Congo-Océan.[2] I am talking about those who, as I write this, are digging the harbor of Abidjan by hand. I am talking about millions of men torn from their gods, their land, their habits, their life – from life, from the dance, from wisdom.

I am talking about millions of men in whom fear has been cunningly instilled, who have been taught to have an inferiority complex, to tremble, kneel, despair, and behave like flunkeys.

They dazzle me with the tonnage of cotton or cocoa that has been exported, the acreage that has been planted with olive trees or grapevines.

I am talking about natural *economies* that have been disrupted – harmonious and viable *economies* adapted to the indigenous population – about food crops destroyed, malnutrition permanently introduced, agricultural development oriented solely toward the benefit of the metropolitan countries, about the looting of products, the looting of raw materials.

They pride themselves on abuses eliminated.

I too talk about abuses, but what I say is that on the old ones – very real – they have superimposed others – very detestable. They talk to me about local tyrants brought to reason; but I note that in general the old tyrants get on very well with the new ones, and that there has been

established between them, to the detriment of the people, a circuit of
mutual services and complicity.

They talk to me about civilization, I talk about proletarianization and
mystification.

For my part, I make a systematic defense of the non-European
civilizations.

Every day that passes, every denial of justice, every beating by the
police, every demand of the workers that is drowned in blood, every
scandal that is hushed up, every punitive expedition, every police van,
every gendarme and every militiaman, brings home to us the value of
our old societies.

They were communal societies, never societies of the many for the few.

They were societies that were not only ante-capitalist, as has been
said, but also *anti-capitalist*.

They were democratic societies, always.

They were cooperative societies, fraternal societies.

I make a systematic defense of the societies destroyed by imperialism.

They were the fact, they did not pretend to be the idea; despite their
faults, they were neither to be hated nor condemned. They were content
to be. In them, neither the word *failure* nor the word *avatar* had any
meaning. They kept hope intact.

Whereas those are the only words that can, in all honesty, be applied
to the European enterprises outside Europe. My only consolation is that
periods of colonization pass, that nations sleep only for a time, and that
peoples remain.

This being said, it seems that in certain circles they pretend to have
discovered in me an 'enemy of Europe' and a prophet of the return to
the ante-European past.

For my part, I search in vain for the place where I could have
expressed such views; where I ever underestimated the importance of
Europe in the history of human thought; where I ever preached a *return*
of any kind; where I ever claimed that there could be a *return*.

The truth is that I have said something very different: to wit, that
the great historical tragedy of Africa has been not so much that it
was too late in making contact with the rest of the world, as the
manner in which that contact was brought about; that Europe began
to 'propagate' at a time when it had fallen into the hands of the most
unscrupulous financiers and captains of industry; that it was our
misfortune to encounter that particular Europe on our path, and that
Europe is responsible before the human community for the highest heap
of corpses in history.

In another connection, in judging colonization, I have added that
Europe has gotten on very well indeed with all the local feudal lords
who agreed to serve, woven a villainous complicity with them, rendered

their tyranny more effective and more efficient, and that it has actually tended to prolong artificially the survival of local pasts in their most pernicious aspects.

I have said – and this is something very different – that colonialist Europe has grafted modern abuse onto ancient injustice, hateful racism onto old inequality.

That if I am attacked on the grounds of intent, I maintain that colonialist Europe is dishonest in trying to justify its colonizing activity *a posteriori* by the obvious material progress that has been achieved in certain fields under the colonial regime – since *sudden change* is always possible, in history as elsewhere; since no one knows at what stage of material development these same countries would have been if Europe had not intervened; since the technical outfitting of Africa and Asia, their administrative reorganization, in a word, their 'Europeanization', was (as is proved by the example of Japan) in no way tied to the European *occupation*; since the Europeanization of the non-European continents could have been accomplished otherwise than under the heel of Europe; since this movement of Europeanization *was in progress*; since it was even slowed down; since in any case it was distorted by the European takeover.

The proof is that at present it is the indigenous peoples of Africa and Asia who are demanding schools, and colonialist Europe which refuses them; that it is the African who is asking for ports and roads, and colonialist Europe which is niggardly on this score; that it is the colonized man who wants to move forward, and the colonizer who holds things back.

To go further, I make no secret of my opinion that at the present time the barbarism of Western Europe has reached an incredibly high level, being only surpassed – far surpassed, it is true – by the barbarism of the United States.

And I am not talking about Hitler, or the prison guard, or the adventurer, but about the 'decent fellow' across the way; not about the member of the SS, or the gangster, but about the respectable bourgeois. In a time gone by, Léon Bloy innocently became indignant over the fact that swindlers, perjurers, forgers, thieves, and procurers were given the responsibility of 'bringing to the Indies the example of Christian virtues'.

We've made progress: today it is the possessor of the 'Christian virtues' who intrigues – with no small success – for the honor of administering overseas territories according to the methods of forgers and torturers.

A sign that cruelty, mendacity, baseness, and corruption have sunk deep into the soul of the European bourgeoisie.

I repeat that I am not talking about Hitler, or the SS, or pogroms, or summary executions. But about a reaction caught unawares, a reflex

permitted, a piece of cynicism tolerated. And if evidence is wanted,
I could mention a scene of cannibalistic hysteria that I have been
privileged to witness in the French National Assembly.

By Jove, my dear colleagues (as they say), I take off my hat to you
(a cannibal's hat, of course).

Think of it! Ninety thousand dead in Madagascar! Indochina trampled
underfoot, crushed to bits, assassinated, tortures brought back from the
depths of the Middle Ages! And what a spectacle! The delicious shudder
that roused the dozing deputies. The wild uproar! Bidault, looking like
a communion wafer covered with shit – unctuous and sanctimonious
cannibalism; Moutet – the cannibalism of shady deals and sonorous
nonsense; Coste-Floret – the cannibalism of an unlicked bear cub, a
blundering fool.

Unforgettable, gentlemen! With fine phrases as cold and solemn
as a mummy's wrappings they tie up the Madagascan. With a few
conventional words they stab him for you. The time it takes to wet
your whistle, and they disembowel him for you. Fine work! Not a
drop of blood will be wasted.

The ones who drink it to the last drop, never adding any water.
The ones like Ramadier, who smear their faces with it in the manner
of Silenus;[3] Fontlup-Esperaber,[4] who starches his moustache with it, the
walrus moustache of an ancient Gaul; old Desjardins bending over the
emanations from the vat and intoxicating himself with them as with new
wine. Violence! The violence of the weak. A significant thing: it is not
the head of a civilization that begins to rot first. It is the heart.

I admit that as far as the health of Europe and civilization is
concerned, these cries of 'Kill! kill!' and 'Let's see some blood', belched
forth by trembling old men and virtuous young men educated by the
Jesuit Fathers, make a much more disagreeable impression on me than
the most sensational bank holdups that occur in Paris.

And that, mind you, is by no means an exception.

On the contrary, bourgeois swinishness is the rule. We've been on
its trail for a century. We listen for it, we take it by surprise, we sniff
it out, we follow it, lose it, find it again, shadow it, and every day it
is more nauseatingly exposed. Oh! the racism of these gentlemen does
not bother me. I do not become indignant over it. I merely examine
it. I note it, and that is all. I am almost grateful to it for expressing
itself openly and appearing in broad daylight, as a sign. A sign that
the intrepid class which once stormed the bastilles is now hamstrung.
A sign that it feels itself to be mortal. A sign that it feels itself to be a
corpse. And when the corpse starts to babble, you get this sort of thing:

There was only too much truth in this first impulse of the Europeans
who, *in the century of Columbus, refused to recognize as their fellow men*

the degraded inhabitants of the new world.... One cannot gaze upon the savage for an instant without reading the anathema written, I do not say upon his soul alone, but *even on the external form of his body.*

And it's signed Joseph de Maistre.
(That's what is ground out by the mystical mill.)
And then you get this:

From the selectionist point of view, I would look upon it as unfortunate if there should be a very great numerical expansion of the yellow and black elements, which would be difficult to eliminate. However, if the society of the future is organized on a dualistic basis, *with a ruling class of dolichocephalic blonds and a class of inferior race confined to the roughest labor, it is possible that this latter role would fall to the yellow and black elements.* In this case, moreover, they would not be an inconvenience for the dolichocephalic blonds but an advantage. *... It must not be forgotten that* [slavery] *is no more abnormal than the domestication of the horse or the ox.* It is therefore possible that it may reappear in the future in one form or another. It is probably even inevitable that this will happen if the simplistic solution does not come about instead – that of a single superior race, leveled out by selection.

That's what is ground out by the scientific mill, and it's signed Lapouge.

And you also get this (from the literary mill this time):

I know that I must believe myself superior to the poor Bayas of the Mambéré. *I know that I must take pride in my blood.* When a superior man ceases to believe himself superior, he actually ceases to be superior.... *When a superior race ceases to believe itself a chosen race, it actually ceases to be a chosen race.*

And it's signed Psichari-soldier-of-Africa.
Translate it into newspaper jargon and you get Faguet:

The barbarian is of the same race, after all, as the Roman and the Greek. He is a cousin. The yellow man, the black man, is not our cousin at all. Here there is a real difference, a real distance, and a very great one: an *ethnological* distance. *After all, civilization has never yet been made except by whites....* If Europe becomes yellow, there will certainly be a regression, a new period of darkness and confusion, that is, another Middle Ages.

And then lower, always lower, to the bottom of the pit, lower than the shovel can go, M. Jules Romains, of the Académie Française and the

Revue des deux mondes. (It doesn't matter, of course, that M. Farigoule changes his name once again and here calls himself Salsette for the sake of convenience.)[5] The essential thing is that M. Jules Romains goes so far as to write this:

> I am willing to carry on a discussion only with people who agree to pose the following hypothesis: a France that had on its metropolitan soil ten million blacks, five or six million of them in the valley of the Garonne. Would our valiant populations of the Southwest never have been touched by race prejudice? Would there not have been the slightest apprehension if the question had arisen of turning all powers over to these Negroes, the sons of slaves? . . . I once had opposite me a row of some twenty pure blacks. . . . I will not even censure our Negroes and Negresses for chewing gum. I will only note . . . that this movement has the effect of emphasizing the jaws, and that the associations which come to mind evoke the equatorial forest rather than the procession of the Panathenaea. . . . The black race has not yet produced, will never produce, an Einstein, a Stravinsky, a Gershwin.

One idiotic comparison for another: since the prophet of the *Revue des deux mondes* and other places invites us to draw parallels between 'widely separated' things, may I be permitted, Negro that I am, to think (no one being master of his free associations) that his voice has less in common with the rustling of the oak of Dodona – or even the vibrations of the cauldron – than with the braying of a Missouri ass.[6]

Once again, I systematically defend our old Negro civilizations: they were courteous civilizations.

So the real problem, you say, is to return to them. No, I repeat. We are not men for whom it is a question of 'either–or'. For us, the problem is not to make a utopian and sterile attempt to repeat the past, but to go beyond. It is not a dead society that we want to revive. We leave that to those who go in for exoticism. Nor is it the present colonial society that we wish to prolong, the most putrid carrion that ever rotted under the sun. It is a new society that we must create, with the help of all our brother slaves, a society rich with all the productive power of modern times, warm with all the fraternity of olden days.

For some examples showing that this is possible, we can look to the Soviet Union.

But let us return to M. Jules Romains:

One cannot say that the petty bourgeois has never read anything. On the contrary, he has read everything, devoured everything.

Only, his brain functions after the fashion of certain elementary types of digestive systems. It filters. And the filter lets through only what can nourish the thick skin of the bourgeois' clear conscience.

Before the arrival of the French in their country, the Vietnamese were people of an old culture, exquisite and refined. To recall this fact upsets the digestion of the Banque d'Indochine. Start the forgetting machine!

These Madagascans who are being tortured today, less than a century ago were poets, artists, administrators? Shhhhh! Keep your lips buttoned! And silence falls, silence as deep as a safe! Fortunately, there are still the Negroes. Ah! the Negroes! Let's talk about the Negroes!

All right, let's talk about them.

About the Sudanese empires? About the bronzes of Benin? Shango sculpture? That's all right with me; it will give us a change from all the sensationally bad art that adorns so many European capitals. About African music. Why not?

And about what the first explorers said, what they saw. . . . Not those who feed at the company mangers! But the d'Elbées, the Marchais, the Pigafettas! And then Frobenius! Say, you know who he was, Frobenius? And we read together: 'Civilized to the marrow of their bones! The idea of the barbaric Negro is a European invention.'

The petty bourgeois doesn't want to hear any more. With a twitch of his ears he flicks the idea away.

The idea, an annoying fly. [. . .]

One of the values invented by the bourgeoisie in former times and launched throughout the world was *man* – and we have seen what has become of that. The other was the nation.

It is a fact: the *nation* is a bourgeois phenomenon.

Exactly; but if I turn my attention from *man* to *nations*, I note that here too there is great danger; that colonial enterprise is to the modern world what Roman imperialism was to the ancient world: the prelude to Disaster and the forerunner of Catastrophe. Come, now! The Indians massacred, the Moslem world drained of itself, the Chinese world defiled and perverted for a good century; the Negro world disqualified; mighty voices stilled forever; homes scattered to the wind; all this wreckage, all this waste, humanity reduced to a monologue, and you think that all that does not have its price? The truth is that this policy *cannot but bring about the ruin of Europe itself,* and that Europe, if it is not careful, will perish from the void it has created around itself.

They thought they were only slaughtering Indians, or Hindus, or South Sea islanders, or Africans. They have in fact overthrown, one after another, the ramparts behind which European civilization could have developed freely.

I know how fallacious historical parallels are, particularly the one I am about to draw. Nevertheless, permit me to quote a page from Edgar Quinet for the not inconsiderable element of truth which it contains and which is worth pondering.

Here it is:

> People ask why barbarism emerged all at once in ancient civilization.
> I believe I know the answer. It is surprising that so simple a cause
> is not obvious to everyone. The system of ancient civilization was
> composed of a certain number of nationalities, of countries which,
> although they seemed to be enemies, or were even ignorant of each
> other, protected, supported, and guarded one another. When the
> expanding Roman empire undertook to conquer and destroy these
> groups of nations, the dazzled sophists thought they saw at the end
> of this road humanity triumphant in Rome. They talked about the
> unity of the human spirit; it was only a dream. It happened that
> these nationalities were so many bulwarks protecting Rome itself.
> ... Thus when Rome, in its alleged triumphal march toward a single
> civilization, had destroyed, one after the other, Carthage, Egypt,
> Greece, Judea, Persia, Dacia, and Cisalpine and Transalpine Gaul, it
> came to pass that it had itself swallowed up the dikes that protected
> it against the human ocean under which it was to perish. The
> magnanimous Caesar, by crushing the two Gauls, only paved the way
> for the Teutons. So many societies, so many languages extinguished,
> so many cities, rights, homes annihilated, created a void around
> Rome, and in those places which were not invaded by the barbarians,
> barbarism was born spontaneously. The vanquished Gauls changed
> into Bagaudes. Thus the violent downfall, the progressive extirpation
> of individual cities, caused the crumbling of ancient civilization. That
> social edifice was supported by the various nationalities as by so
> many different columns of marble or porphyry.
> When, to the applause of the wise men of the time, each of these
> living columns had been demolished, the edifice came crashing
> down; and the wise men of our day are still trying to understand
> how such mighty ruins could have been made in a moment's time.

And now I ask: what else has bourgeois Europe done? It has
undermined civilizations, destroyed countries, ruined nationalities,
extirpated 'the root of diversity'. No more dikes, no more bulwarks.
The hour of the barbarian is at hand. The modern barbarian. The
American hour. Violence, excess, waste, mercantilism, bluff,
gregariousness, stupidity, vulgarity, disorder.

In 1913, Ambassador Page wrote to Wilson:

'The future of the world belongs to us. . . . Now what are we going
to do with the leadership of the world presently when it clearly falls
into our hands?'

And in 1914: 'What are we going to do with this England and this
Empire, presently, when economic forces unmistakably put the
leadership of the race in our hands?'

This Empire. . . . And the others. . . .

And indeed, do you not see how ostentatiously these gentlemen have just unfurled the banner of anti-colonialism?

'*Aid to the disinherited countries*', says Truman. 'The time of the old colonialism has passed.' That's also Truman.

Which means that American high finance considers that the time has come to raid every colony in the world. So, dear friends, here you have to be careful!

I know that some of you, disgusted with Europe, with all that hideous mess which you did not witness by choice, are turning – oh! in no great numbers – toward America and getting used to looking upon that country as a possible liberator.

'What a godsend!' you think.

'The bulldozers! The massive investments of capital! The roads! The ports!'

'But American racism!'

'So what? European racism in the colonies has inured us to it!'

And there we are, ready to run the great Yankee risk.

So, once again, be careful!

American domination – the only domination from which one never recovers. I mean from which one never recovers unscarred.

And since you are talking about factories and industries, do you not see the tremendous factory hysterically spitting out its cinders in the heart of our forests or deep in the bush, the factory for the production of lackeys; do you not see the prodigious mechanization, the mechanization of man: the gigantic rape of everything intimate, undamaged, undefiled that, despoiled as we are, our human spirit has still managed to preserve; the machine, yes, have you never seen it, the machine for crushing, for grinding, for degrading peoples?

So that the danger is immense.

So that unless, in Africa, in the South Sea islands, in Madagascar (that is, at the gates of South Africa), in the West Indies (that is, at the gates of America), Western Europe undertakes on its own initiative a policy of *nationalities*, a new policy founded on respect for peoples and cultures – nay, more – unless Europe galvanizes the dying cultures or raises up new ones, unless it becomes the awakener of countries and civilizations (this being said without taking into account the admirable resistance of the colonial peoples primarily symbolized at present by Vietnam, but also by the Africa of the Rassemblement Démocratique Africain), Europe will have deprived itself of its last chance and, with its own hands, drawn up over itself the pall of mortal darkness.

Which comes down to saying that the salvation of Europe is not a matter of a revolution in methods. It is a matter of the Revolution – the one which, until such time as there is a classless society, will substitute for the narrow tyranny of a dehumanized bourgeoisie the preponderance of the only class that still has a universal mission, because it suffers in its flesh from all the wrongs of history, from all the universal wrongs: the proletariat.

Notes

1. This is a reference to the account of the taking of Thuan-An which appeared in *Le Figaro* in September 1883 and is quoted in N. Serban's book, *Loti, sa vie, son oeuvre*.

   Then the great slaughter had begun. They had fired in double-salvos! and it was a pleasure to see these sprays of bullets, that were so easy to aim, come down on them twice a minute, surely and methodically, on command. . . . We saw some who were quite mad and stood up seized with a dizzy desire to run. . . . They zigzagged, running every which way in this race with death, holding their garments up around their waists in a comical way . . . and then we amused ourselves counting the dead, etc.

2. A railroad line connecting Brazzaville with the port of Pointe-Noire. (Trans.)
3. In classical mythology Silenus was a satyr, the son of Pan. He was the foster-father of Bacchus, the god of wine, and is described as a jolly old man, usually drunk. (Trans.)
4. Not a bad fellow at bottom, as later events proved, but on that day in an absolute frenzy.
5. Jules Romains is the pseudonym of Louis Farigoule, which he legally adopted in 1953. Salsette is a character in one of his books, *Salsette Discovers America* (1942, translated by Lewis Galantiere). The passage quoted, however, appears only in the expanded second edition of the book, published in France in 1950. (Trans.)
6. The responses of the celebrated Greek oracle at Dodona were revealed in the rustling of the leaves of a sacred oak tree. The cauldron, a famous treasure of the temple, consisted of a brass figure holding in its hand a whip made of chains, which, when agitated by the wind, struck a brass cauldron, producing extraordinarily prolonged vibrations. (Trans.)

2 On National Culture*

Frantz Fanon

Fanon's stretching of Marxism, humanism, and nationalism is nowhere more marked than in this chapter from *The Wretched of the Earth*. Fanon describes three stages in the progress of the native writer, from a literature of 'unqualified assimilation', through a 'literature of just-before-the-battle . . . dominated by humour and allegory', but underpinned by 'distress and difficulty', to a 'fighting phase', in which 'death is experienced, and disgust too'. Starting from the premise that 'the native intellectual has thrown himself greedily upon Western culture', a claim that goes to the heart of postcolonial criticism, Fanon proceeds to embark upon a critical cartography that, while privileging the larger collectivities of nation and culture, never loses sight of the way in which these formations impact upon the psyche of the colonized. The essay – and the collection from which it is taken – can usefully be situated between *Black Skin, White Masks* and *Toward the African Revolution*, that is, between the revolutionary psychology elaborated in Fanon's early work and the activism advocated in his most politically engaged writings. In its representation of a crisis for the colonial intellectual, and its insistence on taking sides, Fanon's essay speaks directly to the concerns of Bhabha, Gates, and Said, all of whom have in different ways appropriated him, while in his privileging of nation and class as determining categories, he anticipates critics such as Ahmad and hooks. Especially significant is Fanon's awkward attachment to a humanism that, however much it is extended, radicalized, and revised, arguably remains caught up within a particular Western history of 'Man'. In his fusion of culture and nation Fanon can be seen to disrupt traditional assumptions of the universal application of humanist culture, instead exposing its historical and geographical specificity and political bias. At the same time, his contention

*Reprinted from *The Wretched of the Earth*, trans. Constance Farrington (Harmondsworth: Penguin, 1967; 1990), pp. 167–89.

that national consciousness is the most elaborate form of culture challenges the idea that the nation-state has been superseded, and thus questions the link between postcolonialism and post-nationalism. As for the charge of culturalism frequently levelled at postcolonial critics, Fanon's work here and elsewhere, while maintaining a commitment to political action, places a value on culture and on the individual critic that serves as a reminder of the complex dialectic that obtains between the academy and the outside world, and between critical theory and cultural practice.

Today we know that in the first phase of the national struggle colonialism tries to disarm national demands by putting forward economic doctrines. As soon as the first demands are set out, colonialism pretends to consider them, recognizing with ostentatious humility that the territory is suffering from serious under-development which necessitates a great economic and social effort. And, in fact, it so happens that certain spectacular measures (centres of work for the unemployed which are opened here and there, for example) delay the crystallization of national consciousness for a few years. But, sooner or later, colonialism sees that it is not within its powers to put into practice a project of economic and social reforms which will satisfy the aspirations of the colonized people. Even where food supplies are concerned, colonialism gives proof of its inherent incapability. The colonialist state quickly discovers that if it wishes to disarm the nationalist parties on strictly economic questions then it will have to do in the colonies exactly what it has refused to do in its own country. It is not mere chance that almost everywhere today there flourishes the doctrine of Cartierism.

The disillusioned bitterness we find in Cartier when up against the obstinate determination of France to link to herself peoples which she must feed while so many French people live in want shows up the impossible situation in which colonialism finds itself when the colonial system is called upon to transform itself into an unselfish programme of aid and assistance. It is why, once again, there is no use in wasting time repeating that hunger with dignity is preferable to bread eaten in slavery. On the contrary, we must become convinced that colonialism is incapable of procuring for the colonized peoples the material conditions which might make them forget their concern for dignity. Once colonialism has realized where its tactics of social reform are leading, we see it falling back on its old reflexes, reinforcing police effectives, bringing up troops and setting up a reign of terror which is better adapted to its interests and its psychology.

Inside the political parties, and most often in offshoots from these parties, cultured individuals of the colonized race make their appearance. For these individuals, the demand for a national culture and the affirmation of the existence of such a culture represent a special battlefield. While the politicians situate their action in actual present-day events, men of culture take their stand in the field of history. Confronted with the native intellectual who decides to make an aggressive response to the colonialist theory of pre-colonial barbarism, colonialism will react only slightly, and still less because the ideas developed by the young colonized intelligentsia are widely professed by specialists in the mother country. It is in fact a commonplace to state that for several decades large numbers of research workers have, in the main, rehabilitated the African, Mexican and Peruvian civilizations. The passion with which native intellectuals defend the existence of their national culture may be a source of amazement; but those who condemn this exaggerated passion are strangely apt to forget that their own psyche and their own selves are conveniently sheltered behind a French or German culture which has given full proof of its existence and which is uncontested.

I am ready to concede that on the plane of factual being the past existence of an Aztec civilization does not change anything very much in the diet of the Mexican peasant of today. I admit that all the proofs of a wonderful Songhai civilization will not change the fact that today the Songhais are under-fed and illiterate, thrown between sky and water with empty heads and empty eyes. But it has been remarked several times that this passionate search for a national culture which existed before the colonial era finds its legitimate reason in the anxiety shared by native intellectuals to shrink away from that Western culture in which they all risk being swamped. Because they realize they are in danger of losing their lives and thus becoming lost to their people, these men, hot-headed and with anger in their hearts, relentlessly determine to renew contact once more with the oldest and most pre-colonial springs of life of their people.

Let us go farther. Perhaps this passionate research and this anger are kept up or at least directed by the secret hope of discovering beyond the misery of today, beyond self-contempt, resignation and abjuration, some very beautiful and splendid era whose existence rehabilitates us both in regard to ourselves and in regard to others. I have said that I have decided to go farther. Perhaps unconsciously, the native intellectuals, since they could not stand wonder-struck before the history of today's barbarity, decided to go back farther and to delve deeper down; and, let us make no mistake, it was with the greatest delight that they discovered that there was nothing to be ashamed of in the past, but rather dignity, glory and solemnity. The claim to a national culture in the past does not only rehabilitate that nation and serve as a justification for the hope of a future national culture. In the sphere of psycho-affective equilibrium it is responsible for an important change in the native. Perhaps we have not sufficiently demonstrated that colonialism is not simply content to impose its rule upon the present and the future of a dominated country. Colonialism is not satisfied merely with holding a people in its grip and emptying the native's brain of all form and content. By a kind of perverted logic, it turns to the past of the oppressed people, and distorts, disfigures and destroys it. This work of devaluing pre-colonial history takes on a dialectical significance today.

When we consider the efforts made to carry out the cultural estrangement so characteristic of the colonial epoch, we realize that nothing has been left to chance and that the total result looked for by colonial domination was indeed to convince the natives that colonialism came to lighten their darkness. The effect consciously sought by colonialism was to drive into the natives' heads the idea that if the settlers were to leave, they would at once fall back into barbarism, degradation and bestiality.

On the unconscious plane, colonialism therefore did not seek to be considered by the native as a gentle, loving mother who protects her child from a hostile environment, but rather as a mother who unceasingly restrains her fundamentally perverse offspring from managing to commit suicide and from giving free rein to its evil instincts. The colonial mother protects her child from itself, from its ego, and from its physiology, its biology and its own unhappiness which is its very essence.

In such a situation the claims of the native intellectual are no luxury but a necessity in any coherent programme. The native intellectual who takes up arms to defend his nation's legitimacy and who wants to bring proofs to bear out that legitimacy, who is willing to strip himself naked to study the history of his body, is obliged to dissect the heart of his people.

Such an examination is not specifically national. The native intellectual who decides to give battle to colonial lies fights on the field of the whole continent. The past is given back its value. Culture, extracted from the past to be displayed in all its splendour, is not necessarily that of his own country. Colonialism, which has not bothered to put too fine a point on its efforts, has never ceased to maintain that the Negro is a savage; and for the colonist, the Negro was neither an Angolan nor a Nigerian, for he simply spoke of 'the Negro'. For colonialism, this vast continent was the haunt of savages, a country riddled with superstitions and fanaticism, destined for contempt, weighed down by the curse of God, a country of cannibals – in short, the Negro's country. Colonialism's condemnation is continental in its scope. The contention by colonialism that the darkest night of humanity lay over pre-colonial history concerns the whole of the African continent. The efforts of the native to rehabilitate himself and to escape from the claws of colonialism are logically inscribed from the same point of view as that of colonialism. The native intellectual who has gone far beyond the domains of Western culture and who has got it into his head to proclaim the existence of another culture never does so in the name of Angola or of Dahomey. The culture which is affirmed is African culture. The Negro, never so much a Negro as since he has been dominated by the whites, when he decides to prove that he has a culture and to behave like a cultured person, comes to realize that history points out a well-defined path to him: he must demonstrate that a Negro culture exists.

And it is only too true that those who are most responsible for this racialization of thought, or at least for the first movement towards that thought, are and remain those Europeans who have never ceased to set up white culture to fill the gap left by the absence of other cultures. Colonialism did not dream of wasting its time in denying the existence of one national culture after another. Therefore the reply of the colonized peoples will be straight away continental in its breadth. In Africa, the native literature of the last twenty years is not a national literature but a Negro literature. The concept of Negro-ism, for example, was the emotional if not the logical antithesis of that insult which the white man flung at humanity. This rush of Negro-ism against the white man's contempt showed itself in certain spheres to be the one idea capable of lifting interdictions and anathemas. Because the New Guinean or Kenyan intellectuals found themselves above all up against a general ostracism and delivered to the combined contempt of their overlords, their reaction was to sing praises in admiration of each other. The unconditional affirmation of African culture has succeeded the unconditional affirmation of European culture. On the whole, the poets of Negro-ism oppose the idea of an old Europe to a young Africa, tiresome reasoning to lyricism, oppressive logic to high-stepping nature, and on one side stiffness, ceremony, etiquette and scepticism, while on the other frankness, liveliness, liberty and – why not? – luxuriance: but also irresponsibility.

The poets of Negro-ism will not stop at the limits of the continent. From America, black voices will take up the hymn with fuller unison. The 'black world' will see the light and Busia from Ghana, Birago Diop from Senegal, Hampaté Ba from the Sudan and Saïnt-Clair Drake from Chicago will not hesitate to assert the existence of common ties and a motive power that is identical.

The example of the Arab world might equally well be quoted here. We know that the majority of Arab territories have been under colonial domination. Colonialism has made the same effort in these regions to plant deep in the minds of the native population the idea that before the advent of colonialism their history was one which was dominated by barbarism. The struggle for national liberty has been accompanied by a cultural phenomenon known by the name of the awakening of Islam. The passion with which contemporary Arab writers remind their people of the great pages of their history is a reply to the lies told by the occupying power. The great names of Arabic literature and the great past of Arab civilization have been brandished about with the same ardour as those of the African civilizations. The Arab leaders have tried to return to the famous Dar El Islam which shone so brightly from the twelfth to the fourteenth century.

Today, in the political sphere, the Arab League is giving palpable form to this will to take up again the heritage of the past and to bring it to culmination. Today, Arab doctors and Arab poets speak to each other across the frontiers, and strive to create a new Arab culture and a new Arab civilization. It is in the name of Arabism that these men join together, and that they try to think together. Everywhere, however, in the Arab world, national feeling has preserved, even under colonial domination, a liveliness that we fail to find in Africa. At the same time that spontaneous communion of each with all, present in the African movement, is not to be found in the Arab League. On the contrary, paradoxically, everyone tries to sing the praises of the achievements of his nation. The cultural process is freed from the lack of differentiation which characterized it in the African world, but the Arabs do not always manage to stand aside in order to achieve their aims. The living culture is not national but Arab. The problem is not as yet to secure a national culture, not as yet to lay hold of a movement differentiated by nations, but to assume an African or Arabic culture when confronted by the all-embracing condemnation pronounced by the dominating power. In the African world, as in the Arab, we see that the claims of the man of culture in a colonized country are all-embracing, continental and, in the case of the Arabs, world-wide.

This historical necessity in which the men of African culture find themselves to racialize their claims and to speak more of African culture than of national culture will tend to lead them up a blind alley. Let us take for example the case of the African Cultural Society. This society had been created by African intellectuals who wished to get to know each other and to compare their experiences and the results of their respective research work. The aim of this society was therefore to affirm the existence of an African culture, to evaluate this culture on the plane of distinct nations and to reveal the internal motive forces of each of their national cultures. But at the same time this society fulfilled another need: the need to exist side by side with the European Cultural Society, which threatened to transform itself into a Universal Cultural Society. There was therefore at the bottom of this decision the anxiety to be present at the universal trysting place fully armed, with a culture springing from the very heart of the African continent. Now, this Society will very quickly show its inability to shoulder these different tasks, and will limit itself to exhibitionist demonstrations, while the habitual behaviour of the members of this Society will be confined to showing Europeans that such a thing as African culture exists, and opposing their ideas to those of ostentatious and narcissistic Europeans. We have shown that such an attitude is normal and draws its legitimacy from the lies propagated by men of Western culture. But the degradation of the aims of this Society will become more marked with the elaboration of the concept of Negro-ism. The African Society will become the cultural society of the black world and will come to include the Negro dispersion, that is to say the tens of thousands of black people spread over the American continents.

The Negroes who live in the United States and in Central or Latin America in fact experience the need to attach themselves to a cultural matrix. Their problem is not fundamentally different from that of the Africans. The whites of America did not mete out to them any different treatment from that of the whites that ruled over the Africans. We have seen that the whites were used to putting all Negroes in the same bag. During the first congress of the African Cultural Society which was held in Paris in 1956, the American Negroes of their own accord considered their problems from the same standpoint as those of their African brothers. Cultured Africans, speaking of African civilizations, decreed that there should be a reasonable status within the state for those who had formerly been slaves. But little by little the American Negroes realized that the essential problems confronting them were not the same as those that confronted the African Negroes. The Negroes of Chicago only resemble the Nigerians or the Tanganyikans in so far as they were all defined in relation to the whites. But once the first comparisons had been made and subjective feelings were assuaged, the American Negroes realized that the objective problems were fundamentally heterogeneous. The test cases of civil liberty whereby both whites and blacks in America try to drive back racial discrimination have very little in common in their principles and objectives with the heroic fight of the Angolan people against the detestable Portuguese colonialism. Thus, during the second congress of the African Cultural Society the American Negroes decided to create an American society for people of black cultures.

Negro-ism therefore finds its first limitation in the phenomena which take account of the formation of the historical character of men. Negro and African-Negro culture broke up into different entities because the men who wished to incarnate these cultures realized that every culture is first and foremost national, and that the problems which kept Richard Wright or Langston Hughes on the alert were fundamentally different from those which might confront Leopold Senghor or Jomo Kenyatta. In the same way certain Arab states, though they had chanted the marvellous hymn of Arab renaissance, had nevertheless to realize that their geographical position and the economic ties of their region were stronger even than the past that they wished to revive. Thus we find today the Arab states organically linked once more with societies which are Mediterranean in their culture. The fact is that these states are submitted to modern pressure and to new channels of trade while the network of trade relations which was dominant during the great period of Arab history has disappeared. But above all there is the fact that the political regimes of certain Arab states are so different, and so far away from each other in their conceptions that even a cultural meeting between these states is meaningless.

Thus we see that the cultural problem as it sometimes exists in colonized countries runs the risk of giving rise to serious ambiguities. The lack of culture of the Negroes, as proclaimed by colonialism, and the inherent barbarity of the Arabs ought logically to lead to the exaltation of cultural manifestations which are not simply national but continental, and extremely racial. In Africa, the movement of men of culture is a movement towards the Negro–African culture or the Arab–Moslem culture. It is not specifically towards a national culture. Culture is becoming more and more cut off from the events of today. It finds its refuge beside a hearth that glows with passionate emotion, and from there makes its way by realistic paths which are the only means by which it may be made fruitful, homogeneous and consistent.

If the action of the native intellectual is limited historically, there remains nevertheless the fact that it contributes greatly to upholding and justifying the action of politicians. It is true that the attitude of the native intellectual sometimes takes on the aspect of a cult or of a religion. But if we really wish to analyse this attitude correctly we will come to see that it is symptomatic of the intellectual's realization of the danger that he is running of cutting his last moorings and of breaking adrift from his people. This stated belief in a national culture is in fact an ardent, despairing turning towards anything that will afford him secure anchorage. In order to ensure his salvation and to escape from the supremacy of the white man's culture the native feels the need to turn backwards towards his unknown roots and to lose himself at whatever cost in his own barbarous people. Because he feels he is becoming estranged, that is to say because he feels that he is the living haunt of contradictions which run the risk of becoming insurmountable, the native tears himself away from the swamp that may suck him down and accepts everything, decides to take all for granted and confirms everything even though he may lose body and soul. The native finds that he is expected to answer for everything, and to allcomers. He not

only turns himself into the defender of his people's past; he is willing
to be counted as one of them, and henceforward he is even capable of
laughing at his past cowardice.

This tearing away, painful and difficult though it may be, is, however,
necessary. If it is not accomplished there will be serious psycho-affective
injuries and the result will be individuals without an anchor, without a
horizon, colourless, stateless, rootless – a race of angels. It will be also
quite normal to hear certain natives declare 'I speak as a Senegalese and
as a Frenchman . . .' 'I speak as an Algerian and as a Frenchman. . . .'
The intellectual who is Arab and French, or Nigerian and English, when
he comes up against the need to take on two nationalities, chooses, if
he wants to remain true to himself, the negation of one of these
determinations. But most often, since they cannot or will not make a
choice, such intellectuals gather together all the historical determining
factors which have conditioned them and take up a fundamentally
'universal standpoint'.

This is because the native intellectual has thrown himself greedily
upon Western culture. Like adopted children who only stop investigating
the new family framework at the moment when a minimum nucleus of
security crystallizes in their psyche, the native intellectual will try to
make European culture his own. He will not be content to get to know
Rabelais and Diderot, Shakespeare and Edgar Allen Poe; he will bind
them to his intelligence as closely as possible:

> La dame n'était pas seule
> Elle avait un mari
> Un mari très comme il faut
> Qui citait Racine et Corneille
> Et Voltaire et Rousseau
> Et le Père Hugo et le jeune Musset
> Et Gide et Valéry
> Et tant d'autres encore.[1]

But at the moment when the nationalist parties are mobilizing the
people in the name of national independence, the native intellectual
sometimes spurns these acquisitions which he suddenly feels make him
a stranger in his own land. It is always easier to proclaim rejection than
actually to reject. The intellectual who through the medium of culture
has filtered into Western civilization, who has managed to become part
of the body of European culture – in other words who has exchanged his
own culture for another – will come to realize that the cultural matrix,
which now he wishes to assume since he is anxious to appear original,
can hardly supply any figureheads which will bear comparison with
those, so many in number and so great in prestige, of the occupying
power's civilization. History, of course, though nevertheless written by

the Westerners and to serve their purposes, will be able to evaluate from time to time certain periods of the African past. But, standing face to face with his country at the present time, and observing clearly and objectively the events of today throughout the continent which he wants to make his own, the intellectual is terrified by the void, the degradation and the savagery he sees there. Now he feels that he must get away from white culture. He must seek his culture elsewhere, anywhere at all; and if he fails to find the substance of culture of the same grandeur and scope as displayed by the ruling power, the native intellectual will very often fall back upon emotional attitudes and will develop a psychology which is dominated by exceptional sensitivity and susceptibility. This withdrawal which is due in the first instance to a begging of the question in his internal behaviour mechanism and his own character brings out, above all, a reflex and contradiction which is muscular.

This is sufficient explanation of the style of those native intellectuals who decide to give expression to this phase of consciousness which is in process of being liberated. It is a harsh style, full of images, for the image is the drawbridge which allows unconscious energies to be scattered on the surrounding meadows. It is a vigorous style, alive with rhythms, struck through and through with bursting life; it is full of colour, too, bronzed, sun-baked and violent. This style, which in its time astonished the peoples of the West, has nothing racial about it, in spite of frequent statements to the contrary; it expresses above all a hand-to-hand struggle and it reveals the need that man has to liberate himself from a part of his being which already contained the seeds of decay. Whether the fight is painful, quick or inevitable, muscular action must substitute itself for concepts.

If in the world of poetry this movement reaches unaccustomed heights, the fact remains that in the real world the intellectual often follows up a blind alley. When at the height of his intercourse with his people, whatever they were or whatever they are, the intellectual decides to come down into the common paths of real life, he only brings back from his adventuring formulas which are sterile in the extreme. He sets a high value on the customs, traditions and the appearances of his people; but his inevitable, painful experience only seems to be a banal search for exoticism. The sari becomes sacred, and shoes that come from Paris or Italy are left off in favour of pampooties, while suddenly the language of the ruling power is felt to burn your lips. Finding your fellow countrymen sometimes means in this phase to will to be a nigger, not a nigger like all other niggers but a real nigger, a Negro cur, just the sort of nigger that the white man wants you to be. Going back to your own people means to become a dirty wog, to go native as much as you can, to become unrecognizable, and to cut off those wings that before you had allowed to grow.

The native intellectual decides to make an inventory of the bad habits drawn from the colonial world, and hastens to remind everyone of the good old customs of the people, that people which he had decided contains all truth and goodness. The scandalized attitude with which the settlers who live in the colonial territory greet this new departure only serves to strengthen the native's decision. When the colonialists, who had tasted the sweets of their victory over these assimilated people, realize that these men whom they considered as saved souls are beginning to fall back into the ways of niggers, the whole system totters. Every native won over, every native who had taken the pledge not only marks a failure for the colonial structure when he decides to lose himself and to go back to his own side, but also stands as a symbol for the uselessness and the shallowness of all the work that has been accomplished. Each native who goes back over the line is a radical condemnation of the methods and of the regime; and the native intellectual finds in the scandal he gives rise to a justification and an encouragement to persevere in the path he has chosen.

If we wanted to trace in the works of native writers the different phases which characterize this evolution we would find spread out before us a panorama on three levels. In the first phase, the native intellectual gives proof that he has assimilated the culture of the occupying power. His writings correspond point by point with those of his opposite numbers in the mother country. His inspiration is European and we can easily link up these works with definite trends in the literature of the mother country. This is the period of unqualified assimilation. We find in this literature coming from the colonies the Parnassians, the Symbolists and the Surrealists.

In the second phase we find the native is disturbed; he decides to remember what he is. This period of creative work approximately corresponds to that immersion which we have just described. But since the native is not a part of his people, since he only has exterior relations with his people, he is content to recall their life only. Past happenings of the bygone days of his childhood will be brought up out of the depths of his memory; old legends will be reinterpreted in the light of a borrowed aestheticism and of a conception of the world which was discovered under other skies.

Sometimes this literature of just-before-the-battle is dominated by humour and by allegory; but often too it is symptomatic of a period of distress and difficulty, where death is experienced, and disgust too. We spew ourselves up; but already underneath laughter can be heard.

Finally, in the third phase, which is called the fighting phase, the native, after having tried to lose himself in the people and with the people, will on the contrary shake the people. Instead of according the people's lethargy an honoured place in his esteem, he turns himself into an awakener of the people; hence comes a fighting literature, a revolutionary literature, and a national literature. During this phase a great many men and women who up till then would never have thought of producing a literary work, now that they find themselves in exceptional circumstances – in prison, with the Maquis or on the eve of their execution – feel the need to speak to their nation, to compose the sentence which expresses the heart of the people and to become the mouthpiece of a new reality in action.

The native intellectual nevertheless sooner or later will realize that you do not show proof of your nation from its culture but that you substantiate its existence in the fight which the people wage against the forces of occupation. No colonial system draws its justification from the fact that the territories it dominates are culturally non-existent. You will never make colonialism blush for shame by spreading out little-known cultural treasures under its eyes. At the very moment when the native intellectual is anxiously trying to create a cultural work he fails to realize that he is utilizing techniques and language which are borrowed from the stranger in his country. He contents himself with stamping these instruments with a hall-mark which he wishes to be national, but which is strangely reminiscent of exoticism. The native intellectual who comes back to his people by way of cultural achievements behaves in fact like a foreigner. Sometimes he has no hesitation in using a dialect in order to show his will to be as near as possible to the people; but the ideas that he expresses and the preoccupations he is taken up with have no common yardstick to measure the real situation which the men and the women of his country know. The culture that the intellectual leans towards is often no more than a stock of particularisms. He wishes to attach himself to the people; but instead he only catches hold of their outer garments. And these outer garments are merely the reflection of a hidden life, teeming and perpetually in motion. That extremely obvious objectivity which seems to characterize a people is in fact only the inert, already forsaken result of frequent, and not always very coherent adaptations of a much more fundamental substance which itself is continually being renewed. The man of culture, instead of setting out to find this substance, will let himself be hypnotized by these mummified fragments which because they are static are in fact symbols of negation and outworn contrivances. Culture has never the translucidity of custom; it abhors all simplification. In its essence it is opposed to custom, for custom is always the deterioration of culture. The desire to attach oneself to tradition or bring abandoned traditions to life again does not only mean going against the current of history but also opposing one's own people. When a people undertakes an armed struggle or even a political struggle against a relentless colonialism, the significance of tradition changes. All that has made up the technique of passive resistance in the past may, during this phase, be radically condemned. In an underdeveloped country during the period of struggle traditions are fundamentally unstable and are shot through by centrifugal tendencies. This is why the intellectual often runs the risk of being out of date. The peoples who have carried on the struggle are more impervious to demagogy; and those who wish to follow them reveal themselves as nothing more than common opportunists, in other words late-comers.

In the sphere of plastic arts, for example, the native artist who wishes at whatever cost to create a national work of art shuts himself up in a stereotyped reproduction of details. These artists, who have nevertheless thoroughly studied modern techniques and who have taken part in the main trends of contemporary painting and architecture, turn their back on foreign culture, deny it and set out to look for a true national culture, setting great store on what they consider to be the constant principles of national art. But these people forget that the forms of thought and what it feeds on, together with modern techniques of information, language and dress have dialectically reorganized the people's intelligences and that the constant principles which acted as safeguards during the colonial period are now undergoing extremely radical changes.

The artist who has decided to illustrate the truths of the nation turns paradoxically towards the past and away from actual events. What he ultimately intends to embrace are in fact the cast-offs of thought, its shells and corpses, a knowledge which has been stabilized once and for all. But the native intellectual who wishes to create an authentic work of art must realize that the truths of a nation are in the first place its realities. He must go on until he has found the seething pot out of which the learning of the future will emerge.

Before independence, the native painter was insensible to the national scene. He set a high value on non-figurative art, or more often was specialized in still-lifes. After independence his anxiety to rejoin his people will confine him to the most detailed representation of reality. This is representative art which has no internal rhythms, an art which is serene and immobile, evocative not of life but of death. Enlightened circles are in ecstasies when confronted with this 'inner truth' which is so well expressed; but we have the right to ask if this truth is in fact a reality, and if it is not already outworn and denied, called in question by the epoch through which the people are treading out their path towards history.

In the realm of poetry we may establish the same facts. After the period of assimilation characterized by rhyming poetry, the poetic tom-tom's rhythms break through. This is a poetry of revolt; but it is also descriptive and analytical poetry. The poet ought, however, to understand that nothing can replace the reasoned, irrevocable taking up of arms on the people's side. Let us quote Depestre once more:

> The lady was not alone;
> She had a husband,
> A husband who knew everything,
> But to tell the truth knew nothing,
> For you can't have culture without making concessions.
> You concede your flesh and blood to it,
> You concede your own self to others;
> By conceding you gain
> Classicism and Romanticism,
> And all that our souls are steeped in.[2]

The native poet who is preoccupied with creating a national work of art and who is determined to describe his people fails in his aim, for he is not yet ready to make that fundamental concession that Depestre speaks of. The French poet René Char shows his understanding of the difficulty when he reminds us that 'the poem emerges out of a subjective imposition and an objective choice. A poem is the assembling and moving together of determining original values, in contemporary relation with someone that these circumstances bring to the front.'[3]

Yes, the first duty of the native poet is to see clearly the people he has chosen as the subject of his work of art. He cannot go forward resolutely unless he first realizes the extent of his estrangement from them. We have taken everything from the other side; and the other side gives us nothing unless by a thousand detours we swing finally round in their direction, unless by ten thousand wiles and a hundred thousand tricks they manage to draw us towards them, to seduce us and to imprison us. Taking means in nearly every case being taken: thus it is not enough to try to free oneself by repeating proclamations and denials. It is not enough to try to get back to the people in that past out of which they have already emerged; rather we must join them in that fluctuating movement which they are just giving a shape to, and which, as soon as it has started, will be the signal for everything to be called in question. Let there be no mistake about it; it is to this zone of occult instability where the people dwell that we must come; and it is there that our souls are crystallized and that our perceptions and our lives are transfused with light.

Keita Fodeba, today minister of internal affairs in the Republic of Guinea, when he was the director of the 'African Ballets' did not play any tricks with the reality which the people of Guinea offered him. He reinterpreted all the rhythmic images of his country from a revolutionary standpoint. But he did more. In his poetic works, which are not well known, we find a constant desire to define accurately the historic moments of the struggle and to mark off the field in which were to be unfolded the actions and ideas around which the popular will would crystallize. Here is a poem by Keita Fodeba which is a true invitation to thought, to de-mystification and to battle.

AFRICAN DAWN
(Guitar music)
Dawn was breaking. The little village, which had danced half the night to the sound of its tom-toms was awaking slowly. Ragged shepherds playing their flutes were leading their flocks down into the valley. The girls of the village with their canaries followed one by one along the winding path that leads to the fountain. In the marabout's courtyard a group of children were softly chanting in chorus some verses from the Koran.

(Guitar music)
Dawn was breaking – dawn, the fight between night and day. But the night was exhausted and could fight no more, and slowly died. A few rays of the sun, the forerunners of this victory of the day, still hovered on the horizon, pale and timid, while the last stars gently glided under the mass of clouds, crimson like the blooming flamboyant flowers.

(Guitar music)
Dawn was breaking. And down at the end of the vast plain with its purple contours, the silhouette of a bent man tilling the ground could be seen, the silhouette of Naman the labourer. Each time he lifted his hoe the frightened birds rose, and flew swiftly away to find the quiet banks of the Djoliba, the great Niger river. The man's grey cotton trousers, soaked by the dew, flapped against the grass on either side. Sweating, unresting, always bent over he worked with his hoe; for the seed had to be sown before the next rains came.

(Cora music)
Dawn was breaking, still breaking. The sparrows circled amongst the leaves announcing the day. On the damp track leading to the plain a child, carrying his little quiver of arrows round him like a bandolier, was running breathless towards Naman. He called out: 'Brother Naman, the head man of the village wants you to come to the council tree.'

(Cora music)
The labourer, surprised by such a message so early in the morning, laid down his hoe and walked towards the village which now was shining in the beams of the rising sun. Already the old men of the village were sitting under the tree, looking more solemn than ever. Beside them a man in uniform, a district guard, sat impassively, quietly smoking his pipe.

(Cora music)

Naman took his place on the sheepskin. The head man's spokesman stook up to announce to the assembly the will of the old men: 'The white men have sent a district guard to ask for a man from the village who will go to the war in their country. The chief men, after taking counsel together, have decided to send the young man who is the best representative of our race, so that he may go and give proof to the white men of that courage which has always been a feature of our *Manding.*'

(Guitar music)

Naman was thus officially marked out, for every evening the village girls praised his great stature and muscular appearance in musical couplets. Gentle Kadia, his young wife, overwhelmed by the news, suddenly ceased grinding corn, put the mortar away under the barn, and without saying a word shut herself into her hut to weep over her misfortune with stifled sobs. For death had taken her first husband; and she could not believe that now the white people had taken Naman from her, Naman who was the centre of all her new-sprung hopes.

(Guitar music)

The next day, in spite of her tears and lamentations, the full-toned drumming of the war tom-toms accompanied Naman to the village's little harbour where he boarded a trawler which was going to the district capital. That night, instead of dancing in the market-place as they usually did, the village girls came to keep watch in Naman's outer room, and there told their tales until morning around a wood fire.

(Guitar music)

Several months went by without any news of Naman reaching the village. Kadia was so worried that she went to the cunning fetish-worker from the neighbouring village. The village elders themselves held a short secret council on the matter, but nothing came of it.

(Cora music)

At last one day a letter from Naman came to the village, to Kadia's address. She was worried as to what was happening to her husband, and so that same night she came, after hours of tiring walking, to the capital of the district, where a translator read the letter to her.

Naman was in North Africa; he was well, and he asked for news of the harvest, of the feastings, the river, the dances, the council tree . . . in fact, for news of all the village.

(Balafo music)
That night the old women of the village honoured Kadia by allowing her to come to the courtyard of the oldest woman and listen to the talk that went on nightly among them. The head man of the village, happy to have heard news of Naman, gave a great banquet to all the beggars of the neighbourhood.

(Bafalo music)
Again several months went by and everyone was once more anxious, for nothing more was heard of Naman. Kadia was thinking of going again to consult the fetish-worker when she received a second letter. Naman after passing through Corsica and Italy was now in Germany and was proud of having been decorated.

(Balafo music)
But the next time there was only a postcard to say that Naman had been made prisoner by the Germans. This news weighed heavily on the village. The old men held council and decided that henceforward Naman would be allowed to dance the Douga, that sacred dance of the vultures that no one who has not performed some outstanding feat is allowed to dance, that dance of the Mali emperors of which every step is a stage in the history of the Mali race. Kadia found consolation in the fact that her husband had been raised to the dignity of a hero of his country.

(Guitar music)
Time went by. A year followed another, and Naman was still in Germany. He did not write any more.

(Guitar music)
One fine day, the village head man received word from Dakar that Naman would soon be home. The mutter of the tom-toms was at once heard. There was dancing and singing till dawn. The village girls composed new songs for his homecoming, for the old men who were the devotees of the Douga spoke no more about that famous dance of the *Manding*.

(Tom-toms)
But a month later, Corporal Moussa, a great friend of Naman's, wrote a tragic letter to Kadia: 'Dawn was breaking. We were at Tiaroye-sur-Mer. In the course of a widespread dispute between us and our white officers from Dakar, a bullet struck Naman. He lies in the land of Senegal.'

(Guitar music)
Yes; dawn was breaking. The first rays of the sun hardly touched the surface of he sea, as they gilded its little foam-flecked waves.

Stirred by the breeze, the palm-trees gently bent their trunks down towards the ocean, as if saddened by the morning's battle. The crows came in noisy flocks to warn the neighbourhood by their cawing of the tragedy that was staining the dawn at Tiaroye with blood. And in the flaming blue sky, just above Naman's body, a huge vulture was hovering heavily. It seemed to say to him 'Naman! You have not danced that dance that is named after me. Others will dance it.'
(Cora music)

If I have chosen to quote this long poem, it is on account of its unquestioned pedagogical value. Here, things are clear; it is a precise, forward-looking exposition. The understanding of the poem is not merely an intellectual advance, but a political advance. To understand this poem is to understand the part one has played, to recognize one's advance and to furbish up one's weapons. There is not a single colonized person who will not receive the message that this poem holds. Naman, the hero of the battlefields of Europe, Naman who eternally ensures the power and perenniality of the mother country, Naman is machine-gunned by the police force at the very moment that he comes back to the country of his birth: and this is Sétif in 1945, this is Fort-le-France, this is Saigon, Dakar, and Lagos. All those niggers, all those wogs who fought to defend the liberty of France or for British civilization recognize themselves in this poem by Keita Fodeba.

But Keita Fodeba sees farther. In colonized countries, colonialism, after having made use of the natives on the battlefields, uses them as trained soldiers to put down the movements of independence. The ex-service associations are in the colonies one of the most anti-nationalist elements which exist. The poet Keita Fodeba was training the Minister for Internal Affairs of the Republic of Guinea to frustrate the plots organized by French colonialism. The French secret service intend to use, among other means, the ex-service men to break up the young independent Guinean state.

The colonized man who writes for his people ought to use the past with the intention of opening the future, as an invitation to action and a basis for hope. But to ensure that hope and to give it form, he must take part in action and throw himself body and soul into the national struggle. You may speak about everything under the sun; but when you decide to speak of that unique thing in man's life that is represented by the fact of opening up new horizons, by bringing light to your own country and by raising yourself and your people to their feet, then you must collaborate on the physical plane.

The responsibility of the native man of culture is not a responsibility *vis-à-vis* his national culture, but a global responsibility with regard to the totality of the nation, whose culture merely, after all, represents one

aspect of that nation. The cultured native should not concern himself
with choosing the level on which he wishes to fight or the sector
where he decides to give battle for his nation. To fight for national
culture means in the first place to fight for the liberation of the nation,
that material keystone which makes the building of a culture possible.
There is no other fight for culture which can develop apart from the
popular struggle. To take an example: all those men and women who
are fighting with their bare hands against French colonialism in Algeria
are not by any means strangers to the national culture of Algeria. The
national Algerian culture is taking on form and content as the battles
are being fought out, in prisons, under the guillotine and in every
French outpost which is captured or destroyed.

We must not therefore be content with delving into the past of
a people in order to find coherent elements which will counteract
colonialism's attempts to falsify and harm. We must work and fight
with the same rhythm as the people to construct the future and to
prepare the ground where vigorous shoots are already springing up.
A national culture is not a folklore, nor an abstract populism that
believes it can discover the people's true nature. It is not made up
of the inert dregs of gratuitous actions, that is to say actions which
are less and less attached to the ever-present reality of the people. A
national culture is the whole body of efforts made by a people in the
sphere of thought to describe, justify and praise the action through
which that people has created itself and keeps itself in existence. A
national culture in underdeveloped countries should therefore take its
place at the very heart of the struggle for freedom which these countries
are carrying on. Men of African cultures who are still fighting in the
name of African–Negro culture and who have called many congresses in
the name of the unity of that culture should today realize that all their
efforts amount to is to make comparisons between coins and sarcophagi.

There is no common destiny to be shared between the national
cultures of Senegal and Guinea; but there *is* a common destiny between
the Senegalese and Guinean nations which are both dominated by the
same French colonialism. If it is wished that the national culture of
Senegal should come to resemble the national culture of Guinea, it is
not enough for the rulers of the two peoples to decide to consider
their problems – whether the problem of liberation is concerned, or the
trade-union questions, or economic difficulties – from similar viewpoints.
And even here there does not seem to be complete identity, for the
rhythm of the people and that of their rulers are not the same. There
can be no two cultures which are completely identical. To believe
that it is possible to create a black culture is to forget that niggers are
disappearing, just as those people who brought them into being are
seeing the break-up of their economic and cultural supremacy.[4] There

will never be such a thing as black culture because there is not a single politician who feels he has a vocation to bring black republics into being. The problem is to get to know the place that these men mean to give their people, the kind of social relations that they decide to set up and the conception that they have of the future of humanity. It is this that counts; everything else is mystification, signifying nothing.

In 1959 the cultured Africans who met at Rome never stopped talking about unity. But one of the people who was loudest in the praise of this cultural unity, Jacques Rabemananjara, is today a minister in the Madagascan government, and as such has decided, with his government, to oppose the Algerian people in the General Assembly of the United Nations. Rabemananjara, if he had been true to himself, ought to have resigned from the government and denounced those men who claim to incarnate the will of the Madagascan people. The ninety thousand dead of Madagascar have not given Rabemananjara authority to oppose the aspirations of the Algerian people in the General Assembly of the United Nations.

It is around the peoples' struggles that African–Negro culture takes on substance, and not around songs, poems or folklore. Senghor, who is also a member of the Society of African Culture and who has worked with us on the question of African culture, is not afraid for his part either to give the order to his delegation to support French proposals on Algeria. Adherence to African–Negro culture and to the cultural unity of Africa is arrived at in the first place by upholding unconditionally the peoples' struggle for freedom. No one can truly wish for the spread of African culture if he does not give practical support to the creation of the conditions necessary to the existence of that culture; in other words, to the liberation of the whole continent.

I say again that no speech-making and no proclamation concerning culture will turn us from our fundamental tasks: the liberation of the national territory; a continual struggle against colonialism in its new forms; and an obstinate refusal to enter the charmed circle of mutual admiration at the summit.

Notes

1. The lady was not alone; she had a most respectable husband, who knew how to quote Racine and Corneille, Voltaire and Rousseau, Victor Hugo and Musset, Gide, Valéry and as many more again (René Depestre: 'Face à la nuit').
2. René Depestre: 'Face à la Nuit'.
3. René Char: 'Partage Formel'.

4. At the last school prize-giving in Dakar, the president of the Senegalese Republic, Leopold Senghor, decided to include the study of the idea of Negro-ism in the curriculum. If this decision was due to an anxiety to study historical causes, no one can criticize it. But if on the other hand it was taken in order to create black self-consciousness, it is simply a turning of his back upon history which has already taken cognizance of the disappearance of the majority of Negroes.

3 An Image of Africa: Racism in Conrad's *Heart of Darkness**

CHINUA ACHEBE

Born in Eastern Nigeria in 1930, Chinua Achebe is probably Africa's most widely read novelist. As well as writing novels, most famously *Things Fall Apart* (1958), Achebe has penned many critical essays addressing a wide range of topics in a clear and accessible fashion. The essay reproduced here is of particular interest to the postcolonial critic for a number of reasons. Firstly, there is Achebe's position in relation to the Anglophone novel as a whole in Africa. Secondly, it strikes a blow at the very heart of the canon of English literature in its efforts to dislodge Conrad, a writer whom Leavis placed at the very pinnacle of English literary achievement. For Achebe, the sins of Conrad are deeply connected to a desire in Western psychology to 'set Africa up as a foil to Europe, a place of negations at once remote and vaguely familiar, in comparison with which Europe's own state of spiritual grace will be manifest'. For Achebe, Conrad in this short work is a 'purveyor of comforting myths'.

Having sifted the text for examples of passages where Africa has been denigrated and misrepresented, Achebe poses the questions: Is this the attitude of Conrad himself or merely the fictional narrator, Marlow? Is Conrad not actually holding up to ridicule aspects of the West's perception of Africa? Achebe's answer is a nuanced one, and here he invokes the English liberal tradition (which could be said to stand in for the European Enlightenment tradition, the monster of many postcolonial critics). Yes, there were those shocked by the atrocities of King Leopold of the Belgians in the Congo, but they were only up in arms the better to hide their own disregard for humanity. Conrad's work simply contributes to this particular ideological agenda. Here Achebe is at his most frank. Conrad was, he suggests, a 'thoroughgoing racist'. In the light of this, can *Heart of Darkness* be

*Reprinted from *Hopes and Impediments* (London: Heinemann, 1989) pp. 1–13. First published in the *Massachusetts Review* 18: 4 (Winter 1977).

considered a great work of art? The answer is an unequivocal 'no'. Not everybody will agree with Achebe's assessment, but it is nonetheless a cogently argued one which clearly demonstrates his pivotal role in bridging the gap between colonial fiction and the realm of criticism which is called postcolonial. Furthermore, if our reading is detailed enough it is possible to see that Achebe's essay is strikingly innovative in a number of important ways which prefigure the work of Edward Said in *Orientalism*. We should note his focus on the systems of binary oppositions in Conrad; his argument that Conrad was working in an archive; his focus on the way in which Conrad portrays blacks as victims, the silent Others of Europe's speaking voice; and, finally, his evocation of aspects of psychic projection. In short, Achebe achieves many of the same things as Said without recourse to the work of Foucault and Gramsci.

In the fall of 1974 I was walking one day from the English Department at the University of Massachusetts to a parking lot. It was a fine autumn morning such as encouraged friendliness to passing strangers. Brisk youngsters were hurrying in all directions, many of them obviously freshmen in their first flush of enthusiasm. An older man going the same way as I turned and remarked to me how very young they came these days. I agreed. Then he asked me if I was a student too. I said no, I was a teacher. What did I teach? African literature. Now that was funny, he said, because he knew a fellow who taught the same thing, or perhaps it was African *history*, in a certain community college not far from here. It always surprised him, he went on to say, because he never had thought of Africa as having that kind of stuff, you know. By this time I was walking much faster. 'Oh well', I heard him say finally, behind me: 'I guess I have to take your course to find out.'

A few weeks later I received two very touching letters from high-school children in Yonkers, New York, who – bless their teacher – had just read *Things Fall Apart*. One of them was particularly happy to learn about the customs and superstitions of an African tribe.

I propose to draw from these rather trivial encounters rather heavy conclusions which at first sight might seem somewhat out of proportion to them. But only, I hope, at first sight.

The young fellow from Yonkers, perhaps partly on account of his age but I believe also for much deeper and more serious reasons, is obviously unaware that the life of his own tribesmen in Yonkers, New York, is full of odd customs and superstitions and, like everybody else in his culture, imagines that he needs a trip to Africa to encounter those things.

The other person being fully my own age could not be excused on the grounds of his years. Ignorance might be a more likely reason; but here again I believe that something more wilful than a mere lack of information was at work. For did not that erudite British historian and Regius Professor at Oxford, Hugh Trevor-Roper, also pronounce that African history did not exist?

If there is something in these utterances more than youthful inexperience, more than a lack of factual knowledge, what is it? Quite simply it is the desire – one might indeed say the need – in Western psychology to set Africa up as a foil to Europe, as a place of negations at once remote and vaguely familiar, in comparison with which Europe's own state of spiritual grace will be manifest.

This need is not new; which should relieve us all of considerable responsibility and perhaps make us even willing to look at this phenomenon dispassionately. I have neither the wish nor the competence to embark on the exercise with the tools of the social and biological sciences but do so more simply in the manner of a novelist responding to one famous book of European fiction: Joseph Conrad's *Heart of Darkness*, which better than any other work that I know displays that Western desire and need which I have just referred to. Of course there are whole libraries of books devoted to the same purpose but most of them are so obvious and so crude that few people worry about them today. Conrad, on the other hand, is undoubtedly one of the great stylists of modern fiction and a good story-teller into the bargain. His contribution therefore falls automatically into a different class – permanent literature – read and taught and constantly evaluated by serious academics. *Heart of Darkness* is indeed so secure today that a leading Conrad scholar has numbered it 'among the half-dozen greatest short novels in the English language'.[1] I will return to this critical opinion in due course because it may seriously modify my earlier suppositions about who may or may not be guilty in some of the matters I will now raise.

Heart of Darkness projects the image of Africa as 'the other world', the antithesis of Europe and therefore of civilization, a place where man's vaunted intelligence and refinement are finally mocked by triumphant bestiality. The book opens on the River Thames, tranquil, resting peacefully 'at the decline of day after ages of good service done to the race that peopled its banks'.[2] But the actual story will take place on the River Congo, the very antithesis of the Thames. The River Congo is quite decidedly not a River Emeritus. It has rendered no service and enjoys no old-age pension. We are told that 'going up that river was like travelling back to the earliest beginning of the world'.

Is Conrad saying then that these two rivers are very different, one good, the other bad? Yes, but that is not the real point. It is not the differentness that worries Conrad but the lurking hint of kinship, of common ancestry. For the Thames too 'has been one of the dark places of the earth'. It conquered its darkness, of course, and is now in daylight and at peace. But if it were to visit its primordial relative, the Congo, it would run the terrible risk of hearing grotesque echoes of its own forgotten darkness, and falling victim to an avenging recrudescence of the mindless frenzy of the first beginnings.

These suggestive echoes comprise Conrad's famed evocation of the African atmosphere in *Heart of Darkness*. In the final consideration his method amounts to no more than a steady, ponderous, fake-ritualistic repetition of two antithetical sentences, one about silence and the other about frenzy. We can inspect samples of this on pages 103 and 105 of the New American Library edition: (a) 'It was the stillness of an implacable force brooding over an inscrutable intention' and (b) 'The steamer toiled along slowly on the edge of a black and incomprehensible frenzy.' Of course there is a judicious change of adjective from time to time, so that instead of 'inscrutable', for example, you might have 'unspeakable', even plain 'mysterious', etc., etc.

The eagle-eyed English critic F.R. Leavis[3] drew attention long ago to Conrad's 'adjectival insistence upon inexpressible and incomprehensible mystery'. That insistence must not be dismissed lightly, as many Conrad critics have tended to do, as a mere stylistic flaw; for it raises serious questions of artistic good faith. When a writer while pretending to record scenes, incidents and their impact is in reality engaged in inducing hypnotic stupor in his readers through a bombardment of emotive words and other forms of trickery, much more has to be at stake than stylistic felicity. Generally normal readers are well armed to detect and resist such underhand activity. But Conrad chose his subject well – one which was guaranteed not to put him in conflict with the psychological predisposition of his readers or raise the need for him to contend with their resistance. He chose the role of purveyor of comforting myths.

The most interesting and revealing passages in *Heart of Darkness* are, however, about people. I must crave the indulgence of my reader to quote almost a whole page from about the middle of the story when representatives of Europe in a steamer going down the Congo encounter the denizens of Africa:

> We were wanderers on a prehistoric earth, on an earth that wore the aspect of an unknown planet. We could have fancied ourselves the first of men taking possession of an accursed inheritance, to be subdued at the cost of profound anguish and of excessive toil. But suddenly, as we struggled round a bend, there would be a glimpse of rush walls, of peaked grass-roofs, a burst of yells, a whirl of black limbs, a mass of hands clapping, of feet stamping, of bodies swaying, of eyes rolling, under the droop of heavy and motionless foliage. The steamer toiled along slowly on the edge of the black

and incomprehensible frenzy. The prehistoric man was cursing us, praying to us, welcoming us – who could tell? We were cut off from the comprehension of our surroundings; we glided past like phantoms, wondering and secretly appalled, as sane men would be before an enthusiastic outbreak in a madhouse. We could not understand because we were too far and could not remember because we were travelling in the night of first ages, of those ages that are gone, leaving hardly a sign – and no memories.

The earth seemed unearthly. We are accustomed to look upon the shackled form of a conquered monster, but there – there you could look at a thing monstrous and free. It was unearthly, and the men were – No, they were not inhuman. Well, you know, that was the worst of it – this suspicion of their not being inhuman. It would come slowly to one. They howled and leaped, and spun, and made horrid faces; but what thrilled you was just the thought of their humanity – like yours – the thought of your remote kinship with this wild and passionate uproar. Ugly. Yes, it was ugly enough; but if you were man enough you would admit to yourself that there was in you just the faintest trace of a response to the terrible frankness of that noise, a dim suspicion of there being a meaning in it which you – you so remote from the night of first ages – could comprehend.[4]

Herein lies the meaning of *Heart of Darkness* and the fascination it holds over the Western mind: 'What thrilled you was just the thought of their humanity – like yours . . . Ugly.'

Having shown us Africa in the mass, Conrad then zeros in, half a page later, on a specific example, giving us one of his rare descriptions of an African who is not just limbs or rolling eyes:

And between whiles I had to look after the savage who was fireman. He was an improved specimen; he could fire up a vertical boiler. He was there below me, and, upon my word, to look at him was as edifying as seeing a dog in a parody of breeches and a feather hat, walking on his hind legs. A few months of training had done for that really fine chap. He squinted at the steam gauge and at the water gauge with an evident effort of intrepidity – and he had filed his teeth, too, the poor devil, and the wool of his pate shaved into queer patterns, and three ornamental scars on each of his cheeks. He ought to have been clapping his hands and stamping his feet on the bank, instead of which he was hard at work, a thrall to strange witchcraft, full of improving knowledge.[5]

As everybody knows, Conrad is a romantic on the side. He might not exactly admire savages clapping their hands and stamping their feet but

they have at least the merit of being in their place, unlike this dog in
a parody of breeches. For Conrad things being in their place is of the
utmost importance.

'Fine fellows – cannibals – in their place', he tells us pointedly.
Tragedy begins when things leave their accustomed place, like Europe
leaving its safe stronghold between the policeman and the baker to take
a peep into the heart of darkness.

Before the story takes us into the Congo basin proper we are given
this nice little vignette as an example of things in their place:

> Now and then a boat from the shore gave one a momentary contact
> with reality. It was paddled by black fellows. You could see from afar
> the white of their eyeballs glistening. They shouted, sang; their bodies
> streamed with perspiration; they had faces like grotesque masks
> – these chaps; but they had bone, muscle, a wild vitality, an intense
> energy of movement, that was as natural and true as the surf along
> their coast. They wanted no excuse for being there. They were a great
> comfort to look at.[6]

Towards the end of the story Conrad lavishes a whole page quite
unexpectedly on an African woman who has obviously been some kind
of mistress to Mr Kurtz and now presides (if I may be permitted a little
liberty) like a formidable mystery over the inexorable imminence of his
departure: 'She was savage and superb, wild-eyed and magnificent. . . .
She stood looking at us without a stir and like the wilderness itself,
with an air of brooding over an inscrutable purpose.' This Amazon
is drawn in considerable detail, albeit of a predictable nature, for two
reasons. First, she is in her place and so can win Conrad's special brand
of approval; and second, she fulfils a structural requirement of the story:
a savage counterpart to the refined, European woman who will step
forth to end the story: 'She came forward, all in black with a pale head,
floating toward me in the dusk. She was in mourning. . . . She took both
my hands in hers and murmured, 'I had heard you were coming'. . . .
She had a mature capacity for fidelity, for belief, for suffering.'[7] The
difference in the attitude of the novelist to these two women is conveyed
in too many direct and subtle ways to need elaboration. But perhaps the
most significant difference is the one implied in the author's bestowal of
human expression to the one and the withholding of it from the other.
It is clearly not part of Conrad's purpose to confer language on the
'rudimentary souls' of Africa. In place of speech they made 'a violent
babble of uncouth sounds'. They 'exchanged short grunting phrases'
even among themselves. But most of the time they were too busy with
their frenzy. There are two occasions in the book, however, when
Conrad departs somewhat from his practice and confers speech, even

English speech, on the savages. The first occurs when cannibalism gets the better of them: ' "Catch 'im", he snapped, with a bloodshot widening of his eyes and a flash of sharp white teeth – "catch 'im. Give 'im to us." "To you, eh?" I asked; "what would you do with them?" "Eat 'im!" he said curtly.'[8] The other occasion was the famous announcement: 'Mistah Kurtz – he dead'.[9]

At first sight these instances might be mistaken for unexpected acts of generosity from Conrad. In reality they constitute some of his best assaults. In the case of the cannibals the incomprehensible grunts that had thus far served them for speech suddenly proved inadequate for Conrad's purpose of letting the European glimpse the unspeakable craving in their hearts. Weighing the necessity for consistency in the portrayal of the dumb brutes against the sensational advantages of securing their conviction by clear, unambiguous evidence issuing out of their own mouth Conrad chose the latter. As for the announcement of Mr Kurtz's death by the 'insolent black head in the doorway', what better or more appropriate *finis* could be written to the horror story of that wayward child of civilization who wilfully had given his soul to the powers of darkness and 'taken a high seat amongst the devils of the land' than the proclamation of his physical death by the forces he had joined?

It might be contended, of course, that the attitude to the African in *Heart of Darkness* is not Conrad's but that of his fictional narrator, Marlow, and that far from endorsing it Conrad might indeed be holding it up to irony and criticism. Certainly Conrad appears to go to considerable pains to set up layers of insulation between himself and the moral universe of his story. He has, for example, a narrator behind a narrator. The primary narrator is Marlow but his account is given to us through the filter of a second, shadowy person. But if Conrad's intention is to draw a cordon sanitaire between himself and the moral and psychological *malaise* of his narrator his care seems to me totally wasted because he neglects to hint, clearly and adequately, at an alternative frame of reference by which we may judge the actions and opinions of his characters. It would not have been beyond Conrad's power to make that provision if he had thought it necessary. Conrad seems to me to approve of Marlow, with only minor reservations – a fact reinforced by the similarities between their two careers.

Marlow comes through to us not only as a witness of truth, but one holding those advanced and humane views appropriate to the English liberal tradition which required all Englishmen of decency to be deeply shocked by atrocities in Bulgaria or the Congo of King Leopold of the Belgians or wherever.

Thus Marlow is able to toss out such bleeding-heart sentiments as these:

They were all dying slowly – it was very clear. They were not
enemies, they were not criminals, they were nothing earthly now
– nothing but black shadows of disease and starvation, lying
confusedly in the greenish gloom. Brought from all the recesses
of the coast in all the legality of time contracts, lost in uncongenial
surroundings, fed on unfamiliar food, they sickened, became
inefficient, and were then allowed to crawl away and rest.[10]

The kind of liberalism espoused here by Marlow/Conrad touched all
the best minds of the age in England, Europe and America. It took
different forms in the minds of different people but almost always
managed to sidestep the ultimate question of equality between white
people and black people. That extraordinary missionary, Albert
Schweitzer, who sacrificed brilliant careers in music and theology
in Europe for a life of service to Africans in much the same area as
Conrad writes about, epitomizes the ambivalence. In a comment
which has often been quoted Schweitzer says: 'The African is indeed my
brother but my junior brother.' And so he proceeded to build a hospital
appropriate to the needs of junior brothers with standards of hygiene
reminiscent of medical practice in the days before the germ theory of
disease came into being. Naturally he became a sensation in Europe and
America. Pilgrims flocked, and I believe still flock even after he has
passed on, to witness the prodigious miracle in Lamberéné, on the edge
of the primeval forest.

Conrad's liberalism would not take him quite as far as Schweitzer's,
though. He would not use the word 'brother' however qualified; the
farthest he would go was 'kinship'. When Marlow's African helmsman
falls down with a spear in his heart he gives his white master one final
disquieting look: 'And the intimate profundity of that look he gave me
when he received his hurt remains to this day in my memory – like a
claim of distant kinship affirmed in a supreme moment.'[11] It is important
to note that Conrad, careful as ever with his words, is concerned not so
much about 'distant kinship' as about someone *laying a claim* on it. The
black man lays a claim on the white man which is well-nigh intolerable.
It is the laying of this claim which frightens and at the same time
fascinates Conrad, 'the thought of their humanity – like yours. . . . Ugly'.

The point of my observations should be quite clear by now, namely
that Joseph Conrad was a thoroughgoing racist. That this simple truth is
glossed over in criticisms of his work is due to the fact that white racism
against Africa is such a normal way of thinking that its manifestations
go completely unremarked. Students of *Heart of Darkness* will often tell
you that Conrad is concerned not so much with Africa as with the
deterioration of one European mind caused by solitude and sickness.
They will point out to you that Conrad is, if anything, less charitable to

the Europeans in the story than he is to the natives, that the point of
the story is to ridicule Europe's civilizing mission in Africa. A Conrad
student informed me in Scotland that Africa is merely a setting for the
disintegration of the mind of Mr Kurtz.

Which is partly the point. Africa as setting and backdrop which
eliminates the African as human factor. Africa as a metaphysical
battlefield devoid of all recognizable humanity, into which the
wandering European enters at his peril. Can nobody see the preposterous
and perverse arrogance in thus reducing Africa to the role of props for
the break-up of one petty European mind? But that is not even the
point. The real question is the dehumanization of Africa and Africans
which this age-long attitude has fostered and continues to foster in the
world. And the question is whether a novel which celebrates this
dehumanization, which depersonalizes a portion of the human race, can
be called a great work of art. My answer is: No, it cannot. I do not
doubt Conrad's great talents. Even *Heart of Darkness* has its memorably
good passages and moments: 'The reaches opened before us and closed
behind, as if the forest had stepped leisurely across the water to bar the
way for our return.' Its exploration of the minds of the European
characters is often penetrating and full of insight. But all that has been
more than fully discussed in the last fifty years. His obvious racism has,
however, not been addressed. And it is high time it was!

Conrad was born in 1857, the very year in which the first Anglican
missionaries were arriving among my own people in Nigeria. It was
certainly not his fault that he lived his life at a time when the reputation
of the black man was at a particularly low level. But even after due
allowances have been made for all the influences of contemporary
prejudice on his sensibility there remains still in Conrad's attitude a
residue of antipathy to black people which his peculiar psychology
alone can explain. His own account of his first encounter with a black
man is very revealing: 'A certain enormous buck nigger encountered in
Haiti fixed my conception of blind, furious, unreasoning rage, as
manifested in the human animal to the end of my days. Of the nigger
I used to dream for years afterwards.'[12]

Certainly Conrad had a problem with niggers. His inordinate love of
that word itself should be of interest to psychoanalysts. Sometimes his
fixation on blackness is equally interesting as when he gives us this
brief description: 'A black figure stood up, strode on long black legs,
waving long black arms'[13] – as though we might expect a black figure
striding along on black legs to wave white arms! But so unrelenting is
Conrad's obsession.

As a matter of interest Conrad gives us in *A Personal Record* what
amounts to a companion piece to the buck nigger of Haiti. At the age
of sixteen Conrad encountered his first Englishman in Europe. He calls

him 'my unforgettable Englishman' and describes him in the following manner:

> [his] calves exposed to the public gaze . . . dazzled the beholder by the splendour of their marble-like condition and their rich tone of young ivory. . . . The light of a headlong, exalted satisfaction with the world of men . . . illumined his face . . . and triumphant eyes. In passing he cast a glance of kindly curiosity and a friendly gleam of big, sound, shiny teeth . . . his white calves twinkled sturdily.[14]

Irrational love and irrational hate jostling together in the heart of that talented, tormented man. But whereas irrational love may at worst engender foolish acts of indiscretion, irrational hate can endanger the life of the community. Naturally Conrad is a dream for psychoanalytic critics. Perhaps the most detailed study of him in this direction is by Bernard C. Meyer, MD. In his lengthy book Dr Meyer follows every conceivable lead (and sometime inconceivable ones) to explain Conrad. As an example he gives us long disquisitions on the significance of hair and hair-cutting in Conrad. And yet not even one word is spared for his attitude to black people. Not even the discussion of Conrad's antisemitism was enough to spark off in Dr Meyer's mind those other dark and explosive thoughts. Which only leads one to surmise that Western psychoanalysts must regard the kind of racism displayed by Conrad as absolutely normal despite the profoundly important work done by Frantz Fanon in the psychiatric hospitals of French Algeria.

Whatever Conrad's problems were, you might say he is now safely dead. Quite true. Unfortunately his heart of darkness plagues us still. Which is why an offensive and deplorable book can be described by a serious scholar as 'among the half-dozen greatest short novels in the English language'. And why it is today perhaps the most commonly prescribed novel in twentieth-century literature courses in English departments of American universities.

There are two probable grounds on which what I have said so far may be contested. The first is that it is no concern of fiction to please people about whom it is written. I will go along with that. But I am not talking about pleasing people. I am talking about a book which parades in the most vulgar fashion prejudices and insults from which a section of mankind has suffered untold agonies and atrocities in the past and continues to do so in many ways and many places today. I am talking about a story in which the very humanity of black people is called in question.

Secondly, I may be challenged on the grounds of actuality. Conrad, after all, did sail down the Congo in 1890 when my own father was still a babe in arms. How could I stand up more than fifty years after

his death and purport to contradict him? My answer is that as a
sensible man I will not accept just any traveller's tales solely on
the grounds that I have not made the journey myself. I will not trust
the evidence even of a man's very eyes when I suspect them to be as
jaundiced as Conrad's. And we also happen to know that Conrad
was, in the words of his biographer, Bernard C. Meyer, 'notoriously
inaccurate in the rendering of his own history'.[15]

But more important by far is the abundant testimony about
Conrad's savages which we could gather if we were so inclined from
other sources and which might lead us to think that these people
must have had other occupations besides merging into the evil forest
or materializing out of it simply to plague Marlow and his dispirited
band. For as it happened, soon after Conrad had written his book an
event of far greater consequence was taking place in the art world of
Europe. This is how Frank Willett, a British art historian, describes it:

> Gauguin had gone to Tahiti, the most extravagant individual act of
> turning to a non-European culture in the decades immediately before
> and after 1900, when European artists were avid for new artistic
> experiences, but it was only about 1904–5 that African art began to
> make its distinctive impact. One piece is still identifiable; it is a mask
> that had been given to Maurice Vlaminck in 1905. He records that
> Derain was 'speechless' and 'stunned' when he saw it, bought it
> from Vlaminck and in turn showed it to Picasso and Matisse, who
> were also greatly affected by it. Ambroise Vollard then borrowed it
> and had it cast in bronze.... The revolution of twentieth century art
> was under way![16]

The mask in question was made by other savages living just north of
Conrad's River Congo. They have a name too: the Fang people, and are
without a doubt among the world's greatest masters of the sculptured
form. The event Frank Willett is referring to marked the beginning of
cubism and the infusion of new life into European art that had run
completely out of strength.

The point of all this is to suggest that Conrad's picture of the peoples
of the Congo seems grossly inadequate even at the height of their
subjection to the ravages of King Leopold's International Association
for the Civilization of Central Africa.

Travellers with closed minds can tell us little except about themselves.
But even those not blinkered, like Conrad with xenophobia, can be
astonishingly blind. Let me digress a little here. One of the greatest and
most intrepid travellers of all time, Marco Polo, journeyed to the Far
East from the Mediterranean in the thirteenth century and spent twenty
years in the court of Kublai Khan in China. On his return to Venice he
set down in his book entitled *Description of the World* his impressions of

the peoples and places and customs he had seen. But there were at least two extraordinary omissions in his account. He said nothing about the art of printing, unknown as yet in Europe but in full flower in China. He either did not notice it at all or, if he did, failed to see what use Europe could possibly have for it. Whatever the reason, Europe had to wait another hundred years for Gutenberg. But even more spectacular was Marco Polo's omission of any reference to the Great Wall of China, nearly four thousand miles long and already more than one thousand years old at the time of his visit. Again, he may not have seen it; but the Great Wall of China is the only structure built by man which is visible from the moon![17] Indeed travellers can be blind.

As I said earlier Conrad did not originate the image of Africa which we find in his book. It was and is the dominant image of Africa in the Western imagination and Conrad merely brought the peculiar gifts of his own mind to bear on it. For reasons which can certainly use close psychological inquiry the West seems to suffer deep anxieties about the precariousness of its civilization and to have a need for constant reassurance by comparison with Africa. If Europe, advancing in civilization, could cast a backward glance periodically at Africa trapped in primordial barbarity it could say with faith and feeling: there go I but for the grace of God. Africa is to Europe as the picture is to Dorian Gray – a carrier on to whom the master unloads his physical and moral deformities so that he may go forward, erect and immaculate. Consequently Africa is something to be avoided just as the picture has to be hidden away to safeguard the man's jeopardous integrity. Keep away from Africa, or else! Mr Kurtz of *Heart of Darkness* should have heeded that warning and the prowling horror in his heart would have kept its place, chained to its lair. But he foolishly exposed himself to the wild irresistible allure of the jungle and lo! the darkness found him out.

In my original conception of this essay I had thought to conclude it nicely on an appropriately positive note in which I would suggest from my privileged position in African and Western cultures some advantages the West might derive from Africa once it rid its mind of old prejudices and began to look at Africa not through a haze of distortions and cheap mystifications but quite simply as a continent of people – not angels, but not rudimentary souls either – just people, often highly gifted people and often strikingly successful in their enterprise with life and society. But as I thought more about the stereotype image, about its grip and pervasiveness, about the wilful tenacity with which the West holds it to its heart; when I thought of the West's television and cinema and newspapers, about books read in its schools and out of school, of churches preaching to empty pews about the need to send help to the heathen in Africa, I realized that no easy optimism was possible. And there was in any case something totally wrong in offering bribes to the

West in return for its good opinion of Africa. Ultimately the abandonment of unwholesome thoughts must be its own and only reward. Although I have used the word 'wilful' a few times here to characterize the West's view of Africa it may well be that what is happening at this stage is more akin to reflex action that calculated malice. Which does not make the situation more but less hopeful.

The *Christian Science Monitor*, a paper more enlightened than most, once carried an interesting article written by its Education Editor on the serious psychological and learning problems faced by little children who speak one language at home and then go to school where something else is spoken. It was a wide-ranging article taking in Spanish-speaking children in America, the children of migrant Italian workers in Germany, the quadrilingual phenomenon in Malaysia and so on. And all this while the article speaks unequivocally about language. But then out of the blue sky comes this: 'In London there is an enormous immigration of children who speak Indian or Nigerian dialects, or some other native language.'[18] I believe that the introduction of 'dialects', which is technically erroneous in the context, is almost a reflex action caused by an instinctive desire of the writer to downgrade the discussion to the level of Africa and India. And this is quite comparable to Conrad's withholding of language from his rudimentary souls. Language is too grand for these chaps; let's give them dialects!

In all this business a lot of violence is inevitably done not only to the image of despised peoples but even to words, the very tools of possible redress. Look at the phrase 'native language' in the *Science Monitor* excerpt. Surely the only *native* language possible in London is Cockney English. But our writer means something else – something appropriate to the sounds Indians and Africans make!

Although the work of redressing which needs to be done may appear too daunting, I believe it is not one day too soon to begin. Conrad saw and condemned the evil of imperial exploitation but was strangely unaware of the racism on which it sharpened its iron tooth. But the victims of racist slander who for centuries have had to live with the inhumanity it makes them heir to have always known better than any casual visitor, even when he comes loaded with the gifts of a Conrad.

Notes

1. ALBERT J. GUERARD, Introduction to *Heart of Darkness* (New York: New American Library, 1950), p. 9.
2. JOSEPH CONRAD, *Heart of Darkness and The Secret Sharer* (New York: New American Library, 1950), p. 66.
3. F.R. LEAVIS, *The Great Tradition* (London: Chatto & Windus, 1948; second impression 1950), p. 177.

4. CONRAD, *Heart of Darkness*, pp. 105–6.
5. Ibid., p. 106.
6. Ibid., p. 78.
7. Ibid.
8. Ibid., p. 148.
9. Ibid., p. 153.
10. Ibid., p. 82.
11. Ibid., p. 124.
12. Conrad, quoted in JONAH RASKIN, *The Mythology of Imperialism* (New York: Random House, 1971), p. 143.
13. CONRAD, *Heart of Darkness*, p. 142.
14. Conrad, quoted in BERNARD C. MEYER, MD, *Joseph Conrad: A Psychoanalytic Biography* (Princeton NJ: Princeton University Press, 1967), p. 30.
15. Ibid.
16. FRANK WILLETT, *African Art* (New York: Praeger, 1971), pp. 35–6.
17. About the omission of the Great Wall of China I am indebted to 'The Journey of Marco Polo' as recreated by artist MICHAEL FOREMAN, published by *Pegasus* magazine (New York, 1974).
18. *Christian Science Monitor* (Boston, 25 November 1974): 11.

4 Orientalism Reconsidered*

EDWARD W. SAID

In this essay, Said provides an important set of reflections on
Orientalism (1978) and some early critical responses to it. (It also
provides the basis for the afterword to the new edition of *Orientalism*
which appeared in 1995.) In so quickly dismissing the critics he
identifies in the second paragraph of the essay, Said by and large
confirms many of the main arguments of the book. Once again, he
insists on the threefold nature of Orientalism, on the intimate relationship between Western knowledge and its will-to-power over the rest
of the world, on the necessarily interdisciplinary nature of colonial
discourse analysis and on the continuing influence of earlier traditions
of Orientalism on current politics in the Middle East. Many of these
arguments are fleshed out in the context of contemporary Israeli–
Palestinian relations, reminding one that *Orientalism* was 'simply' part
of a trilogy made up of *The Question of Palestine* and *Covering Islam*.

The essay also, however, points to important developments in Said's
thinking – at both the methodological and political level – which
prepare the way for the at times marked contrasts between *Orientalism*
and more recent work such as *Culture and Imperialism* (1993). At the
methodological level, for example, contrary to what one might at
times infer from *Orientalism*, Said now recognizes that the critic cannot
'by an act of pure will or of sovereign understanding stand at some
Archimedean point' outside the object of study. There are also clear
signs that Said will henceforth modify the programmatic, system-
building ambition of the earlier text. At a thematic level, there are
three principal developments. Firstly, to a greater extent than is
characteristically the case in *Orientalism*, Said admits to significant
variations in the histories of Orientalism and offers a more nuanced
account of the way textuality shapes or modifies, rather than simply

---

*Reprinted from FRANCIS BARKER et al. (eds), *Europe and Its Others* (Colchester:
University of Essex, 1985), vol. 1, pp. 14–27.

constructs, the objects it describes. Secondly, Said now accepts more explicitly that there was resistance to Orientalism and that such resistance must be registered in both the colonizing and colonized formations. The essay also marks Said's increasing recognition of earlier kinds of anti-colonial critical analysis, including the work of Fanon and Césaire. Finally, Said sketches out elements of a way forward from the confrontational and dichotomizing political vision of Orientalism and 'nativist' counter-discourse alike, proposing a reconstituted vision of humanism as a basis for breaking down essentialist conceptions of cultural difference and thus avoiding the 'politics of blame' to which they lead. Perhaps for the first time in the history of postcolonial criticism, there is an explicit recognition of two crucial problems. On the one hand, how to negotiate between a recognition of the heterogeneity of the experiences and identities of the (formerly) colonized and the necessity of finding common ground against the obstacles to decolonization; on the other, how to transcend the 'politics of blame' without underplaying the historical realities of colonial oppression.

There are two sets of problems that I'd like to take up, each of them deriving from the general issues addressed in *Orientalism*,[1] of which the most important are: the representation of other cultures, societies, histories; the relationship between power and knowledge; the role of the intellectual; the methodological questions that have to do with the relationships between different kinds of texts, between text and context, between text and history.

I should make a couple of things clear at the outset, however. First of all, I shall be using the word 'Orientalism' less to refer to my book than to the problems to which my book is related; moreover I shall be dealing, as will be evident, with the intellectual and political territory covered both by *Orientalism* (the book) as well as the work I have done since. This imposes no obligation on my audience to have read me since *Orientalism*; I mention it only as an index of the fact that since writing *Orientalism* I have thought of myself as continuing to look at the problems that first interested me in that book but which are still far from resolved. Second, I would not want it to be thought the license afforded me by the present occasion – for which of course I am grateful – is an attempt to answer my critics. Fortunately, *Orientalism* elicited a great deal of comment, much of it positive and instructive, yet a fair amount of it hostile and in some cases (understandably) abusive. But the fact is that I have not digested and understood everything that was either written or said. Instead I have grasped some of the problems and answers proposed by some of my critics, and because they strike me as useful in focusing an argument, these are the ones I shall be taking into account in the comments that follow. Others – like my exclusion of German Orientalism, which no one has given any reason for me to have *included* – have frankly struck me as superficial or trivial, and there seems no point in even responding to them. Similarly the claims made by Dennis Porter, among others, that I am ahistorical and inconsistent, would have more interest if the virtues of consistency (whatever may be intended by the term) were subjected to rigorous analysis; as for my ahistoricity that too is a charge more weighty in assertion than it is in proof.

Now let me quickly sketch the two sets of problems I'd like to deal with here. As a department of thought and expertise Orientalism of course refers to several overlapping domains: firstly, the changing historical and cultural relationship between Europe and Asia, a relationship with a 4,000-year-old history; secondly, the scientific discipline in the West according to which beginning in the early nineteenth century one specialized in the study of various Oriental cultures and traditions; and, thirdly, the ideological suppositions, images and fantasies about a currently important and politically urgent region of the world called the Orient. The relatively common denominator between these three aspects of Orientalism is the line separating Occident from Orient and this, I have argued, is less a fact of nature than it is a fact of human production, which I have called imaginative geography. This is, however, neither to say that the division between Orient and Occident is unchanging nor is it to say that it is simply fictional. It is to say – emphatically – that as with aspects of what Vico calls the world of nations, the Orient and the Occident are facts produced by human beings, and as such must be studied as integral components of the social, and not the divine or natural, world. And because the social world includes the person or subject doing the studying as well as the object or realm being studied, it is imperative to include them both in any consideration of Orientalism for, obviously enough, there could be no Orientalism without, on the one hand, the Orientalists, and on the other, the Orientals.

Far from being a crudely political apprehension of what has been called the problem of Orientalism, this is in reality a fact basic to any theory of interpretation, or hermeneutics. Yet, and this is the first set of problems I want to consider, there is still a remarkable unwillingness to discuss the problems of Orientalism in the political or ethical or even epistemological contexts proper to it. This is as true of professional literary critics who have written about my book, as it is of course of the Orientalists themselves. Since it seems to me patently impossible to dismiss the truth of Orientalism's political origin and its continuing political actuality, we are obliged on intellectual as well as political grounds to investigate the resistance to the politics of Orientalism, a resistance that is richly symptomatic of precisely what is denied.

If the first set of problems is concerned with the problems of Orientalism reconsidered from the standpoint of local issues like who writes or studies the Orient, in what institutional or discursive setting, for what audience, and with what ends in mind, the second set of problems takes us to a wider circle of issues. These are the issues raised initially by methodology and then considerably sharpened by questions as to how the production of knowledge best serves communal, as opposed to factional, ends, how knowledge that is non-dominative and non-coercive can be produced in a setting that is deeply inscribed with the politics, the considerations, the positions, and the strategies of power. In these methodological and moral reconsiderations of Orientalism I shall quite consciously be alluding to similar issues raised by the experiences of feminism or women's studies, black or ethnic studies, socialist and anti-imperialist studies, all of which take for their point of departure the right of formerly un- or mis-represented human groups to speak for and represent themselves in domains defined, politically and intellectually, as normally excluding them, usurping their signifying and representing functions, overriding their historical reality. In short, Orientalism reconsidered in this wider and libertarian optic entails nothing less than the creation of new objects for a new kind of knowledge.

But let me now return to the local problems I referred to first. The hindsight of authors not only stimulates in them a sense of regret at what they could or ought to have done but did not; it also gives them a wider perspective in which to comprehend what they did. In my own case I have been helped to achieve this broader understanding by nearly everyone who wrote about my book, and who saw it – for better or worse – as being part of current debates, conflicts and contested interpretations in the Arab–Islamic world, as that world interacts with the United States and Europe. Certainly there can be no doubt that – in my own rather limited case – the consciousness of being an Oriental goes back to my youth in colonial Palestine and Egypt, although the impulse to resist its accompanying impingements was nurtured in the heady atmosphere of the post-World War II period of independence when Arab nationalism, Nasserism, the 1967 War, the rise of the Palestine national movement, the 1973 War, the Lebanese Civil War, the Iranian Revolution and its horrific aftermath, produced that extraordinary series of highs and lows which has neither ended nor allowed us a full understanding of its remarkable revolutionary impact.

The interesting point here is how difficult it is to try to understand a region of the world whose principal features seem to be, first, that it is in perpetual flux, and second, that no one trying to grasp it can by an

act of pure will or of sovereign understanding stand at some
Archimedean point outside the flux. That is, the very reason for
understanding the Orient generally and the Arab world in particular,
was first that it prevailed upon one, beseeched one's attention urgently,
whether for economic, political, cultural, or religious reasons, and
second, that it defied neutral, disinterested, or stable definition.

Similar problems are commonplace in the interpretation of literary
texts. Each age, for instance, re-interprets Shakespeare, not because
Shakespeare changes, but because, despite the existence of numerous
and reliable editions of Shakespeare, there is no such fixed and
non-trivial object as Shakespeare independent of his editors, the actors
who played his roles, the translators who put him in other languages,
the hundreds of millions of readers who have read him or watched
performances of his plays since the late sixteenth century. On the
other hand, it is too much to say that Shakespeare has no independent
existence at all, and that he is completely reconstituted every time
someone reads, acts, or writes about him. In fact Shakespeare leads
an institutional or cultural life that among other things has guaranteed
his eminence as a great poet, his authorship of thirty-odd plays, his
extraordinary canonical powers in the West. The point I am making
here is a rudimentary one: that even so relatively inert an object as a
literary text is commonly supposed to gain some of its identity from
its historical moment interacting with the attentions, judgements,
scholarship and performances of its readers. But, I discovered, this
privilege was rarely allowed the Orient, the Arabs, or Islam, which
separately or together were supposed by mainstream academic thought
to be confined to the fixed status of an object frozen once and for all in
time by the gaze of Western percipients.

Far from being a defense either of the Arabs or Islam – as my book
was taken by many to be – my argument was that neither existed
except as 'communities of interpretation' which gave them existence,
and that, like the Orient itself, each designation represented interests,
claims, projects, ambitions and rhetorics that were not only in violent
disagreement, but were in a situation of open warfare. So saturated
with meanings, so overdetermined by history, religion and politics are
labels like 'Arab' or 'muslim' as subdivisions of 'The Orient' that no one
today can use them without some attention to the formidable polemical
mediations that screen the objects, if they exist at all, that the labels
designate.

I do not think it is too much to say that the more these observations
have been made by one party, the more routinely they are denied by
the other; this is true whether it is Arabs or Muslims discussing the
meaing of Arabism or Islam, or whether an Arab or Muslim disputes
these designations with a Western scholar. Anyone who tries to suggest

that nothing, not even a simple descriptive label, is beyond or outside
the realm of interpretation, is almost certain to find an opponent
saying that science and learning are designed to transcend the vagaries
of interpretation, and that objective truth is in fact attainable. This
claim was more than a little political when used against Orientals who
disputed the authority and objectivity of an Orientalism intimately allied
with the great mass of European settlements in the Orient. At bottom,
what I said in *Orientalism* had been said before me by A.L. Tibawi, by
Abdullah Laroui, by Anwar Abdel Malek, by Talal Asad, by S.H. Alatas,
by Fanon and Césaire, by Pannikar, and Romila Thapar, all of whom
had suffered the ravages of imperialism and colonialism, and who in
challenging the authority, provenance, and institutions of the science
that represented them to Europe, were also understanding themselves
as something more than what this science said they were.

Nor was this all. The challenge to Orientalism and the colonial era of
which it is so organically a part, was a challenge to the muteness imposed
upon the Orient as object. In so far as it was a science of incorporation
and inclusion by virtue of which the Orient was constituted and then
introduced into Europe, Orientalism was a scientific movement whose
analogue in the world of empirical politics was the Orient's colonial
accumulation and acquisition by Europe. The Orient was therefore not
Europe's interlocutor, but its silent Other. From roughly the end of
the eighteenth century, when in its age, distance and richness the Orient
was rediscovered by Europe, its history had been a paradigm of
antiquity and originality, functions that drew Europe's interests in acts
of recognition or acknowledgement but *from* which Europe moved as its
own industrial, economic and cultural development seemed to leave the
Orient far behind. Oriental history – for Hegel, for Marx, later for
Burkhardt, Nietzsche, Spengler, and other major philosophers of history
– was useful in portraying a region of great age, and what had to be
left behind. Literary historians have further noted in all sorts of
aesthetic writing and plastic portrayals that a trajectory of 'Westering',
found for example in Keats and Holderlin, customarily saw the Orient
as ceding its historical pre-eminence and importance to the world spirit
moving westwards away from Asia and towards Europe.

As primitivity, as the age-old antetype of Europe, as a fecund night
out of which European rationality developed, the Orient's actuality
receded inexorably into a kind of paradigmatic fossilization. The origins
of European anthropology and ethnography were constituted out of this
radical difference and, to my knowledge, as a discipline anthropology
has not yet dealt with this inherent political limitation upon its
supposedly disinterested universality. This, by the way, is one reason
Johannes Fabian's book, *Time and the Other: How Anthropology Constitutes
its Object* is both so unique and so important; compared, say, with the

standard disciplinary rationalizations and self-congratulatory clichés about hermeneutic circles offered by Clifford Geertz, Fabian's serious effort to redirect anthropologists' attention back to the discrepancies in time, power and development between the ethnographer and his/her constituted object is all the more remarkable. In any event, what for the most part got left out of Orientalism was precisely the very history that resisted its ideological as well as political encroachments, and that repressed or resistant history has returned in the various critiques and attacks upon Orientalism, which has uniformly and polemically been represented by these critiques as a science of imperialism.

The divergences between the numerous critiques made of Orientalism as ideology and praxis, at least so far as their aims are concerned, are very wide nonetheless. Some attack Orientalism as a prelude to assertions about the virtues of one or another native culture: these are the nativists. Others criticize Orientalism as a defense against attacks on one or another political creed: these are the nationalists. Still others criticize Orientalism for falsifying the nature of Islam: these are, grosso modo, the fundamentalists. I will not adjudicate between these claims, except to say that I have explicitly avoided taking stands on such matters as the real, true or authentic Islamic or Arab world, except as issues relating to conflicts involving partisanship, solidarity, or sympathy, although I have always tried never to forsake a critical sense or reflective detachment. But in common with all the recent critics of Orientalism I think that two things are especially important – one, a rigorous methodological vigilance that construes Orientalism less as a positive than as a critical discipline and therefore makes it subject to intense scrutiny, and two, a determination not to allow the segregation and confinement of the Orient to go on without challenge. My own understanding of this second point has led me to the extreme position of entirely refusing designations like 'Orient' and 'Occident', but this is something I shall return to a little later.

Depending on how they construed their roles as Orientalists, critics of the critics of Orientalism have either reinforced the affirmations of positive power lodged within Orientalism's discourse, or much less frequently alas, they have engaged Orientalism's critics in a genuine intellectual exchange. The reasons for this split are self-evident: some have to do with power and age, as well as institutional or guild defensiveness; others have to do with religious or ideological convictions. All, irrespective of whether the fact is acknowledged or not, are political – something that not everyone has found easy to acknowledge. If I may make use of my own example, when some of my critics in particular agreed with the main premises of my argument they tended to fall back on encomia to the achievements of what one of their most distinguished individuals, Maxime Rodinson, called 'la science orientaliste'. This view

lent itself to attacks on an alleged Lysenkism lurking inside the polemics
of Muslims or Arabs who lodged a protest with 'Western' Orientalism,
despite the fact that all the recent critics of Orientalism have been quite
explicit about using such 'Western' critiques as Marxism or structuralism
in an effort to override invidious distinctions between East and West,
between Arab and Western truth, and the like.

Sensitized to the outrageous attacks upon an august and formerly
invulnerable science, many accredited members of the certified
professional cadre whose division of study is the Arabs and Islam have
disclaimed any politics at all, while pressing a rigorous, but for the
most part intellectually empty and ideologically intended counter-attack.
Although I said I would not respond to critics here, I need to mention
a few of the more typical imputations made against me so that you can
see Orientalism extending its nineteenth-century arguments to cover a
whole incommensurate set of late twentieth-century eventualities, all of
them deriving from what to the nineteenth-century mind is the
preposterous situation of an Oriental responding to Orientalism's
asseverations. For sheer heedless anti-intellectualism unrestrained or
unencumbered by the slightest trace of critical self-consciousness no
one, in my experience, has achieved the sublime confidence of Bernard
Lewis, whose almost purely political exploits require more time to
mention than they are worth. In a series of articles and one particularly
weak book – *The Muslim Discovery of Europe* – Lewis has been busy
responding to my argument, insisting that the Western quest for
knowledge about other societies is unique, that it is motivated by pure
curiosity, and that in contrast Muslims neither were able nor interested
in getting knowledge about Europe, as if knowledge about Europe was
the only acceptable criterion for true knowledge. Lewis's arguments
are presented as emanating exclusively from the scholar's apolitical
impartiality whereas at the same time he has become an authority
drawn on for anti-Islamic, anti-Arab, Zionist and Cold War crusades, all
of them underwritten by a zealotry covered with a veneer of urbanity
that has very little in common with the 'science' and learning Lewis
purports to be upholding.

Not quite as hypocritical, but no less uncritical, are younger
ideologues and Orientalists like Daniel Pipes whose expertise as
demonstrated in his book *In the Path of God: Islam and Political Power*
is wholly at the service not of knowledge but of an aggressive and
interventionary State – the US – whose interests Pipes helps to define.
Even if we leave aside the intellectually scandalous generalizing that
allows Pipes to speak of Islam's anomie, its sense of inferiority, its   blow
defensiveness, as if Islam were one simple thing, and as if the quality
of his either absent or impressionistic evidence were of the most
secondary importance, Pipes's book testifies, I think, to Orientalism's

unique resilience, its insulation from intellectual developments
everywhere else in the culture, and its antediluvian imperiousness as
it makes its assertions and affirmations with little regard for logic and
argument. I doubt that any expert anywhere in the world would speak
today of Judaism or Christianity with quite that combination of force
and freedom that Pipes allows himself about Islam, although one would
have thought that a book about Islamic revival would allude to parallel
and related developments in styles of religious resurgence in, for
example, Lebanon, Israel, and the US. Nor is it likely that anyone
anywhere, writing about material for which, in his own words, 'rumour,
hearsay, and other wisps of evidence' are the only proof, will in the
very same paragraph alchemically transmute rumour and hearsay into
'facts' on whose 'multitude' he relies in order 'to reduce the importance
of each'. This is magic quite unworthy even of high Orientalism, and
although Pipes pays his obeisance to imperialist Orientalism he masters
neither its genuine learning nor its pretense at disinterestedness. For
Pipes, Islam is a volatile and dangerous business, a political movement
intervening in and disrupting the West, stirring up insurrection and
fanaticism everywhere else.

The core of Pipes's book is not simply its highly expedient sense of
its own political relevance to Reagan's America where terrorism and
communism fade imperceptibly into the media's image of Muslim
gunners, fanatics and rebels, but its thesis that Muslims themselves are
the worst source for their own history. The pages of *In the Path of God*
are dotted with references to Islam's incapacity for self-representation,
self-understanding, self-consciousness, and with praise for witnesses like
V. S. Naipaul who are so much more useful and clever in understanding
Islam. Here, of course, is perhaps the most familiar of Orientalism's
themes – they cannot represent themselves, they must therefore be
represented by others who know more about Islam than Islam knows
about itself. Now it is often the case that you can be known by others
in different ways than you know yourself, and that valuable insights
might be generated accordingly. But that is quite a different thing than
pronouncing it as immutable law that outsiders *ipso facto* have a better
sense of you as an insider than you do of yourself. Note that there is
no question of an *exchange* between Islam's views and an outsider's: no
dialogue, no discussion, no mutual recognition. There is a flat assertion
of quality, which the Western policy-maker, or his faithful servant
possesses by virtue of his being Western, white, non-Muslim.

Now this, I submit, is neither science, nor knowledge, nor
understanding: it is a statement of power and a claim for relatively
absolute authority. It is constituted out of racism, and it is made
comparatively acceptable to an audience prepared in advance to listen
to its muscular truths. Pipes speaks to and for a large clientele for

whom Islam is not a culture, but a nuisance; most of Pipes's readers will, in their minds, associate what he says about Islam with the other nuisances of the 1960s and the 1970s – blacks, women, post-colonial Third World nations that have tipped the balance against the US in such places as UNESCO and the UN, and for their pains have drawn forth the rebuke of Senator Moynihan and Mrs Kirkpatrick. In addition, Pipes – and the rows of like-minded Orientalists and experts he represents as their common denominator – stands for programmatic ignorance. Far from trying to understand Islam in the context of imperialism and the revenge of an abused, but internally very diverse, segment of humanity, far from availing himself of the impressive recent work on Islam in different histories and societies, far from paying some attention to the immense advances in critical theory, in social science and humanistic research, in the philosophy of interpretation, far from making some slight effort to acquaint himself with the vast imaginative literature produced in the Islamic world, Pipes obdurately and explicitly aligns himself with colonial Orientalists like Snouck Hurgronje and shamelessly pre-colonial renegades like V.S. Naipaul, so that from the eyrie of the State Department and the National Security Council he might survey and judge Islam at will.

I have spent this much time talking about Pipes only because he usefully serves to make some points about Orientalism's large political setting, which is routinely denied and suppressed in the sort of claim proposed by its main spokesman, Bernard Lewis, who has the effrontery to disassociate Orientalism from its 200-year-old partnership with European imperialism and associate it instead with modern classical philology and the study of ancient Greek and Roman culture. Perhaps it is also worth mentioning about this larger setting that it comprises two other elements, about which I'd like to speak very briefly, namely the recent (but at present uncertain) prominence of the Palestinian movement, and secondly, the demonstrated resistance of Arabs in the United States and elsewhere against their portrayal in the public realm.

As for the Palestinian issue, between them the question of Palestine and its fateful encounter with Zionism on the one hand, and the guild of Orientalism, its professional caste-consciousness as a corporation of experts protecting their terrain and their credentials from outside scrutiny on the other hand, these two account for much of the animus against my critique of Orientalism. The ironies here are rich, and I shall restrict myself to enumerating a small handful. Consider the case of one Orientalist who publicly attacked my book, he told me in a private letter, not because he disagreed with it – on the contrary, he felt that what I said was just – but because he had to defend the honor of his profession!! Or, take the connection – explicitly made by two of the authors I cite in *Orientalism*, Renan and Proust – between Islamophobia and anti-Semitism. Here, one would have expected many scholars and critics to have seen the conjuncture, that hostility to Islam in the modern Christian West has historically gone hand in hand with, has stemmed from the same source, has been nourished at the same stream as anti-Semitism, and that a critique of the orthodoxies, dogmas, and disciplinary procedures of Orientalism contribute to an enlargement of our understanding of the cultural mechanisms of anti-Semitism. No such connection has ever been made by critics, who have seen in the critique of Orientalism an opportunity for them to defend Zionism, support Israel, and launch attacks on Palestinian nationalism. The reasons for this confirm the history of Orientalism for, as the Israeli commentator Dani Rubenstein has remarked, the Israeli occupation of the West Bank and Gaza, the destruction of Palestinian society, and the sustained Zionist assault upon Palestinian nationalism has quite literally been led and staffed by Orientalists. Whereas in the past it was European Christian Orientalists who supplied European culture with arguments for colonizing and suppressing Islam, as well as for despising Jews, it is now the Jewish national movement that produces a cadre of colonial officials whose ideological theses about the Islamic or Arab mind are implemented in the administration of the Palestinian Arabs, an oppressed minority within the white-European-democracy that is Israel. Rubenstein notes with some sorrow that the Hebrew University's Islamic studies department has produced every one of the colonial officials and Arab experts who run the Occupied Territories.

One further irony should be mentioned in this regard: just as some Zionists have construed it as their duty to defend Orientalism against its critics, there has been a comic effort by some Arab nationalists to see the Orientalist controversy as an imperialist plot to enhance American control over the Arab world. According to this seriously argued but extraordinarily implausible scenario, we are informed that critics of Orientalism turn out not to be anti-imperialist at all, but covert agents of imperialism. The next step from this is to suggest that the best way to attack imperialism is either to become an Orientalist or not to say anything critical about it. At this stage, however, I concede that we have left the world of reality for a world of such illogic and derangement that I cannot pretend to understand its structure or sense.

Underlying much of the discussion of Orientalism is a disquieting realization that the relationship between cultures is both uneven and irremediably secular. This brings us to the point I alluded to a moment ago, about recent Arab and Islamic efforts, well-intentioned for the most part, but sometimes motivated by unpopular regimes, who in attracting attention to the shoddiness of the Western media in representing the Arabs or Islam divert scrutiny from the abuses of their rule and therefore make efforts to improve the so-called image of Islam and the

Arabs. Parallel developments have been occurring, as no one needs to be told, in UNESCO, where the controversy surrounding the world information order – and proposals for its reform by various Third World and Socialist governments – has taken on the dimensions of a major international issue. Most of these disputes testify, first of all, to the fact that the production of knowledge, or information, of media images, is unevenly distributed: its locus, and the centers of its greatest force are located in what, on both sides of the divide, has been polemically called the metropolitan West. Second, this unhappy realization on the part of weaker parties and cultures, has reinforced their grasp of the fact that although there are many divisions within it, there is only one secular and historical world, and that neither nativism, nor divine intervention, nor regionalism, nor ideological smokescreens can hide societies, cultures and peoples from each other, especially not from those with the force and will to penetrate others for political as well as economic ends. But, third, many of these disadvantaged post-colonial states and their loyalist intellectuals have, in my opinion, drawn the wrong set of conclusions, which in practice is that one must either attempt to impose control upon the production of knowledge at the source, or, in the worldwide media economy, to attempt to improve, enhance, ameliorate the images currently in circulation without doing anything to change the political situation from which they emanate and on which to a certain extent they are based.

The failings of these approaches strike me as obvious, and here I don't want to go into such matters as the squandering of immense amounts of petro-dollars for various short-lived public relations scams, or the increasing repression, human-rights abuses, outright gangsterism that has taken place in many formerly colonial countries, all of them occurring in the name of national security and fighting neo-imperialism. What I do want to talk about is the much larger question of what, in the context recently provided by such relatively small efforts as the critique of Orientalism, is to be done, and on the level of politics and criticism how we can speak of intellectual work that isn't merely reactive or negative.

I come finally now to the second and, in my opinion, the more challenging and interesting set of problems that derive from the reconsideration of Orientalism. One of the legacies of Orientalism, and indeed one of its epistemological foundations, is historicism, that is, the view propounded by Vico, Hegel, Marx, Ranke, Dilthey and others, that if humankind has a history it is produced by men and women, and can be understood historically as, at each given period, epoch or moment, possessing a complex, but coherent unity. So far as Orientalism in particular and the European knowledge of other societies in general have been concerned, historicism meant that the one human history

137

uniting humanity either culminated in or was observed from the vantage point of Europe, or the West. What was neither observed by Europe nor documented by it was therefore 'lost' until, at some later date, it too could be incorporated by the new sciences of anthropology, political economics, and linguistics. It is out of this later recuperation of what Eric Wolf has called people without history, that a still later disciplinary step was taken, the founding of the science of world history, whose major practitioners include Braudel, Wallerstein, Perry Anderson and Wolf himself.

But along with the greater capacity for dealing with – in Ernst Bloch's phrase – the non-synchronous experiences of Europe's Other, has gone a fairly uniform avoidance of the relationship between European imperialism and these variously constituted, variously formed and articulated knowledges. What, in other words, has never taken place is an epistemological critique at the most fundamental level of the connection between the development of a historicism which has expanded and developed enough to include antithetical attitudes such as ideologies of Western imperialism and critiques of imperialism on the one hand, and on the other, the actual practice of imperialism by which the accumulation of territories and population, the control of economies, and the incorporation and homogenization of histories are maintained. If we keep this in mind we will remark, for example, that in the methodological assumptions and practice of world history – which is ideologically anti-imperialist – little or no attention is given to those cultural practises like Orientalism or ethnography affiliated with imperialism, which in genealogical fact fathered world history itself; hence the emphasis in world history as a discipline has been on economic and political practices, defined by the processes of world historical writing, as in a sense separate and different from, as well as unaffected by, the knowledge of them which world history produces. The curious result is that the theories of accumulation on a world scale, or the capitalist world state, or lineages of absolutism depend (a) on the same displaced percipient and historicist observer who had been an Orientalist or colonial traveller three generations ago; (b) they depend also on a homogenizing and incorporating world historical scheme that assimilated non-synchronous developments, histories, cultures, and peoples to it; and (c) they block and keep down latent epistemological critiques of the institutional, cultural and disciplinary instruments linking the incorporative practice of world history with partial knowledges like Orientalism on the one hand, and on the other, with continued 'Western' hegemony of the non-European, peripheral world.

In fine, the problem is once again historicism and the universalizing and self-validating [logic] that has been endemic to it. Bryan Turner's exceptionally important little book *Marx and the End of Orientalism* went a very great part of the distance towards fragmenting, dissociating, dislocating and decentering the experiential terrain covered at present by universalizing historicism; what he suggests in discussing the epistemological dilemma is the need to go beyond the polarities and binary oppositions of Marxist-historicist thought (voluntarisms v. determinism, Asiatic v. Western society, change v. stasis) in order to create a new type of analysis of plural, as opposed to single, objects. Similarly, in a whole series of studies produced in a number of both interrelated and frequently unrelated fields, there has been a general advance in the process of, as it were, breaking up, dissolving and methodologically as well as critically re-conceiving the unitary field ruled hitherto by Orientalism, historicism, and what could be called essentialist universalism.

I shall be giving examples of this dissolving and decentering process in a moment. What needs to be said abut it immediately is that it is neither purely methodological nor purely reactive in intent. You do not respond, for example, to the tyrannical conjuncture of colonial power with scholarly Orientalism simply by proposing an alliance between nativist sentiment buttressed by some variety of native ideology to combat them. This, it seems to me, has been the trap into which many Third World and anti-imperialist activists fell in supporting the Iranian and Palestinian struggles, and who found themselves either with nothing to say about the abominations of Khomeini's regime or resorting, in the Palestine case, to the time-worn clichés of revolutionism and, if I might coin a deliberately barbaric phrase, rejectionary armed-strugglism after the Lebanese debacle. Nor can it be a matter simply of recycling the old Marxist or world-historical rhetoric which only accomplishes the dubiously valuable task of re-establishing [the] intellectual and theoretical ascendancy of the old, by now impertinent and genealogically flawed, conceptual models. No: we must, I believe, think both in political and above all theoretical terms, locating the main problems in what Frankfurt theory identified as domination and division of labor, and along with those, the problem of the absence of a theoretical and utopian as well as libertarian dimension in analysis. We cannot proceed unless therefore we dissipate and redispose the material of historicism into radically different objects and pursuits of knowledge, and we cannot do that until we are aware clearly that no new projects of knowledge can be constituted unless they fight to remain free of the dominance and professionalized particularism that comes with historicist systems and reductive, pragmatic, or functionalist theories.

These goals are less grand and difficult than my description sounds. For the reconsideration of Orientalism has been intimately connected with many other activities of the sort I referred to earlier, and which it now becomes imperative to articulate in more detail. Thus, for example, we can now see that Orientalism is a praxis of the same sort, albeit in different territories, as male gender dominance, or patriarchy, in metropolitan societies: the Orient was routinely described as feminine, its riches as fertile, its main symbols the sensual woman, the harem, and the despotic – but curiously attractive – ruler. Moreover, Orientals like Victorian housewives were confined to silence and to unlimited enriching production. Now much of this material is manifestly connected to the configurations of sexual, racial and political asymmetry underlying mainstream modern Western culture, as adumbrated and illuminated respectively by feminists, by black studies critics, and by anti-imperialist activists. To read, for example, Sandra Gilbert's recent and extraordinarily brilliant study of Rider Haggard's *She* is to perceive the narrow correspondence between suppressed Victorian sexuality at home, its fantasies abroad, and the tightening hold on the male late-nineteenth-century imagination of imperialist ideology. Similarly a work like Abdul JanMohamed's *Manichean Aesthetics* investigates the parallel, but unremittingly separate artistic worlds of white and black fictions of the same place, Africa, suggesting that even in imaginative literature a rigid ideological system operates beneath a freer surface. Or in a study like Peter Gran's *The Islamic Roots of Capitalism*, which is written out of a polemically although meticulously researched and scrupulously concrete anti-imperialist and anti-Orientalist historical stance, one can begin to sense what a vast invisible terrain of human effort and ingenuity lurks beneath the frozen Orientalist surface formerly carpeted by the discourse of Islamic or Oriental economic history.

There are many more examples that one could give of analyses and theoretical projects undertaken out of similar impulses as those fuelling the anti-Orientalist critique. All of them are interventionary in nature, that is, they self-consciously situate themselves at vulnerable conjunctural nodes of ongoing disciplinary discourses where each of them posits nothing less than new objects of knowledge, new praxes of humanist (in the broad sense of the word) activity, new theoretical models that upset or at the very least radically alter the prevailing paradigmatic norms. One might list here such disparate efforts as Linda Nochlin's explorations of nineteenth-century Orientalist ideology as working within major art-historical contexts; Hanna Batatu's immense restructuring of the terrain of the modern Arab state's political behavior; Raymond Williams's sustained examinations of structures of feeling, communities of knowledge, emergent or alternative cultures, patterns of geographical thought (as in his remarkable *The Country and the City*); Talal Asad's account of anthropological self-capture in the work of major theorists, and along with that his own studies in the field; Eric Hobsbawm's new formulation of 'the invention of tradition' or invented practices studied by historians as a crucial index both of the historian's craft and, more

important, of the invention of new emergent nations; the work produced
in re-examination of Japanese, Indian and Chinese culture by scholars
like Masao Miyoshi, Eqbal Ahmad, Tariq Ali, Romila Thapar, the group
around Ranajit Guha (*Subaltern Studies*), Gayatri Spivak, and younger
scholars like Homi Bhabha and Partha Mitter; the freshly imaginative
reconsideration by Arab literary critics – the *Fusoul* and *Mawakif* groups,
Elias Khouri, Kamal Abu Deeb, Mohammad Bannis, and others – seeking
to redefine and invigorate the reified classical structures of Arabic
literary performance, and as a parallel to that, the imaginative works of
Juan Goytisolo and Salman Rushdie whose fictions and criticism are self-
consciously written against the cultural stereotypes and representations
commanding the field. It is worth mentioning here too the pioneering
efforts of the *Bulletin of Concerned Asian Scholars,* and the fact that twice
recently, in their presidential addresses an American Sinologist (Benjamin
Schwartz) and Indologist (Ainslee Embree) have reflected seriously upon
what the critique of Orientalism means for their fields, a public reflection
as yet denied Middle Eastern scholars; perennially, there is the work
carried out by Noam Chomsky in political and historical fields, an
example of independent radicalism and uncompromising severity
unequalled by anyone else today; or in literary theory, the powerful
theoretical articulations of a social, in the widest and deepest sense,
model for narrative put forward by Fredric Jameson, Richard Ohmann's
empirically arrived-at definitions of canon privilege and institution in
his recent work, revisionary Emersonian perspectives formulated in the
critique of contemporary technological and imaginative, as well as
cultural ideologies by Richard Poirier, the decentering, redistributive
ratios of intensity and drive studied by Leo Bersani.

One could go on mentioning many more, but I certainly do not wish
to suggest that by excluding particular examples I have thought them
less eminent or less worth attention. What I want to do in conclusion is
to try to draw them together into a common endeavor which, it has
seemed to me, can inform the larger enterprise of which the critique
of Orientalism is a part. First, we note a plurality of audiences and
constituencies; none of the works and workers I have cited claims to
be working on behalf of One audience which is the only one that
counts, or for one supervening, overcoming Truth, a truth allied to
Western (or for that matter Eastern) reason, objectivity, science. On the
contrary, we note here a plurality of terrains, multiple experiences and
different constituencies, each with its admitted (as opposed to denied)
interest, political desiderata, disciplinary goals. All these efforts work
out of what might be called a decentered consciousness, not less
reflective and critical for being decentered, for the most part non- and
in some cases anti-totalizing and anti-systematic. The result is that
instead of seeking common unity by appeals to a center of sovereign

authority, methodological consistency, canonicity, and science, they offer the possibility of common grounds of assembly between them. They are therefore planes of activity and praxis, rather then one topography commanded by a geographical and historical vision locatable in a known center of metropolitan power. Second, these activities and praxes are consciously secular, marginal and oppositional with reference to the mainstream, generally authoritarian systems from which they emanate, and against which they now agitate. Thirdly, they are political and practical in as much as they intend – without necessarily succeeding in implementing – the end of dominating, coercive systems of knowledge. I do not think it too much to say that the political meaning of analysis, as carried out in all these fields, is uniformly and programmatically libertarian by virtue of the fact that, unlike Orientalism, it is not based on the finality and closure of antiquarian or curatorial knowledge, but on investigative open models of analysis, even though it might seem that analyses of this sort – frequently difficult and abstruse – are in the final count paradoxically quietistic. I think we must remember the lesson provided by Adorno's negative dialectics, and regard analysis as in the fullest sense being *against* the grain, deconstructive, utopian.

But there remains the one problem haunting all intense, self-convicted and local intellectual work, the problem of the division of labor, which is a necessary consequence of that reification and commodification first and most powerfully analysed in this century by George Lukács. This is the problem sensitively and intelligently put by Myra Jehlen for women's studies, whether in identifying and working through anti-dominant critiques, subaltern groups – women, blacks, and so on – can resolve the dilemma of autonomous fields of experience and knowledge that are created as a consequence. A double kind of possessive exclusivism could set in: the sense of being an excluding insider by virtue of experience (only women can write for and about women, and only literature that treats women or Orientals well is good literature), and second, being an excluding insider by virtue of method (only Marxists, anti-Orientalists, feminists can write about economics, Orientalism, women's literature).

This is where we are now, at the threshold of fragmentation and specialization, which impose their own parochial dominations and fussy defensiveness, or on the verge of some grand synthesis which I for one believe could very easily wipe out both the gains and the oppositional consciousness provided by these counter-knowledges hitherto. Several possibilities propose themselves, and I shall conclude simply by listing them. A need for greater crossing of boundaries, for greater interventionism in cross-disciplinary activity, a concentrated awareness of the situation – political, methodological, social, historical – in which intellectual and cultural work is carried out. A clarified political and methodological commitment to the dismantling of systems of domination which since they are collectively maintained must, to adopt and transform some of Gramsci's phrases, be collectively fought, by mutual siege, war of manoeuvre *and* war of position. Lastly, a much sharpened sense of the intellectual's role both in the defining of a context and in changing it, for without that, I believe, the critique of Orientalism is simply an ephemeral pastime.

Note

1. EDWARD SAID, *Orientalism* (London, 1978). Some pertinent reviews have appeared in: *Race and Class*, XXI (1979); *Journal of Asian Studies*, XXXIX (1980); *History and Theory*, XIX (1980).

References

ABDEL, ANWAR MALEK, *Idéologie et renaissance nationale* (Paris, 1969); 'Orientalism in Crisis', *Diogenes* 44 (1963).
—— *Social Dialectics*, 2 vols (London, 1981).
ALATAS, S.H., *Intellectuals in Developing Societies* (London, 1977).
—— *The Myth of the Lazy Native* (London, 1977).
ANDERSON, PERRY, *Lineages of the Absolutist State* (London, 1974).
ASAD, TALAL (ed.), *Anthropology and the Colonial Encounter* (London, 1979).
BERSANI, LEO, *A Future for Astyanax: Character and Desire in Literature* (Cambridge, 1978).
BHABHA, HOMI, 'Difference, Discrimination and the Discourse of Colonialism', in *The Politics of Theory*, ed. Francis Barker et al. (Colchester, 1983).
—— 'Of Mimicry and Men: the Ambivalence of Colonial Discourse', *October* 28 (1984).
BRAN, PETER, *The Islamic Roots of Capitalism: Egypt 1760–1840* (Austin, 1979).
BRAUDEL, FERNAND, *The Mediterranean and the Mediterranean World in the Age of Philip II*, 2 vols (New York, 1972–73).
—— *Civilization and Capitalism* (London, 1981–82).
CESAIRE, AIME, *Discourse on Colonialism* (New York, 1972).
CHOMSKY, NOAM, *American Power and the New Mandarins* (New York, 1969).
—— *For Reasons of State* (New York, 1973).
—— *The Fateful Triangle: Israel, the United States and the Palestinians* (New York, 1983).
FABIAN, JOHANNES, *Time and the Other* (New York, 1983).
FANON, FRANTZ, *The Wretched of the Earth* (London, 1965).
—— *Black Skin White Masks* (New York, 1967).
HOBSBAWM, ERIC (ed., with TERENCE RANGER), *The Invention of Tradition* (Cambridge, 1983).
JAMESON, FREDRIC, *The Political Unconscious* (London, 1981).
JANMOHAMED, ABDUL, *Manichean Aesthetics: The Politics of Literature in Colonial Africa* (Amherst, 1983).
LAROUI, ABDULLAH, *The Crisis of the Arab Intellectuals* (Berkeley, 1976).
—— *The History of the Maghrib* (Princeton, 1977).

LEWIS, BERNARD, *The Muslim Discovery of Europe* (New York, 1982). Cf. the exchange of letters between Said and Lewis in the *New York Review of Books*, XXIX (1982), 24 June and 12 August.

MIYOSHI, MASAO, *The Divided Self: A Perspective on the Literature of the Victorians* (New York, 1969).

NOCHLIN, LINDA, 'The Imaginary Orient', *Art in America* (May, 1983).

OHMANN, RICHARD, *English in America: A Radical View of the Profession* (Oxford, 1976).

PANNIKAR, K.M., *Asia and Western Dominance* (London, 1959).

PIPES, DANIEL, *In the Path of God* (New York, 1983).

POIRIER, RICHARD, *Performing Self: Composition and Decomposition in the Language of Contemporary Life* (Oxford, 1971).

RUSHDIE, SALMAN, *Midnight's Children* (London, 1979).

—— *Shame* (London, 1983).

SPIVAK, GAYATRI, ' "Draupaudi" by Mahasveta Devi', in *Writing and Sexual Difference*, ed. Elizabeth Abel (Chicago, 1982).

—— 'Displacement and the Discourse of Woman', in *Displacement: Derrida and After*, ed. Mark Krupnick (Bloomington, 1983).

THAPAR, ROMILA (with PERCIVAL SPEAR), *A History of India*, 2 vols (Harmondsworth, 1965–66).

TIBAWI, A.L., *British Interests in Palestine, 1800–1901* (London, 1961).

—— 'English-Speaking Orientalists', *Islamic Quarterly* 8 (1964).

—— *American Interests in Syria, 1800–1901* (Oxford, 1966).

TURNER, BRYAN, *Marx and the End of Orientalism* (London, 1978).

WALLERSTEIN, IMMANUEL, *The Modern World System*, 2 vols (New York, 1974–80).

WILLIAMS, RAYMOND, *The Country and the City* (London, 1973).

WOLF, ERIC, *Europe and the People Without History* (Berkeley, 1982).

5 Three Women's Texts and a Critique of Imperialism*

Gayatri C. Spivak

'Orientalism Reconsidered' testifies to Said's belated recognition of the importance of issues of gender in both colonial discourse and its analysis. 'Three Women's Texts', published in the same year, is only one of many essays in which such issues are central. Here, Spivak provides a critique of the ethnocentrism of Western feminism and its complicity in the regimes of (neo-)colonial knowledge, in a piece which extends the key arguments of 'French Feminism in an International Frame' (1981) to the Anglo-American context. In this general respect, she can be linked to other postcolonial women critics such as Mohanty, hooks and Katrak. Spivak centres her critique of Western feminism on what she describes as its 'basically isolationist admiration for the literature of the female subject' and, more particularly, on texts like *Jane Eyre*, which record the triumphant emergence of the (proto-)feminist Western subject. For Spivak what gets left out of such accounts is the historical role played by the non-Western woman in this narrative of empowerment. In Brontë's text, for instance, Spivak tracks the process by which Jane's emergence as feminist heroine is accompanied by, indeed dependent upon, the effacement of Bertha Mason, 'the woman from the colonies'. Even a sensitive contemporary writer like Jean Rhys reveals the limitations of Western feminism in the way that the dissenting voice of the colonized woman is silenced through Christophine's 'expulsion' from *Wide Sargasso Sea*.

In methodological terms, Spivak's essay is highly innovative. Drawing on Derrida (she translated his *Of Grammatology* in 1976), Spivak demonstrates the usefulness of deconstruction to postcolonial criticism in a number of ways. Firstly it provides a strategic safeguard against Western feminism's 'benevolence', in other words its assumption that it is necessarily allied with the non-Western subject against

*Reprinted from H.L. Gates jr (ed.), *'Race', Writing and Difference* (Chicago: Chicago University Press, 1986), pp. 262–88.

the patriarchal (neo-)colonial centre. Secondly, Derrida furnishes two important tactical manoeuvres. The first is the procedure of reading the text against the grain, or contrary to its ostensible logic. Spivak's emphasis on 'catachresis' is exemplified here by the way that she reads Bertha 'allegorically', making her representative of the colonized woman, despite the fact that Bertha is 'objectively' a member of the former slave-owning plantocracy. Secondly, Spivak follows Derrida in taking apparently marginal material (Bertha is a minor character in Brontë's text, the empire is barely referred to in *Frankenstein*) and using it to expose the presuppositions informing the 'obvious' or privileged meanings and structure of the novel. (Compare Said's reading of Jane Austen's *Mansfield Park* in *Culture and Imperialism*.) The effect is to demonstrate how all narratives – fictional, political, economic – construct themselves (like empire itself) by suppressing, or marginalizing, competing possibilities, viewpoints or material. Despite its obvious difficulties, such work justifies Spivak's status as the first major postcolonial feminist critic.

It should not be possible to read nineteenth-century British literature without remembering that imperialism, understood as England's social mission, was a crucial part of the cultural representation of England to the English. The role of literature in the production of cultural representation should not be ignored. These two obvious 'facts' continue to be disregarded in the reading of nineteenth-century British literature. This itself attests to the continuing success of the imperialist project, displaced and dispersed into more modern forms.

If these 'facts' were remembered, not only in the study of British literature but in the study of the literatures of the European colonizing cultures of the great age of imperialism, we would produce a narrative, in literary history, of the 'worlding' of what is now called 'the Third World'. To consider the Third World as distant cultures, exploited but with rich intact literary heritages waiting to be recovered, interpreted, and curricularized in English translation fosters the emergence of 'the Third World' as a signifier that allows us to forget that 'worlding', even as it expands the empire of the literary discipline.[1]

It seems particularly unfortunate when the emergent perspective of feminist criticism reproduces the axioms of imperialism. A basically isolationist admiration for the literature of the female subject in Europe and Anglo-America establishes the high feminist norm. It is supported and operated by an information-retrieval approach to 'Third World' literature which often employs a deliberately 'nontheoretical' methodology with self-conscious rectitude.

In this essay, I will attempt to examine the operation of the 'worlding' of what is today 'the Third World' by what has become a cult text of feminism: *Jane Eyre*.[2] I plot the novel's reach and grasp, and locate its structural motors. I read *Wide Sargasso Sea* as *Jane Eyre*'s reinscription and *Frankenstein* as an analysis – even a deconstruction – of a 'worlding' such as *Jane Eyre*'s.[3]

I need hardly mention that the object of my investigation is the printed book, not its 'author'. To make such a distinction is, of course, to ignore the lessons of deconstruction. A deconstructive critical approach would loosen the binding of the book, undo the opposition between verbal text and the bio-graphy of the named subject 'Charlotte Brontë', and see the two as each other's 'scene of writing'. In such a reading, the life that writes itself as 'my life' is as much a production in psychosocial space (other names can be found) as the book that is written by the holder of that named life – a book that is then consigned to what *is* most often recognized as genuinely 'social': the world of publication and distribution.[4] To touch Brontë's 'life' in such a way, however, would be too risky here. We must rather strategically take shelter in an essentialism which, not wishing to lose the important advantages won by US mainstream feminism, will continue to honor the suspect binary oppositions – book and author, individual and history – and start with an assurance of the following sort: my readings here do not seek to undermine the excellence of the individual artist. If even minimally successful, the readings will incite a degree of rage against the imperialist narrativization of history, that it should produce so abject a script for her. I provide these assurances to allow myself some room to situate feminist individualism in its historical determination rather than simply to canonize it as feminism as such.

Sympathetic US feminists have remarked that I do not do justice to Jane Eyre's subjectivity. A word of explanation is perhaps in order. The broad strokes of my presuppositions are that what is at stake, for feminist individualism in the age of imperialism, is precisely the making of human beings, the constitution and 'interpellation' of the subject not only as individual but as 'individualist'.[5] This stake is represented on two registers: childbearing and soul-making. The first is domestic-society-through-sexual-reproduction cathected as 'companionate love'; the second is the imperialist project cathected as civil-society-through-social-mission. As the female individualist, not-quite/not-male, articulates herself in shifting relationship to what is at stake, the 'native female' as such (*within* discourse, *as* a signifier) is excluded from any share in this emerging norm.[6] If we read this account from an isolationist perspective in a 'metropolitan' context, we see nothing there but the psychobiography of the militant female subject. In a reading such as mine, in contrast, the effort is to wrench oneself away from the mesmerizing focus of the 'subject-constitution' of the female individualist.

To develop further the notion that my stance need not be an accusing one, I will refer to a passage from Roberto Fernández Retamar's 'Caliban'.[7] José Enrique Rodó had argued in 1900 that the model for the Latin American intellectual in relationship to Europe could be Shakespeare's Ariel.[8] In 1971 Retamar, denying the possibility of an identifiable 'Latin American Culture', recast the model as Caliban. Not surprisingly, this powerful exchange still excludes any specific consideration of the civilizations of the Maya, the Aztecs, the Incas, or the smaller nations of what is now called Latin America. Let us note carefully that, at this stage of my argument, this 'conversation' between Europe and Latin America (without a specific consideration of the political economy of the 'worlding' of the 'native') provides a sufficient thematic description of our attempt to confront the ethnocentric and reverse-ethnocentric benevolent double bind (that is, considering the 'native' as object for enthusiastic information-retrieval and thus denying its own 'worlding') that I sketched in my opening paragraphs.

In a moving passage in 'Caliban', Retamar locates both Caliban and Ariel in the postcolonial intellectual:

> There is no real Ariel–Caliban polarity: both are slaves in the hands of Prospero, the foreign magician. But Caliban is the rude and unconquerable master of the island, while Ariel, a creature of the air, although also a child of the isle, is the intellectual.
>
> The deformed Caliban – enslaved, robbed of his island, and taught the language by Prospero – rebukes him thus: 'You taught me language, and my profit on't/Is, I know how to curse.'
>
> ('C', pp. 28, 11)

As we attempt to unlearn our so-called privilege as Ariel and 'seek from [a certain] Caliban the honor of a place in his rebellious and glorious ranks', we do not ask that our students and colleagues should emulate us but that they should attend to us ('C', p. 72). If, however, we are driven by a nostalgia for lost origins, we too run the risk of effacing the 'native' and stepping forth as 'the real Caliban', of forgetting that he is a name in a play, an inaccessible blankness circumscribed by an interpretable text.[9] The stagings of Caliban work alongside the narrativization of history: claiming to *be* Caliban legitimizes the very individualism that we must persistently attempt to undermine from within.

Elizabeth Fox-Genovese, in an article on history and women's history, shows us how to define the historical moment of feminism in the West in terms of female access to individualism.[10] The battle for female individualism plays itself out within the larger theater of the establishment of meritocratic individualism, indexed in the aesthetic field by the ideology of 'the creative imagination'. Fox-Genovese's presupposition will guide us into the beautifully orchestrated opening of *Jane Eyre*.

It is a scene of the marginalization and privatization of the protagonist: 'There was no possibility of taking a walk that day.... Out-door exercise was now out of the question. I was glad of it', Brontë writes (*JE*, p. 9). The movement continues as Jane breaks the rules of the appropriate topography of withdrawal. The family at the center withdraws into the sanctioned architectural space of the withdrawing room or drawing room; Jane inserts herself – 'I slipped in' – into the margin – 'A small breakfast-room *adjoined* the drawing room' (*JE*, p. 9; my emphasis).

The manipulation of the domestic inscription of space within the upwardly mobilizing currents of the eighteenth- and nineteenth-century bourgeoisie in England and France is well known. It seems fitting that the place to which Jane withdraws is not only not the withdrawing room but also not the dining room, the sanctioned place of family meals. Nor is it the library, the appropriate place for reading. The breakfast room 'contained a book-case' (*JE*, p. 9). As Rudolph Ackerman wrote in his *Repository* (1823), one of the many manuals of taste in circulation in nineteenth-century England, these low bookcases and stands were designed to 'contain all the books that may be desired for a sitting-room without reference to the library'.[11] Even in this already triply off-center place, 'having drawn the red moreen curtain nearly close, I [Jane] was shrined in double retirement' (*JE*, pp. 9–10).

Here in Jane's self-marginalized uniqueness, the reader becomes her accomplice: the reader and Jane are united – both are reading. Yet Jane still preserves her odd privilege, for she continues never quite doing the proper thing in its proper place. She cares little for reading what is *meant* to be read: the 'letter-press'. *She* reads the pictures. The power of this singular hermeneutics is precisely that it can make the outside inside. 'At intervals, while turning over the leaves of my book, I studied the aspect of that winter afternoon.' Under 'the clear panes of glass', the rain no longer penetrates, 'the drear November day' is rather a one-dimensional 'aspect' to be 'studied', not decoded like the 'letter-press' but, like pictures, deciphered by the unique creative imagination of the marginal individualist (*JE*, p. 10).

Before following the track of this unique imagination, let us consider the suggestion that the progress of *Jane Eyre* can be charted through a sequential arrangement of the family/counter-family dyad. In the novel, we encounter, first, the Reeds as the legal family and Jane, the late Mr Reed's sister's daughter, as the representative of a near incestuous counter-family; second, the Brocklehursts, who run the school Jane is sent to, as the legal family and Jane, Miss Temple, and Helen Burns as a counter-family that falls short because it is only a community of women; third, Rochester and the mad Mrs Rochester as the legal family and Jane and Rochester as the illicit counter-family. Other items may be added to the thematic chain in this sequence: Rochester and Céline Varens as structurally functional counter-family; Rochester and Blanche Ingram as dissimulation of legality – and so on. It is during this sequence that Jane is moved from the counter-family to the family-in-law. In the next sequence, it is Jane who restores full family status to the as-yet-incomplete community of siblings, the Riverses. The final sequence of the book is a *community of families*, with Jane, Rochester, and their children at the center.

In terms of the narrative energy of the novel, how is Jane moved from the place of the counter-family to the family-in-law? It is the active ideology of imperialism that provides the discursive field.

(My working definition of 'discursive field' must assume the existence of discrete 'systems of signs' at hand in the socius, each based on a specific axiomatics. I am identifying these systems as discursive fields. 'Imperialism as social mission' generates the possibility of one such axiomatics. How the individual artist taps the discursive field at hand with a sure touch, if not with transhistorical clairvoyance, in order to make the narrative structure move I hope to demonstrate through the following example. It is crucial that we extend our analysis of this example beyond the minimal diagnosis of 'racism'.)

Let us consider the figure of Bertha Mason, a figure produced by the axiomatics of imperialism. Through Bertha Mason, the white Jamaican Creole, Brontë renders the human/animal frontier as acceptably indeterminate, so that a good greater than the letter of the Law can be broached. Here is the celebrated passage, given in the voice of Jane:

> In the deep shade, at the further end of the room, a figure ran backwards and forwards. What it was, whether beast or human being, one could not . . . tell: it grovelled, seemingly, on all fours; it snatched and growled like some strange wild animal: but it was covered with clothing, and a quantity of dark, grizzled hair, wild as a mane, hid its head and face.
>
> (*JE*, p. 295)

In a matching passage, given in the voice of Rochester speaking *to* Jane, Brontë presents the imperative for a shift beyond the Law as divine injunction rather than human motive. In the terms of my essay, we might say that this is the register not of mere marriage or sexual reproduction but of Europe and its not-yet-human Other, of soul making. The field of imperial conquest is here inscribed as Hell:

> 'One night I had been awakened by her yells . . . it was a fiery West Indian night. . . .

'This life', said I at last, 'is hell! – this is the air – those are the sounds of the bottomless pit! *I have a right* to deliver myself from it if I can. . . . Let me break away, and go home to God!' . . .

A wind fresh from Europe blew over the ocean and rushed through the open casement: the storm broke, streamed, thundered, blazed, and the air grew pure. . . . It was true Wisdom that consoled me in that hour, and showed me the right path. . . .

The sweet wind from Europe was still whispering in the refreshed leaves, and the Atlantic was thundering in glorious liberty. . . .

'Go', said Hope, 'and live again in Europe. . . . You have done all that God and Humanity require of you.'

(*JE*, pp. 310–11; my emphasis)

It is the unquestioned ideology of imperialist axiomatics, then, that conditions Jane's move from the counter-family set to the set of the family-in-law. Marxist critics such as Terry Eagleton have seen this only in terms of the ambiguous *class* position of the governess.[12] Sandra Gilbert and Susan Gubar, on the other hand, have seen Bertha Mason only in psychological terms, as Jane's dark double.[13]

I will not enter the critical debates that offer themselves here. Instead, I will develop the suggestion that nineteenth-century feminist individualism could conceive of a 'greater' project than access to the closed circle of the nuclear family. This is the project of soul making beyond 'mere' sexual reproduction. Here the native 'subject' is not almost an animal but rather the object of what might be termed the terrorism of the categorical imperative.

I am using 'Kant' in this essay as a metonym for the most flexible ethical moment in the European eighteenth century. Kant words the categorical imperative, conceived as the universal moral law given by pure reason, in this way: 'In all creation every thing one chooses and over which one has any power, may be used *merely as means*; man alone, and with him every rational creature, is an *end in himself.*' It is thus a moving displacement of Christian ethics from religion to philosophy. As Kant writes: 'With this agrees very well the possibility of such a command as: *Love God above everything, and thy neighbor as thyself.* For as a command it requires respect for a law which *commands love* and does not leave it to our own arbitrary choice to make this our principle.'[14]

The 'categorical' in Kant cannot be adequately represented in determinately grounded action. The dangerous transformative power of philosophy, however, is that its formal subtlety can be travestied in the service of the state. Such a travesty in the case of the categorical imperative can justify the imperialist project by producing the following formula: *make* the heathen into a human so that he can be treated as an end in himself.[15] This project is presented as a sort of tangent in *Jane Eyre*, a tangent that escapes the closed circle of the *narrative* conclusion. The tangent narrative is the story of St John Rivers, who is granted the important task of concluding the *text*.

At the novel's end, the *allegorical* language of Christian psychobiography – rather than the textually constituted and seemingly *private* grammar of the creative imagination which we noted in the novel's opening – marks the inaccessibility of the imperialist project as such to the nascent 'feminist' scenario. The concluding passage of *Jane Eyre* places St John Rivers within the fold of *Pilgrim's Progress*. Eagleton pays no attention to this but accepts the novel's ideological lexicon, which establishes St John Rivers' heroism by identifying a life in Calcutta with an unquestioning choice of death. Gilbert and Gubar, by calling *Jane Eyre* 'Plain Jane's progress', see the novel as simply replacing the male protagonist with the female. They do not notice the distance between sexual reproduction and soul-making, both actualized by the unquestioned idiom of imperialist presuppositions evident in the last part of *Jane Eyre*:

> Firm, faithful, and devoted, full of energy, and zeal, and truth, [St John Rivers] labours for his race. . . . His is the sternness of the warrior Greatheart, who guards his pilgrim convoy from the onslaught of Apollyon. . . . His is the ambition of the high master-spirit[s] . . . who stand without fault before the throne of God; who share the last mighty victories of the Lamb; who are called, and chosen, and faithful.
> (*JE*, p. 455)

Earlier in the novel, St John Rivers himself justifies the project: 'My vocation? My great work? . . . My hopes of being numbered in the band who have merged all ambitions in the glorious one of bettering their race – of carrying knowledge into the realms of ignorance – of substituting peace for war – freedom for bondage – religion for superstition – the hope of heaven for the fear of hell? (*JE*, p. 376). Imperialism and its territorial and subject-constituting project are a violent deconstruction of these oppositions.

When Jean Rhys, born on the Caribbean island of Dominica, read *Jane Eyre* as a child, she was moved by Bertha Mason: 'I thought I'd try to write her a life.'[16] *Wide Sargasso Sea*, the slim novel published in 1965, at the end of Rhys's long career, is that 'life'.

I have suggested that Bertha's function in *Jane Eyre* is to render indeterminate the boundary between human and animal and thereby to weaken her entitlement under the spirit if not the letter of the Law. When Rhys rewrites the scene in *Jane Eyre* where Jane hears 'a snarling, snatching sound, almost like a dog quarrelling' and then encounters a bleeding Richard Mason (*JE*, p. 210), she keeps Bertha's humanity, indeed her sanity as critic of imperialism, intact. Grace Poole, another character originally in *Jane Eyre*, describes the incident to Bertha in *Wide Sargasso Sea*: 'So you don't remember that you attacked this gentleman with a knife? . . . I didn't hear all he said except "I cannot interfere legally between yourself and your husband." It was when he said "legally" that you flew at him' (*WSS*, p. 150). In Rhys's retelling, it is the dissimulation that Bertha discerns in the word 'legally' – not an innate bestiality – that prompts her violent *re*action.

In the figure of Antoinette, whom in *Wide Sargasso Sea* Rochester violently renames Bertha, Rhys suggests that so intimate a thing as personal and human identity might be determined by the politics of imperialism. Antoinette, as a white Creole child growing up at the time of emancipation in Jamaica, is caught between the English imperialist and the black native. In recounting Antoinette's development, Rhys reinscribes some thematics of Narcissus.

There are, noticeably, many images of mirroring in the text. I will quote one from the first section. In this passage, Tia is the little black servant girl who is Antoinette's close companion: 'We had eaten the same food, slept side by side, bathed in the same river. As I ran, I thought, I will live with Tia and I will be like her. . . . When I was close I saw the jagged stone in her hand but I did not see her throw it. . . . We stared at each other, blood on my face, tears on hers. It was as if I saw myself. Like in a looking glass' (*WSS*, p. 38).

A progressive sequence of dreams reinforces this mirror imagery. In its second occurrence, the dream is partially set in a *hortus conclusus*, or 'enclosed garden' – Rhys uses the phrase (*WSS*, p. 50) – a Romance rewriting of the Narcissus topos as the place of encounter with Love.[17] In the enclosed garden, Antoinette encounters not Love but a strange threatening voice that says merely 'in here', inviting her into a prison which masquerades as the legalization of love (*WSS*, p. 50).

In Ovid's *Metamorphoses*, Narcissus' madness is disclosed when he recognizes his Other as his self: 'Iste ego sum.'[18] Rhys makes Antoinette see her *self* as her Other, Brontë's Bertha. In the last section of *Wide Sargasso Sea*, Antoinette acts out *Jane Eyre*'s conclusion and recognizes herself as the so-called ghost in Thornfield Hall: 'I went into the hall again with the tall candle in my hand. It was then that I saw her – the ghost. The woman with streaming hair. She was surrounded by a gilt frame but I knew her' (*WSS*, p. 154). The gilt frame encloses a mirror: as Narcissus' pool reflects the selfed Other, so this 'pool' reflects the Othered self. Here the dream sequence ends, with an invocation of none other than Tia, the Other that could not be selfed, because the fracture of imperialism rather than the Ovidian pool intervened. (I will return to this difficult point.) 'That was the third time I had my dream, and it ended. . . . I called "Tia" and jumped and woke' (*WSS*, p. 155). It is now, at the very end of the book, that Antoinette/Bertha can say: 'Now at last

I know why I was brought here and what I have to do' (*WSS*, pp. 155–6).
We can read this as her having been brought into the England of
Brontë's novel: 'This cardboard house' – a book between cardboard
covers – 'where I walk at night is not England' (*WSS*, p. 148). In this
fictive England, she must play out her role, act out the transformation
of her 'self' into that fictive Other, set fire to the house and kill herself,
so that Jane Eyre can become the feminist individualist heroine of
British fiction. I must read this as an allegory of the general epistemic
violence of imperialism, the construction of a self-immolating colonial
subject for the glorification of the social mission of the colonizer. At
least Rhys sees to it that the woman from the colonies is not sacrificed
as an insane animal for her sister's consolidation.

Critics have remarked that *Wide Sargasso Sea* treats the Rochester
character with understanding and sympathy.[19] Indeed, he narrates
the entire middle section of the book. Rhys makes it clear that he is
a victim of the patriarchal inheritance law of entailment rather than
of a father's natural preference for the firstborn: in *Wide Sargasso Sea*,
Rochester's situation is clearly that of a younger son dispatched to the
colonies to buy an heiress. If in the case of Antoinette and her identity,
Rhys utilizes the thematics of Narcissus, in the case of Rochester and
his patrimony, she touches on the thematics of Oedipus. (In this she
has her finger on our 'historical moment'. If, in the nineteenth century,
subject-constitution is represented as childbearing and soul making,
in the twentieth century psychoanalysis allows the West to plot the
itinerary of the subject from Narcissus (the 'imaginary') to Oedipus
(the 'symbolic'). This subject, however, is the normative male subject.
In Rhys' reinscription of these themes, divided between the female and
the male protagonist, feminism and a critique of imperialism become
complicit.)

In place of the 'wind from Europe' scene, Rhys substitutes the scenario
of a suppressed letter to a father, a letter which would be the 'correct'
explanation of the tragedy of the book.[20] 'I thought about the letter
which should have been written to England a week ago. Dear Father . . .'
(*WSS*, p. 57). This is the first instance: the letter not written. Shortly
afterward:

> Dear Father. The thirty thousand pounds have been paid to me
> without question or condition. No provision made for her (that must
> be seen to). . . . I will never be a disgrace to you or to my dear brother
> the son you love. No begging letters, no mean requests. None of the
> furtive shabby manoeuvres of a younger son. I have sold my soul or
> you have sold it, and after all is it such a bad bargain? The girl is
> thought to be beautiful, she is beautiful. And yet. . . .
>
> (*WSS*, p. 59)

This is the second instance: the letter not sent. The formal letter is uninteresting; I will quote only a part of it:

> Dear Father, we have arrived from Jamaica after an uncomfortable few days. This little estate in the Windward Island is part of the family property and Antoinette is much attached to it. . . . All is well and has gone according to your plans and wishes. I dealt of course with Richard Mason. . . . He seemed to become attached to me and trusted me completely. This place is very beautiful but my illness has left me too exhausted to appreciate it fully. I will write again in a few days' time.
>
> (*WSS*, p. 63)

And so on.

Rhys's version of the Oedipal exchange is ironic, not a closed circle. We cannot know if the letter actually reaches its destination. 'I wondered how they got their letters posted', the Rochester figure muses. 'I folded mine and put it into a drawer of the desk. . . . There are blanks in my mind that cannot be filled up' (*WSS*, p. 64). It is as if the text presses us to note the analogy between letter and mind.

Rhys denies to Brontë's Rochester the one thing that is supposed to be secured in the Oedipal relay: the Name of the Father, or the patronymic. In *Wide Sargasso Sea*, the character corresponding to Rochester has no name. His writing of the final version of the letter to his father is supervised, in fact, by an image of the *loss* of the patronymic: 'There was a crude bookshelf made of three shingles strung together over the desk and I looked at the books, Byron's poems, novels by Sir Walter Scott, *Confessions of an Opium Eater* . . . and on the last shelf, *Life and Letters of* . . . The rest was eaten away' (*WSS*, p. 63).

Wide Sargasso Sea marks with uncanny clarity the limits of its own discourse in Christophine, Antoinette's black nurse. We may perhaps surmise the distance between *Jane Eyre* and *Wide Sargasso Sea* by remarking that Christophine's unfinished story is the tangent to the latter narrative, as St John Rivers' story is to the former. Christophine is not a native of Jamaica; she is from Martinique. Taxonomically, she belongs to the category of the good servant rather than that of the pure native. But within these borders, Rhys creates a powerfully suggestive figure.

Christophine is the first interpreter and named speaking subject in the text. 'The Jamaican ladies had never approved of my mother, "because she pretty like, pretty self" Christophine said', we read in the book's opening paragraph (*WSS*, p. 15). I have taught this book five times, once in France, once to students who had worked on the book with the well-known Caribbean novelist Wilson Harris, and once at a prestigious institute where the majority of the students were faculty from other universities. It is part of the political argument I am making that all these students blithely stepped over this paragraph without asking or knowing what Christophine's patois, so-called incorrect English, might mean.

Christophine is, of course, a commodified person. ' "She was your father's wedding present to me" ' explains Antoinette's mother, ' "one of his presents" ' (*WSS*, p. 18). Yet Rhys assigns her some crucial functions in the text. It is Christophine who judges that black ritual practices are culture-specific and cannot be used by whites as cheap remedies for social evils, such as Rochester's lack of love for Antoinette. Most important, it is Christophine alone whom Rhys allows to offer a hard analysis of Rochester's actions, to challenge him in a face-to-face encounter. The entire extended passage is worthy of comment. I quote a brief extract:

> 'She is Creole girl, and she have the sun in her. Tell the truth now. She don't come to your house in this place England they tell me about, she don't come to your beautiful house to beg you to marry with her. No, it's you come all the long way to her house – it's you beg her to marry. And she love you and she give you all she have. Now you say you don't love her and you break her up. What you do with her money, eh?' [And then Rochester, the white man, comments silently to himself] Her voice was still quiet but with a hiss in it when she said 'money'.
>
> (*WSS*, p. 130)

Her analysis is powerful enough for the white man to be afraid: 'I no longer felt dazed, tired, half hypnotized, but alert and wary, ready to defend myself' (*WSS*, p. 130).

Rhys does not, however, romanticize individual heroics on the part of the oppressed. When the Man refers to the forces of Law and Order, Christophine recognizes their power. This exposure of civil inequality is emphasized by the fact that, just before the Man's successful threat, Christophine had invoked the emancipation of slaves in Jamaica by proclaiming: 'No chain gang, no tread machine, no dark jail either. This is free country and I am free woman' (*WSS*, p. 131).

As I mentioned above, Christophine is tangential to this narrative. She cannot be contained by a novel which rewrites a canonical English text within the European novelistic tradition in the interest of the white Creole rather than the native. No perspective *critical* of imperialism can turn the Other into a self, because the project of imperialism has always already historically refracted what might have been the absolutely Other into a domesticated Other that consolidates the imperialist self.[21] The Caliban of Retamar, caught between Europe and Latin America, reflects this predicament. We can read Rhys's reinscription of Narcissus as a thematization of the same problematic.

Of course, we cannot know Jean Rhys' feelings in the matter. We can, however, look at the scene of Christophine's inscription in the text. Immediately after the exchange between her and the Man, well before the conclusion, she is simply driven out of the story, with neither narrative nor characterological explanation or justice. '"Read and write I don't know. Other things I know." She walked away without looking back' (*WSS*, p. 133).

Indeed, if Rhys rewrites the madwoman's attack on the Man by underlining of the misuse of 'legality', she cannot deal with the passage that corresponds to St John Rivers' own justification of his martyrdom, for it has been displaced into the current idiom of modernization and development. Attempts to construct the 'Third World Woman' as a signifier remind us that the hegemonic definition of literature is itself caught within the history of imperialism. A full literary reinscription cannot easily flourish in the imperialist fracture or discontinuity, covered over by an alien legal system masquerading as Law as such, an alien ideology established as only Truth, and a set of human sciences busy establishing the 'native' as self-consolidating Other.

In the Indian case at least, it would be difficult to find an ideological clue to the planned epistemic violence of imperialism merely by rearranging curricula or syllabi within existing norms of literary pedagogy. For a later period of imperialism – when the constituted colonial subject has firmly taken hold – straightforward experiments of comparison can be undertaken, say, between the functionally witless India of *Mrs Dalloway*, on the one hand, and literary texts produced in India in the 1920s, on the other. But the first half of the nineteenth century resists questioning through literature or literary criticism in the narrow sense, because both are implicated in the project of producing Ariel. To reopen the fracture without succumbing to a nostalgia for lost origins, the literary critic must turn to the archives of imperial governance.

In conclusion, I shall look briefly at Mary Shelley's *Frankenstein*, a text of nascent feminism that remains cryptic, I think, simply because it does not speak the language of feminist individualism which we have come to hail as the language of high feminism within English literature. It is interesting that Barbara Johnson's brief study tries to rescue this recalcitrant text for the service of feminist autobiography.[22] Alternatively, George Levine reads *Frankenstein* in the context of the creative imagination and the nature of the hero. He sees the novel as a book about its own writing and about writing itself, a Romantic allegory of reading within which Jane Eyre as unselfconscious critic would fit quite nicely.[23]

I propose to take *Frankenstein* out of this arena and focus on it in terms of that sense of English cultural identity which I invoked at the opening of this essay. Within that focus we are obliged to admit that, although *Frankenstein* is ostensibly about the origin and evolution of man in society, it does not deploy the axiomatics of imperialism.

Let me say at once that there is plenty of incidental imperialist sentiment in *Frankenstein*. My point, within the argument of this essay, is that the discursive field of imperialism does not produce unquestioned ideological correlatives for the narrative structuring of the book. The discourse of imperialism surfaces in a curiously powerful way in Shelley's novel, and I will later discuss the moment at which it emerges.

Frankenstein is not a battleground of male and female individualism articulated in terms of sexual reproduction (family and female) and social subject-production (race and male). That binary opposition is undone in Victor Frankenstein's laboratory – an artificial womb where both projects are undertaken simultaneously, though the terms are never openly spelled out. Frankenstein's apparent antagonist is God himself as Maker of Man, but his real competitor is also woman as the maker of children. It is not just that his dream of the death of mother and bride and the actual death of his bride are associated with the visit of his monstrous homoerotic 'son' to his bed. On a much more overt level, the monster is a bodied 'corpse', unnatural because bereft of a determinable childhood: 'No father had watched my infant days, no mother had blessed me with smiles and caresses; or if they had, all my past was now a blot, a blind vacancy in which I distinguished nothing' (F, pp. 57, 115). It is Frankenstein's own ambiguous and miscued understanding of the real motive for the monster's vengefulness that reveals his own competition with woman as maker:

> I created a rational creature and was bound towards him to assure, as far as was in my power, his happiness and well-being. This was my duty, but there was another still paramount to that. My duties towards the beings of my own species had greater claims to my attention because they included a greater proportion of happiness or misery. Urged by this view, I refused, and I did right in refusing, to create a companion for the first creature.
>
> (F, p. 206)

It is impossible not to notice the accents of transgression inflecting Frankenstein's demolition of his experiment to create the future Eve. Even in the laboratory the woman-in-the-making is not a bodied corpse but 'a human being'. The (il)logic of the metaphor bestows on her a prior existence which Frankenstein aborts, rather than an anterior death which he reembodies: 'The remains of the half-finished creature, whom I had destroyed, lay scattered on the floor, and I almost felt as if I had mangled the living flesh of a human being' (F, p. 163).

In Shelley's view, man's hubris as soul-maker both usurps the place of God and attempts – vainly – to sublate woman's physiological prerogative.[24] Indeed, indulging a Freudian fantasy here, I could urge that, if to give and withhold to/from the mother a phallus is *the* male fetish, then to give and withhold to/from the man a womb might be the female fetish.[25] The icon of the sublimated womb in man is surely his productive brain, the box in the head.

In the judgment of classical psychoanalysis, the phallic mother exists only by virtue of the castration-anxious son; in *Frankenstein*'s judgment, the hysteric father (Victor Frankenstein gifted with his laboratory – the womb of theoretical reason) cannot produce a daughter. Here the language of racism – the dark side of imperialism understood as social mission – combines with the hysteria of masculism into the idiom of (the withdrawal of) sexual reproduction rather than subject-constitution. The roles of masculine and feminine individualists are hence reversed and displaced. Frankenstein cannot produce a 'daughter' because 'she might become ten thousand times more malignant than her mate . . . [and because] one of the first results of those sympathies for which the demon thirsted would be children, and a race of devils would be propagated upon the earth who might make the very existence of the species of man a condition precarious and full of terror' (*F*, p. 158). This particular narrative strand also launches a thoroughgoing critique of the eighteenth-century European discourses on the origin of society through (Western Christian) man. Should I mention that, much like Jean-Jacques Rousseau's remark in his *Confessions*, Frankenstein declares himself to be 'by birth a Genevese' (*F*, p. 31)?

In this overly didactic text, Shelley's point is that social engineering should not be based on pure, theoretical, or natural-scientific reason alone, which is her implicit critique of the utilitarian vision of an engineered society. To this end, she presents in the first part of her deliberately schematic story three characters, childhood friends, who seem to represent Kant's three-part conception of the human subject: Victor Frankenstein, the forces of theoretical reason or 'natural philosophy'; Henry Clerval, the forces of practical reason or 'the moral relations of things'; and Elizabeth Lavenza, that aesthetic judgment – 'the aerial creation of the poets' – which, according to Kant, is 'a suitable mediating link connecting the realm of the concept of nature and that of the concept of freedom . . . (which) promotes . . . *moral feeling*' (*F*, pp. 37, 36).[26]

This three-part subject does not operate harmoniously in *Frankenstein*. That Henry Clerval, associated as he is with practical reason, should have as his 'design . . . to visit India, in the belief that he had in his knowledge of its various languages, and in the views he had taken of its society, the means of materially assisting the progress of European colonization and trade' is proof of this, as well as part of the incidental imperialist sentiment that I speak of above (*F*, pp. 151–2). I should perhaps point out that the language here is entrepreneurial rather than missionary:

> He came to the university with the design of making himself complete master of the Oriental languages, as thus he should open a field for the plan of life he had marked out for himself. Resolved to pursue no inglorious career, he turned his eyes towards the East as affording scope for his spirit of enterprise. The Persian, Arabic, and Sanskrit languages engaged his attention.
>
> (*F*, pp. 66–7)

But it is of course Victor Frankenstein, with his strange itinerary of obsession with natural philosophy, who offers the strongest demonstration that the multiple perspectives of the three-part Kantian subject cannot co-operate harmoniously. Frankenstein creates a putative human subject out of natural philosophy alone. According to his own miscued summation: 'In a fit of enthusiastic madness I created a rational creature' (*F*, p. 206). It is not at all far fetched to say that Kant's categorical imperative can most easily be mistaken for the hypothetical imperative – a command to ground in cognitive comprehension what can be apprehended only by moral will – by putting natural philosophy in the place of practical reason.

I should hasten to add here that just as readings such as this one do not necessarily accuse Charlotte Brontë the named individual of harboring imperialist sentiments, so also they do not necessarily commend Mary Shelley the named individual for writing a successful Kantian allegory. The most I can say is that it is possible to read these texts, within the frame of imperialism and the Kantian ethical moment, in a politically useful way. Such an approach presupposes that a 'disinterested' reading attempts to render transparent the interests of the hegemonic readership. (Other 'political' readings – for instance, that the monster is the nascent working class – can also be advanced.)

Frankenstein is built in the established epistolary tradition of multiple frames. At the heart of the multiple frames, the narrative of the monster (as reported by Frankenstein to Robert Walton, who then recounts it in a letter to his sister) is of his almost learning, clandestinely, to be human. It is invariably noticed that the monster reads *Paradise Lost* as true history. What is not so often noticed is that he also reads Plutarch's *Lives*, 'the histories of the first founders of the ancient republics', which he compares to 'the patriarchal lives of my protectors' (*F*, pp. 123, 124). And his *education* comes through 'Volney's *Ruins of Empires*', which purported to be a prefiguration of the French Revolution, published after the event and after the author had rounded off his theory with practice (*F*, p. 113). It is an attempt at an enlightened universal secular, rather than a Eurocentric Christian, history, written from the perspective of a narrator 'from below', somewhat like the attempts of Eric Wolf or Peter Worsley in our own time.[27]

This Caliban's education in (universal secular) humanity takes place through the monster's eavesdropping on the instruction of an Ariel – Safie, the Christianized 'Arabian' to whom 'a residence in Turkey was abhorrent' (*F*, p. 121). In depicting Safie, Shelley uses some commonplaces of eighteenth-century liberalism that are shared by many today: Safie's Muslim father was a victim of (bad) Christian religious prejudice and yet was himself a wily and ungrateful man not as morally refined as her (good) Christian mother. Having tasted the emancipation of woman, Safie could not go home. The confusion between 'Turk' and 'Arab' has its counterpart in present-day confusion about Turkey and Iran as 'Middle Eastern' but not 'Arab'.

Although we are a far cry here from the unexamined and covert axiomatics of imperialism in *Jane Eyre*, we will gain nothing by celebrating the time-bound pieties that Shelley, as the daughter of two anti-evangelicals, produces. It is more interesting for us that Shelley differentiates the Other, works at the Caliban–Ariel distinction, and *cannot* make the monster identical with the proper recipient of these lessons. Although he had 'heard of the discovery of the American hemisphere and *wept with Safie* over the helpless fate of its original inhabitants', Safie cannot reciprocate his attachment. When she first catches sight of him, 'Safie, unable to attend to her friend [Agatha], rushed out of the cottage' (*F*, pp. 114 [my emphasis], 129).

In the taxonomy of characters, the Muslim–Christian Safie belongs with Rhys's Antoinette/Bertha. And indeed, like Christophine the good servant, the subject created by the fiat of natural philosophy is the tangential unresolved moment in *Frankenstein*. The simple suggestion that the monster is human inside but monstrous outside and only provoked into vengefulness is clearly not enough to bear the burden of so great a historical dilemma.

At one moment, in fact, Shelley's Frankenstein does try to tame the monster, to humanize him by bringing him within the circuit of the Law. He 'repair[s] to a criminal judge in the town and . . . relate[s his] history briefly but with firmness' – the first and disinterested version of the narrative of Frankenstein – 'marking the dates with accuracy and never deviating into invective or exclamation. . . . When I had concluded my narration I said, "This is the being whom I accuse and for whose seizure and punishment I call upon you to exert your whole power. It is your duty as a magistrate"' (*F*, pp. 189, 190). The sheer social reasonableness of the mundane voice of Shelley's 'Genevan magistrate' reminds us that the absolutely Other cannot be selfed, that the monster has 'properties' which will not be contained by 'proper' measures:

I will exert myself [he says], and if it is in my power to seize the
monster, be assured that he shall suffer punishment proportionate
to his crimes. But I fear, from what you have yourself described to
be his properties, that this will prove impracticable; and thus, while
every proper measure is pursued, you should make up your mind to
disappointment.

(*F*, p. 190)

In the end, as is obvious to most readers, distinctions of human
individuality themselves seem to fall away from the novel. Monster,
Frankenstein, and Walton seem to become each others' relays.
Frankenstein's story comes to an end in death; Walton concludes his
own story within the frame of his function as letter writer. In the
narrative conclusion, he is the natural philosopher who learns from
Frankenstein's example. At the end of the *text*, the monster, having
confessed his guilt toward his maker and ostensibly intending to
immolate himself, is borne away on an ice raft. We do not see the
conflagration of his funeral pile – the self-immolation is not
consummated in the text: he too cannot be contained by the text. In
terms of narrative logic, he is 'lost in darkness and distance' (*F*, p. 211)
– these are the last words of the novel – into an existential temporality
that is coherent with neither the territorializing individual imagination
(as in the opening of *Jane Eyre*) nor the authoritative scenario of
Christian psychobiography (as at the end of Brontë's work). The very
relationship between sexual reproduction and social subject-production
– the dynamic nineteenth-century topos of feminism-in-imperialism
– remains problematic within the limits of Shelley's text and,
paradoxically, constitutes its strength.

Earlier, I offered a reading of woman as womb-holder in *Frankenstein*.
I would now suggest that there is a framing woman in the book who
is neither tangential, nor encircled, nor yet encircling. 'Mrs Saville',
'excellent Margaret', 'beloved Sister' are her address and kinship
inscriptions (*F*, pp. 15, 17, 22). She is the occasion, though not the
protagonist, of the novel. She is the feminine *subject* rather than the
female individualist: she is the irreducible *recipient*-function of the
letters that constitute *Frankenstein*. I have commented on the singular
appropriative hermeneutics of the reader reading with Jane in the
opening pages of *Jane Eyre*. Here the reader must read with Margaret
Saville in the crucial sense that she must *intercept* the recipient-function,
read the letters *as* recipient, in order for the novel to exist.[28] Margaret
Saville does not respond to close the text as frame. The frame is thus
simultaneously not a frame, and the monster can step 'beyond the text'
and be 'lost in darkness'. Within the allegory of our reading, the place
of both the English lady and the unnameable monster are left open by

this great flawed text. It is satisfying for a postcolonial reader to consider this a noble resolution for a nineteenth-century English novel. This is all the more striking because, on the anecdotal level, Shelley herself abundantly 'identifies' with Victor Frankenstein.[29]

I must myself close with an idea that I cannot establish within the limits of this essay. Earlier I contended that *Wide Sargasso Sea* is necessarily bound by the reach of the European novel. I suggested that, in contradistinction, to reopen the epistemic fracture of imperialism without succumbing to a nostalgia for lost origins, the critic must turn to the archives of imperialist governance. I have not turned to those archives in these pages. In my current work, by way of a modest and inexpert 'reading' of 'archives', I try to extend, outside of the reach of the European novelistic tradition, the most powerful suggestion in *Wide Sargasso Sea*: that *Jane Eyre* can be read as the orchestration and staging of the self-immolation of Bertha Mason as 'good wife'. The power of that suggestion remains unclear if we remain insufficiently knowledgeable about the history of the legal manipulation of widow-sacrifice in the entitlement of the British government in India. I would hope that an informed critique of imperialism, granted some attention from readers in the First World, will at least expand the frontiers of the politics of reading.

Notes

1. My notion of the 'worlding of a world' upon what must be assumed to be uninscribed earth is a vulgarization of MARTIN HEIDEGGER's idea; see 'The Origin of the Work of Art', *Poetry, Language, Thought*, trans. Albert Hofstadter (New York, 1977), pp. 17–87.
2. See CHARLOTTE BRONTË, *Jane Eyre* (New York, 1960); all further references to this work, abbreviated *JE*, will be included in the text.
3. See JEAN RHYS, *Wide Sargasso Sea* (Harmondsworth, 1966); all further references to this work, abbreviated *WSS*, will be included in the text. And see MARY SHELLEY, *Frankenstein; or, The Modern Prometheus* (New York, 1965); all further references to this work, abbreviated *F*, will be included in the text.
4. I have tried to do this in my essay 'Unmaking and Making in *To the Lighthouse*', in *Women and Language in Literature and Society*, ed. Sally McConnell-Ginet, Ruth Borker, and Nelly Furman (New York, 1980), pp. 310–27.
5. As always, I take my formula from LOUIS ALTHUSSER, 'Ideology and Ideological State Apparatuses (Notes towards an Investigation)', *'Lenin and Philosophy' and Other Essays*, trans. Ben Brewster (New York, 1971), pp. 127–86. For an acute differentiation between the individual and individualism, see V.N. VOLOSINOV, *Marxism and the Philosophy of Language*, trans. Ladislav Matejka and I.R. TITUNIK, Studies in Language, vol. 1 (New York, 1973), pp. 93–4 and 152–3. For a 'straight' analysis of the roots and ramifications of English 'individualism', see C.B. MACPHERSON, *The Political Theory of*

Possessive Individualism: Hobbes to Locke (Oxford, 1962). I am grateful to Jonathan Rée for bringing this book to my attention and for giving a careful reading of all but the very end of the present essay.

6. I am constructing an analogy with HOMI BHABHA's powerful notion of 'not-quite/not-white' in his 'Of Mimicry and Man: The Ambiguity of Colonial Discourse', *October* 28 (Spring 1984): 132. I should also add that I use the word 'native' here in reaction to the term 'Third World Woman'. It cannot, of course, apply with equal historical justice to both the West Indian and the Indian contexts nor to contexts of imperialism by transportation.

7. See ROBERTO FERNÁNDEZ RETAMAR, 'Caliban: Notes towards a Discussion of Culture in Our America', trans. Lynn Garafola, David Arthur McMurray and Robert Márquez, *Massachusetts Review* 15 (Winter–Spring 1974): 7–72; all further references to this work, abbreviated 'C', will be included in the text.

8. See JOSÉ ENRIQUE RODÓ, *Ariel*, ed. Gordon Brotherston (Cambridge, 1967).

9. For an elaboration of 'an inaccessible blankness circumscribed by an interpretable text', see my 'Can the Subaltern Speak?' *Marxist Interpretations of Culture*, ed. Cary Nelson (Urbana, Ill., forthcoming).

10. See ELIZABETH FOX-GENOVESE, 'Placing Women's History in History,' *New Left Review* 133 (May–June 1982): 5–29.

11. RUDOLPH ACKERMAN, *The Repository of Arts, Literature, Commerce, Manufactures, Fashions, and Politics* (London, 1823), p. 310.

12. See TERRY EAGLETON, *Myths of Power: A Marxist Study of the Brontës* (London, 1975); this is one of the general presuppositions of his book.

13. See SANDRA M. GILBERT and SUSAN GUBAR, *The Madwoman in the Attic: The Woman Writer and the Nineteenth-Century Literary Imagination* (New Haven, Conn., 1979), pp. 360–2.

14. IMMANUEL KANT, *Critique of Practical Reason, The 'Critique of Pure Reason', the 'Critique of Practical Reason' and Other Ethical Treatises, the 'Critique of Judgement'*, trans. J.M.D. Meiklejohn et al. (Chicago, 1952), pp. 328, 326.

15. I have tried to justify the reduction of sociohistorical problems to formulas or propositions in my essay 'Can the Subaltern Speak?' The 'travesty' I speak of does not befall the Kantian ethic in its purity as an accident but rather exists within its lineaments as a possible supplement. On the register of the human being as child rather than heathen, my formula can be found, for example, in 'What Is Enlightenment?' in KANT, *'Foundations of the Metaphysics of Morals', 'What Is Enlightenment?' and a Passage from 'The Metaphysics of Morals'*, trans. and ed. Lewis White Beck (Chicago, 1950). I have profited from discussing Kant with Jonathan Rée.

16. Jean Rhys, in an interview with Elizabeth Vreeland, quoted in NANCY HARRISON, *An Introduction to the Writing Practice of Jean Rhys: The Novel as Women's Text* (Rutherford, NJ, forthcoming). This is an excellent, detailed study of Rhys.

17. See LOUISE VINGE, *The Narcissus Theme in Western European Literature Up to the Early Nineteenth Century*, trans. Robert Dewsnap et al. (Lund, 1967), Chapter 5.

18. For a detailed study of this text, see JOHN BRENKMAN, 'Narcissus in the Text', *Georgia Review* 30 (Summer 1976): 293–327.

19. See, e.g., THOMAS F. STALEY, *Jean Rhys: A Critical Study* (Austin, Texas 1979), pp. 108–16; it is interesting to note Staley's masculinist discomfort with this and his consequent dissatisfaction with Rhys's novel.

20. I have tried to relate castration and suppressed letters in my 'The Letter

As Cutting Edge', in *Literature and Psychoanalysis; The Question of Reading: Otherwise*, ed. Shoshana Felman (New Haven, Conn., 1981), pp. 208–26.

21. This is the main argument of my 'Can the Subaltern Speak?'

22. See BARBARA JOHNSON, 'My Monster/My Self', *Diacritics* 12 (Summer 1982): 2–10.

23. See GEORGE LEVINE, *The Realistic Imagination: English Fiction from Frankenstein to Lady Chatterley* (Chicago, 1981), pp. 23–35.

24. Consult the publications of the Feminist International Network for the best overview of the current debate on reproductive technology.

25. For the male fetish, see SIGMUND FREUD, 'Fetishism', *The Standard Edition of the Complete Psychological Works of Sigmund Freud*, ed. and trans. James Strachey et at., 24 vols (London, 1953–74), 21: 152–7. For a more 'serious' Freudian study of *Frankenstein*, see MARY JACOBUS, 'Is There a Woman in This Text?' *New Literary History* 14 (Autumn 1982): 117–41. My 'fantasy' would of course be disproved by the 'fact' that it is more difficult for a woman to assume the position of fetishist than for a man; see MARY ANN DOANE, 'Film and the Masquerade: Theorising the Female Spectator', *Screen* 23 (Sept.–Oct. 1982): 74–87.

26. KANT, *Critique of Judgement*, trans. J.H. Bernard (New York, 1951), p. 39.

27. See [CONSTANTIN FRANÇOIS CHASSEBOEUF DE VOLNEY], *The Ruins; or, Meditations on the Revolutions of Empires*, trans. pub. (London, 1811). JOHANNES FABIAN has shown us the manipulation of time in 'new' secular histories of a similar kind; see *Time and the Other: How Anthropology Makes Its Object* (New York, 1983). See also ERIC R. WOLF, *Europe and the People without History* (Berkeley and Los Angeles, 1982), and PETER WORSLEY, *The Third World*, 2nd edn. (Chicago, 1973); I am grateful to Dennis Dworkin for bringing the latter book to my attention. The most striking ignoring of the monster's education through Volney is in GILBERT's otherwise brilliant 'Horror's Twin: Mary Shelley's Monstrous Eve', *Feminist Studies* 4 (June 1980): 48–73. GILBERT's essay reflects the absence of race-determinations in a certain sort of feminism. Her present work has most convincingly filled in this gap; see, e.g., her recent piece on H. RIDER HAGGARD's *She* ('Rider Haggard's Heart of Darkness', *Partisan Review* 50: 3 (1983): 444–53).

28. 'A letter is always and *a priori* intercepted, . . . the "subjects" are neither the senders nor the receivers of messages. . . . The letter is constituted . . . by its interception' (JACQUES DERRIDA, 'Discussion', after Claude Rabant, 'Il n'a aucune chance de l'entendre', in *Affranchissement: Du transfert et de la lettre*, ed. René Major (Paris, 1981), p. 106; my translation). Margaret Saville is not made to appropriate the reader's 'subject' into the signature of her own 'individuality'.

29. The most striking 'internal evidence' is the admission in the 'Author's Introduction' that, after dreaming of the yet-unnamed Victor Frankenstein figure and being terrified (through, yet not quite through, him) by the monster in a scene she later reproduced in Frankenstein's story, SHELLEY began her tale 'on the morrow . . . with the words "It was on a dreary night of November"' (*F*, p. xi). Those are the opening words of Chapter 5 of the finished book, where Frankenstein begins to recount the actual making of his monster (see *F*. p. 56).

6 'Race', Time and the Revision of Modernity*

Homi K. Bhabha

This essay has a special significance in Bhabha's work, reappearing as the Conclusion to *The Location of Culture* (1994), his own choice of his most important essays up to that date. The dominant themes of both phases of Bhabha's career are represented here in so far as colonial discourse and its analysis are brought to bear upon exploration of the relationship between the postcolonial and the postmodern. Returning to the work of Fanon, who demonstrates how 'Man' comes to be authorized or defined in the Enlightenment episteme, Bhabha provides a comparable critique of the implicit ethnocentrism of contemporary postmodern decentrings of the Sovereign Subject inaugurated by modernity. Just as Fanon reveals the constructed and relative nature of the figure of Enlightenment Man, which could claim to be 'universal' only by representing non-Westerners as 'belatedly' entering History (always defined, of course, in Eurocentric terms) through contact with the West, so Bhabha takes a number of more recent Western thinkers to task for failing to take sufficient account of the histories and legacies of colonialism in their narratives of postmodernity. Foucault, Benedict Anderson and Fredric Jameson (among others) are criticized for this oversight which, for Bhabha, reveals the same sort of limitations in much postmodern theory that Spivak discovers in Western feminism.

Methodologically, the essay is striking for its attempt to negotiate between systems of fixed binary oppositions (whether West vs. non-West, modernity vs. postmodernity, the public sphere vs. the psychic, private or 'domestic' spheres, for example), without also producing teleologically driven syntheses or resolutions which do not sufficiently respect the differences between the various pairs of terms. The essay also suggests that postcolonial identity is always differential and relational, rather than fixed and essential, and that postcolonial politics

---

*Reprinted from *The Oxford Literary Review* 9: 12–13 (1991): 193–219.

are subversive rather than directly oppositional. Both aspects of this argument are illustrated in Bhabha's emphasis on the tactical 'translation' of dominant metropolitan narratives about, and definitions of, the non-West. Bhabha maintains that the most effective response to such work is not simple rejection, or a nostalgic retreat back to one's 'roots'. Rather it lies in seizing the dominant narratives (whether in literature, anthropology or history) and opening them up to a re-articulation from postcolonial perspectives. For instance, the Western narratives of modernity (and 'progress' more generally) should be forced to confront the fact that colonialism accompanied the Enlightenment or even, indeed, made it possible (the West could only be 'enlightened' in relation to a 'benighted' or 'pre-modern' non-West.) Thus modernity remains an incomplete project in so far as this process of 'translation' is still unfinished, and postmodernism represent a new phase of the West's will to knowledge over the non-Western world so long as it, too, fails to properly and fully address the current predicaments and historical experiences of the rest of the globe.

I

'Dirty nigger!' Or simply, 'Look, a Negro!'

Whenever these words are said in anger or in hate, whether of the Jew in that estaminet in Antwerp, or of the Palestinian on the West Bank, or the Zaïrian student eking out a wretched existence selling fake fetishes on the Left Bank; whether they are said of the body of woman or the man of colour; whether they are quasi-officially spoken in South Africa or officially prohibited in London or New York, but inscribed nevertheless in the severe staging of the statistics of educational performance and crime, visa violations, immigration irregularities; whenever 'Dirty nigger!' or, 'Look a Negro!' is not said at all, but you can see it in a gaze, or hear it in the solecism of a still silence; whenever and wherever I am when I hear a racist, or catch his look, I am reminded of Fanon's evocatory essay 'The Fact of Blackness' and its unforgettable opening lines.[1]

I want to start by returning to that essay, to explore only one scene in its remarkable staging, Fanon's phenomenological performance of what it means to be *not only a nigger* but a member of the marginalized, the displaced, the diasporic. Those whose very presence is both 'overlooked' – in the double sense of social surveillance and psychic disavowal. And, at the same time 'overdetermined' – psychically projected, made stereotypical and symptomatic. Despite its very specific location – a Martinican subjected to the racist gaze on a street corner in Lyons – I claim a generality for Fanon's argument because he talks not simply of the historicity of the Black man, as much as he writes in 'The Fact of Blackness' about the temporality of modernity within which the figure of the 'human' comes to be *authorized*. It is Fanon's temporality of emergence – his sense of the *belatedness of the Black man* – that does not simply make the question of 'ontology' inappropriate for Black identity, but somehow *impossible* for the very understanding of humanity in the world of modernity: '*You come too late, much too late, there will always be a world – a white world between you and us.*' It is the opposition to the ontology of that white world – to its assumed, hierarchical forms of rationality and universality – that Fanon turns in a *performance* that is iterative and interrogative – a repetition that is *initiatory*, instating a differential history that will not return to the power of the Same. Between *you and us* Fanon opens up an enunciative space that does not simply contradict the metaphysical Ideas of Progress or Racism or Rationality; he distantiates them by 'repeating' these ideas, makes them uncanny by displacing them in a number of culturally contradictory and discursively estranged locations.

What Fanon shows up is the liminality of those ideas – their ethnocentric margin – by revealing the *historicity* of its most universal symbol – Man. From the perspective of a postcolonial 'belatedness', Fanon disturbs the *punctum* of man as the signifying, subjectifying category of Western culture, as a unifying referent of ethical value. Fanon performs the desire of the colonized to identify with the humanistic, Enlightenment ideal of Man: 'all I wanted was to be a man among other men. I wanted to come lithe and young into a world that was ours and build it together.' Then, in a catachrestic reversal he shows how, despite the pedagogies of human history, the performative discourse of the 'liberal' West, its quotidian conversation and comments, reveal the cultural supremacy and racial typology upon which the universalism of Man is founded: 'But of course, come in, sir, there is no colour prejudice among us. . . . Quite, the Negro is a man like ourselves. . . . It is not because he is black that he is less intelligent than we are. . . .'

Fanon uses the fact of blackness, of belatedness, to destroy the binary structure of power and identity: the *imperative* that 'the Black man must be Black; he must be Black in relation to the white man'. Elsewhere he has written: 'The Black man is not. [caesura] Any more than the white man' (my interpolation). Fanon's discourse of the 'human' emerges from that temporal 'break' or caesura effected in the continuist, progressivist myth of Man. He too speaks from the signifying time-lag of cultural difference that I have been attempting to develop as a structure for the representation of subaltern and postcolonial agency. Fanon writes from that temporal caesura, the time-lag of cultural difference, in a space between the symbolization of the social and the 'sign' of its representation of subjects and agencies. Fanon destroys two time-schemes in which the historicity of the human is thought. He rejects the 'belatedness' of the Black man because it is only the opposite of the framing of the white man as universal, normative – *the white sky all around me*: the Black man refuses to occupy the past of which the white man is the future. But Fanon also refuses the Hegelian–Marxist dialectical schema whereby the Black man is part of a transcendental sublation: a minor term in a dialectic that will emerge into a more equitable universality. Fanon, I believe, suggests another time, another space.

It is a space of being that is wrought from the interruptive, interrogative, tragic experience of blackness, of discrimination, of despair. It is the apprehension of the social and psychic question of 'origin' – and its erasure – in a negative side that 'draws its worth from an almost substantive absoluteness ... [which has to be] ignorant of the essences and determinations of its being ... an absolute density ... an abolition of the ego by desire'. What may seem primordial or timeless is, I believe, a moment of a kind of 'projective past' whose history and signification I shall attempt to explore here. It is a mode of 'negativity' that makes the enunciatory present of modernity disjunctive. It opens up a time-lag at the point at which we speak of humanity through its differentiations – gender, race, class – that mark an excessive marginality of modernity. It is the enigma of this form of temporality which emerges from what Du Bois also called the 'swift and slow of human doing', to face Progress with some unanswerable questions, and suggest some answers of its own.

In destroying the 'ontology of man', Fanon suggests that 'there is not merely one Negro, there are *Negroes*'. This is emphatically not a 'postmodern' celebration of pluralistic identities. As my argument will make clear, for me the project of modernity is itself rendered so contradictory and unresolved through the insertion of the 'time-lag' in which colonial and postcolonial moments emerge as sign and history, that I am sceptical of those transitions to postmodernity in the West which theorize the experience of this 'new historicity' through the appropriation of a 'Third World' metaphor; 'the First World ... in a peculiar dialectical reversal, begins to touch some features of third-world experience. . . . The United States is . . . the biggest third-world country because of unemployment, nonproduction, etc.'[2]

Fanon's sense of social contingency and indeterminacy, made from the perspective of a postcolonial belatedness, is not a celebration of fragmentation, *bricolage, pastiche* or the 'simulacrum'. It is a vision of social contradiction and cultural difference – as the disjunctive space of modernity – that is best seen in a fragment of a poem he cites towards the end of 'The Fact of Blackness':

As the contradiction among the features
creates the harmony of the face
we proclaim the oneness of the suffering
and the revolt.

II

The discourse of race that I am trying to develop displays the *problem of the ambivalent temporality of modernity* that is often overlooked in the more 'spatial' traditions of some aspects of postmodern theory.[3] Under the rubric 'the discourse of modernity', I do not intend to reduce a complex and diverse historical moment, with varied national genealogies and different institutional practices, into a singular shibboleth – be it the 'idea' of Reason, Historicism, Progress – for the critical convenience of postmodern literary theory. My interest in the question of modernity resides in the influential discussion generated by the work of Habermas, Foucault, Lyotard, and Lefort, amongst many others, that has generated a critical discourse around historical modernity as an epistemological structure.[4] To put it succinctly, the question of ethical and cultural judgement, central to the processes of subject formation and the objectification of social knowledge, is challenged at its 'cognitivist' core. Habermas characterizes it as a form of Occidental self-understanding that enacts a cognitive reductionism in the relation of the human being to the social world:

> Ontologically the world is reduced to a world of entities *as a whole* (as the totality of objects . . .); epistemologically, our relationship to that world is reduced to the capacity of know[ing] . . . states of affairs . . . in a purposive-rational fashion; semantically it is reduced to fact-stating discourse in which assertoric sentences are used.[5]

Although this may be a stark presentation of the problem, it highlights the fact that the challenge to such a 'cognitivist' consciousness displaces the problem of truth or meaning from the disciplinary confines of epistemology – the problem of the referential as 'objectivity' reflected in that celebrated Rortyesque trope, the mirror of nature. What results could be figuratively described as a preoccupation not simply with the reflection in the glass – the idea or concept in itself – but with the frameworks of meaning as they are revealed in what Derrida has called the 'supplementary necessity of a parergon'. That is the performative, living description of the *writing* of a concept or theory, 'a relation to the history of its writing and the writing of its history also'.[6]

If we take even the most cursory view of influential 'postmodern' perspectives, we find that there is an increasing *narrativization* of the question of social ethics and subject formation. Whether it is in the conversational procedures and 'final vocabularies' of liberal ironists like Richard Rorty, or the 'moral fictions' of Alisdair Macintyre that are the sustaining myths 'after virtue'; whether it is the *petits récits* and *phrases* that remain from the fall-out of the grand narratives of modernity in Lyotard; or the projective but ideal speech community that is rescued *within* modernity by Habermas in his concept of communicative reason that is expressed in its pragmatic logic or argument and a 'decentered' understanding of the world: what we encounter in all these accounts are proposals for what is considered to be the essential gesture of Western modernity, an 'ethics of self-construction' – or, as Mladan Dolar cogently describes it: 'What makes this attitude typical of modernity is the constant reconstruction and the reinvention of the self. . . . The subject and the present it belongs to have no objective status, they have to be perpetually (re)constructed.'[7]

I want to ask whether this synchronous constancy of reconstruction and reinvention of the subject does not assume a cultural temporality that may not be 'universalist' in its 'epistemological' moment of judgement, but may, indeed, be ethnocentric in its construction of cultural 'difference'. It is certainly true, as Robert Young argues, that the 'inscription of alterity within the self can allow for a new relation to ethics';[8] but does that *necessarily* entail the more general case argued by Dolar, that 'the persisting split [of the subject] is the condition of freedom'?

If so, how do we specify the historical conditions and theoretical configurations of 'splitting' in political situations of 'unfreedom' – in the colonial and postcolonial margins of modernity? I am persuaded that it is the catachrestic postcolonial agency of 'seizing the value-coding' – as I have argued elsewhere – that opens up an interruptive time-lag in the 'progressive' myth of modernity, and enables the diasporic and the postcolonial to be represented. But this makes it all the more crucial to specify the discursive and historical temporality that interrupts the enunciative 'present' in which the self-inventions of modernity take place. And it is this 'taking place' of modernity, this insistent and incipient *spatial* metaphor in which the social relations of modernity are conceived, that introduces a temporality of the 'synchronous' in the structure of the 'splitting' of modernity. It is this 'synchronous and spatial' representation of cultural difference that must be reworked as a *framework* for cultural otherness *within* the general dialectic of doubling that postmodernism proposes. Otherwise we are likely to find ourselves beached amidst Jameson's 'cognitive mappings' of the Third World, which might work for the Bonaventura Hotel in Los Angeles, but will leave you somewhat eyeless in Gaza.[9] Or if, like Terry Eagleton, your taste is more 'other Worldly' than Third World, you will find yourself

171

somewhat dismissive of the 'real' history of the 'other' – women, foreigners, homosexuals, the natives of Ireland – on the basis 'of certain styles, values, life-experiences which can be appealed to now as a form of political critique' because 'the fundamental political question is that of demanding an equal right with others of what one might become, not of assuming some fully-fashioned identity which is merely repressed'.[10]

It is to establish a *sign of the present*, of modernity, that is not that 'now' of transparent immediacy, and to found a form of social individuation where communality is *not predicated on a transcendent becoming*, that I want to pose my questions of a contra-modernity: what is modernity in those colonial conditions where its imposition is itself the denial of historical freedom, civic autonomy and the 'ethical' choice of refashioning?

III

I am posing these questions from within the problematic of modernity because of a shift within contemporary critical traditions of postcolonial writing. No longer is there an influential separatist emphasis on simply elaborating an anti-imperialist or Black nationalist tradition 'in-itself'. There is an attempt to interrupt the Western discourses of modernity through these displacing, interrogative subaltern or post-slavery narratives and the critical–theoretical perspectives they engender. For example, Houston Baker's reading of the modernity of the Harlem Renaissance strategically elaborates a 'deformation of mastery', a vernacularism, based on the enunciation of the subject as 'never a simple coming into being, but a release from being possessed'.[11] The revision of Western modernism, he suggests, requires both the linguistic investiture of the subject and a practice of diasporic performance that is metaphorical. The 'public culture' project that Carol Breckenridge and Arjun Appadurai have initiated focuses on the transnational dissemination of cultural modernity. What becomes properly urgent for them is that the 'simultaneous' global locations of such a modernity should not lose sense of the conflictual, contradictory locutions of those cultural practices and products that follow the 'unequal development' of the tracks of international or multinational capital. Any transnational cultural study must 'translate', each time locally and specifically, what decentres and subverts this transnational globality, so that it does not become enthralled by the new global technologies of ideological transmission and cultural consumption.[12] Paul Gilroy proposes a form of populist modernism to comprehend both the aesthetic and political transformation of European philosophy and letters by Black writers, but also to 'make sense of the secular and spiritual *popular* forms – music and dance – that have handled the anxieties and dilemmas involved in a response to the *flux of modern life*.[13]

The power of the postcolonial translation of modernity rests in its *performative, deformative* structure that does not simply revalue the 'contents' of a cultural tradition, or transpose values 'cross-culturally' or multiculturally. The cultural inheritance of slavery or colonialism is brought *before* modernity *not* to resolve its historic differences into a new totality, nor to forego its traditions. It is to introduce another locus of inscription and intervention, another hybrid, 'inappropriate' enunciative site, through that temporal split – or time-lag – that I have opened up (specifically in 'The Postcolonial and the Postmodern') for the signification of postcolonial agency, and the differences in culture and power that constitute its social conditions of enunciation: the temporal caesura, *which is also the historically transformative moment*, when a lagged space opens up *in*-between the *inter*subjective 'reality of signs . . . deprived of subjectivity'* and the historical development of the subject in the order of social symbols.[14] This transvaluation of the symbolic structure of the cultural sign is absolutely necessary so that in the renaming of modernity there may ensue that process of the active agency of translation – the moment of 'making a name for oneself' that emerges through 'the undecidability . . . [at work] in a struggle for the proper name within a scene of genealogical indebtedness'.[15] Without such a reinscription of the sign itself – without a transformation of the site of *enunciation* – there is the danger that the mimetic contents of a discourse will conceal the fact that the hegemonic structures of power are maintained in a position of authority through a *shift in vocabulary* in the position of authority. There is for instance a kinship between the normative paradigms of 'colonial' anthropology and the contemporary discourse of aid and development agencies. The 'transfer of technology' has not resulted in the transfer of power or the displacement of a 'colonial' tradition of political control through philanthropy – a celebrated missionary position. Cultural translation must change the value of culture *as a sign*, as the 'time signature' of the present:

> Where were the courts of Castile?
> Versailles' colonnades
> Supplanted by cabbage palms
> With Corinthian crests
> belittling diminutives
> then, little Versailles
> meant plans for a pigsty. . . .
> Being men they could not live
> except they presumed
> the right of everything to be a noun

The African acquiesced,
repeated and changed them . . .
moubain: the hog-plum . . .
baie-la: the bay . . .
in the way the wind bends
our natural inflections.[16]

What is the struggle of translation in the name of modernity? How
do we catachrestically seize the genealogy of modernity and open it
to the postcolonial translation? The 'value' of modernity is not located,
a priori, in the passive fact of an epochal event or idea – of progress,
civility, the law – but has to be negotiated *within* the 'enunciative'
present of the discourse. The brilliance of Claude Lefort's account
of the genesis of ideology in modern societies is to suggest that the
representation of the rule, or the discourse of generality that symbolizes
authority, is ambivalent because it is split off from its effective
operation.[17] The *new or the contemporary* appear through the splitting
of modernity as event and enunciation, the epochal and the everyday.
Modernity as a *sign* of the present emerges in that process of splitting,
that *lag*, that gives the practice of everyday life its consistency as *being
contemporary*. It is because the present has the value of a 'sign' that
modernity is iterative; a continual questioning of the conditions of
existence; making problematic its own discourse not simply 'as ideas'
but as the position and status of the *locus* of social enunciation.

IV

'It is not enough . . . to follow the teleological thread that makes progress
possible; one must isolate, within the history [of modernity], an event
that will have the value of a sign.[18] In his reading of Kant's *Was ist
Aufklärung?* Foucault suggests that the sign of modernity is a form of
decipherment whose value must be sought in *petits récits*, imperceptible
events, in signs apparently *without* meaning and value – empty and
excentric – in events that are outside the 'great events' of history, in
supplementary framings: 'belittling diminutives . . . / The African
acquiesced / repeated and changed them . . . / *baie-la*: the bay . . .'.

The sign of history does not consist in an essence of the 'event itself',
nor exclusively in the *immediate consciousness* of its agents and 'actors',
but in its form as a *spectacle*; spectacle that signifies *because of* the
distanciation and displacement between the event and those who are
its spectators. The 'indeterminacy' of modernity, where the struggle of
translation takes place, is not simply around the 'ideas' of progress or
truth. Modernity, I suggest, is about the historical construction of a
specific position of historical enunciation and address. It privileges those

who 'bear witness', those who are 'subjected', or in the Fanonian sense
with which I began, historically belated. It gives them a representative
position through the spatial distance, or the *time-lag* between the Great
Event and its circulation as a historical sign of the 'people' or an
'epoch', that constitutes the memory and the moral of the event *as a
narrative*, a disposition to cultural communality, a form of social and
psychic identification. The discursive address of modernity – its
structure of *authority* – decentres the Great Event, and speaks from
that moment of 'imperceptibility', the supplementary space 'outside'
or uncannily beside (*Abseits*).

Through Kant, Foucault traces 'the ontology of the present' to the
exemplary event of the French Revolution and it is there that he stages
his sign of modernity. But it is the spatial dimension of 'distance' – *the
perspectival distance from which the spectacle is seen* – that installs a cultural
homogeneity into the sign of modernity; a eurocentric perspective at
the point at which modernity installs 'moral disposition in mankind'.
The eurocentricity of Foucault's theory of cultural difference is revealed
in his insistent spatializing of the time of modernity. Avoiding the
problems of the sovereign subject and linear causality, he nonetheless
falls prey to the notion of the 'cultural' as a social formation whose
discursive doubleness – the transcendental and empirical dialectic
– are contained in a temporal frame that makes differences repetitively
'contemporaneous', regimes of sense-as-synchronous. It is a kind of
cultural 'contradictoriness' that always presupposes a correlative
spacing. Foucault's *spatial distancing* seals the sign of modernity in 1789
into a 'correlative', overlapping temporality. Progress brings together the
three moments of the sign as:

> a *signum rememorativum*, for it reveals that disposition [of progress]
> which has been present from the beginning; it is a *signum
> demonstrativum* because it demonstrates the present efficacity of
> this disposition; and it is also *signum prognosticum* for, although the
> Revolution may have certain questionable results, one cannot forget
> the disposition [of modernity] that is revealed through it.[19]

What if the effects of 'certain questionable results' of the Revolution
create a disjunction, between the *signum demonstrativum* and the *signum
prognosticum*? What if in the geopolitical space of the colony,
genealogically (in Foucault's sense) related to the Western metropolis,
the symbol of the Revolution is partially visible as an unforgettable,
tantalizing promise – a *pedagogy* of the values of modernity, while the
'present efficacy' of the sign of everyday life – its *political performativity*
– repeats the archaic aristocratic racism of the *ancien régime*?

The ethnocentric limitations of Foucault's spatial sign of modernity
become immediately apparent if we take our stand, in the immediate

post-revolutionary period, in San Domingo with the Black Jacobins, rather than Paris. What if the 'distance' that constitutes the meaning of the Revolution as sign, the *signifying lag* between event and enunciation, stretches not across the Place de la Bastille or the rue des Blancs-Monteaux, but spans the temporal difference of the colonial space? What if we heard the 'moral disposition of mankind' uttered by Toussaint L'Ouverture for whom, as C.L.R. James so vividly recalls, the signs of modernity, 'liberty, equality, fraternity... what the French Revolution signified, was perpetually on his lips, in his correspondence, in his private conversations'.[20] What do we make of the figure of Toussaint – James invokes Phèdre, Ahab, Hamlet – at the moment when he grasps the tragic lesson that the moral, *modern* disposition of mankind, enshrined in the sign of the Revolution, only fuels the archaic racial factor in the society of slavery? What do we learn from that split consciousness, that 'colonial' disjunction of modern times and colonial and slave histories, where the reinvention of the self and the remaking of the social are strictly out of joint? What do we learn when we realize that the subaltern agency of the chapati flour mixed with bone-dust, emerges uncannily, antagonistically alongside the great event of the modernization of the Indian Army and the 'rationalization' of land tenures in Northern India?

These are the issues of the catachrestic, postcolonial translation of modernity. They force us to introduce the question of subaltern agency, *Che vuoi?*, into the question of modernity: what is this 'now' of modernity? Who defines this present from which we speak? This leads to a more challenging question: *What is the desire of this repeated demand to modernize? Why does it insist, so compulsively, on its contemporaneous reality, its spatial dimension, its spectatorial distance?* What happens to the sign of modernity in those repressive places like San Domingo where progress is only heard (of) and not 'seen', is that it reveals the problem of the disjunctive moment of its utterance: the space which enables a postcolonial contra-modernity to emerge. For the discourse of modernity is *signified* from the time-lag, or temporal caesura, that emerges in the tension between the epochal 'event' of modernity as the symbol of the continuity of progress, and the interruptive temporality of the sign of the present, the contingency of modern times that Habermas has aptly described as its 'forward gropings and shocking encounters'.[21]

In this 'time' of repetition there circulates a contingent tension within modernity: a tension between the *pedagogy* of the symbols of progress, historicism, modernization, homogeneous empty time, the narcissism of organic culture, the onanistic search for the origins of race, and what I shall call the 'sign of the present', the performativity of discursive practice, the *récits* of the everyday, the repetition of the empirical, the ethics of self-enactment, the iterative signs that mark the non-synchronic *passages* of time in the archives of the 'new'. This is the space in which the question of modernity *emerges as a form of interrogation*: what do I belong to in this present? In what terms do I identify with the 'we', the intersubjective realm of society? This process cannot be represented in the binary relation of archaism/modernity, inside/outside, past/present, because it blocks off the 'forward drive' or teleology of modernity. It suggests that what is read as the 'futurity' of the modern, its ineluctable progress, its cultural hierarchies, may be an 'excess', a disturbing alterity, a process of the marginalization of the symbols of modernity.

Time-lag is not a circulation of nullity, the endless slippage of the signifier or the theoretical anarchy of aporia. It is a concept that does not collude with current fashions for claiming the heterogeneity of ever-increasing 'causes', multiplicities of subject positions, endless supplies of subversive 'specificities', 'localities', 'territories'. These are the power-dressers of contemporary critical jargon who end up by becoming its abominable snowmen – all shoulderpads, no solar plexus! The problem of the articulation of cultural difference is not the problem of free-wheeling pragmatist pluralism or the 'diversity' of the many; it is the problem of the not-one, the minus in the origin and repetition of cultural signs in a doubling that will not be sublated into a similitude. What is *in* modernity *more* than modernity is this signifying 'cut' or temporal break: it cuts into the plenitudinous notion of Culture splendidly reflected in the mirror of Nature; equally it 'halts' the 'endless' signification of difference. The process I have described as the sign of the present – *within modernity* – erases and interrogates those ethnocentric forms of cultural modernity that 'contemporize' cultural difference: it opposes both cultural pluralism with its spurious egalitarianism – different cultures in the same time (*The Magicians of the Earth*, Pompidou, Paris, 1989) – or cultural relativism – different cultural temporalities in the same 'universal' space (*The Primitivism Show*, MOMA, New York, 1984).

V

This caesura in the narrative of modernity reveals something of what de Certeau has famously described as the non-place from which all historiographical operation starts, the lag which all histories must encounter in order to make a beginning.[22] For the emergence of modernity – as an ideology of *beginning, modernity as the new* – the template of this 'non-place' becomes the colonial space. It signifies this in a double way. The colonial space is the *terra incognita* or the *terra nulla*, the empty or wasted land whose history has to be begun, whose archives must be filled out; whose future progress must be secured in modernity. But the colonial space also stands for the *despotic* time of the Orient that becomes a great problem for the definition of modernity and its inscription of the history of the colonized from the perspective of the West. Despotic time, as Althusser has brilliantly described it, is 'space without places, time without duration'.[23] In that double-figure which haunted the moment of the Enlightenment in its relation to the *otherness* of the Other, you can see the historical formation of the time-lag of modernity. And lest it be said that this disjunctive present of modernity is merely my theoretical abstraction, let me also remind you that a similar, signifying caesura occurs within the invention of progress in the 'long imperialist nineteenth century'. At the mid-point of the century questions concerning the 'origin of races' provided modernity with an ontology of its present and a justification of cultural hierarchy within the West and in the East. In the structure of the discourse there was always an antagonism between the developmental, organic notion of cultural and racial 'indigenism' as the guarantee of progress, and the notion of evolution as abrupt cultural transition, discontinuous progress, the periodic eruption of invading tribes from somewhere mysterious in Asia, as the guarantee of progress: 'French and German anthropologists blackened each other's racial ancestry as readily as the English denigrated the Irish Celts . . . whose character made it impossible for its members ever to govern themselves.'[24]

The 'subalterns and ex-slaves' who now seize the spectacular event of modernity do so in a catachrestic gesture of reinscription, of 'seizing the value coding' and transforming the locus of thought and writing in their postcolonial critique. Listen to the ironic naming, the interrogative repetitions, of the critical terms themselves: Black 'vernacularism' repeats the minor term used to designate the language of the native and the housebound slave to make demotic the grander narratives of progress. Black 'expressivism' reverses the stereotypical affectivity and sensuality of the stereotype to suggest that 'rationalities are produced *endlessly*' in populist modernism.[25] 'New ethnicity' is used by Stuart Hall in the Black British context to create a discourse of cultural difference that 'marks' ethnicity as the struggle against ethnicist 'fixing' and in favour of a wider minority discourse that represents sexuality and class. Cornel West's genealogical materialist view of race and Afro-American oppression is, he writes, 'both continuous and discontinuous with the Marxist tradition' and shares an equally contingent relation to Nietzsche and Foucault.[26] More recently, he has constructed a prophetic pragmatic tradition from William James, Niebuhr and Du Bois suggesting that 'it is possible to be a prophetic pragmatist and belong to different political movements, e.g. feminist, Black, chicano, socialist, left-liberal ones'.[27] The Indian historian Gyan Prakash, in a recent essay on postorientalist histories of the Third World, claims that:

it is difficult to overlook the fact that ... third world voices ... speak within and to discourses familiar to the 'West'. ... The Third World, far from being confined to its assigned space, has penetrated the inner sanctum of the 'First World' in the process of being 'Third Worlded' – arousing, inciting, and affiliating with the subordinated others in the First World ... to connect with minority voices.[28]

The intervention of postcolonial or Black critique is aimed at transforming the conditions of enunciation at the level of the sign – where the intersubjective realm is constituted – not simply setting up new symbols of identity, new 'positive images' that fuel an unreflective 'identity politics'. The challenge to modernity comes in redefining the signifying relation to a disjunctive 'present': staging the 'past' as *symbol*, myth, memory, history, the ancestral – but a 'past' whose iterative *value as sign* reinscribes the 'lessons of the past' into the very textuality of the present that determines both the identification with, and the interrogation of, modernity: what is the 'we' that defines the prerogative of my present? The possibility of inciting cultural translations across minority discourses – athwart the margins of the First and Third Worlds – arises because of the disjunctive present of modernity. It ensures that what *seems* the 'same' within cultures is negotiated in the time-lag of the 'sign' which constitutes the intersubjective, social realm. Because that lag is indeed the very structure of difference and splitting within the discourse of modernity, turning it into a performative process, then each repetition of the sign of modernity is different, specific to its historical and cultural conditions of enunciation.

This process is most clearly apparent in the work of those 'postmodern' writers who, in pushing the paradoxes of modernity to its limits, reveal the margins of the West.[29] From the postcolonial perspective we can only assume a disjunctive and displaced relation to these works; we cannot accept them until we subject them to a *lagging*: both in the temporal sense of postcolonial agency with which you are now (over)familiar, and in the obscurer sense in which, in the early days of settler colonization, to be lagged was to be transported to the colonies for penal servitude!

In Foucault's Introduction to the *History of Sexuality*, racism emerges in the nineteenth century in the form of an historical retroversion that Foucault finally disavows. In the 'modern' shift of power from the juridical politics of death to the biopolitics of life, race produces a historical temporality of interference, overlapping, and the displacement of sexuality. It is, for Foucault, the great historical irony of modernity that the Hitlerite annihilation of the Jews was carried out in the name of the archaic, pre-modern signs of race and sanguinity – the oneiric exaltation of blood, death, skin – rather than through the politics of

sexuality. What is profoundly revealing is Foucault's complicity with
the logic of the 'contemporaneous' within Western modernity.
Characterizing the 'symbolics of blood' as being retroverse, Foucault
disavows the time-lag of race as the sign of cultural difference and its
mode of repetition.

The *temporal* disjunction that the 'modern' question of race would
introduce into the discourse of disciplinary and pastoral power is
disallowed because of Foucault's spatial critique: 'we must conceptualize
the deployment of sexuality on the basis of the techniques of power that
are *contemporary* with it' (my emphasis).[30] However subversive 'blood'
and race may be they are in the last analysis merely an 'historical
retroversion'. Elsewhere Foucault directly links the 'flamboyant
rationality' of Social Darwinism to Nazi ideology, entirely ignoring
colonial societies which were the proving grounds for social Darwinist
administrative discourses all through the nineteenth and early twentieth
centuries.[31]

If Foucault normalizes time-lagged, 'retroverse' sign of race, Benedict
Anderson places the 'modern' dreams of racism 'outside history'
altogether. For Foucault race and blood interfere with sexuality. For
Anderson racism has its origins in antique ideologies of class that
belong to the aristocratic 'pre-history' of the modern nation. Race
represents an archaic ahistorical moment outside the 'modernity' of the
imagined community: 'nationalism thinks in historical destinies, while
racism dreams of eternal contaminations . . . outside history'.[32] Foucault's
spatial notion of the conceptual contemporaneity of power-as-sexuality
limits him from seeing the double and overdetermined structure of
race and sexuality that has a long history in the *peuplement* (politics
of settlement) of colonial societies; for Anderson the 'modern' anomaly
of racism finds its historical modularity, and its phantasmatic scenario,
in the colonial space which is a belated and hybrid attempt to 'weld
together dynastic legitimacy and national community . . . to shore up
domestic aristocratic bastions'.[33]

The racism of colonial empires is then part of an archaic acting out,
a dream-text of a form of historical retroversion that 'appeared to
confirm on a global, modern stage antique conceptions of power and
privilege'.[34] What could have been a way of understanding the limits
of Western imperialist ideas of progress within the genealogy of a
'colonial metropolis' – a hybridizing of the Western nation – is quickly
disavowed in the language of the *opera bouffe* as a grimly amusing
tableau vivant of 'the [colonial] bourgeois gentilhomme speaking poetry
against a backcloth of spacious mansions and gardens filled with
mimosa and bougainvillea'.[35] It is in that 'weld' of the colonial site
as, contradictorily, both 'dynastic and national', that the modernity
of Western national society is confronted by its colonial double. Such

a moment of temporal disjunction, which would be crucial for understanding the colonial history of contemporary metropolitan racism in the West, is placed 'outside history'. It is obscured by Anderson's espousal of 'a simultaneity across homogenous empty time' as the modal narrative of the imagined community. It is this kind of evasion, I think, that makes Partha Chatterjee, the Indian 'subaltern' scholar, suggest, from a different perspective, that Anderson 'seals up his theme with a sociological determinism . . . without noticing the twists and turns, the suppressed possibilities, the contradictions still unresolved'.[36]

These accounts of the modernity of power and national community become strangely symptomatic at the point at which they create a rhetoric of 'retroversion' for the emergence of racism. In placing the representations of race 'outside' modernity, in the space of historical retroversion, Foucault reinforces his 'correlative spacing'; by relegating the social fantasy of racism to an archaic daydream, Anderson further universalizes his homogeneous empty time of the 'modern' social imaginary. Lurking in the symbol of racism as part of a perverse political 'unconscious' is a disavowal of the sign of cultural difference, its colonial and postcolonial genealogy. Hidden in the disavowing narrative of historical retroversion and its archaism, is a notion of the time-lag that displaces Foucault's spatial analytic of modernity and Anderson's homogeneous temporality of the modern nation. In order to extract the one from the other we have to see how they form a double, catachrestic boundary: rather like the more general intervention and seizure of the history of modernity that has been attempted by postcolonial critics.

Retroversion and archaic doubling, attributed to the ideological 'contents' of racism, do not remain at the ideational or pedagogical level of the discourse. Their inscription of a structure of retroaction returns to disrupt the enunciative function of this discourse and produce a different 'value' of the sign and time of race and modernity as figured in the time-lag of representation. At the level of content the archaism and phantasy of racism is represented as 'ahistorical', outside the progressive myth of modernity. This is an attempt, I would argue, to universalize the spatial fantasy of modern cultural communities as living their history 'contemporaneously', in a 'homogeneous empty time' of the People-as-One that deprives minorities of that marginal, liminal space from which they can intervene in the unifying and totalizing *myths* of the national culture.

However, each time such a homogeneity of cultural identification is established there is a marked disturbance of temporality in the *writing of modernity*. For Foucault it is the awareness that retroversion of race or sanguinity haunts and doubles the contemporary analytic of power and sexuality and may be subversive of it: we may need to think the

181

disciplinary powers of race as sexuality in a hybrid cultural formation that will not be contained within Foucault's logic of the contemporary. Anderson goes further in acknowledging that colonial racism introduces an awkward weld, a strange historical 'suture', in the narrative of the nation's *modernity*. The archaism of colonial racism, as a form of cultural signification (rather than simply an ideological content), reactivates nothing less than the 'primal scene' of the modern Western nation: that is, the problematic historical transition between dynastic, lineage societies and horizontal, homogenous 'secular' communities. What Anderson designates as racism's 'timelessness', its location 'outside history', is in fact that form of time-lag, a mode of repetition and reinscription, that *performs* the ambivalent historical temporality of modern national cultures – the *aporetic coexistence*, within the cultural history of the *modern* imagined community, of both the dynastic, hierarchical, prefigurative 'medieval' traditions (the past), and the secular, homogeneous, synchronous cross-time of modernity (the present). Anderson resists a reading of the modern nation that suggests – in an iterative time-lag – that the hybridity of the colonial space may provide a pertinent problematic within which to write the history of the 'postmodern' national formations of the West.

To take this perspective would mean that we see 'racism' not simply as a hangover from archaic conceptions of the aristocracy, but as part of the historical traditions of 'civic' and liberal humanism that create ideological matrices of 'national' aspiration, together with their concepts of 'a people' and its imagined community. Such a privileging of ambivalence in the social imaginaries of nation*ness*, and its forms of collective affiliation, would enable us to understand the coeval, often *incommensurable*, tension between the influence of traditional 'ethnicist' identifications that coexist with 'contemporary' secular, modernizing aspirations. The enunciative 'present' of modernity that I am proposing, would provide a political space to articulate and negotiate such culturally hybrid social identities. Questions of cultural difference would not be dismissed – with a barely concealed racism – as atavistic 'tribal' instincts that afflict Irish Catholics in Belfast or 'Muslim fundamentalists' in Bradford. It is precisely such unresolved, transitional moments within the disjunctive 'present' of modernity that are then projected into a time of historical retroversion or an inassimilable place 'outside history'.

The *history* of modernity's antique dreams is to be found in the *writing out* of the colonial and postcolonial moment. In resisting these attempts to normalize the time-lagged colonial moment, we may provide a *genealogy* for postmodernity that is at least as important as the 'aporetic' history of the Sublime or the nightmare of rationality in Auschwitz. For colonial and postcolonial texts do not merely tell the modern history of 'unequal development' or evoke memories of underdevelopment. I have tried to suggest that they provide modernity with a modular moment of *enunciation* as *time-lag*: the locus and locution of cultures caught in the transitional and disjunctive temporalities of modernity. What is in modernity *more* than modernity is the disjunctive 'postcolonial' time and space that makes its presence felt *at the level of enunciation*. It figures, in an influential contemporary fictional instance, as the contingent margin between Toni Morrison's indeterminate moment of the 'not there' – a 'Black' space that she distinguishes from the Western sense of synchronous tradition – which then turns into the 'first stroke' of slave rememory, the *time* of communality and the narrative of a history of slavery. This translation of the meaning of time into the discourse of space; this catachrestic seizure of the signifying 'caesura' of modernity's presence and *present*; this insistence that power must be thought in the hybridity of race and sexuality; that nation must be reconceived liminally as the dynastic-in-the-democratic, race-difference doubling and splitting the teleology of class-consciousness: it is through these iterative interrogations and *historical initiations* that the cultural location of modernity shifts to the postcolonial site.

I have attempted, then, to designate a postcolonial 'enunciative' present that moves beyond Foucault's reading of the task of modernity as providing an ontology of the present. I have tried to open up a cultural space in the temporal caesura of sign and symbol: from the stroke of the sign that establishes the intersubjective world of truth 'deprived of subjectivity', back to the rediscovery of that moment of agency and individuation in the social imaginary of the order of historic symbols. I have attempted to provide a form of the writing of cultural difference in the midst of modernity that is inimical to binary boundaries: whether these be between past and present, inside and outside, subject and object, signifier and signified. This spatial-time of cultural difference – with its postcolonial genealogy – erases the Occidental 'culture of common sense' that Derrida aptly describes as 'ontologizing the limit between outside and inside, between the biophysical and the psychic'.[37] In his essay 'The Uncolonized Mind: Postcolonial India and the West', Ashis Nandy provides a more descriptive illustration of a postcolonial India that is neither modern nor anti-modern but non-modern. What this entails for the 'modern antonyms' of cultural difference between the First and Third Worlds, requires a form of time-lagged signification, for as he writes:

> this century has shown that in every situation of organized
> oppression the true antonyms are always the exclusive part versus
> the inclusive whole. . . . [N]ot the past versus the present but either of
> them versus the timelessness in which the past is the present and the

present is the past, not the oppressor versus the oppressed but both of them versus the rationality which turns them into co-victims.[38]

In splitting open those 'welds' of modernity, a postcolonial contra-modernity becomes visible. What Foucault and Anderson disavow as 'retroversion' emerges as a retroactivity, a form of cultural reinscription that moves *back to the future*. I shall call it a 'projective' past, a form of the future anterior. Without the postcolonial *time-lag* the discourse of modernity cannot, I believe, be written; with the *projective past* it can only be written as a narrative of alterity that explores forms of social antagonism and contradiction that are not yet properly represented, political identities in the process of being formed, cultural enunciations in the act of hybridity, in the process of translating and transvaluing cultural differences. The political space for such a social imaginary is that marked out by Raymond Williams in his distinction between emergent and residual practices of oppositionality that require a 'non-metaphysical and non-subjectivist' socio-historical positionality.[39] This largely unexplored and undeveloped aspect of Williams's work has a contemporary relevance for those burgeoning forces of the 'cultural' Left who are attempting to formulate (the unfortunately entitled) 'politics of difference', grounded in the experience and theory of the 'new social movements'. Williams suggests that in certain historical moments, the 'profound deformation' of the dominant culture will prevent it from recognizing 'practices and meanings that are not reached for' and these potentially empowering perspectives, and their political constituencies, will remain profoundly unsignified and silent within the political culture. Stuart Hall takes this argument forward in his attempt to construct an alternative 'modernity' where, he suggests, 'organic' ideologies are neither consistent nor homogeneous and the subjects of ideology are not unitarily assigned to a singular social position. Their 'strangely composite' construction requires a redefinition of the public sphere to take account of the historical transformation by which

> it follows that an alternative conception of socialism must embrace this struggle to democratize power across all the centres of social activity – in private as well as in public life, in personal associations as well as in public obligations. . . . If the struggle for socialism in modern societies is a war of position, then our conception of society must be of a *society of positions* – different places from which we can all begin the reconstruction of society of which the state is only the anachronistic caretaker.[40]

Such a form of the social (or socialist) imaginary 'blocks' the totalization of the site of social utterance by confronting it with the 'non-place' (the time-lag) that the narrative has to encounter in its construction of the 'sign' (not *simply* the event) of its historicity. This encounter through the time-lag of representation insists that any representation of 'historical beginning' must encounter the *contingent place* from where its narrative *begins* in relation to the temporalities of other marginal 'minority' histories that are seeking their 'individuation', their vivid realization. There is a focus on what Houston Baker has emphasized, for Black Renaissancism, as 'the processual quality [of meaning]... not material instantiation at any given moment but the efficacy of passage'.[41] And such a passage of historical experience lived through the time-lag opens up quite suddenly in a poem by the Afro-American poet, Sonia Sanchez:

> life is obscene with crowds
> of black on white
> death is my pulse.
> what might have been
> is not for him/or me
> but what could have been
> floods the womb until i drown

You can hear it in the ambiguity between 'what *might* have been' and 'what *could* have been' – the contingency, the closeness of those rhetorics of indeterminacy. You read it in that considerable shift in historical time between the conditions of an obscene past – *might have been* – and the conditionality of a new birth – *could have been*; you barely see it in the almost imperceptible shift in tense and syntax – *might:could* – that makes all the difference between the pulse of death and the flooded womb of birth. It is the repetition of the 'could-in-the-might' that expresses the marginalized disjunctive experience of the subject of racism – *obscene with crowds / of black on white*: the passage of a 'projective past' in the very time of its performance.

The postcolonial passage through modernity produces that form of repetition – the past as projective. It emerges through the ambivalence within the present of enunciation. It is not a cyclical form of repetition that circulates around a lack. The time-*lag* of postcolonial modernity moves *forward*, erasing that compliant past tethered to the myth of progress, ordered in the binarisms of its cultural logic: past/present, inside/outside. This *forward* is neither teleological nor is it an endless slippage. It is the function of the *lag* to slow down the linear, progressive time of modernity to reveal its 'gesture', its *tempi*, 'the pauses and stresses of the whole performance'. This can only be achieved – as Walter Benjamin remarked of Brecht's epic theatre – by damming the stream of real life, by bringing the flow to a standstill in a reflux of astonishment. When the dialectic of modernity is brought to a standstill, then the temporal action of modernity – its progressive, future drive – is *staged*, revealing 'everything that is involved in the act of staging *per se*'.[42] This slowing down, or lagging, *impels* the 'past', *projects* it, gives its 'dead' symbols the circulatory life of the 'sign' of the present, of *passage*, the quickening of the quotidian. Where these temporalities touch contingently, their spatial boundaries metonymically overlapping, at that moment their margins are lagged, sutured, by the indeterminate articulation of the 'disjunctive' present. *Time-lag keeps alive the making of the past.* As it negotiates the levels and liminalities of that spatial time that I have tried to unearth in the postcolonial archaeology of modernity, you might think that it 'lacks' time or history. Don't be fooled!

It may appear 'timeless' only in that sense in which, for Toni Morrison, Afro-American art is 'astonished' by the figure of the ancestor: 'the timelessness is there, this person who represented this ancestor'.[43] And when the ancestor rises from the dead in the guise of the murdered daughter, Beloved, then we see the furious emergence of the projective past. Beloved is not the ancestor as the 'elder' whom Morrison describes as benevolent, instructive and protective. Her presence, which is profoundly time-lagged, moves forward while continually encircling that moment of the 'not there' which Morrison sees as the stressed, dislocatory absence that is crucial for the rememoration of the narrative of slavery. Ella, a member of the chorus, standing at that very distance from the 'event' from which modernity produces its 'sign', now describes the projective past:

> The future was sunset; the past something to leave behind. And if it didn't stay behind you might have to stomp it out. . . . As long as the ghost showed out from its ghostly place. . . . Ella respected it. But if it took flesh and came in her world, well, the shoe was on the other foot. She didn't mind a little communication between the two worlds, but this was an invasion.[44]

Ella bears witness to this invasion of the projective past. Toussaint bears witness to the tragic dissolution, in San Domingo, of the sign of the Revolution. In these forms of witness there is no passivity; there is a violent turning from interrogation to *initiation*. We have not simply opposed the idea of progress with other 'ideas': the battle has been waged on hybrid territory, in the discontinuity and *distanciation* between event and enunciation, in the time-lag *in between* sign and symbol. I have attempted to constitute a postcolonial, critical discourse that contests modernity through the establishment of other temporal sites, other forms of enunciation.

In the figure of the witness of a postcolonial modernity we have another wisdom: it comes from those who have seen the nightmare of racism and oppression in the banal daylight of the everyday. They represent an idea of action and agency more complex than either the nihilism of despair or the utopia of progress. They speak of the reality of survival and negotiation that constitutes the moment of resistance, its sorrow and its salvation, but is rarely spoken in the heroisms or the horrors of history. Ella says it, plainly: *'What is to be done in a world where even when you were a solution you were a problem.'* This is not defeatism. It is an enactment of the limits of the 'idea' of progress, the marginal displacement of the ethics of modernity. The sense of Ella's words, and my essay, echo in that great prophet of the double consciousness of modern America who spoke across the veil, against what he called 'the colour-line'. Nowhere has the historical problem of cultural temporality as constituting the 'belatedness' of subjects of oppression and dispossession been spoken more pertinently than in the words of W.E. Du Bois – I like to think that they are the prophetic precursor of my discourse of the time-lag:

> So woefully unorganized is sociological knowledge that the meaning of progress, the meaning of swift and slow in human doing, and the limits of human perfectibility, are veiled, unanswered sphinxes on the shores of science. Why should Aeschylus have sung two thousand years before Shakespeare was born? Why has civilization flourished in Europe and flickered, flamed and died in Africa? So long as the world stands meekly dumb before such questions, shall this nation proclaim its ignorance and unhallowed prejudices by denying freedom of opportunity to those who brought the Sorrow Songs to the Seats of the Mighty?[45]

Du Bois makes a fine answer in the threnody of the Sorrow Songs, their eloquent omissions and silences that 'conceal much of real poetry beneath conventional theology and unmeaning rhapsody'.[46] In the inversion of our catachrestic, critical process, we find that the 'unmeaning', the non-sense of the sign discloses a symbolic vision of a form of progress beyond modernity and its sociology – but not without the enigmatic riddle of the sphinx. To turn Ella's words: what do we do in a world where even when there is a resolution of meaning there is a problem of its performativity? An indeterminacy which is also the condition of its being historical? A contingency which is also the possibility of cultural translation? You heard it in the song of the seagrapes, in Walcott's evocation of the African who acquiesces only to create his own names, to establish his historical revisions; you heard it in the repetition of Sonia Sanchez as she turned the historical obscenity of 'what might have been' into the projective past, the empowering vision of 'what could have been'.

Now you see it in the gaze of the unanswered sphinxes: Du
Bois' answer comes through rhythm of the swift and slow of human
doing itself as he commands the certain shores of 'modern' science
to recede. The problem of progress is not simply an unveiling of
human perfectibility, not simply the hermeneutic of progress. In the
performance of human doing, through the veil, emerges a figure of
cultural time where perfectibility is not ineluctably tied to the myth of
progressivism. The rhythm of the Sorrow Songs may at times be swift
– like the projective past – at other times it may be slow – like the
time-lag. What is crucial to such a vision of the future is the belief that
we must not merely change the *narratives* of our histories, but transform
our sense of what it means to live, to be, in other times and different
spaces, both human and historical.

Notes

1. All citations from FANON in the following pages come from 'The Fact of
   Blackness', in *Black Skin, White Masks*, Foreword by Homi Bhabha (London:
   Pluto Press, 1986), pp. 109–40.
2. 'A Conversation with Fredric Jameson', in A. Ross (ed.), *Universal Abandon:
   The Politics of Postmodernism* (Edinburgh: Edinburgh University Press, 1988),
   p. 17.
3. See my reading of Renan in 'DissemiNation' in *Nation and Narration*,
   ed. Homi K. Bhabha (London: Routledge, 1990), 291–322.
4. Each of these writers has addressed the problem of modernity in a number
   of works so that selection becomes invidious. However, some of the most
   directly relevant are the following: J. HABERMAS, *The Philosophical Discourse
   of Modernity* (Cambridge: Polity Press, 1990), especially Chapters 11 and 12;
   M. FOUCAULT, *The History of Sexuality. Volume One: An Introduction* (London:
   Allen Lane, 1979); see also 'The Art of Telling the Truth', in *Politics, Philosophy
   and Culture*, ed. L.D. Kritzman (New York: Routledge, 1990); J.-F. LYOTARD,
   The Differend (Minneapolis: Minnesota University Press, 1988); C. LEFORT,
   The Political Forms of Modern Society, ed. J.B. Thompson (Cambridge: Polity
   Press, 1978), especially Part II, 'History, Ideology, and the Social Imaginary'.
5. HABERMAS, *The Philosophical Discourse of Modernity*, p. 311.
6. JACQUES DERRIDA, *The Post Card: From Socrates to Freud and Beyond*, trans. Alan
   Bass (Chicago: Chicago University Press, 1987), pp. 303–4.
7. M. DOLAR, *The Legacy of the Enlightenment: Foucault and Lacan* (unpublished
   manuscript).
8. ROBERT YOUNG, *White Mythologies: Writing History and the West* (London:
   Routledge, 1990), pp. 16–17. Young argues a convincing case against the
   eurocentrism of historicism through his exposition of a number of 'totalizing'
   historical doctrines, particularly in the Marxist tradition, while demonstrating
   at the same time that the spatializing anti-historicism of Foucault remains
   equally eurocentric.
9. Cf. YOUNG, *White Mythologies*, pp. 116–17.
10. T. EAGLETON, *Ideology of the Aesthetic* (Oxford: Basil Blackwell, 1989), p. 414.

11. H.A. BAKER, JR, *Modernism and the Harlem Renaissance* (Chicago: Chicago University Press, 1987), p. 56.

12. C. BRECKENRIDGE and A. APPADURAI, 'The Situation of Public Culture' (unpublished manuscript). For the general elaboration of this thesis see various issues of *Public Culture: Bulletin of the Project for Transnational Cultural Studies* (University of Pennsylvania).

13. P. GILROY, 'One Nation Under a Groove', in *Anatomy of Racism*, ed. D.T. Goldberg (Minneapolis: University of Minnesota Press, 1990), p. 280.

14. Although I introduce the term 'time-lag' more specifically in recent essays ('DissemiNation', 'The Postmodern and the Postcolonial: The Question of Agency'), it is a structure of the 'splitting' of colonial discourse that I have been elaborating and illustrating – without giving it a name – from my very earliest essays.

15. J. DERRIDA, 'Des Tours de Babel', in *Difference in Translation*, ed. J.F. Graham (Ithaca: Cornell University Press, 1985), p. 174.

16. DEREK WALCOTT, 'Sea Grapes', *Collected Poems 1948–1984* (Toronto: The Noonday Press, 1986), p. 307.

17. C. LEFORT, *The Political Forms of Modern Society*, p. 212.

18. M. FOUCAULT, 'The Art of Telling the Truth', in *Politics, Philosophy and Culture*, p. 90.

19. Ibid., p. 93.

20. C.L.R. JAMES, *The Black Jacobins* (London: Alison & Busby, 1980), pp. 290–1.

21. J. HABERMAS, 'Modernity: An Incomplete Project', in Hal Foster (ed.), *Postmodern Culture* (London: Pluto Press, 1985).

22. M. DE CERTEAU, 'The Historiographical Operation', in *The Writing of History*, trans. Tom Conley (New York: Columbia University Press, 1988), p. 91.

23. L. ALTHUSSER, *Montesquieu, Rousseau, Marx* (London: Verso, 1972), p. 78.

24. P.J. BOWLER, *The Invention of Progress* (Oxford: Basil Blackwell, 1990), Chapter 4.

25. P. GILROY, 'One Nation Under a Groove', p. 278.

26. C. WEST, 'Race and Social Theory: Towards a Genealogical Materialist Analysis', in *Towards a Rainbow Socialism*, ed. M. Davis et al. (London: Verso, 1987), pp. 86ff.

27. C. WEST, *The American Evasion of Philosophy* (London: Macmillan, 1990), pp. 232–3.

28. G. PRAKASH, 'Post-Orientalist Third-World Histories', *Comparative Studies in Society and History* 32:2 (1990): 403.

29. ROBERT YOUNG, in *White Mythologies*, also suggests that, as I have been arguing, the colonial and postcolonial moment is the liminal point, or the limit-text, of the holistic demands of historicism.

30. M. FOUCAULT, *The History of Sexuality: An Introduction*, p. 150.

31. M. FOUCAULT, *Foucault Live*, trans. J. Johnstone and S. Lotringer (New York: Semiotext(e), 1989), p. 269.

32. B. ANDERSON, *Imagined Communities* (London: Verso, 1983), p. 136.

33. Ibid., p. 137.

34. Ibid.

35. Ibid.

36. PARTHA CHATTERJEE, *Nationalist Thought and the Colonial World* (London: Zed Books, 1986), pp. 21–2.

37. J.H. SMITH and W. KERRIGAN (eds), *Taking Chances: Derrida, Psychoanalysis, Literature* (Baltimore: Johns Hopkins University Press, 1984), p. 27.

38. Ashis Nandy, *The Intimate Enemy* (Delhi: Oxford University Press, 1983), p. 99.
39. R. Williams, *Problems in Materialism and Culture* (London: Verso, 1980), p. 43.
40. S. Hall, *The Hard Road to Renewal* (London: Verso, 1988), pp. 10–11, 231–2.
41. H. Baker, 'Our Lady: Sonia Sanchez and the Writing of a Black Renaissance', in *Reading Black, Reading Feminist*, ed. H.L. Gates (New York: Meridian, 1990).
42. W. Benjamin, *Understanding Brecht*, trans. S. Mitchell (London: New Left Books, 1973), pp. 11–13. I have freely adapted some of Benjamin's phrases and interpolated the problem of modernity in the midst of his argument on epic theatre. I do not think that I have misrepresented his argument.
43. Toni Morrison, 'The Ancestor as Foundation', in *Black Women Writers*, ed. Mari Evans (London: Pluto Press, 1985), p. 343.
44. Toni Morrison, *Beloved* (New York: Plume, 1987), pp. 256–7.
45. W.E. Du Bois, *The Souls of Black Folk* (New York: Signet Classics, 1969), p. 275.
46. Ibid., p. 271.

7 West Indian Literature and the Australian Comparison*

DIANA BRYDON, HELEN TIFFIN

Brydon, a Canadian critic, and Tiffin, herself Australian, here attempt to trace the similarities between the literatures of Australia and the English-speaking Caribbean. Their stated aim is to examine the 'counter-discursive' qualities of national and regional literatures in relation to the ' "mainstream" hegemonies' of the metropolitan canon. The objective of the particular comparison that they make is not to posit a direct similarity between the Caribbean and Australian instances, but, rather, 'to emphasise the way(s) in which British imperialism in vastly different regions, ones differing in racial, ethnic, social and class circumstances has produced similar traces . . .'. Both regions, they argue, share a predicament based on what another critic, Avis McDonald, has termed 'enforced exile and conditions of bondage'. Furthermore, they suggest that 'conditions of literary production in both regions follow comparable patterns'. Their account begins with a discussion of the early histories of the two regions, the one of slavery, the other of the convict system, and the role that this plays on the formulation of contemporary ideologies in both regions. While colonialism can be found in history, Brydon and Tiffin argue that it is also present in the very culture of England. It is in this area that they pursue their comparative analysis of imperial fictions, the stories which Empire told itself and which were exported to the various colonies. A key text in this regard is Defoe's *Robinson Crusoe*. Such works served to justify and bolster the whole process of conquest and colonization. As they suggest 'Within the entire field of colonialist enterprise, the texts of Europe, its fictions, were as decisive as the gun.' One reading of Defoe, that privileged by Empire, portrays Crusoe as an explorer hero, an archetype of the bravery necessary to colonize other worlds. There is, however, a rather more unflattering view of Crusoe which sees him as a murderer and exploiter. This transformation

---

*Reprinted from *Decolonising Fictions* (Mundelstrup: Dangaroo), pp. 35–53.

from explorer–hero to murderer is literally embodied in the figure of one man who links Australia to the Caribbean directly. He was Edward Eyre. In the Australian context he was regarded as a great explorer and hero but, later in his life, when he moved to Jamaica he is transformed into the notorious Governor who brutally suppressed the Morant Bay uprising in 1865. Such a change is possible because both, in their way, are Imperial myths, both are two sides of the same imperial coin. All such imperial fictions have long been propagated by the colonial education systems established by the British and it is this fact too which links the countries of the former 'British'.Caribbean to Australia. As they suggest, both remain 'tied to Imperial history and its collusive textuality'. In relation to the task of generating 'decolonizing fictions' there are two roads open to both regions. The first is the actual dismantling of the original 'fictions', such as *Robinson Crusoe*, which continue to exert their baleful influence and subjecting them to critical analysis. The second is to actually rewrite these fictions, but now 'from a basis of a history of subversive activities' which transgress the original Imperial narratives. Indeed, in both the West Indies and Australia, they argue, a 'literary revolution' has occurred, one based on 'the conscious dismantling and rewriting of the Anglo-European fictions of conquest and colonisation'. It is this rewriting which emerges as the final point of comparison. Contemporary 'Australian' and 'West Indian' literatures share a 'counter-discursive stance towards imperial textuality'.

The similarities between the literatures of Australia and of the English-speaking Caribbean do not at first seem as obvious or important as those between Canadian and Australian literatures. But the juxtaposing of these two literatures reveals, even more clearly than in the case of Australia and Canada, the ways in which the power relations of empire and colonisation determine the nature and course of literary production.

The term 'Caribbean' is generally used to refer to all island countries of the region. The term 'West Indies' (or 'West Indian') usually refers to those English-speaking countries formerly colonised by Britain, and hence island territories such as Jamaica, Trinidad, Barbados, St Lucia, as well as Guyana and Belize on the mainland, are generally considered together as a region. Even though the attempted West Indian federation failed, there remain close cultural and political links between many of the nations. In sport the West Indies still fields a regional cricket team, while in education the University of the West Indies has campuses in Jamaica, Trinidad and Barbados, all of which are closely affiliated with the University of Guyana.

'West Indian Literature' is here used to include texts written in English by West Indians, whatever their racial origin or nationality, just as 'Australian literature' includes works written in English by Aboriginal writers as well as by descendants of the original Anglo-Saxon invaders and later migrants from Europe or Asia. In conflating all these groups, it is not our intention to assent to nationalist or regionalist constructions, or to occlude the power relations *between* races or classes within these nations or regions. Clearly, Aboriginal writing, in being 'incorporated' within mainstream white writing as 'Australian' is necessarily disadvantaged, in the way in which the incorporation of white and black Australian writing as 'English' is inevitably distorting. But by keeping this clearly in mind in terms of our own constructions of the field of English studies, and in theorising relationships within national or regional literatures as *counter-discursive* to 'mainstream' hegemonies rather than as minor contributory parts of a single field, we wish to stress the relations between power and textuality in these postcolonial areas.

In constructing this comparison between two such areas we wish then to emphasise the way(s) in which British imperialism in vastly different regions, ones differing in racial, ethnic, social and class circumstances has produced similar traces, both through its original impositions on the colonised and through postcolonial strategies of resistance. This moves us away from racialist or nationalist typologies towards a structuring of English studies. Our comparison thus deliberately transgresses the 'boundaries' of three major contemporary discourses: (1) internationalist constitutions which 'naturalise' difference to various 'universalist' criteria; (2) nationalist literary studies which, while they deny the internationalist stance, often lay claim to an essentialist exclusivity, one which inevitably invokes implicit comparison with a British 'mainstream'; and (3) the discourse of Black Literary Studies where a racialist essentialism replaces the nationalist.

Cross-cultural comparisons within and between the postcolonial literatures then, offer radical interrogations of both the traditional constitutions of the field, and of consolidating contemporary ones. And we deliberately use the plural 'literatures' to stress that we are not engaged in a covert re-introduction of universalist paradigms or criteria, but are proposing a framework for the study of literatures in English wherein significant differences as well as significant similarities provide the ground for a 'negotiated' counter-discursive network whose differing subversive strategies are directed towards the decolonising of those imperial fictions which underwrote the colonising process, and which continue to ratify and energise that traditional hegemony in economic and social relations, as well as through the field of English Studies. The roots of the particular correspondences between Australia and the West

Indies which are explored here lie in language, in history, and in education, both in terms of British intrusion and imposition and in the various strategies of textual decolonisation deployed in both these postcolonial areas.

Language and colonisation

West Indian writing in English is not, in general, second language writing by those who have access to an alternative 'mother' tongue, but is, as in the case of English Canada and Australia, a *de facto* first language. The practices of slave-selling and plantation economy ensured (as they did elsewhere in the Americas) the virtual destruction of African language communities within one or two generations. Jamaican, Barbadian or Trinidadian Creoles attest to the survival of some West African vocabulary, grammatical constructions and pronunciation, but in general the language of the European master *per force* replaced that of the kidnapped African. Although, as Alleyne has noted[1] some African languages did survive in Jamaica, the pressures of the slave system and several centuries of deracination ensured the status of a modified English as a 'first' language, in all its variants, along the Creole continuum.

While this is generally the rule for the present-day majority black population of the West Indian islands and Guyana, minority groups – for instance Indians and Chinese brought to the Caribbean as indentured labourers after the abolition of slavery – do still acquire English as a 'second' language even if the 'mother tongue' is increasingly replaced in one or two generations by a dominant Creole or standard West Indian English.

In spite of the above exceptions and qualifications, English, then, has been the dominant language in the West Indies since the mid 1500s. Varieties of English have thus been spoken in Jamaica for over four hundred years as against barely two hundred in Australia, and consequently its interactions with the local geopolitical environment present a more complex picture.

In both places people have faced the problem of voicing a 'strange' land in terms of an unfamiliar language – a foreign language in the case of African slaves and Indian indentured labourers, and in Australia, Aboriginal peoples; and one rendered foreign by its application to totally unfamiliar circumstances in the case of white Australian settler-invaders, or white West Indians.

History

As Philip Sherlock notes, 'Colonialism, however important, was an incident in the history of Nigeria and Ghana, Kenya or Uganda; but it is the whole history of the West Indies and . . . it has a deeper meaning for the West Indian than for the African.'[2] The same might also be said of Australia, both for its Aboriginal inhabitants since 1788 and for the descendants of the white invader-settlers. In both Australia and the West Indies the present day majority populations are ones in ancestral exile. In both areas, European invaders annihilated or decimated the indigenous populations, and plundered and colonised the land. European crops and cattle destroyed a native landscape[3] as surely as their diseases, militia, governments and settlers destroyed the original inhabitants and their way of life, condemning those who survived to be outcasts on their own soil. In Australia the descendants of the invaders and subsequent immigrant populations continue to marginalise the Aboriginal minority, while in the West Indies the descendants of the indigenous survivors of the original European genocidal incursions are now restricted to a small reservation (Saliba) on Dominica and to a remnant population on the Guyanese mainland.

Present-day majority populations in both areas, then, are ones whose relationship with the lands they inhabit is relatively recent, is characterised not by a 'timeless' and 'balanced' accommodation with its 'natural' resources, but by rootlessness and exploitation and a tainted history of genocidal confrontations between invader and indigene; and whose 'geneses' are in two violent European 'systems', slavery and convictism. And until well into the present century both areas remained locked to their British/European designers as service 'industries', minor terms in England's economic and historical 'narrative', created at and for her convenience.

Australia and the West Indies, in spite of their obvious differences of race, class structures, economies, share with Canada not just a common language root – and a particular tendency (especially in Australia and the Caribbean) to deliberate subversion of this language – but a common heritage of British colonialism. But Australia and the Caribbean countries also share what Avis McDonald has characterised as 'creation' on the basis of 'enforced exile and conditions of bondage'.[4]

Within approximately one hundred and fifty years of Columbus's arrival in the Caribbean, the original Carib and Arawak inhabitants had been virtually annihilated in the greedy European quest for gold (specifically the search for the legendary 'El Dorado') and for strategic territory. A period of legalised piracy amongst the European powers was gradually succeeded by more permanent settlement as the demand for sugar in Europe established the West Indies as supply colonies, economic outposts of empire. (Like Australia, the Caribbean was of strategic importance in the internecine rivalries of Europe, and it was not until the end of the Napoleonic wars that the islands ceased changing European owners.) Labour was needed to work the sugar plantations and so the future demography of the islands was dictated by Europe's need for a luxury substance. After largely abortive attempts at using (often shanghaied) white labour to work the estates, Europeans began to import kidnapped Africans as slaves. During the period 1680–1786 alone, approximately two million Africans were abducted from their homelands and shipped across the Atlantic in chains to the English colonies in the Caribbean. West Indian (and Caribbean) history for over two hundred years is thus a history of a white minority elite ruling over an enslaved African population. Although this white elite in the Caribbean came increasingly to differ from (and with) their European (or British) ancestors, they did not in any sense 'share' economically, politically, even psychically, their new environment with the Africans, whose experience of enslavement on foreign soil differed so drastically from that of the white planters that they could hardly be said to be experiencing the same world at all. The history of this period in the Caribbean is recorded by Europeans – travellers, or absentee landlords like M.G. Lewis;[5] in the diaries of resident dignitaries like Lady Nugent[6] (and later through the politically interested pens of Froude[7] and Spencer St John).[8] Although slave rebellions occurred, these were ruthlessly put down and their motivation, course and result incorporated within an 'authoritative' European record. It is not really until the late nineteenth and twentieth centuries that a history of the West Indies begins to be written from a black rather than a European or white resident/planter viewpoint.

With the abolition of the slave trade in 1807 and of the system of slavery approximately thirty years later, labour to work the less profitable but still viable estates was brought from China and India under indenture contracts whose return clauses were usually dishonoured. Thus the present-day populations of the West Indies are composed of remnant native peoples, a small minority of the descendants of European planters and settlers and later white residents; a majority population of African descent, and, particularly in Guyana and Trinidad, substantial numbers of people of particularly, Indian, and to a lesser degree, Chinese and Middle-Eastern origin.

Cook's 'discovery' of the east coast of the Australian continent, coincident with the closure of the American colonies as a dumping ground for the undesirables of British society, plus the increasing interest in strategic ownership of territory underwrote the first fleet settlement of 1788. Settlement, and the spread of the white population to other strategic points along the East Coast was followed by a lengthy but relentless guerrilla warfare against indigenous Aboriginal populations. Australian Aboriginal peoples are only in the twentieth century returning from the brink of near-extinction to which they were driven by European incursion and settlement, and recovering, through

Land Rights claims, some small portion of the territory that was once originally theirs.

But the first settlement by Europeans on Australian Aboriginal land was itself one of British outcasts and their jailors – whites who had been, deservedly or undeservedly, rejected by a society which now saw fit to export them from the prisons of London and the overcrowded hulks of the Thames, some twelve thousand miles to an unfamiliar 'hell' of penal servitude. Many of the Irish convicts were political victims of an English colonialism which remains in place to this day. But whether they were political prisoners, murderers, forgers or pickpockets from whatever part of Britain, they began settlement, like the slaves, after a long sea voyage in chains[9] in conditions of exile and bondage; and unlike Canadian settlements, theirs did not form, or seek to form a community independent of its continuing function as part (if an unwanted part) of the British social system. Australia provided a jail (and a strategic base) – it was not seen at first, except in mythological American refractions – as redolent of Edenic promise, or as offering new beginnings. For the first Europeans its metaphysical associations were of hell, unnatural inversions (for instance of the seasons) and imprisonment, and, as Avis McDonald has noted, this similarity of settlement origins and attitudes, between slaves and convicts, has itself influenced the subsequent course of both literatures, through image patterns, themes, forms, and in complex love/hate relations with, and attitudes to, the English literary tradition, producing comparable tendencies to rebel against and subvert imposed authority. Although then there are obvious and profound differences in levels of brutality, in the cultural relations between slaves and planters, in the racisms which increasingly empowered the slave trade and enabled and encouraged the near extinction of Aboriginal and Arawak peoples, it is nevertheless possible to draw significant comparisons between the twentieth century literatures of a predominantly white Australia and a predominantly black Caribbean because the conditions of literary production and consumption in both regions follow comparable patterns inevitably implicated in, though not wholly dependent on, the imperial 'centre'.

The early brutal histories of the two regions continue to figure in modern consciousness, not only as remote antecedent, but as active formulation for contemporary ideology. Popular history and sociology in Australia ascribe an anti-authoritarian streak in the Australian character to the legacy of the convict experience, while the modern West Indian's black consciousness constantly keeps the experience of slavery to the fore. Modern novels (e.g. Patrick White's *A Fringe of Leaves* and George Lamming's *Natives of My Person*) continue to explore the slave and convict pasts for allegorical leverage on the present. But colonialism does not have to be sought in history. It is still propagated in both regions today through the literature and language (however altered) of England, and in the electronic media.

Imperial fictions

In the latter part of the twentieth century both Australian and West Indian economies remain prey to a variety of economic colonisations – in particular that of the United States and Canada in the Caribbean and the United States and Japan in Australia – and to an allied political neo-colonialism by the United States and the associated cultural fictions of its global politics. A study of current weekly programmes on both Australian and West Indian television indicates further areas of comparability, ones they share, to a greater or lesser degree with the rest of the postcolonial English speaking world (outside the United States). What popular television patterns indicate is a world in which the fictions of the old imperialist, though still persisting, are giving place to those of the new.

With the exception of the Special Broadcasting Service, Australian channels carry predominantly American, Australian and English programmes, increasingly in that order, although fifteen years ago, the Australian would have approximated, say, the Jamaican pattern of American, English, local.[10] Some Australian series (*Neighbours*, *The Flying Doctors*) also appear in Jamaica, but this represents more a refraction of current 'frontier nostalgia' in the United States than either Jamaican preferences or the birth of any Australian media hegemony.

But if the fictions of the United States are beginning to replace those of Britain, film versions of traditional imperialist classics like *King Solomon's Mines* or *Robinson Crusoe* are not only re-run but continue to underpin modern inanities such as *Gilligan's Island*. Televised English productions of Shakespeare's plays are still staples of the networks, particularly in Jamaica where, before the major public exams, JBC offers regular Sunday morning showings of the English 'set' texts. Imperial fictions, old and new, still constantly inform popular culture, while much formal literary education in Australia and the West Indies, particularly at secondary and tertiary levels, continues its traditional emphasis on British texts, in spite of increasing study of the local national cultures.

Thus while older forms of textual imperialism shade into the new, and power centres change, the myths which have constructed us and our views of the world persist. Martin Green has argued that

> the adventure tales that formed the light reading of Englishmen for two hundred years and more after *Robinson Crusoe* were, in fact, the

energising myth of English imperialism. They were, collectively, the story England told itself as it went to sleep at night; and, in the form of its dreams, they charged England's will with the energy to go out into the world and explore, conquer, and rule.[11]

Ironically they became also the inhibiting visions of many of the peoples who were conquered and ruled, or who though descended from such explorers and conquerors had come to identify with the conquered land. Green is not simply describing a moment of imperial expansionism, but a much longer period of ideational subjection which extends up to the present.

Fictions of conquest and colonisation

As Peter Hulme has noted, the conquest and colonisation of much of the world by the European powers, was preceded, accompanied, and justified by its own philosophical texts and their inscriptions of 'otherness'. Columbus's 'discovery' of the 'New' World was less a genuine 'discovery' than a reinscription of that domestic archive within which 'difference' had already been interpreted and placed, i.e. captured and contained.[12] The journals of explorers, imaginative accounts by medieval travellers who never left home, Hakluyt's voyages, the subsequent histories of exploration and conquest facilitated the 'othering'[13] of the rest of the world, and the bolstering of Europe's idea of itself as the centre of civilisation, one morally and materially superior to all others, and having the 'divine' right or religious duty to convert or destroy. Within the entire field of colonialist enterprise, the texts of Europe, its fictions, were as decisive a weapon as the gun.

Secular fictions of all kinds, together with those of Christianity were used to justify the profitable trade in slaves. Self-referring and self-serving definitions of 'humanity' and 'civilisation' enabled the exclusion or inclusion of blacks within the charmed circle depending on European need (and greed). Indeed the very savagery that lay at the heart of the white colonialist enterprise was projected, through a series of psychological manoeuvres traced in textual shifts, onto that otherness which was the object of European exploitation. Neil Heims notes the ways in which this is effected in a text like Defoe's *Robinson Crusoe* over the particularly charged subject of cannibalism. 'Through its fable', Heims claims, '*Robinson Crusoe* shows the justifying fantasy of the Europeans for their brutal consumption of human lives.'[14]

At first the novel appears to be tending towards being an even-handed condemnation of savages and Europeans. Crusoe makes a savagery similar to that of the cannibals adhere to the Europeans with several observations on the similarity of some Christians to the cannibals. . . . Overt comparison between Christians and cannibals is invited when Crusoe, thinking of the risk of falling into Spanish hands, dread 'to be made a *sacrifice*' (emphasis added) to the Inquisition.

Thus the European savagery is admitted, but only after it has been effectively projected onto the cannibals. Then the narrator can accuse the Europeans of acting *like* the savages. But the fundamental savagery itself has been alienated from them.

(p. 243)

The persisting popularity of the topos of *Robinson Crusoe* within all English-speaking cultures is a testament to the interpellative power of such texts, and the persistence of their mythologies over time. I recently asked one hundred first year university students how many had actually read *Robinson Crusoe* – fewer than fifteen. But when asked what could they tell me *about Robinson Crusoe*, almost all could tell me that the setting was an island; that Crusoe was white; that he had a black or 'native' servant Friday; and that there was something about cannibals and Crusoe saving Friday's life. Naturally none mentioned that Crusoe was wrecked while on a slaving enterprise, or would have been likely, as E. Pearlman does, to characterise Crusoe as a murderer and exploiter, although they might condemn comparable practices in the history of their own country.

The mystery is not that this is the most popular novel in English, but that so many readers have blinded themselves to the character of the hero. . . . He is a radical individualist and the prototype of new economic man, but he is also an authoritarian of a dangerous kind, and an unredeemed, uncivilised colonialist. For when the novel is stripped of its ethnocentric biases, what is left is the essence of the colonial encounter. A weak individual, unable to succeed in his own country, of restless and unstable character, moves to an exotic locale where the technological advantage of his civilisation gives him immediate superiority over the indigenous population. There he exploits the land, slaughters the heathens and makes instruments (military and otherwise) of selected converts. He despises the natives, but is also terrified of them, and is prepared to justify massacre if he can fantasise a threat to himself. It is on this foundation that expansion and colonialism is reared, and it is for these reasons that *Robinson Crusoe* demands our continual attention.[15]

Like *The Tempest, Jane Eyre* and *Heart of Darkness*, this fiction of European encounters with others has received the attention of Caribbean and Australian writers like Samuel Selvon, Randolph Stow and Patrick White who have re-entered Defoe's text not just to rewrite its terms

and interrogate the b(i)ases underlying the narrative, but to unlock
the whole of that complex field within which such texts operate(d)
in colonialist discourse, not just in the initial phases of conquest and
colonisation, but in their re/sitations at the colonial periphery (whether
through formal education or popular reading) where they naturalise(d)
for the colonised the terms of their own conquest and exploitation.

The refusal of the Caribs (Caribals/cannibals) to convert to
Christianity justified European genocide in the Caribbean. Native 'other'
and 'cannibal' became linked concepts in a European psyche already
politically and religiously alert for signs of this ultimate sacrilege/
sacrament. Myths of African savagery and 'heathen rites' justified a
racism rendered necessary by the economic promise of the slave trade.
White planters in the Caribbean were vastly outnumbered by their
slaves and their fear of uprisings was fuelled not only by (unconscious)
guilt about those they held in bondage, but by the prior European
constructions of Africans. These vaguer fears were given immediate
form and direction in the success of Toussaint L'Ouverture in Haiti in
1803. As the first successful slave revolt in history, the Haitian
revolution inspired European and white Caribbean writers to re-circulate
– now with felt political intent – the myths of African savagery. Eighty
years after the rebellion, Spencer St John[16] and other writers were still
'demonising' Haitian blacks. (Herman Melville in 'Benito Cereno' drew
on previous portraits of Toussaint for his more complex, yet still
'demonic' portrait of Babo.)[17]

The charge of cannibalism resurfaced and invoked particular fears
for white planters throughout the Caribbean in the Morant Bay uprising
in Jamaica in 1865. The paradoxes of racist stereotyping were replayed:
the leaders were fools, the people lazy, starving and disorganised yet, as
in Haiti, the black peasants (led in Jamaica by a Christian pastor) were
demonism incarnate; their rebellion threatening, organised, widespread.
Black freedom and a 'return' to African 'savagery' would be synonymous.
Domestic planter myths, and the accounts of eighteenth and nineteenth
century English travellers, like Froude's, drew from, and localised, the
often contradictory myths of otherness and difference as old as European
exploration, ones now also refracted from the southern United States.[18]

In the controversy surrounding the Morant Bay Rebellion in Jamaica
in October 1865, these mythologies powered much of the continuing
debate. Both black (Revd Paul Bogle) and white (Governor Edward
Eyre) protagonists have been depicted by black and white historians
as, variously, demon and saviour. Evidence for both positions has been
adduced from psychological readings of character and meticulous inquiry
into event. But the history of textuality, the nature of imperial fictions
and the part they played in the interpretation of the uprising have less
often been considered.

Before resorting to action, the black Jamaican peasantry had appealed to Queen Victoria against the inaction of the white (and coloured) Jamaica House of Assembly. When Victoria proved no help, the Revd Paul Bogle led an uprising which invoked a bloody suppression by troops under the direction of the colonial governor, Edward Eyre. 'In the course of the purification of the Island by the army, during a month-long reign of terror, a thousand homes were burnt, nearly five hundred negroes were killed, and more than that number were flogged and tortured.'[19] Eyre also managed to secure the court martial and execution of George William Gordon, a personal and political enemy, and a mulatto member of the Jamaica House of Assembly (p. 13). In England Eyre's actions in suppressing the revolt and in executing Gordon created a three-year controversy which became, in Leonard Huxley's words, 'the touchstone of ultimate political convictions'.

But there are two other aspects of the uprising which are relevant here, aside from the black peasantry's vain belief in the goodness and fairness of the English Crown (and Bogle's Christian justifications for the uprising). The first is the way in which the successful Haitian rebellion and the European fictions associated with it had contributed to the hysteria of the white Jamaican settlers. Semmel notes that

> The first news of the Jamaica insurrection had come to England in the bundles of Kingston newspapers which had come aboard the West-Indian mail-packet in November 1865. The planter journals wrote hysterically of the prospect of a slaughter of the white population of the island such as had occurred at Haiti over half a century earlier. The passengers aboard the packet added stories of Savageries committed by the rebellious blacks . . . Upon closer questioning, it turned out that none of these persons had actually witnessed the atrocities of which they spoke, and much of the British public tended rather to discount the tale of their Creole cousins. . . . It was . . . difficult to believe that thirty years after emancipation, Jamaica's black men, so often charged with an indolent apathy, would erupt in so terrifying a manner.

(p. 15)

But Semmel goes on to note that what disturbed the English public most was the vengefulness and 'bloodthirstiness' of the packet's white planter–settler passengers and of the white-run Kingston newspapers they brought with them.

With the refractive play of textuality in colonialist discourse, a paradoxical shift in attitudes can be seen here. The white Jamaican settler-planters, having been deeply influenced by traditional European fictions about Africans, now contribute to and reinforce them by their own accounts, becoming in the process more convinced believers in the blacks' essential savagery than the English themselves. Moreover, the parent culture, manifesting a typically ambiguous attitude towards one of its settler colonies, regards the white creole as bloodthirsty and demonic, thereby replicating the terms in which the native and black colonised were 'othered' from the outset. This is not to deny that the settler-planters were brutal and bloodthirsty, but simply to note the metropolitan English tendency to attribute to its own colonising agents the alleged human debasement with which they had come in contact. As Peter Hulme notes, British attitudes to colonials began to take this cast very early,[20] a symptomatic later example in Victorian fiction being the picture of the debased and demonic Bertha Mason in *Jane Eyre* (1847). It is to this portrait of the 'savage, barbaric' white creole that Jean Rhys replied in *Wide Sargasso Sea*.

The second aspect of the uprising which calls for comment is the contrasting portrayals of Edward John Eyre in two different imperial contexts. In 1967 the Australian writer Geoffrey Dutton published *The Hero as Murderer: The Life of Edward John Eyre Australian Explorer and Governor of Jamaica 1815–1901.* 'The name of Edward John Eyre has been familiar to me since I was a child. Every Australian child knows the name of one of their country's greatest explorers.'[21] However, through the predictable ironies of empire, Dutton was in Leeds in 1960, and there met the Jamaican anthropologist Fernando Henriques.

> After chatting for a few minutes in his usual affable way, Henriques suddenly asked 'Why did you send us that bastard Eyre?'
> The noun is a term of endearment in Australia, but clearly not in Jamaica. I had a vague idea that Eyre had got into some sort of trouble in Jamaica, but I did not know that our Australian hero had allegedly turned into a monster there.
>
> (p. 9)

While Dutton's 1960 championing of the explorer–hero would probably not have been as enthusiastically endorsed by quite the popular majority he claims, nevertheless until very recently, the imperial fiction of the 'hero–explorer' was prominent in white Australian self-consciousness, and had an essential place in the teaching of Australian history and 'origins' to both Aboriginal and white Australians. Cast as a founding-father (always father) of the nation, the hero–explorer in Australia 'penetrated' 'virgin territory', 'opening up' vast acres to settlement (and eco-catastrophe). On the journey the hero endured privations of all kinds, but his iron will, self-sacrifice and determination to succeed won through; or, faced with overwhelming odds, (the vastness of the land; the vagaries of the climate), he perished heroically in desert or bush.

This portrait of the explorer–hero depended on a wilful amnesia on the part of its constructors and perpetrators, about the Aboriginal presence. Explorers never 'found' anything Aboriginal peoples had not already known of. Indeed most expeditions of any duration were dependent on Aboriginal guides (voluntary or coerced) for supplies of food and water and other eco-geographical knowledges without which such 'explorations' would inevitably have foundered. Robinson Crusoe's 'virgin' island represents the wish-fulfilment of an expansionist imperial culture and its determined amnesia in relation to prior ownership, an amnesia savagely addressed in George Lamming's *Natives of My Person*. Like the fiction of 'virgin territory' then, 'exploration' is one of the most important imperial fictions, essential to the narrative of colonisation, and the hero–explorer as ancestor/originator of settler colonies is a myth not easily relinquished.

The problematic Dutton was addressing lay not, as he believed, in the apparent transformation of 'hero' into 'murderer', but in Eyre's imperial/ Australian construction as hero–explorer. Once the hero–explorer is seen in his true role as agent of empire, harbinger of colonisation, and hence 'murderer' (actual or precursorial) of indigenous peoples, Eyre's role as governor and his part in the Morant Bay killings becomes less problematic; less a question of interpretation of character and event, than an exposé of the fictions which condition both the interpretations and the events themselves. Dutton's investigation of Eyre's character and his publication of the 1967 apologia – without any real questioning of the basis of Eyre's construction within imperial ideology as explorer– hero – attests to the persisting power of imperial fictions in settler colonies, in spite of the radical interrogations of the these fictions undertaken by both black and white writers over the last fifty years.

Allied to the myth of the explorer in settler colonies was that of the pioneer. Celebration of the hardihood with which pioneers faced suffering and privation in establishing European 'civilisation' on the territory of the 'other', similarly occluded prior Aboriginal ownership and authorised their murder and dispossession by the pioneers or by troops called in to 'protect' them. In the second section of his *Dusklands*, the white South African writer J.M. Coetzee savagely deconstructs the myth of the pioneer explorer, presenting in Jacobus Coetzee, a portrait of the explorer–murderer as self-constructed hero.

Fictions of education

But imperial fictions are deeply implanted in colonialism in another important way. We have already considered some examples of the historical, anthropological and literary texts which preceded and

powered conquest and colonisation and those subsequently written
at the sites of colonisation which were collusive in the maintenance
and continuation of the colonialist enterprise. But we also need to
consider the part played by British colonial education systems in the
subjectification of the colonised (both white and black) and in the
maintenance of imperial domination and control. For it is to the
whole of this complex discursive field within which texts operated
and continue to operate in colonial and postcolonial worlds, that the
interrogative and deconstructive strategies of contemporary West Indian
and Australian writers are addressed.

Until very recently, primary, secondary and tertiary curricula in both
the English-speaking Caribbean and in Australia were Anglo-centred
and Anglo-dominated. At primary school level geography meant the
detailed topography of Britain; a study of the local nation or region;
and the economic geography of the British Empire. Outside their own
region and the British Isles, the countries of the rest of the world were
depicted as 'mere producers'[22] notable for what they exported to Britain.
Canada 'gave' timber; Katanga, copper; Trinidad, pitch. But Trinidad's
pitch lake was mentioned in Australian school books for another reason.
Sir Walter Ralegh had caulked his ships there on his expeditions of
legalised piracy and the quest for El Dorado. (These expeditions were
not of course described in these terms. They were part of the heroic
explorer-narrative of England).

Literary education as it was promulgated at primary level through
the local adaptations of the *Royal Readers*[23] (for almost half a century in
parts of the Caribbean and a number of Australian States) combined
historical sketches, anthropological data on indigenous peoples, folklore
of Britain, natural history, poems, short stories, and extracts from novels.
In general the literary material (in contrast to the natural history or
anthropology which provided the illusion of localisation) was British,
with a heavy emphasis on nineteenth- and early twentieth-century
writing: Wordsworth's now notorious 'daffodils';[24] Keats's 'To Autumn',
Newbolt's desperate cricketers. If in Australia Henry Kendall's 'Bell
Birds' was included, the exception only served to point the contrast
between the wealth of a 'great tradition' and the local lack of one. Even
Dorothea Mackellar's nationalist 'My Country' (like Kipling's 'Christmas
in India') began with the English connection and the 'norm' of the
English climate and seasons before rejecting these in favour of the
'sunburnt country'. In the Caribbean similar literary pieces were
interspersed with pirate legends and 'exotic' (as the underlying
perspective revealed) 'natural' history. The Australian equivalent was
the life of the koala or kangaroo. And just as Australian children of
varying ethnic backgrounds for over half a century began the school
day by singing 'God Save the King/Queen' so West Indians, schooled

like Australians in British values and Empire loyalty through learning by heart 'How Horatius Kept the Bridge'[25] and 'Vite Lampada', were obliged to stand in the playground and sing 'Rule Britannia' with its triumphant conclusion of 'Britons, Britons Never Never Shall be Slaves'.

Until independence in most West Indian territories, the history of British slaving was not officially taught in schools, the origin of the black presence in the Caribbean deliberately obscured. West Indians were taught that their history had nothing to do with a 'jungle' and 'uncivilised' Africa. Barbados, Britain's long-term possession in the area was 'Little England', the colony successfully interpellated as loyal daughter/son of Britain. The history of England was also Barbados' history, or all of it that mattered. Margaret Atwood's summary of the learning acquired through a British colonial education in Canada (from a child's perspective) might as easily have come from Australia or the West Indies:

> In countries that are not the British Empire, they cut out children's tongues, especially those of boys. Before the British Empire there were no railroads or postal services in India, and Africa was full of tribal warfare, with spears, and had no proper clothing. The Indians in Canada did not have the wheel or telephones, and ate the hearts of their enemies in the heathenish belief that it would give them courage. The British Empire changed all that. It brought in electric lights.[26]

Australia's history was also England's (and Europe's as a lesser term). Aboriginal peoples had no right to a 'history' and no written records. Australian history began with Cook's 'discovery'. But since the Aborigines were cast as unworthy foes, and since most wars of conquest in Australia consisted in massacre, or in relentless if 'scattered guerrilla warfare, even this potential 'history' remained largely unacknowledged and unwritten. With no traditions (outside that of Britain), no 'ruins' and no 'civilisation' (all these were literary as well as historical disqualifications) Australia was, like Barbados, a brief chapter in England's glorious narrative, and most of that brief chapter was devoted to explorers. The Aboriginal past and the genocidal and eco-catastrophes of white invasion were not considered. The dates of the reigns of English Kings and Queens, however, mattered.

In *In the Castle of My Skin* George Lamming depicted the efforts of Barbadian schoolchildren in coping with these educational 'disinformation' programmes. With slave history and slave trading absorbed into the convenient amnesia of empire, the boys must manufacture their own pasts out of a confusing mixture of Sunday-school teachings, empire loyalty propaganda, and vague notions of Queen Victoria as 'saviour', responsible for their restitution after some sort of 'fall'. But just what these terms allegorise remains lost in the deliberately obscured African connection. The school teacher assures the boys: 'People talked of slaves a long time ago. It had nothing to do with the old lady. She wouldn't be old enough. And moreover it had nothing to do with people in Barbados. No one there was ever a slave, the teacher said. It was in another part of the world that those things happened. Not in Little England.'[27]

But while the specifics of slave history were officially denied to the descendants of that history in schools, these same primary, secondary and tertiary pupils had black–white and empire–colony relations *naturalised* for them through the reading and teaching of classic English texts like *The Tempest, Robinson Crusoe, Jane Eyre,* the novels of Dickens, *Heart of Darkness*. Not only did Britain have the best, indeed the only tradition of English literature (American literature only began to be taught in Caribbean and Australian universities in the 1960s), its greatest works were 'Universal'. Literary texts which had both reflected and energised the vilification and capture of alterity formed part of a curriculum devoted to naturalising the colonial as 'other' within an English/European code assumed or proffered as a 'norm'. The teaching and general dissemination of works like *Robinson Crusoe* and *The Tempest* at the colonial 'peripheries', formed an important part of material imperial practice in continually reiterating for the colonised the original capture of his/her alterity and the processes of its annihilation and marginalisation as if this were axiomatic, culturally ungrounded, natural.

In Australia continuing white prejudice against Aboriginal peoples was fuelled by this perpetuation of imperial values. But white Australians themselves were also represented in England's nineteenth century literature as convicts, thieves, uncouth frontiersmen, boorish and ignorant settlers and drifters. Australia was the country to which unwanted or difficult relatives could be conveniently exiled – the 'ends' of the earth. As a character in Henry Kingsley's *The Hillyars and the Burtons* (rather ironically) notes, Australia had turned out to be 'the most wonderfully scentless cesspool for a vast quantity of nameless rubbish, convicted and unconvicted' and from the point of view of England, its discovery 'ranks next in importance, after the invention of soda water' as 'a sort of way of escaping cheaply from the consequences of debauchery for a time'.[28] Algernon, of Oscar Wilde's popular *The Importance of Being Earnest*, expresses the not unrelated view of Australia as 'fate worse than death':

> *Algernon*: I certainly wouldn't let Jack buy my outfit. He has no taste in neckties at all.
> *Cecily*: I don't think you will require neckties. Uncle Jack is sending you to Australia.

Algernon: Australia? I'd sooner die.
Cecily: Well he said . . . that you would have to choose between this
world, the next world, and Australia.
Algernon: Oh, well! The accounts I have received of Australia and the
next world are not particularly encouraging.[29]

In spite of apparently rebellious assertiveness, all Australians, black
and white, still suffer from the 'cultural cringe' induced by the complex
of imperial fictions, while many white Australians continue to collude,
as willing subjects, in their own interpellation as the 'natural' inferiors
of Britain or Europe. And although the countries of the former 'British'
Caribbean are, like Australia, now 'independent' territories, they remain,
at least in part, tied to Imperial history and its collusive textuality.

Decolonising fictions

In spite of a history of continuing political, economic and cultural
domination (and hence dependence and apparent powerlessness) the
West Indies and Australia offer two comparable areas of significant
cultural possibility. These possibilities bear on the decolonising of those
European 'fictions' which powered the material forces of conquest and
colonisation, and which structured notions of selfhood and nationhood,
and which continue to influence their destinies. The perverse energies
of violence and genocide which conditioned origin and settlement in
Australia and the Caribbean inevitably produced racially and ethnically
mixed hybrid societies. In these societies values of cultural purity and
denigration of difference and otherness, issuing in the savage bias of
race, are necessarily eroded, a process characterised as 'catalysis'[30] by
Denis Williams, one invoking the creative cross-cultural capacities of
Wilson Harris's 'womb of space'.[31] Although most of the theoretical
writing on cross-cultural imperatives (which paradoxically grow out
of and necessarily undermine the 'fictions' which underwrite invasion
and genocide) has been done in the Caribbean, (particularly in Guyana),
the processes of 'Creolisation'[32] are also evident in Australia, and
increasingly work is being done in this field.[33] Neither Williams's,
Harris's nor Edward Kamau Brathwaite's particular formulations of this
process, however, ignores the persisting inequalities between various
communities undergoing catalysis, nor the destructive and divisive
legacies of history on which they are contingent. Nevertheless, all three
writers envision in material as well as imaginative terms, and through
material and imaginative agencies, the energetics of a revolutionary
transformation resident in cultural hybridisations and syncretisms that
are the complex legacy of European conquest and colonisation of 'other'
worlds.

Secondly, both Australian and West Indian peoples, whatever their origin, have long histories of subversion and rebellion (material, cultural, and psychic) directed against those oppressive systems of social control – slavery, convictism, settler, militia – which precluded revolution. And in the latter half of this century they have begun to rewrite the fictions of Empire which represented, through the centuries, so intimate a part of their construction and oppression. Postcolonial Caribbean and Australian historians, anthropologists, geographers, creative writers and critics have now begun to interrogate and rewrite the narrative of English and European colonisation, and they do so from a basis of a history of subversive activities.

It has become fashionable to ascribe the notion of subverting dominant discourses to a Euro-American postmodernism, but subversion of the dominant, in convict ballads and convict language, characterises early white Australian culture, as it does that of slave culture in the West Indies. The outlawed drumming, parodic dancing and play acting undermined, in subtle and conscious mimicry and in undisguised abuse, the normative 'claims' of dominant Anglo-planter culture. And the subversion of English from within its own vocabulary and grammar which characterised slave (and to a lesser degree, convict) usage has direct intentional affinities with contemporary Rastafarian experiments in the decolonisation of the English language.

'Textual revolution' is theorised by Richard Terdiman as conditional (or partly conditional) on the 'blockage of energy directed to structural change in the social formation'. The 'Literary revolution' which is the redirected issue of this blockage is not, Terdiman argues, 'revolution by homology, but by intended function'.[34] Literary revolution in the West Indies and Australia has issued, particularly since the 1950s, in the conscious dismantling and rewriting of the Anglo-European fictions of conquest and colonisation. In the West Indies C.L.R. James reclaimed Toussaint L'Ouverture[35] and the successful Haitian slave rebellion from accounts like those of Spencer St John, J.J. Thomas, at a much earlier period, exposed J.A. Froude's stereotyping and racism in *Froudacity*.[36] Eric Williams, Elsa Goveia and other Caribbean historians have reclaimed their own past from its capture within European interpretation, and interrogated those interpretations in works like *British Historians and the West Indies*.[37] Michael Dash's recent *Haiti and the United States: National Stereotypes and the Literary Imagination*[38] examines specifically American constructions of Haiti and Haitians and traces the relationship between these 'local' fictions and the European archive.

In Australia both Aboriginal and white historians and anthropologists have turned to oral sources to refute 'authoritative' accounts of European invasion and settlement. Documentary evidence has been reinterpreted, and a picture of both white atrocity and Aboriginal resistance on scales vaster than had been previously acknowledged is emerging.[39] Aboriginal perspectives on history, on space and time, in which European incursion becomes but a chapter in a continuing Aboriginal narrative of place are increasingly influencing white Australian self perceptions.[40] Settler and pioneer mythologies are being undermined, and in both the West Indies and Australia, fictions of race and cultural purity are being directly challenged by writers like Wilson Harris and Sally Morgan. The role of the English language in the colonising project has been explored in Selvon's rewriting of *Robinson Crusoe* (and to a lesser extent *The Tempest*) in *Moses Ascending*. Jessica Anderson has looked at the part played by role of English texts in alienating the colonial subject from her creative local base in *Tirra Lirra by the River*, while in Patrick White's *Voss* and Peter Carey's *Oscar and Lucinda* (amongst many others) the character of the explorer hero and the 'value' of his explorations is being interrogated and dismantled. The Aboriginal writer, Mudrooroo Noongar (Colin Johnson) in *Dr Wooreddy's Prescription for Enduring the Ending of the World* and in *Master of the Ghost Dreaming* has recast those empire and settler fictions as the genocide and dispossession they represented from the Aboriginal viewpoint. In *My Place* Sally Morgan has rewritten the terms of A.B. Facey's *A Fortunate Life*,[41] the most recently influential of the portraits of white (male) pioneer as hero. And although Facey's intention is apparently not to construct himself or his career in heroic terms, his account cannot (and did not) escape its generic history. Like Erna Brodber's *Jane and Louisa Will Soon Come Home*, Morgan's *My Place* traces a black ancestry back through a family history of white interpellation and obfuscation. This journey of recovery involves, significantly, a more away from the written world to oral sources and an informal education in personal and communal history.

The comparisons that can and are being made between contemporary 'Australian' and 'West Indian' literatures are numerous. But what characterises both is a counter-discursive stance towards imperial textuality evident both across and within each tradition. However different the strategies engaged (and there are remarkable similarities as well) the complex fictions of empire are being radically interrogated by writers in both areas, both as they relate directly to the English tradition, and to the local traditions in which these fictions were deployed and promulgated.

In attempting to work towards a literature which seeks to 'consume [its] own biases'[42] as well as exposing those inherent in their European fictive geneses, Australian and West Indian writers have produced a body of contemporary works which are counter-discursive, allegorical, allusive, and metacritical. More detailed analyses of the ways in which they decolonise imperial fictions, then, form the comparative core of this book.

Notes

1. MERVYN C. ALLEYNE, *Roots of Jamaican Culture* (London: Pluto Press, 1988).
   Alleyne argues that:

   > Among the most widespread fallacies about slave societies in the
   > New World is the belief that slaves were unable to communicate with
   > each other because of the wide diversity and mutual non-intelligibility
   > of African languages and dialects and because they (slaves) were
   > systematically separated so that members of the same ethnic/linguistic
   > group would not find themselves on the same plantation. The fact is that
   > African languages were routinely used on slave plantations and have
   > survived in Jamaica up to today.
   >
   > (p. 120)

2. PHILIP SHERLOCK, *West Indies* (London: Thames & Hudson, 1966) pp. 13–14.
3. See ALFRED W. CROSBY, *Ecological Imperialism: The Biological Expansion of Europe 900–1900* (Cambridge: Cambridge University Press, 1968).
4. AVIS G. MCDONALD, 'Patterns of Exile and Bondage in Selected Australian and West Indian Fiction' (dissertation, Macquarie University, 1986), Preface.
5. M.G. LEWIS, *Journal of a Residence Among the Negroes in the West Indies* (London: Murray, 1845).
6. LADY MARIA NUGENT, *Lady Nugent's Journal of Her Residence in Jamaica from 1801 to 1805*, ed. Philip Wright (Kingston: Institute of Jamaica, 1966).
7. JAMES ANTHONY FROUDE, *The English in the West Indies or The Bow of Ulysses* (London: Longmans, Green, 1888).
8. SPENSER ST JOHN, *Hayti or The Black Republic* (London: Smith, Elder, 1884).
9. After the abolition of the slave trade in 1807, at least four slave ships were employed as convict carriers to Australia. The origins of Australian 'mateship' have sometimes been traced to friendships formed and convict 'codes' evolved during this long voyage. Here is another possible analogy with the African experience. MICHAEL CRATON (*Searching for the Invisible Man: Slaves and Plantation Life in Jamaica* [Cambridge, Mass: Harvard University Press, 1978]) notes that for the slaves, being 'shipmates' was a link said to be more binding even than common tribal origin, and he cites BRYAN EDWARDS (*The History, Civil and Commercial of the British Colonies in the West Indies*, 2nd edn, London, 1801, Vol. 2, 156): 'We find that negroes in general are strongly attached to their countrymen, but above all to such of their companions as came in the same ship with them from Africa. . . . The term *shipmate* is understood among them as signifying a relationship of the most enduring nature.'
10. In 1968 MUNGO MACCALLUM estimated that 'ninety-seven per cent of the drama on our screens comes packaged from abroad, mainly the US' (Mungo MacCallum (ed.), *Ten Years of Television* (Melbourne: Sun Books, 1968), p. 67).
11. MARTIN GREEN, *Dreams of Adventure, Deeds of Empire* (London: Routledge, 1980), p. 3.
12. See PETER HULME, *Colonial Encounters: Europe and the Native Caribbean 1492–1797* (London: Methuen, 1986).
13. The term is Gayatri Spivak's.
14. NEIL HEIMS, '*Robinson Crusoe* and the Fear of Being Eaten', *Colby Library Quarterly* 19: 4 (December 1983): 191–2.

15. E. Pearlman, 'Robinson Crusoe and the Cannibals', *Mosaic* 10: 1 (Fall 1976): 54–5.
16. Spenser St John, *Hayti or the Black Republic*.
17. Herman Melville, 'Benito Cereno' (1855), *Billy Budd, Sailor and Other Stories* (Harmondsworth: Penguin, 1967).
18. J. Michael Dash, *Haiti and the United States: National Stereotypes and the Literary Imagination* (London: Macmillan, 1988).
19. Bernard Semmel, *The Governor Eyre Controversy* (London: Macgibbon Kee, 1962), p. 15.
20. See Peter Hulme, 'Polytropic Man: Tropes of Sexuality and Mobility in Early Colonial Discourse', *Europe and its Others*, ed. Francis Barker et al. (Colchester: Essex University Press, 1985), vol. 2, pp. 17–32.
21. Geoffrey Dutton, *The Hero as Murderer: The Life of Edward John Eyre Australian Explorer and Governor of Jamaica 1815–1901* (London: Collins, 1967), p. 9.
22. The phrase is used by John Hearne in his review of Jean Rhys's *Wide Sargasso Sea*, 'The Wide Sargasso Sea: A West Indian Reflection', *Cornhill Magazine* 180 (Summer 1974): 325–6.
23. In Queensland *Royal Readers* were used in primary schools 1893–1913. The *Queensland Reader* (1913–38) and the subsequent *Queensland School Reader* (1938–1960) formed the basis of primary school language/literature teaching till the early 1960s. See also Frances Helen Cristie, 'The Teaching of English in Elementary Schools in New South Wales 1848–1900', dissertation, Sydney University, 1977, and Kelvin Edwards, 'Basic Reading Books in the Primary School Past and Present: A Content Analysis of Cultural, Social and Literary Themes', dissertation, La Trobe University, 1981. I am not aware of detailed work published on West Indian primary curricula, but see M.K. Bacchus, 'Education and Decolonization', University of West Indies: Dept Education (Unpublished paper given at UWI, Mona, Jamaica). For a summary of the Canadian situation, see Satu Repo, 'From Pilgrims Progress to Sesame Street: 125 Years of Colonial Readers', *This Magazine* 7: 2 (August 1973): 11–15.
24. Brydon, Diana. 'Wordsworth's Daffodils: A Recurring Motif in Contemporary Canadian Literature', *Kunapipi* 4: 2 (1984): 6–14.
25. Analogies between the British Empire and the Roman were common in Victorian writing, and were used in texts like the *Queensland Reader* in the promotion of a British Empire loyalty.
26. Margaret Atwood, *Cat's Eye* (Toronto: McClelland & Stewart, 1988), p. 79.
27. George Lamming, *In the Castle of My Skin* (London: Michael Joseph, 1953), p. 57.
28. Henry Kingsley, *The Hillyars and the Burtons* (1865) (Sydney: Sydney University Press, 1973), pp. 238–9.
29. Oscar Wilde, *The Importance of Being Earnest* (1895), Act I. The Indian 'economy' and the Indian climate are also satirised in the play.
30. Denis Williams, *Image and Idea in the Arts of Guyana* (Georgetown, Guyana: Edgar Mittelholzer Memorial Lectures, National History and Arts Council Ministry of Information, 1969). In Williams's formulation, the attachment to the parent, 'the security of being thoroughbred' is not for New World cultures. Rather, a creative social 'catalysis' occurs in which 'each racial group qualifies, and diminishes, the self-image of the other' (p. 19). Williams

draws a distinction between the Guyanese situation (or that in the Caribbean generally) and Australia, Canada and New Zealand, societies which he sees as more 'filiastic' with a subservient relationship to the 'parent' culture, and hence with less capacity for creative hybridity. At the time Williams was writing, this did seem a more valid distinction than it does twenty years later.

31. WILSON HARRIS, *The Womb of Space: The Cross-Cultural Imagination* (Westport, Connecticut: Greenwood, 1983). Harris also associates cultural hybridity/catalysis with creativity, but extends the 'model' to embrace other social groups within which there is the potential for an energising meeting of cultures, and he offers intuitive cross-cultural *readings* of various postcolonial texts. Harris, like Williams, is concerned to erode the destructive monoliths of race purity and attachment to pure-line ancestry, and sees this as being achieved – imaginatively and actually – not just through hybridity within particular societies, but *between* and *across* societies.

32. EDWARD KAMAU BRATHWAITE, *The Development of Creole Society in Jamaica 1770–1820* (London: Oxford University Press, 1971). Although Edward Kamau Brathwaite is concerned to revive the occluded ancestral connection with Africa, he has increasingly moved towards theorising a Caribbean aesthetic which necessarily implies a 'creolisation' (and hence cultural hybridity). See for instance 'The Love Axe/1: Developing a Caribbean Aesthetic 1962–1974', *Bim* 16 (June 1977): 53–65; *Bim* 17 (December 1977): 100–6; *Bim* 17 (June 1978): 181–92; 'Caliban, Ariel and Unprospero in the Conflict of Creolisation: A Study of the Slave Revolt in Jamaica in 1831–32', *Comparative Perspectives on Slavery in New World Plantation Societies*, ed. Vera Ruben and Arthur Turden (New York: New York Academy of Sciences, 1977); *Sun Poem* (London: Oxford University Press, 1982); and *History of the Voice* (London: New Beacon, 1984).

33. For a rather less positive view see SNEJA GUNEW, 'Australia 1914: A Moment in the Archaeology of Multiculturalism', *Europe and its Others*, ed. Francis Barker et al. (Colchester: University of Essex Press, 1985), and in a slightly different vein, JULIAN CROFT, 'Is *Geoffry Hamlyn* a Creole Novel?', *Australian Literary Studies*, 6 (May 1974): 269–76.

34. RICHARD TERDIMAN, *Discourse/Counter-Discourse: The Theory and Practice of Symbolic Resistance in Nineteenth-Century France* (Ithaca: Cornell University Press, 1985), p. 80.

35. C.L.R. JAMES, *The Black Jacobins: Toussaint L'Ouverture and the San Domingo Revolution* (New York: Random House, 1963).

36. J.J. THOMAS, *Froudacity: West Indian Fables Explained* (1889; London: New Beacon, 1969). See also his *The Theory and Practice of Creole Grammar* (1869; London: New Beacon, 1969) which codifies and thus authorises Jamaican language use against an English 'standard'.

37. ERIC WILLIAMS, *British Historians and the West Indies* (1964; London: André Deutsch, 1966).

38. J. MICHAEL DASH, *Haiti and the United States: National Stereotypes and the Literary Imagination* (London: Macmillan, 1988).

39. See HENRY REYNOLDS, *The Other Side of the Frontier: Aboriginal Resistance to the European Invasion of Australia* (Ringwood, Vic: Penguin, 1982) and *The Law of the Land* (Ringwood, Vic: Penguin, 1987).

40. KRIM BENTERRAK, STEPHEN MUECKE, and PADDY ROE, *Reading the Country: Introduction to Nomadology* (Fremantle: Fremantle Arts Centre Press, 1984).

41. For some significant distinctions between these two works see JOAN NEWMAN, 'Reader-response to Transcribed Oral Narrative: *A Fortunate Life* and *My Place*', *Southerly* 48 (1988): 376–89.

42. WILSON HARRIS 'Adversarial Contexts and Creativity', *New Left Review* 154 (November–December 1985): 128.

8 Revolutionary Black Women: Making Ourselves Subject*

BELL HOOKS

In this essay, bell hooks displays what she has called elsewhere 'the joy of being polyphonic, of multi-vocality'. The piece is typical of hooks's varied style and critical approach, mixing memory and desire, using different voices, and transgressing the boundaries of genre and form. It epitomizes her charged advocacy of a radical black female subjectivity. She opens with an anecdote set in a non-academic space, moving from there to a review of several black women writers – including Audre Lorde, Toni Morrison and Zora Neale Hurston – before ending with a call for more autobiographical works by black women on the Left. hooks regards theory and fiction as crucial components in the formation of a radical subjectivity, but no substitutes for confessional narrative, a key mode in the African–American context. Specifically, the essay develops ideas rehearsed in an earlier article in *Yearning: Race, Gender, and Cultural Politics*, entitled 'The Politics of Radical Black Subjectivity'. In that earlier essay, hooks maintains, in a familiar refrain, that: 'Opposition is not enough.' Throughout her writings, hooks promotes the construction of a self that is not defined negatively, over and against white supremacy, a self that is active rather than merely reactive, resistant in positive and creative ways. In this project her work recalls the revolutionary psychology of Fanon. The danger of becoming like the thing one opposes and repeating the exclusionary procedures of the dominant culture are risks to which hooks is constantly alert. In essays such as 'Choosing the Margin as a Space of Radical Openness', in 'Postmodern Blackness', and indeed throughout her work, hooks argues that while taking theory on board, black writers must be wary of jettisoning identity politics. At the same time, they must seek to formulate identities based on a respect for difference rather than an opposition

---

*Reprinted from *Black Looks: Race and Representation* (London: Turnaround, 1992), pp. 41–60.

to whiteness. Again, the focus is on an interlocking pattern of dominance and subservience that involves a reconfiguration of race, gender, class, as well as self, family, and community. hooks's primary concern here and elsewhere is with the decolonization of the mind and the development of a critical consciousness, leading toward a concept of identity that values rather than suppresses difference. In this respect, although her language and presentation is different, she can be instructively compared with Spivak. What hooks offers in her more informal discourse is not an alternative to theory, but another way – complex and multilayered, for all its directness – of framing its premises.

Sitting in a circle with several black women and one black man, children running in and out, on a hot Saturday evening at the office of the Council on Battered Women, after working all day, my spirits are renewed sharing with this group aspects of my development as a feminist thinker and writer. I listen intently as a sister comrade talks about her responses to my work. Initially she was disturbed by it. 'I didn't want to hear it', she says. 'I resented it.' The talk in the group is about black women and violence, not just the violence inflicted by black men, but the violence black women do to children, and the violence we do to one another. Particularly challenged by the essay in *Talking Back*, 'Violence in Intimate Relationships: A Feminist Perspective', because of its focus on a continuum of dominating violence that begins not with male violence against women but with the violence parents do to children, individual black women in the group felt they had to interrogate their parental practice.

There is little feminist work focusing on violence against children from a black perspective. Sharing our stories, we talked about the ways styles of parenting in diverse black communities support and perpetuate the use of violence as a means of domestic social control. We connected common acceptance of violence against children with community acceptance of male violence against women. Indeed, I suggested many of us were raised in families where we completely accepted the notion that violence was an appropriate response to crisis. In such settings it was not rare for black women to be verbally abusive and physically violent with one another. Our most vivid memories (in the group) of black women fighting one another took place in public settings where folks struggled over men or over gossip. There was no one in the group who had not witnessed an incident of black women doing violence to one another.

I shared with the group the declaration from Nikki Giovanni's 'Woman Poem': 'I ain't shit. You must be lower than that to care.'

This quote speaks directly to the rage and hostility oppressed/exploited people can turn inward on themselves and outward towards those who care about them. This has often been the case in black female encounters with one another. A vast majority of black women in this society receive sustained care only from other black women. That care does not always mediate or alter rage, or the desire to inflict pain; it may provoke it. Hostile responses to care echo the truth of Giovanni's words. When I first puzzled over them, I could hear voices in the background questioning, 'How can you be worth anything if you care about me, who is worth nothing?' Among black women, such deeply internalized pain and self-rejection informs the aggression inflicted on the mirror image – other black women. It is this reality Audre Lorde courageously describes in her essay 'Eye to Eye: Black Women, Hatred, and Anger'. Critically interrogating, Lorde asks:

> . . . why does that anger unleash itself most tellingly against another Black woman at the least excuse? Why do I judge her in a more critical light than any other, becoming enraged when she does not measure up? And if behind the object of my attack should lie the face of my own self, unaccepted, then what could possibly quench a fire fueled by such reciprocating passions?

I was reminded of Lorde's essay while seated among black women, listening to them talk about the intensity of their initial 'anger' at my work. Retrospectively, that anger was vividly evoked so that I would know that individual black women present had grappled with it, moved beyond it, and come to a place of political awareness that allowed us to openly acknowledge it as part of their process of coming to consciousness and go on to critically affirm one another. They wanted me to understand the process of transformation, the movement of their passions from rage to care and recognition. It is this empowering process that enables us to meet face to face, to greet one another with solidarity, sisterhood, and love. In this space we talk about our different experiences of black womanhood, informed by class, geographical location, religious backgrounds, etc. We do not assume that all black women are violent or have internalized rage and hostility.

In contrast, Lorde writes in 'Eye to Eye':

> We do not love ourselves, therefore we cannot love each other. Because we see in each other's face our own face, the face we never stopped wanting. Because we survived and survival breeds desire for more self. A face we never stopped wanting at the same time as we try to obliterate it. Why don't we meet each other's eyes? Do we expect betrayal in each other's gaze, or recognition.

Lorde's essay chronicles an understanding of ways 'wounded' black women, who are not in recovery, interact with one another, helping us to see the way in which sexism and racism as systems of domination can shape and determine how we regard one another. Deeply moved by her portrait of the way internalized racism and sexism informs the formation of black female social identity, the way it can and often does affect us, I was simultaneously disturbed by the presumption, expressed by her continual use of a collective 'we', that she was speaking to an experience all black women share. The experience her essay suggests black women share is one of passively receiving and absorbing messages of self-hate, then directing rage and hostility most intensely at one another. While I wholeheartedly agree with Lorde that many black women feel and act as she describes, I am interested in the reality of those black women, however few, who even if they have been the targets of black female rage do not direct hostility or rage toward other black women.

Throughout 'Eye to Eye', Lorde constructs a monolithic paradigm of black female experience that does not engage our differences. Even as her essay urges black women to openly examine the harshness and cruelty that may be present in black female interaction so that we can regard one another differently, an expression of that regard would be recognition, without hatred or envy, that not all black women share the experience she describes. To some extent Lorde's essay acts to shut down, close off, erase, and deny those black female experiences that do not fit the norm she constructs from the location of her experience. Never in Lorde's essay does she address the issue of whether or not black women from different cultural backgrounds (Caribbean, Latina, etc.) construct diverse identities. Do we all feel the same about black womanhood? What about regional differences? What about those black women who have had the good fortune to be raised in a politicized context where their identities were constructed by resistance and not passive acceptance? By evoking this negative experience of black womanhood as 'commonly' shared, Lorde presents it in a way that suggests it represents 'authentic' black female reality. To not share the critique she posits is to be made an 'outsider' yet again. In Donna Haraway's essay 'A Manifesto for Cyborgs', she warns feminist thinkers against assuming positions that 'appear to be the telos of the whole', so that we do not 'produce epistemologies to police deviation from official women's experience'. Though Haraway is speaking about mainstream feminist practice, her warning is applicable to marginalized groups who are in the process of making and remaking critical texts that name our politics and experience.

Years ago I attended a small gathering of black women who were meeting to plan a national conference on black feminism. As we sat in a circle talking about our experiences, those individuals who were most listened to all told stories of how brutally they had been treated by 'the' black community. Speaking against the construction of a monolithic experience, I talked about the way my experience of black community differed, sharing that I had been raised in a segregated rural black community that was very supportive. Our segregated church and schools were places where we were affirmed. I was continually told that I was 'special' in those settings, that I would be 'somebody' someday and do important work to 'uplift' the race. I felt loved and cared about in the segregated black community of my growing up. It gave me the grounding in a positive experience of 'blackness' that sustained me when I left that community to enter racially integrated settings, where racism informed most social interactions. Before I could finish speaking, I was interrupted by one of the 'famous' black women present, who chastised me for trying to erase another black woman's pain by bringing up a different experience. Her voice was hostile and angry. She began by saying she was 'sick of people like me'. I felt both silenced and misunderstood. It seemed that the cathartic expression of collective pain wiped out any chance that my insistence on the diversity of black experience would be heard.

My story was reduced to a competing narrative, one that was seen as trying to divert attention from the 'true' telling of black female experience. In this gathering, black female identity was made synonymous again and again with 'victimization'. The black female voice that was deemed 'authentic' was the voice in pain; only the sound of hurting could be heard. No narrative of resistance was voiced and respected in this setting. I came away wondering why it was these black women could only feel bonded to each other if our narratives echoed, only if we were telling the same story of shared pain and victimization. Why was it impossible to speak an identity emerging from a different location?

A particular brand of black feminist 'essentialism' had been constructed in that place. It would not allow for difference. Any individual present who was seen as having inappropriate thoughts or lingering traces of politically incorrect ideas was the target for unmediated hostility. Not surprisingly, those who had the most to say about victimization were also the ones who judged others harshly, who silenced others. Individual black women who were not a part of that inner circle learned that if they did not know the 'right' thing to say, it was best to be silent. To speak against the grain was to risk punishment. One's speech might be interrupted or one might be subjected to humiliating verbal abuse.

At the close of this gathering, many black women gave testimony about how this had been a wonderful experience of sisterhood and black woman-bonding. There was no space for those individuals whose spirits had been assaulted and attacked to name their experience. Ironically, they were leaving this gathering with a sense of estrangement, carrying with them remembered pain. Some of them felt that this was the first time in their lives that they had been so cruelly treated by other black women. The oldest black woman present, an academic intellectual who had often been the target for verbal assault, who often wept in her room at night, vowed never again to attend such a gathering. The memory of her pain has lingered in my mind. I have not forgotten this collective black female 'rage' in the face of difference, the anger directed at individual black women who dared to speak as though we were more than our pain, more than the collective pain black females have historically experienced.

Sitting at the offices of the Council on Battered Women was different. After many years of feminist movement, it seems to me that black women can now come together in ways that allow for difference. At the Council, women could speak openly and honestly about their experience, describe their negative and positive responses to my work without fear of rebuke. They could name their rage, annoyance, frustration, and simultaneously critique it. In a similar setting where black women had talked openly about the way my work 'enraged' them, I had asked a sister if she would talk about the roots of her hostility. She responded by telling me that I was 'daring to be different, to have a different response to the shit black women were faced with everyday'. She said, 'It's like you were saying, this is what the real deal is and this what we can do about it. When most of us have just been going along with the program and telling ourselves that's all we could do. You were saying that it don't have to be that way.' The rage she articulated was in response to the demand that black women acknowledge the impact of sexism on our lives and engage in feminist movement. That was a demand for transformation. At the offices of the Council, I was among black comrades who were engaged in a process of transformation. Collectively, we were working to problematize our notions of black female subjectivity. None of us assumed a fixed essential identity. It was so evident that we did not all share a common understanding of being black and female, even though some of our experiences were similar. We did share the understanding that it is difficult for black women to construct radical subjectivity within white supremacist capitalist patriarchy, that our struggle to be 'subject', though similar, also differs from that of black men, and that the politics of gender create that difference.

Much creative writing by contemporary black women authors highlights gender politics, specifically black male sexism, poverty, black female labor, and the struggle for creativity. Celebrating the 'power' of black women's writing in her essay 'Women Warriors: Black Women

Writers Load the Canon' in the *Voice Literary Supplement*, dated May 1990, Michelle Cliff asserts:

There is continuity in the written work of many African–American women, whether writer is their primary identity or not. You can draw a line from the slave narrative of Linda Brent to Elizabeth Keckley's life to *Their Eyes Were Watching God* to *Coming of Age in Mississippi* to *Sula* to *The Salteaters* to *Praisesong for the Widow*. All of these define a response to power. All structure that response as a quest, a journey to complete, to realize the self; all involve the attempt to break out of expectations imposed on black and female identity. All work against the odds to claim the *I*.

Passionate declarations like this one, though seductive, lump all black female writing together in a manner that suggests there is indeed a totalizing *telos* that determines black female subjectivity. This narrative constructs a homogenous black female subject whose subjectivity is most radically defined by those experiences she shares with other black women. In this declaration, as in the entire essay, Cliff glorifies black women writers even though she warns against the kind of glorification (particularly that accorded a writer that is expressed by sustained academic literary critique of their work) that has the potential to repress and contain.

Cliff's piece also contains. Defining black women's collective work as a critical project that problematizes the quest for 'identity', she subsumes that quest solely by focusing on rites of passages wherein black women journey to find themselves. She does not talk about whether that journeying is fruitful. By focusing attention primarily on the journey, she offers paradigms for reading and understanding black women writers that invite readers (critics included) to stop there, to romanticize the journey without questioning the location of that journey's end. Sadly, in much of the fiction by contemporary black women writers, the struggle by black female characters for subjectivity, though forged in radical resistance to the status quo (opposition to racist oppression, less frequently to class and gender) usually takes the form of black women breaking free from boundaries imposed by others, only to practice their newfound 'freedom' by setting limits and boundaries for themselves. Hence though black women may make themselves 'subject' they do not become radical subjects. Often they simply conform to existing norms, even ones they once resisted.

Despite all the 'radical' shifts in thought, location, class position, etc., that Celie undergoes in Alice Walker's novel *The Color Purple*, from her movement from object to subject to her success as a capitalist entrepreneur, Celie is reinscribed within the context of family and

221

domestic relations by the novel's end. The primary change is that those relations are no longer abusive. Celie has not become a 'feminist', a civil rights activist, or a political being in any way. Breaking free from the patriarchal prison that is her 'home' when the novel begins, she creates her own household, yet radical politics of collective struggle against racism or sexism do not inform her struggle for self-actualization.

Earlier writing by black women, Linda Brent's slave narrative for example, records resistance struggles where black women confront and overcome incredible barriers in the quest to be self-defining. Often after those barriers have been passed, the heroines settle down into conventional gender roles. No tale of woman's struggle to be self-defining is as powerful as the Brent narrative. She is ever conscious of the way in which being female makes slavery 'far more grievous'. Her narrative creates powerful groundwork for the construction of radical black female subjectivity. She engages in a process of critical thinking that enables her to rebel against the notion that her body can be sold, and insists on placing the sanctity of black ontological being outside modes of exchange. Yet this radical, visionary 'take' on subjectivity does not inform who she becomes once she makes her way to freedom. After breaking the bonds of slavery, Harriet Jacobs takes on the pseudonym Linda Brent when she writes about the past and falls into the clutches of conventional notions of womanhood. Does the radical invented self 'Linda Brent' have no place in the life of Harriet Jacobs? Freed, descriptions of her life indicate no use of the incredible oppositional imagination that has been a major resource enabling her to transgress boundaries, to take risks, and dare to survive. Does Jacobs's suppression of the radical self chart the journey that black women will follow, both in real life and in their fictions?

More than any other novel by a contemporary black woman writer, Toni Morrison's *Sula* chronicles the attempt by a black female to constitute radical black female subjectivity. Sula challenges every restriction imposed upon her, transgressing all boundaries. Defying conventional notions of passive female sexuality, she asserts herself as desiring subject. Rebelling against enforced domesticity, she chooses to roam the world, to remain childless and unmarried. Refusing standard sexist notions of the exchange of female bodies, she engages in the exchange of male bodies as part of a defiant effort to displace their importance. Asserting the primacy of female friendship, she attempts to break with patriarchal male identification and loses the friendship of her 'conservative' buddy Nel, who has indeed capitulated to convention.

Even though readers of *Sula* witness her self-assertion and celebration of autonomy, which Sula revels in even as she is dying, we also know that she is not self-actualized enough to stay alive. Her awareness of what it means to be a radical subject does not cross the boundaries of public and private; hers is a privatized self-discovery. Sula's death at an early age does not leave the reader with a sense of her 'power', instead she seems powerless to assert agency in a world that has no interest in radical black female subjectivity, one that seeks to repress, contain, and annihilate it. Sula is annihilated. The reader never knows what force is killing her, eating her from the inside out. Since her journey has been about the struggle to invent herself, the narrative implies that it is the longing for 'selfhood' that leads to destruction. Those black women who survive, who live to tell the tale, so to speak, are the 'good girls', the ones who have been self-sacrificing, hardworking black women. Sula's fate suggests that charting the journey of radical black female subjectivity is too dangerous, too risky. And while Sula is glad to have broken the rules, she is not a triumphant figure. Sula, like so many other black female characters in contemporary fiction, has no conscious politics, never links her struggle to be self-defining with the collective plight of black women. Yet this novel was written at the peak of contemporary feminist movement. Given the 'power' of Sula's black female author/creator, Toni Morrison, why does she appear on the page as an 'artist without an art form'? Is it too much like 'treason' – like disloyalty to black womanhood – to question this portrait of (dare I say it) 'victimization', to refuse to be seduced by Sula's exploits or ignore their outcome?

There are black female characters in contemporary fictions who are engaged in political work. Velma, the radical activist in Toni Cade Bambara's *The Salteaters*, has grounded her struggle for meaning within activist work for black liberation. Overwhelmed by responsibility, by the sense of having to bear too much, too great a weight, she attempts suicide. This novel begins with older radical black women problematizing the question of black female subjectivity. Confronting Velma's attempt at self-destruction and self-erasure, they want to know, 'are you sure, sweetheart, that you want to be well?' Wellness here is synonymous with radical subjectivity. Indeed, the elders will go on to emphasize that Velma's plight, and that of other black women like her, reflects the loss of 'maps' that will chart the journey for black females. They suggest that it is the younger generation's attempt to assimilate, to follow alien maps, that leads to the loss of perspective. Velma only came back to life (for though she fails to kill herself, she is spiritually dead) when she testifies to herself that she indeed will choose wellness, will claim herself and nurture that radical subjectivity. Like Paule Marshall's *Praisesong for the Widow* and Gloria Naylor's *Mama Day*, the 'radical' black women elders with fresh memories of slavery holocaust, of the anguish of reconstruction, who sustain their courage in resistance, live fruitfully outside conventional gender roles. They either do not

conform or they acknowledge the way conformity rarely enables black
female self-actualization.

Representing a new generation of 'modern' black women, Velma, even
as she is in the process of recovery, critiques her desire to make a self
against the grain, and questions 'what good did wild do you, since there
was always some low-life gruesome gang-bang raping lawless careless
petty last straw nasty thing ready to pounce – put your shit under total
arrest and crack your back?' Wild is the metaphoric expression of that
inner will to rebel, to move against the grain, to be out of one's place.
It is the expression of radical black female subjectivity. Law professor
Regina Austin calls black women to cultivate this 'wildness' as a survival
strategy in her piece 'Sapphire Bound'. Significantly, she begins the essay
by calling attention to the fact that folks seem to be more eager to read
about wild black women in fictions than to make way for us in real life.
Reclaiming that wildness, she declares:

> Well, I think the time has come for us to get truly hysterical, to take
> on the role of 'professional Sapphires' in a forthright way, to declare
> that we are serious about ourselves, and to capture some of the
> intellectual power and resources that are necessary to combat the
> systematic denigration of minority women. It is time for Sapphire to
> testify on her own behalf, *in writing*, complete with footnotes.

If the writers of black women's fiction are not able to express the
wilder, more radical dimensions of themselves, in sustained and fruitful
ways, it is unlikely that they will create characters who 'act up' and
flourish. They may doubt that there is an audience for fictions where
black women are not first portrayed as victims. Though fictions portray
black women being wild in resistance, confronting barriers that impede
self-actualization, rarely is the new 'self' defined. Though Bambara
includes passages that let the reader know Velma lives, there are no
clues that indicate how her radical subjectivity will emerge in the
context of 'wildness'.

Consistently, contemporary black women writers link the struggle to
become subject with a concern with emotional and spiritual well-being.
Most often the narcissistic-based individual pursuit of self and identity
subsumes the possibility of sustained commitment to radical politics.
This tension is played out again and again in Alice Walker's *The Third
Life of Grange Copeland*. While the heroine, Ruth, is schooled by her
grandfather to think critically, to develop radical political consciousness,
in the end he fights against whites alone. It is not clear what path Ruth
will take in the future. Will she be a militant warrior for the revolution
or be kept in her place by 'strong' black male lovers/patriarchs who,
like her grandfather, will be convinced that they can best determine what
conditions are conducive to producing black female well-being? Ironically,

Meridian takes up where Ruth's story ends, yet the older black woman activist, like Ruth, remains confined and contained by a self-imposed domesticity. Is Meridian in hiding because there is no place where her radical black subjectivity can be expressed without punishment? Is the non-patriarchal home the only safe place?

Contemporary fiction by black women focusing on the construction of self and identity breaks new ground in that it clearly names the ways structures of domination, racism, sexism, and class exploitation, oppress and make it practically impossible for black women to survive if they do not engage in meaningful resistance on some level. Defiantly naming the condition of oppression and personal strategies of opposition, such writing enables the individual black woman reader who has not yet done so to question, and/or critically affirms the efforts of those readers who are already involved in resistance. Yet these writings often fail to depict any location for the construction of new identities. It is this textual gap that leads critic Sondra O'Neale to ask in her essay 'Inhibiting Midwives, Usurping Creators: The Struggling Emergence of Black Women in American Fiction':

> For instance, where are the Angela Davises, Ida B. Wellses, and Daisy Bateses of black feminist literature? Where are the portraits of those women who fostered their own action to liberate themselves, other black women, and black men as well? We see a sketch of such a character in *Meridian*, but she is never developed to a social and political success.

In an earlier essay, 'The Politics of Radical Black Subjectivity', I emphasized that opposition and resistance cannot be made synonymous with self-actualization on an individual or collective level: 'Opposition is not enough. In that vacant space after one has resisted there is still the necessity to become – to make oneself anew.' While contemporary writing by black women has brought into sharp focus the idea that black females must 'invent' selves, the question – what kind of self? – usually remains unanswered. The vision of selfhood that does emerge now and then is one that is in complete concordance with conventional western notions of a 'unitary' self. Again it's worth restating Donna Haraway's challenge to feminist thinkers to resist making 'one's own political tendencies to be the telos of the whole' so we can accept different accounts of female experience and also face ourselves as complex subjects who embody multiple locations. In 'A Manifesto for Cyborgs', she urges us to remember that, 'The issue is dispersion. The task is to survive in diaspora.'

Certainly, collective black female experience has been about the struggle to survive in diaspora. It is the intensity of that struggle, the fear of failure (as we face daily the reality that many black people do not and are not surviving) that has led many black women thinkers, especially within feminist movement, to wrongly assume that strength in unity can only exist if difference is suppressed and shared experience is highlighted. Though feminist writing by black women is usually critical of the racism that has shaped and defined the parameters of much contemporary feminist movement, it usually reiterates, in an uncritical manner, major tenets of dominant feminist thought. Admonishing black women for wasting time critiquing white female racism, Sheila Radford-Hill, in 'Considering Feminism as a Model for Social Change', urges black feminists:

> ... to build an agenda that meets the needs of black women by helping black women to mobilize around issues that they perceive to have a direct impact on the overall quality of their lives. Such is the challenge that defined our struggle and constitutes our legacy ... Thus, black women need to develop their own leadership and their own agenda based on the needs of their primary constituent base; that is, based around black women, their families, and their communities. This task cannot be furthered by dialoging with white women about their inherent racism.

While I strongly agree with Radford-Hill's insistence that black critical thinkers engaged in feminist movement develop strategies that directly address the concerns of our diverse black communities, she constructs an either/or proposition that obscures the diversity of our experiences and locations. For those black women who live and work in predominantly white settings (and of course the reality is that most black women work jobs where their supervisors are white women and men), it is an appropriate and necessary political project for them to work at critical interrogations and interventions that address white racism. Such efforts do not preclude simultaneous work in black communities. Evocations of an 'essentialist' notion of black identity seek to deny the extent to which all black folk must engage with whites as well as exclude individuals from 'blackness' whose perspectives, values, or lifestyles may differ from a totalizing notion of black experience that sees only those folk who live in segregated communities or have little contact with whites as 'authentically' black.

Radford-Hill's essay is most insightful when she addresses 'the crisis of black womanhood', stating that 'the extent to which black feminists can articulate and solve the crisis of black womanhood is the extent to which black women will undergo a feminist transformation'. The crisis Radford-Hill describes is a crisis of identity and subjectivity. When the major struggle black women addressed was opposition to racism and the goal of that struggle was equality in the existing social structures, when most black folks were poor and lived in racially segregated neighborhoods, gender roles for black women were more clearly defined. We had a place in the 'struggle' as well as a place in the social institutions of our communities. It was easier for black women to chart the journey of selfhood. With few job options in the segregated labor force, most black women knew that they would be engaged in service work or become teachers. Today's black woman has more options even though most of the barriers that would keep her from exercising those options are still in place. Racial integration, economic changes in black class relations, the impact of consumer capitalism, as well as a male-centered contemporary black liberation struggle (which devalued the contributions of black females) and a feminist movement which called into question idealized notions of womanhood have radically altered black female reality. For many black women, especially the underclass, the dream of racial equality was intimately linked with the fantasy that once the struggle was over, black women would be able to assume conventional sexist gender roles. To some extent there is a crisis in black womanhood because most black women have not responded to these changes by radically reinventing themselves, by developing new maps to chart future journeys. And more crucially, most black women have not responded to this crisis by developing critical consciousness, by becoming engaged in radical movements for social change.

When we examine the lives of individual black women who did indeed respond to contemporary changes, we see just how difficult it is for black women to construct radical subjectivity. Two powerful autobiographies of radical black women were published in the early 1970s. In 1970, Shirley Chisholm published *Unbought and Unbossed*, chronicling the events that led to her becoming the first black congresswoman. In 1974, *Angela Davis: An Autobiography* was published. Both accounts demonstrate that the construction of radical black female subjectivity is rooted in a willingness to go against the grain. Though many folks may not see Chisholm as 'radical', she was one of the first black female leaders to speak against sexism, stressing in the introduction to her book: 'Of my two "handicaps", being female put many more obstacles in my path than being black.' An outspoken advocate of reproductive and abortion rights for women, Chisholm responded to black males who were not opposed to compulsory pregnancy for black women by arguing: 'Which is more like genocide, I have asked some of my black brothers – this, the way things are, or the conditions I am fighting for in which the full range of family planning service is fully available to women of all classes and colors; starting with effective contraception and extending to safe, legal termination of undesired pregnancies, at a price they can afford?'

Militant in her response to racism, Chisholm also stressed the need for education for critical consciousness to help eradicate internalized racism:

> It is necessary for our generation to repudiate Carver and all the lesser-known black leaders who cooperated with the white design to keep their people down. We need none of their kind today. Someday, when, God willing, the struggle is over and its bitterness has faded, those men and woman may be rediscovered and given their just due for working as best they could see to do in their time and place, for their brothers and sisters. But at present their influence is pernicious, and where they still control education in the North or the South, they must be replaced with educators who are ready to demand full equality for the oppressed races and fight for it at any cost.

As a radical black female subject who would not allow herself to be the puppet of any group, Chisholm was often harassed, mocked, and ridiculed by colleagues. Psychological terrorism was often the weapon used to try and coerce her into silence, to convince her she knew nothing about politics, or worse yet that she was 'crazy'. Often her colleagues described her as mad if she took positions they could not understand or would not have taken. Radical black female subjects are constantly labeled crazy by those who hope to undermine our personal power and our ability to influence others. Fear of being seen as insane may be a major factor keeping black women from expressing their most radical selves. Just recently, when I spoke against the omnipresent racism and sexism at a conference, calling it terroristic, the organizers told folks I was 'crazy'. While this hurt and angered, it would have wounded me more had I not understood the ways this appellation is used by those in power to keep the powerless in their place. Remembering Chisholm's experience, I knew that I was not alone in confronting racist, sexist attacks that are meant to silence. Knowing that Chisholm claimed her right to subjectivity without apology inspires me to maintain courage.

Recently rereading the autobiography of Angela Davis, I was awed by her courage. I could appreciate the obstacles she confronted and her capacity to endure and persevere in a new way. Reading this work in my teens, her courage seemed like 'no big deal'. At the beginning of the work, Davis eschews any attempt to see herself as exceptional. Framing the narrative in this way, it is easy for readers to ignore the specificity of her experience. In fact, very few black females at the time had gone to radical high schools where they learned about socialism or traveled to Europe and studied at the Sorbonne. Yet Davis insists that her situation is like that of all black people. This gesture of solidarity, though important, at times obscures the reality that Davis's radical understanding of politics was learned as was her critical consciousness.

Had she voiced her solidarity with underclass black people, while simultaneously stressing the importance of learning, of broadening one's perspective, she would have shared with black females tools that enable one to be a radical subject.

Like Chisholm, Davis confronted sexism when she fully committed herself to working for political change:

> I became acquainted very early with the widespread presence of an unfortunate syndrome among some Black male activists – namely to confuse their political activity with an assertion of their maleness. They saw – and some continue to see – Black manhood as something separate from Black womanhood. These men view Black women as a threat to their attainment of manhood – especially those Black women who take initiative and work to become leaders in their own right.

Working in the radical black liberation movement, Davis constantly confronted and challenged sexism even as she critiqued the pervasive racism in mainstream feminist movement. Reading her autobiography, it is clear that reading and studying played a tremendous role in shaping her radical political consciousness. Yet Davis understood that one needed to go beyond books and work collectively with comrades for social change. She critiqued self-focused work to emphasize the value of working in solidarity:

> Floating from activity to activity was no revolutionary anything. Individual activity – sporadic and disconnected – is not revolutionary work. Serious revolutionary work consists of persistent and methodical efforts through a collective of other revolutionaries to organize the masses for action. Since I had long considered myself a Marxist, the alternatives open to me were very limited.

Despite limited options, Davis's decision to advocate communism was an uncommon and radical choice.

When the Davis autobiography was written, she was thirty years old; her most militant expression of subjectivity erupted in her twenties. Made into a cultural icon, a gesture that was not in line with her insistence on the importance of collectivity and fellowship, she came to be represented in mass media as an 'exceptional' black woman. Her experience was not seen as a model young black women could learn from. Many parents pointed to the prison sentence she served as reason enough for black women not to follow in her footsteps. Black males who wanted the movement to be male-centered were not trying to encourage other black women to be on the Left, to fully commit themselves to a revolutionary black liberation struggle. At public appearances, Angela Davis was not and is not flanked by other black women on the Left. Constantly projected as an 'isolated' figure, her presence, her continued commitment to critical thinking and critical pedagogy, had not had the galvanizing impact on black females that it could have. Black women 'worship' Davis from a distance, see her as exceptional. Though young black women adore Davis, they do not often read her work nor seek to follow her example. Yet learning about those black women who have dared to assert radical subjectivity, is a necessary part of black female self-actualization. Coming to power, to selfhood, to radical subjectivity cannot happen in isolation. Black women need to study the writings, both critical and autobiographical, of those women who have developed their potential and chosen to be radical subjects.

Critical pedagogy, the sharing of information and knowledge by black women with black women, is crucial for the development of radical black female subjectivity (not because black women can only learn from one another, but because the circumstances of racism, sexism, and class exploitation ensure that other groups will not necessarily seek to further our self-determination). This process requires of us a greater honesty about how we live. Black females (especially students) who are searching for answers about the social formation of identity want to know how radical black women think but they also want to know about our habits of being. Willingness to share openly one's personal experience ensures that one will not be made into a deified icon. When black females learn about my life, they also learn about the mistakes I make, the contradictions. They come to know my limitations as well as my strengths. They cannot dehumanize me by placing me on a pedestal. Sharing the contradictions of our lives, we help each other learn how to grapple with contradictions as part of the process of becoming a critical thinker, a radical subject.

The lives of Ella Baker, Fannie Lou Hamer, Septima Clark, Lucy Parson, Ruby Doris Smith Robinson, Angela Davis, Bernice Reagon, Alice Walker, Audre Lorde, and countless others bear witness to the difficulty of developing radical black female subjectivity even as they attest to the joy and triumph of living with a decolonized mind and participating in ongoing resistance struggle. The narratives of black women who have militantly engaged in radical struggles for change offer insights. They let us know the conditions that enable the construction of radical black female subjectivity as well as the obstacles that impede its development. In most cases, radical black female subjects have willingly challenged the status quo and gone against the grain. Despite the popularity of Angela Davis as a cultural icon, most black women are 'punished' and 'suffer' when they make choices that go against the prevailing societal sense of what a black woman should be and do. Most radical black female subjects are not caught up in consumer capitalism. Living simply is often the price one pays for choosing to be different. It was no accident that Zora Neale Hurston died poor. Radical black female subjects have had to educate ourselves for critical consciousness, reading, studying, engaging in critical pedagogy, transgressing boundaries to acquire the knowledge we need. Those rare radical black women who have started organizations and groups are attempting to build a collective base that will support and enable their work. Many of these black women create sites of resistance that are far removed from conservatizing institutions in order to sustain their radical commitments. Those of us who remain in institutions that do not support our efforts to be radical subjects are daily assaulted. We persevere because we believe our presence is needed, is important.

Developing a feminist consciousness is a crucial part of the process by which one asserts radical black female subjectivity. Whether she has called herself a feminist or not, there is no radical black woman subject who has not been forced to confront and challenge sexism. If, however, that individual struggle is not connected to a larger feminist movement, then every black woman finds herself reinventing strategies to cope when we should be leaving a legacy of feminist resistance that can nourish, sustain, and guide other black women and men. Those black women who valiantly advocate feminism often bear the brunt of severe critique from other black folks. As radical subject, the young Michele Wallace wrote one of the first book-length, polemical works on feminism that focused on black folks. She did not become a cultural icon; to a great extent she was made a pariah. Writing about her experience in 'The Politics of Location: Cinema/Theory/Literature/Ethnicity/Sexuality/Me', she remembers the pain.

> I still ponder the book I wrote, *Black Macho and The Myth of the Superwoman*, and the disturbance it caused; how black women are not allowed to establish their own intellectual terrain, to make their own mistakes, to invent their own birthplace in writing. I still ponder my book's rightness and wrongness, and how its reception almost destroyed me so that I vowed never to write political and/or theoretical statements about feminism again.

Wallace suffered in isolation, with no group of radical black women rallying to her defense, or creating a context where critique would not lead to trashing.

Without a context of critical affirmation, radical black female subjectivity cannot sustain itself. Often black women turn away from the radicalism of their younger days as they age because the isolation, the sense of estrangement from community, becomes too difficult to bear. Critical affirmation is a concept that embraces both the need to affirm one another and to have a space for critique. Significantly, that critique is not rooted in negative desire to compete, to wound, to trash.

Though I began this piece with critical statements about Audre Lorde's essay, I affirm the value of her work. The 'Eye to Eye' essay remains one of the most insightful discussions of black female interaction. Throughout the essay, Lorde emphasizes the importance of affirmation, encouraging black women to be gentle and affectionate with one another. Tenderness should not simply be a form of care extended to those black women who think as we do. Many of us have been in situations where black females are sweet to the folks in their clique and completely hostile to anyone deemed an outsider.

In 'Eye to Eye', Lorde names this problem. Offering strategies black women might use to promote greater regard and respect, she says that 'black women must love ourselves'. Loving ourselves begins with understanding the forces that have produced whatever hostility toward blackness and femaleness that is felt, but it also means learning new ways to think about ourselves. Often the black women who speak the most about love and sisterhood are deeply attached to essentialist notions of black female identity that promote a 'policing' of anyone who does not conform. Ironically, of course, the only way black women can construct radical subjectivity is by resisting set norms and challenging the politics of domination based on race, class, and sex. Essentialist perspectives on black womanhood often perpetuate the false assumption that black females, simply by living in white supremacist/capitalist/ patriarchy, are radicalized. They do not encourage black women to develop their critical thinking. Individual black women on the Left often find their desire to read or write 'theory', to be engaged in critical dialogues with diverse groups, mocked and ridiculed. Often, I am criticized for studying feminist theory, especially writing by white women. And I am seen as especially 'naïve' when I suggest that even though a white woman theorist may be 'racist', she may also have valuable information that I can learn from. Until black women fully recognize that we must collectively examine and study our experience from a feminist standpoint, there will always be lags and gaps in the structure of our epistemologies. Where are our feminist books on mothering, on sexuality, on feminist film criticism? Where are our autobiographies that do not falsely represent our reality in the interest of promoting monolithic notions of black female experience or celebrating how wonderfully we have managed to overcome oppression?

Though autobiography or any type of confessional narrative is often devalued in North American letters, this genre has always had a privileged place in African American literary history. As a literature of resistance, confessional narratives by black folks were didactic. More than any other genre of writing, the production of honest confessional narratives by black women who are struggling to be self-actualized and to become radical subjects are needed as guides, as texts that affirm our fellowship with one another. (I need not feel isolated if I know that there are other comrades with similar experiences. I learn from their strategies of resistance and from their recording of mistakes.) Even as the number of novels published by black women increase, this writing cannot be either a substitute for theory or for autobiographical narrative. Radical black women need to tell our stories; we cannot document our experience enough. Works like *Lemon Swamp, Balm in Gilead, Ready From Within* and *Every Goodbye Ain't Gone*, though very different, and certainly not all narratives of radical black female subjectivity, enable readers to understand the complexity and diversity of black female experience.

There are few contemporary autobiographies by black women on the Left. We need to hear more from courageous black women who have gone against the grain to assert nonconformist politics and habits of being, folks like Toni Cade Bambara, Gloria Joseph, Faye Harrison, June Jordan, and so many others. These voices can give testimony and share the process of transformation black women undergo to emerge as radical subjects. Black females need to know who our revolutionary comrades are. Speaking about her commitment to revolution, Angela Davis notes:

> For me revolution was never an interim 'thing-to-do' before settling down: it was no fashionable club with newly minted jargon, or a new kind of social life – made thrilling by risk and confrontation, made glamorous by costume. Revolution is a serious thing, the most serious thing about a revolutionary's life. When one commits oneself to the struggle, it must be for a lifetime.

The crisis of black womanhood can only be addressed by the development of resistance struggles that emphasize the importance of decolonizing our minds, developing critical consciousness. Feminist politics can be an integral part of a renewed black liberation struggle. Black women, particularly those of us who have chosen radical subjectivity, can move toward revolutionary social change that will address the diversity of our experiences and our needs. Collectively bringing our knowledge, resources, skills, and wisdom to one another, we make the site where radical black female subjectivity can be nurtured and sustained.

9 Toward a Theory of Minority Discourse: What is to be Done?*

ABDUL JANMOHAMED AND DAVID LLOYD

In this essay, the introduction to the volume entitled *The Nature and Context of Minority Discourse*, the authors outline an approach to minority cultures aimed at finding their points of contact. What links minority cultures is their shared antagonism to the dominant culture. One weakness of their argument here might be the assumption that the dominant is singular while minorities are plural. Minority discourse is a way of speaking about minority cultures collectively, a task that is bound up with the role of the minority intellectual. This essay can be seen to bring together earlier work by JanMohamed on colonialism such as a 'Manichaean allegory', and Lloyd's study of the Irish poet James Clarence Mangan as the author of a 'minor literature'. Opposition and subordination are integral parts of minority discourse. Its pitfalls are integration or assimilation, and pluralism. JanMohamed and Lloyd insist on minority cultures in place of multiculturalism. Three key components of minority discourse are its attention to class, its insistence on a network rather than a hierarchy of differences, and its emphasis on pedagogical innovation, and in all of these particulars it has affiliations with the work of bell hooks. In their foregrounding of the role of the 'twice marginalized' intellectual JanMohamed and Lloyd touch on the issue of the place of the postcolonial critic within academe, recalling the work of Said and Spivak, while their treatment of the alienation experienced by such an intellectual bears directly on the comments of Fanon on the crisis experienced by the colonial intellectual caught between two cultures. Another Fanonian theme is the argument for a new or revised humanism, which they term 'a Utopian exploration of human potentiality'. In their attempts to close the gap between theory and practice, and in their call for

*Reprinted from ABDUL R. JANMOHAMED and DAVID LLOYD (eds), *The Nature and Context of Minority Discourse* (Oxford and New York: Oxford University Press, 1990), pp. 1–16.

'ever-more-inclusive solidarities', JanMohamed and Lloyd tackle problems central to postcolonialism. The concept of minority status with which JanMohamed and Lloyd work is reminiscent of the use of the term 'subaltern' by Spivak, in so far as both categories can be seen to represent political resistance, absolute exteriority, and irreducible difference. It is finally this idea of a non-appropriable colonial subject that is the most pressing and problematic element of their argument, because the inclusive solidarities that JanMohamed and Lloyd call for depend precisely upon a perception of the exclusiveness of a dominant culture whose greatest strength may lie in its ability to incorporate opposition and subsume the marginal. It is to their credit that the authors endeavour to avoid as far as possible what they call 'the pathos of alienation', a risk implicit in minority discourse and in postcolonial theory. A difficulty that is arguably not resolved here is whether in seeking to distinguish the pathos of alienation experienced by the traditional humanist from the 'objective alienation' of the minority intellectual JanMohamed and Lloyd are speaking of a difference of kind or a difference of degree. Finally, what the authors impress upon their readers is that it is not essence but position that matters most.

I

At a moment when the liberation and celebration of differences and polyvocality are central features of critical endeavors, it is perhaps best to begin by defining the term 'minority discourse' and justifying its singularity. In the past two decades, intellectuals involved in ethnic and feminist studies have enabled fresh examinations of a variety of minority voices engaged in retrieving texts repressed or marginalized by a society that espouses universalistic, univocal, and monologic humanism. Although this archival work has generated provocative theoretical analysis (in the best instances dialectical), it still remains true that the dispersal of the intellectuals in underfunded 'special programs' has perpetuated and reinforced the fragmentation and marginalization of nonhegemonic cultures and communities in academic as well as in other spheres. Thus various minority discourses and their theoretical exegesis continue to flourish, but the relations between them remain to be articulated. Such articulation is precisely the task of minority discourse, in the singular: to describe and define the common denominators that link various minority cultures. Cultures designated as minorities have certain shared experiences by virtue of their similar antagonistic relationship to the dominant culture, which seeks to marginalize them all. Thus bringing together these disparate voices in a common forum is not merely a polemical act; it is an attempt to prefigure practically what should already be the case: that those who, despite their marginalization, in fact constitute the majority should be able collectively to examine the nature and content of their common marginalization and to develop strategies for their re-empowerment.

The need for such forums for comparative studies of minority cultures and for the definition of a common political agenda cannot be overemphasized, because the denial of such spaces and of any but a negative value to minority cultures continues to be central to the agenda of Western, Eurocentric humanism. For instance, in one chapter Henry Louis Gates, Jr, provides a fascinating example of a minority intellectual. Alexander Crummell accepted Euro-American hegemony so thoroughly that, after learning Greek to prove that he was civilized, he dismissed all African languages as 'the speech of rude barbarians' and as 'marked by brutal and vindictive sentiments, and those principles which show a predominance of the animal propensities'. To the extent that we minority intellectuals still communicate professionally in European languages and within the 'truth' of Western discourse rather than in our own languages and discourses, we are heirs of Crummell. Every time we speak or write in English, French, German, or another dominant European language, we pay homage to Western intellectual and political hegemony. Many such examples of how minority intellectuals were subjugated and 'subjectified' by Western 'humanistic' discursive practices can be adduced. Usually, however, we tend to distance such 'subjectification', either historically – it used to happen in the past – or spatially – it happens to other people.

Given this tendency to repress the current political context of minority cultures, one cannot overemphasize that Western humanism still considers us barbarians beyond the pale of civilization; we are forever consigned to play the role of the ontological, political, economic, and cultural Other according to the schema of a Manichaean allegory that seems the central trope not only of colonialist discourse but also of Western humanism. The hegemonic pressures that forced Crummell to reconstruct his entire world in accordance with the values of the Manichaean allegory – that allowed him to define the African past in totally negative terms and the European past in totally positive ones – are just as prevalent today, in spite of what we have been led to believe by the abolition of slavery, the 'success' of the Civil Rights movement, and the admission of a handful of minorities and women to the academy. Apt evidence of this state of affairs was ironically provided by the negative response of the National Endowment for the Humanities (NEH) to our application for funding the 1986 conference 'The Nature and Context of Minority Discourse'.

Documents furnished by NEH clearly show the determining criterion for its decision to reject our application. Of the external reviews solicited by NEH, five were to be returned to NEH by 7 November 1985, and one was to be returned 'ASAP'. Some of the initial five reviewers had minor reservations about our proposal, but all recommended funding the conference. However, the review solicited in haste recommended rejection, and the summary of the NEH panel discussion makes clear that our proposal was indeed rejected on the basis of this evaluation. After praising the credentials of the conference organizer, the 'ASAP' reviewer provides fascinating reasons for his negative evaluation.

> I cannot but feel that a conference that would bring together in a few days of papers and discussion specialists on Chicano, Afro-American, Asian-American, Native-American, Afro-Caribbean, African, Indian, Pacific island, Aborigine, Maori, and other ethnic literature would be anything but diffuse. A conference on ONE of these literatures might be in order; but even with the best of planning, the proposed conference would almost certainly devolve into an academic tower of Babel. It is not at all clear that a specialist on Native-American literature, for example, will have much to say to someone specializing in African literature. It is also unlikely that the broad generalizations Professor JanMohamed would have them address would bring them any closer.

The ideological implications of this evaluation are self-evident. First, when Europeans come together to discuss their various national literatures, they are seen as being able to communicate coherently across linguistic barriers, and such coherence is not only encouraged in conferences but even institutionalized in the form of comparative literature departments in various universities across the country; in contrast, when ethnic minorities and Third World peoples want to have similar discussions, their dialogue is represented, according to the ideology of humanism, as incoherent babble, even though they propose to use a single dominant European language for this purpose. Second, Western humanists find it inconceivable that Native-Americans, Africans, and others who have been brutalized by Euro-American imperialism and marginalized by its hegemony can have anything relevant to say to each other. Third, ethnic minorities must be prevented from getting 'close' to each other, through broad generalizations or any other means. Eighteenth-century statutes in South Carolina and other states made the desire of black Americans to acquire literacy a criminal offense, and various colonialist educational policies systematically repressed native education, as South Africa still does. We are now allowed to learn the master's language, but our use of it to discuss the issues that most concern us is still defined as babble, an 'incoherence' that Eurocentric humanist discourse still needs to pose as a foil to its own civilized coherence.

II

Given such a historically sustained negation of minority voices, we must realize that minority discourse is, in the first instance, the product of damage – damage more or less systematically inflicted on cultures produced as minorities by the dominant culture. The destruction involved is manifold, bearing down on variant modes of social formation, dismantling previously functional economic systems, and deracinating whole populations at best or decimating them at worst. In time, with this material destruction, the cultural formations, languages, and diverse modes of identity of the 'minoritized peoples' are irreversibly affected, if not eradicated, by the effects of their material deracination from the historically developed social and economic structures in terms of which alone they 'made sense'. With a certain savage consistency, this very truncation of development becomes both the mark and the legitimation of marginalization. The diverse possible modes of cultural development that these societies represent are displaced by a single model of historical development within which other cultures can only be envisaged as underdeveloped, imperfect, childlike, or – when already deracinated by material domination – inauthentic, perverse, or criminal. From this perspective, such cultures are seen as capable of development toward a higher level of cultural achievement only through assimilation to that already attained by those of European stock. Even the majority culture's recognition of the damage already inflicted can be converted, with a *frisson* of charitable pathos, into a stimulus toward the more rapid assimilation of 'disadvantaged' minorities to the dominant culture's modes of being.

It is crucial, especially in the context of a volume that seeks in a sense to celebrate the positive achievements and potential of minority discourse, to stress the real and continuing damage inflicted on minorities. The pathos of hegemony is frequently matched by its interested celebration of differences, but only of differences in the aestheticized form of recreations. Detached from the site of their production, minority cultural forms become palatable: a form of practical struggle like *capoeira*, a form of defense developed by Brazilian slaves whose physical movements were severely restricted by chains, becomes recuperable first as a Hollywood spectacle of break dancing and then as a form of aerobics. Attending to minority cultural forms requires accordingly a double vigilance, both with respect to their availability for hegemonic recuperation and to their strategies of resistance (strategies that will always be referable to the specific material conditions from which such forms are produced). Minority discourse is in this respect a mode of ideology in the sense in which Marx in 'On the Jewish Question' described religion – at once the sublimation and the expression of misery – but with the critical difference that in the case of minority forms even the sublimation of misery needs to be understood as primarily a strategy for survival, for the preservation in some form or other of cultural identity, *and* for political critique. For example, the Afro-American culture, to the extent that African slaves were deprived of their own cultures and prevented from entering white American culture, can function as a paradigm of minority cultures. Houston Baker, Jr, has pointed out that in Afro-American culture this sublimation and expression of misery – a comprehension and a critique – find their unique form in the blues matrix, 'a mediational site where familiar antinomies are resolved . . . in the office of adequate cultural understanding'. This sublimation and expression, then, are not imposed from above by the dominant culture, nor are they the form in which that culture misrecognizes or legitimates its oppressive practices. Rather, cultural practices are an intrinsic element of the economic and political struggles of Third World and minority peoples. Indeed, exactly to the extent that such peoples are systematically marginalized *vis-à-vis* the global economy, one might see the resort to cultural modes of struggle as all the more necessary, even within the framework of a Marxist analysis of such struggles. For many minorities, culture is not a mere superstructure; all too often, in an ironic twist of a Sartrean phenomenology, the physical survival of minority groups depends on the recognition of its culture as viable.

One aspect of the struggle between hegemonic culture and minorities is the recovery and mediation of cultural practices that continue to be subjected to 'institutional forgetting', which, as a form of control of one's memory and history, is one of the gravest forms of damage done to minority cultures. Archival work, as a form of counter-memory, therefore is essential to the critical articulation of minority discourse. Since ethnic and women's studies departments and programs were instituted in the late sixties, such archival work has continued apace. However, if the previously marginalized production of minority cultures is not to be relegated by the force of dominant culture to the mere repetition of ethnic or feminine exotica, theoretical reflection cannot be omitted. Such theory would be obliged to provide a sustained critique of the historical conditions and formal qualities of the institutions that have continued to legitimize exclusion and marginalization in the name of universality. One must always keep in mind that the universalizing humanist project has been highly selective, systematically valorizing certain texts and authors as *the* humanist tradition while ignoring or actively repressing alternative traditions and attitudes.

The 'inadequacy' or 'underdevelopment' ascribed to minority texts and authors by a dominant humanism in the end only reveals the limiting (and limited) ideological horizons of that dominant, ethnocentric perspective. Because the dominant culture occludes minority discourse by making minority texts unavailable – either literally through publishers and libraries or, more subtly, through an implicit theoretical perspective that is structurally blind to minority concerns – one of the first tasks of a re-emergent minority culture is to break out from such ideological encirclement. In such an endeavor, theoretical and archival work of minority culture must always be concurrent and mutually reinforcing: a sustained theoretical critique of the dominant culture's apparatus both eases the task of recovering and mediating marginalized work and permits us to elucidate the full significance of the specific modes of resistance – and celebration – those works contain. However, neither the theoretical nor the archival work can afford to stop with establishing the validity of the achievements and values of marginalized cultures. The danger remains that these cultures will thus be recuperated, as Deleuze and Guattari put it, into 'performing a major function'. Unmediated by a theoretical perspective, the mere affirmation of achievement lends itself too easily to selective recuperation into the dominant culture, which always regards individual minority achievement as symptomatic of what (given a certain level of 'development') a depoliticized 'humanity' in general is capable.

As the affirmation of a universal humanity, which is always an ideological postulate in so far as its real conditions are not yet given, such premature integration is exactly what is to be avoided. Those who argue for the creation of canons of various ethnic and feminist writings do so with the full awareness that the formation of different canons permits the self-definition and, eventually, self-validation that must be completed before any consideration of integration. To date, integration and assimilation have never taken place on equal terms, but always as assimilation by the dominant culture. In relations with the dominant culture, the syncretic movement is always asymmetrical: although members of the dominant culture rarely feel obliged to comprehend various ethnic cultures, minorities are always obliged, in order to survive, to master the hegemonic culture (without thereby necessarily gaining access to the power that circulates within the dominant sector). To believe otherwise is either naïve or self-serving and denies the fact that cultural struggle continues at every level, in many ways, and, most importantly, at the theoretical level. For example, to argue that one has never considered oneself 'minor' and then to complain that ethnic literatures have traditionally been marginalized is to confuse cultural pride with the nature of current political reality (for, surely, it is the political situation of an ethnic literature, not the strength or weakness of one's pride, that renders it 'minor'). This kind of conflation can be avoided when theory works in conjunction with archival projects: the theoretical and archival struggle must continue jointly so long as the culture of domination persists globally.

Minority discourse must similarly be wary of 'pluralism', which, along
with assimilation, continues to be the Great White Hope of conservatives
and liberals alike. The semblance of pluralism disguises the perpetuation
of exclusion in so far as it is enjoyed only by those who have already
assimilated the values of the dominant culture. For this pluralism, ethnic
or cultural difference is merely an exoticism, an indulgence that can be
relished without significantly modifying the individual who is securely
embedded in the protective body of dominant ideology. Such pluralism
tolerates the existence of salsa, it even enjoys Mexican restaurants, but
it bans Spanish as a medium of instruction in American schools. Above
all, it refuses to acknowledge the class basis of discrimination and the
systematic economic exploitation of minorities that underlie postmodern
culture.

However, an emergent theory of minority discourse must not be
merely negative in its implications. Rather, the critique of the apparatus
of universalist humanism entails a second theoretical task permitted by
the recovery of excluded or marginalized practices. The positive
theoretical work involves a critical-discursive articulation of alternative
practices and values that are embedded in the often-damaged,
-fragmentary, -hampered, or -occluded works of minorities. This is
not to reassert the exclusive claim of the dominant culture that
objective grounds for marginalization can be read in the inadequacy or
underdevelopment of 'minority' work. On the contrary, it is to assert
that even the very differences that have always been read as symptoms
of inadequacy can be reread transformatively as indications and
figurations of values radically opposed to those of the dominant culture.
A theory of minority discourse is essential precisely for the purposes of
such a reinterpretation, for, in practice, the blindness of dominant theory
and culture towards the positive values of minority culture can easily
engulf us. Because we, the critics of minority culture, have been formed
within the dominant culture's educational apparatus and continue to
operate under its (relatively tolerant) constraints, we are always in
danger of reproducing the dominant ideology in our reinterpretations
unless we theoretically scrutinize our critical tools and methods and
the very categories of our epistemology, aesthetics, and politics. In the
task of re-evaluating values, our marginality can be our chief asset.

For example, in rejecting the premature avowal of humanist
pluralism, the theory of minority discourse should neither fall back
on ethnicity or gender as an a priori essence nor rush into inculcating
some 'non-humanist' celebration of diversity for its own sake. Rather,
ethnic or gender differences must be perceived as one of many residual
cultural elements; they retain the memory of practices that have had to
be (and still have to be) repressed so that the capitalist economic subject
may be more efficiently produced. The theoretical project of minority

discourse involves drawing out solidarities in the form of similarities between modes of repression and struggle that all minorities experience separately but experience precisely as minorities. 'Becoming minor' is not a question of essence (as the stereotypes of minorities in dominant ideology would want us to believe) but a question of position: a subject-position that in the final analysis can be defined only in 'political' terms – that is, in terms of the effects of economic exploitation, political disenfranchisement, social manipulation, and ideological domination on the cultural formation of minority subjects and discourses. The project of systematically articulating the implications of that subject-position – a project of exploring the strengths and weaknesses, the affirmations and negations that are inherent in that position – must be defined as *the* central task of the theory of minority discourse.

Deleuze and Guattari's observation that 'minor' literature is necessarily collective here gains its validity. Out of the damage inflicted on minority cultures, which, as Fanon so clearly recognized, prevents their 'development' according to the Western model of individual and racial identity, emerges the possibility of a collective subjectivity formed in practice rather than contemplation. For the collective nature of minority discourse is due not to the scarcity of talent, as Deleuze and Guattari claim, but to other cultural and political factors. In those societies caught in the transition from oral, mythic, and collective cultures to the literate, 'rational', and individualistic values and characteristics of Western cultures, the writer more often than not manifests the collective nature of social formation in forms such as the novel, thus transforming what were once efficacious vehicles for the representation of individually, atomistically oriented experiences into collective modes of articulation. However, more importantly, the collective nature of all minority discourse also derives from the fact that minority individuals are always treated and forced to experience themselves generically. Coerced into a negative, generic subject-position, the oppressed individual responds by transforming that position into a positive, collective one. Therein lies the basis of a broad minority coalition: in spite of the enormous differences among various minority cultures, which must be preserved, all of them occupy the same oppressed and 'inferior' cultural, political, economic, and material subject-position in relation to the Western hegemony. Just as it is vitally important to avoid the homogenization of cultural differences, so it is equally important to recognize the common political basis of a minority struggle. The minority's attempt to negate the prior hegemonic negation of itself is one of its most fundamental forms of affirmation.

The theory of minority discourse raises yet another question: what does the 'becoming minor' of theory and pedagogy entail? Clearly, it necessitates far-reaching transformations of cultural or 'humanist' education. At the level of content, what is required in the way of introducing new material to syllabi and new courses to major programs is simple enough to outline but in practice significantly difficult to achieve, as any who have made the attempt will testify. At the level of form, the emerging theoretical synthesis entails not only the study of different material but also the effective transgression of current disciplinary divisions. For example, the study of minority cultures cannot be conducted without at least a relevant knowledge of sociology, political theory, economics, and history; otherwise, the specifics of the struggles embodied in cultural forms remain invisible. The ground for such changes in the form of pedagogy is the refusal of the assumption of the timeless universality of cultural products and of the concomitant tendency to read cultural texts exclusively for their representation of 'aesthetic' effects and 'essential' human values. For the premature claim to represent a realm of aesthetic freedom and disinterest has time and again legitimated the political quietism of academic institutions. That claim must be rejected as masking the very real damage inflicted by dominant culture on its minorities.

III

In this inevitably gradual process of revaluing values, which perforce advances only by glimpse and paradox toward systematic formulations, the role of the intellectual becomes doubly problematic, for the intellectual is twice marginalized by the institutional structures within which he or she must work (and which are as much a part of the quotidian world of practice in contemporary Western society as factory or home). The intellectual appreciates the collective nature of minority cultures yet is cut off from those cultures by virtue of the relative privilege offered by educational institutions as part of their hegemonizing function. More often than not, the minority intellectual is also marginalized within the institution, in part individually as a direct result of continuing racial or sexual discrimination, but more importantly (since it is here a question of an effect of structure) as a result of the systemic relegation of minority concerns to the periphery of academic work. No moral pathos attaches to this double alienation of the minority intellectual, unpleasant as its effects may be, for both forms of alienation spring as inevitably from the modes of late capitalist society as do the systematic exploitation of less-privileged minority groups, the feminization of poverty, the demonization of Third World peoples, and homophobic hysteria. The dual alienation of minority intellectuals derives not from the universal anomie of spirits in the material world nor even from the intrinsic 'difficulties' of the theoretical work in which they may be engaged. Both aspects derive, rather, from the division of labor required by economic rationalization and by the need to denigrate alternative modes of rationality as, in Sylvia Wynter's phrase, the 'ontological Other'.

Unfortunately, an alienation so systematically produced cannot be overcome simply by wishful identification with an abstractly idealized 'minority collective', because both the alienation of the minority intellectual and the collective identity that can emerge in the struggle against domination are recto and verso of the same process of rational division of labor – two complementary modes of the damage it inflicts. To overcome the situation will entail a mutually complementary work of theoretical critique and practical struggle, which clearly will take different forms in different spheres. Although the intellectual cannot prescribe what is to be done in other spheres, within the academic sphere there are transformations to be effected that will necessarily complement those undertaken by minorities elsewhere.

The foremost of these transformations is the critique and reformulation of the traditional role of humanist intellectuals and of the disciplinary divisions that sanction that role. The systemic function of the traditional humanist intellectual has always ultimately been the legitimation of the sets of discriminations required for economic and social domination. The very claim to universality that humanism makes, while utopian in itself, is annulled by the developmental schema of world history through which it is to be achieved. Accordingly, actual exploitation is legitimated from the perspective of a perpetually deferred universality. Although the phenomena of exploitation may without doubt be criticized well-meaningly on individual grounds, a critique of the rationale underlying the distinctions that legitimate exploitation cannot be produced systematically out of traditional humanism.

Herein lies the specific difference between the objective alienation, which the minority intellectual seeks to overcome, and the pathos of alienation, which afflicts the traditional humanist: the minority intellectual is situationally opposed to the alienation, while the traditional intellectual seeks either to make the characteristics of the alien prefigurative of deferred universality or (in a recent, insidiously logical development of the former version) to accept positivistically as merely given the alienated conditions of labor in the glorified form of 'professionalism'. Knowing that exploitation and discrimination are neither the inevitable products of universal history nor rationally justifiable but, rather, are the products of concrete and contestable historical developments, the minority intellectual is committed to the critique of the structures that continue to legitimate them.

The minority intellectual must also be committed to a reappraisal of 'affirmative action', which in the humanities has meant either the creation of special units – separate departments of ethnic studies, women's studies, and (with conspicuous scarcity) gay–lesbian studies – that have been relegated to the margins of the universities or the employment of one or two minority individuals in a large department. At best, such action has confined itself to the quantitative level; it has resulted in a few more minority intellectuals in the academy. However, we must now move beyond numerical presence and special programs. What we must require from the institutions and from ourselves is the intellectual equivalent of 'affirmative action'. In the first place, we must see that a 'humanism' that systematically ignores all issues concerned with the relations of domination, as it has done at least since Matthew Arnold consigned the dominated to the realm of anarchy, is in a sense profoundly bankrupt. Because relations of domination permeate every facet of our personal and social lives as well as of our literature and culture, a critique of culture that ignores such relations can be, at best, a distorted one. From a minority viewpoint, a viable humanism must be centered on a critique of domination. In the second place, it follows that most of those who hold power and those whose subject-positions are protected by the prevailing hegemony will be more interested in the efficacious use of power than in examining its misuse. In contrast, those who are dominated will understand the devastating effects of misused power; they are in a better position to document and analyse, as the contemporary resurgence in black women's writing illustrates, how relations of domination can destroy the 'human' potential of its victims. The concerns of the victims of domination must be at the center not only of a minority discourse but also of non-Eurocentric, non-aestheticizing 'humanism' – that is, of a Utopian exploration of human potentiality.

IV

Minority discourse implies that it is the perpetual return of theory to the concrete givens of domination, rather than the separation of culture as a discrete sphere, that militates against the reification of any dominated group's experience as in some sense 'privileged'. Just as domination works by constant adjustment, so the strategies of the dominated must remain fluid in their objects as in their solidarities. Apposite here is Sylvia Wynter's critique in her chapter of the various 'isms' that single out particular specifications of 'ontological otherness' as a unique field of political action: the tactical necessities that determine such maneuvers ossify only too rapidly into new domains of relative privilege, leaving, as the racial bias of even the feminization of poverty indicates, a bottom line of discrimination and exclusion that imposes all the more on those who suffer from it. This critique of former and current practices of minority groups implies, on the one hand, that minority groups need constantly to form and to re-form ever-more-inclusive solidarities and, on the other, that the material and intellectual formations by which 'minorities' are constituted must be put under ever-increasing pressure. The two programs are complementary of course; the critique of the current basis of disciplinary divisions within the academic institutions and the consequent, at first experimental, production of other syntheses or bodies of knowledge will lead inevitably to the erosion of those structures by which the marginalization of 'special programs' is justified. In time, the experimental nature of these new syntheses will give way to an increasingly systematic refutation of the pseudoscientific and pseudorational formulations on whose basis minorities continue to be oppressed.

From the present, necessarily limited perspective, it seems sure that, whatever shifts of this nature minorities will prove capable of effecting, they will at least be unsatisfactory in so far as they do not permit a far greater real acceptance of difference and diversity than is currently evident in any sphere of Western society. The realization of the goal of true acceptance will depend not on an epochal rupture at the discursive level – a hope that would retain a large element of idealism – but on radical transformations of the material structures of exploitation. The effectiveness of any new formations we can intellectually project could be predicated on such transformations alone, and to think otherwise in the context of continuing genocide, exploitation, and technological destruction is to risk an impermissible disproportion. But this is not, at the other extreme, to relegate intellectual work to perpetual adventism, an idealistic waiting for some historically inevitable precipitation of a class formation powerful enough to 'smash the system'. Openings for intervention are various and multiple at any moment, and indeed most of the terms of a critical minority discourse have been forged precisely in the practices of engaged minority groups. To cling solely to the role of an 'intellectual' as to a singular and determinate identity would be fatuous where the process of the rational division of labor has made of every modern subject a fragmented or multiple identity, who functions now as a professor, now as one among women, now as a tenant, now as a black employee, now as a lesbian feminist. The gain that can be located in this situation by a critical minority discourse lies in the recognition that these multiple identities are neither reducible nor impermeable to one another, that there is no sphere of universal and objective knowledge or of purely economic rationality, that what is worked out in one sphere can be communicated in another, and that institutional boundaries will always need to be transgressed in the interests of political and cultural struggle. In so far as the practices that emerge in any of these spheres remain referable to the fundamental goal of a society based on the possibility of uncoerced *economic* self-determination (the only foundation on which effective political or cultural self-determination can be based), they do not become isolated and abstract Utopian activities.

The effort of critical minority discourse to produce social and cultural formations genuinely tolerant of difference and to critique the dominant structures that tend to reduce the human to a single universal mode accounts for its apparent affinities to post-structuralism and postmodernism. It is essential not to collapse the distinction between the discourses of minorities and Third World groups and those of Western intellectuals; above all, apparently postmodern minority texts must not be seen as representations of the dissolving bourgeois subject. Certainly there is an overlap, especially in the realm of gender issues, and virtually without exception the contributors to this volume owe much methodologically to the critical reading of post-structuralist writings. But where the point of departure of post-structuralism lies within the Western tradition and tries to deconstruct its identity formations 'from within', the critical difference is that minorities, by virtue of their very social being, must begin from a position of objective non-identity that is rooted in their economic and cultural marginalization *vis-à-vis* the 'West'. The non-identity that the critical Western intellectual seeks to (re)produce discursively is for minorities a given of their social existence. But as such a given, it is not yet by any means an index of liberation, not even of the formal and abstract liberation, which is all that post-structuralism, in itself and disarticulated from any actual process of struggle, could offer. On the contrary, the non-identity of minorities remains the sign of material damage to which the only coherent response is struggle, not ironic distance. To be sure, the fact that the material damage is legitimated by humanist institutions and their universal claims entails as its logical corollary the demystification of 'the figure of man'. And to be sure, the non-identity experienced by minorities as the oppressive effects of Western philosophies of identity is the strongest reason that a rigorously critical minority discourse, in its positive transformation of the discourses emerging from that non-identity, should not merely fall back on the oppositional affirmation of an essential ethnic or gender identity. In minority discourse, the abstract philosophical questions of essence and ethics are transformed into questions of practice; the only meaningful response to the question, 'What is or ought to be?', has to be the question, 'What is to be done?'

10 From *In Theory:*
*Classes, Nations, Literatures**

AIJAZ AHMAD

Of the various critiques of postcolonial criticism, whether from those outside or within the field, Ahmad's text is probably the most substantial, interesting and systematic and certainly the most biting. For Ahmad, postcolonial theory in particular (Said and Bhabha are the principal targets here, though African–American criticism and Commonwealth literary studies also receive a mauling), represents a disastrous domestication of 'real' material struggles against Western domination into a safely discursive realm which exists comfortably as a new branch of the West's traditional culture industries (of which Orientalism is equally a part). In Ahmad's eyes, postcolonial criticism sees reading (or literary criticism) as the most appropriate and effective form of resistance and by virtue of its focus on colonial discourse as the privileged object of analysis, it avoids having to grapple with the much more pressing questions raised by contemporary global cultural relations. Postcolonial theory is, moreover, deemed to be radically compromised in so far as it is, in general, addressed to a Western audience and methodologically dependent on contemporary European 'high' theory which, Ahmad points out, achieved the high point of its influence in the Anglo-American academy in the era of Thatcher and Reagan. From this perspective, Ahmad sees postcolonial critics as a new kind of collaborationist class of 'interpreters' or 'native inform-ants', who function as intermediaries between their Western masters and cultures of origin.

Ahmad proposes to replace postcolonial criticism altogether and subsume its objects of interest into a much older (but, his critics might argue, nonetheless equally 'academic') tradition of cultural criticism, namely Marxism. For Ahmad, Marxism provides a number of sig-nificant advantages over the current configurations of postcolonial

---

*Extracts from *In Theory: Classes, Nations, Literatures* (London: Verso, 1992), pp. 34–42, 64–71, 84–94.

criticism. First of all, its focus on class dispenses with the necessity of the 'Three Worlds' theory. Ahmad argues persuasively that the world economy now functions as an integrated unit in which the world's workers must unite in a common struggle against a globally-dispersed bourgeoisie and the flows of international capital. This kind of approach also avoids the pitfalls of organizing against the dominant order through the mediation of 'Third World' nationalisms. Ahmad sees these as largely shaped, even determined, by the same epistemologies and political values as the colonizing formations, which perpetuated their authority while ceding the outward forms of power to a compliant local national(ist) bourgeoisie. Ahmad also argues that privileging nationalism as the prime locus of the struggle against (neo-)colonialism downplays other forms of resistance, such as those based on identities defined by gender and sexuality as well as class. The force of Ahmad's argument derives in large part from his insistence on the continuing legitimacy of a traditional conception of what constitutes 'the political'. In his eyes, the relationship between the West and non-West continues to be exploitative to a degree which means that opposition to the international division of labour must necessarily take material, 'public', even confrontational forms.

Facts require explanations, and all explanations, even bad ones, presume a configuration of concepts, which we provisionally call 'theory'. In other words, theory is not simply a desirable but a *necessary* relation between facts and their explanations. That anti-colonial nationalism was a tremendous historical force until about the mid 1970s is a fact. That this force declined sharply in the succeeding years is also a fact. So is the defeat of the revolutionary movements which sought to replace colonial societies with socialist societies, and so is the assimilation of the nationalism of the national bourgeoisie into the globally overarching imperialist structure. It is also a fact that a very unequal kind of war between imperialism and socialism has raged in a great many places around the globe throughout most of this century, and that this war has now been won by imperialism, for the remainder of this century at least. It is not possible to pose questions about colony and empire, and about their representations in cultural products, without possessing a theory of such facts.

Marxism provides a particular constellation of concepts to account for facts of this order. Within this conceptual apparatus, there is plenty of room for internal development and debate – which accounts for the most intense kinds of disagreements among Marxists themselves, as can be seen in a small way in the severity of my criticisms of Fredric Jameson [Chapter 3, *In Theory: Classes, Nations, Literatures*]. The

preceding two sections of this [Introduction] offer an outline of my
own understanding of recent history in accordance with the way I
understand those concepts, and this brief (non-literary) detour has been
necessary because the way we pose questions of colony and empire, in
literary or any other theory, depends very much on how we understand
the history of materialities within which these questions obtain their
objects and densities. The objective, in other words, is to make explicit
the premisses from which I offer my own readings of literary theory, as
well as to prepare the theoretical ground from which it is then possible
to argue that both Third-Worldist cultural nationalism and the more
recently fashionable postmodernisms offer false knowledges of real facts.

Other Marxists may well disagree with at least part of my account,
and shared understanding may well be the richer for such disagreements.
But a theoretical position that dismisses the history of materialities as a
'progressivist modes-of-production narrative', historical agency itself as
a 'myth of origins', nations and states (all nations and all states) as
irretrievably coercive, classes as simply discursive constructs, and political
parties themselves as fundamentally contaminated with collectivist
illusions of a stable subject position – a theoretical position of that
kind, from which no post-structuralism worth the name can escape,
is, in the most accurate sense of these words, *repressive* and *bourgeois*.[1]
It suppresses the very conditions of intelligibility within which the
fundamental facts of our time can be theorized; and in privileging the
figure of the reader, the critic, the theorist, as the guardian of the texts
of this world, where everything becomes a text, it recoups the main
cultural tropes of bourgeois humanism – especially in its Romantic
variants, since the dismissal of class and nation as so many 'essentialisms'
logically leads towards an ethic of non-attachment as the necessary
condition of true understanding, and because breaking away from
collective socialities of that kind inevitably leaves only the 'individual'
– in the most abstract sense epistemologically, but in the shape of the
critic/theorist concretely – as the locus of experience and meaning,
while the well-known poststructuralist scepticism about the possibility
of rational knowledge impels that same 'individual' to maintain only
an ironic relation with the world and its intelligibility.[2] I might add
that this issue of irony and non-attachment as regards literary post-
structuralism of the kind under discussion here surfaces in a variety of
ways: in the actual practice of the individual critics, in the ideological
positions they advocate, and in the heavily charged ways in which
conditions of postmodern 'migrancy' and the image of the theorist as
'traveler' are foregrounded.[3]

As one now examines that branch of literary theory which poses
those questions, one is struck by the fact that while the privileging
of cultural nationalism as the determinate political energy of our time

takes place under one or another variant of the Three Worlds Theory, the subsequent move *against* nationalism – all of it – is made under a completely different theoretical signature, that of post-structuralism. The two moments – politically, for and against nationalism; theoretically, Third-Worldism and post-structuralism – remain discrete and epiphenomenal, even though the more outlandish of the post-structuralists have tried to combine them. What this branch of literary theory has lacked is a larger configuration of concepts that may produce a systematic periodization of its own practices and of that world to which it constantly refers, so that it may overcome the discreteness of *moments* and their second-order explanations.[4] That is, I suppose, another way of saying that in renouncing Marxism and in developing a shrill rhetoric against historicism – not just the positivist and geneticist current in it, but historicism as such – avant-gardist literary theory has turned its back on modes of thought that might help it to grasp at least its own history.

My starting point [...], briefly put, is that the sizeable changes we have witnessed in the situation(s) of literary theory over the past quarter-century have occurred within the context of monumental and extremely rapid shifts in the economic and political orderings of the world, and that the surrender, in rapid succession, first to a Third-Worldist kind of nationalism and then to deconstruction – to post-structuralism generally, in fact – on the part of that branch of literary theory which is most engaged with questions of colony and empire conceals, instead of explaining, the relationships between literature, literary theory and that world of which these purport to be the literature and the theory. By the same token, then, the vicissitudes and even re-enactments of those more global realities in the shifting frames of literary theory become intelligible only if we connect the theory with the determinate and shaping forces of our time, not *through* post-structuralism but by examining, as a considerable issue in itself, the historical co-ordinates of the rise and fall of cultural nationalism as the master-code of this theory in its earlier phase, and then the turn away from activist kinds of politics – even nationalist politics – as this theory fully develops its post-structuralist complicities. I can illustrate this point with reference to a phenomenon that will be summarized here in very general outline but will receive considerable elaboration in the main body of this book.

We know that this branch of literary theory privileged cultural nationalism as the determinate ideological form of resistance against the dominant imperialist culture throughout the 1970s; but then, increasingly in the 1980s, nationalism itself, in all its forms, came to be discarded as an oppressive, coercive mechanism. I write at considerable length in Chapters 1 and 2 [of *In Theory, Classes, Nations, Literatures*]

251

about factors which contributed to the predominance of cultural nationalism for a time, and the sea-change in the fortunes of nationalist ideology within literary theory in the later years – as we go, for instance, from *Orientalism* to the later work of Said himself, or from Fredric Jameson to a whole host of lesser and later critics like Homi Bhabha – needs, of course, to be traced in relation to developments internal to literary theory itself. But the precise terms in which this shift away from cultural nationalism has taken place would be unintelligible without taking into account the ascendancy of post-structuralism, with its debunking of all myths of origin, totalizing narratives, determinate and collective historical agents – even the state and political economy as key sites for historical narrativization.

The newly dominant position of post-structuralist ideology is the fundamental enabling condition for a literary theory which debunks nationalism not on the familiar Marxist ground that nationalism in the present century has frequently suppressed questions of gender and class and has itself been frequently complicit with all kinds of obscurantisms and revanchist positions, but in the patently postmodernist way of debunking *all* efforts to speak of origins, collectivities, determinate historical projects. The upshot, of course, is that critics working within the post-structuralist problematic no longer distinguish, in any foregrounded way, between the progressive and retrograde forms of nationalism with reference to particular histories, nor do they examine the even more vexed question of how progressive and retrograde elements may be (and often are) combined within particular nationalist trajectories; what gets debunked, rather, is nationalism *as such*, in more or less the same apocalyptic manner in which cultural nationalism was, only a few years earlier, declared the determinate answer to imperialism.

Needless to add, a number of tendencies within 'Western Marxism', especially as they developed in the 1960s, contributed considerably to the latter ascendancy of post-structuralism. If Marcuse finally came to abandon the category of class and to locate the revolutionary dynamic in the realms of the erotic and the aesthetic, Adorno's extreme pessimism in *Minima Moralia* found its analogue in Sartre's proposition, in *Critique of Dialectical Reason*, that the category of 'scarcity' makes it virtually inevitable that any 'fused group' which comes to power will undergo bureaucratic degeneration. The central case, so far as literary theory is concerned, was of course that of Althusser, who has exercised very considerable influence on 'theory' on both sides of the Atlantic and whose affinities with structuralism are well enough known.[5] It is also significant that Althusser's conception of ideology simultaneously as an 'unconscious', as 'a system (with its own logic and rigour) of representations', as 'the "lived" relation between men and the world',[6] and as something which saturates virtually all conceivable 'apparatuses' in political society (the state),[7] makes it remarkably homologous with the concept of 'discourse' as it was to be developed in post-structuralist thought – chiefly by his renegade pupil Michel Foucault, with whom he shared a deep antipathy towards humanism, even though the two clashed on the status of Marxism, the historic role of the working class and, above all, the issue of practical involvement in communist politics.[8] And there is, of course, the accidental matter of temporal adjacency; even though the historical moment of 'Western Marxism' in its continental unfolding was largely different, its moment of arrival in the Anglo-American academy in fact coincided with the arrival of post-structuralism itself, in the mid to late 1970s. Philosophical affinity of discrete elements facilitated, then, the acceptance of [a] great many poststructuralist positions among literary theorists who came to it through the Althusserian route.

That post-structuralism, arising initially in fields as diverse as anthropology and philosophy, has given literary theory its present terms of thought, is obvious enough. But these changing fortunes of the nationalist ideology in the trajectories of literary theory are determined also – more decisively though less self-consciously on [the] part of the theorists themselves – by the actual fortunes of the national-bourgeois state in the decolonized countries. The years between 1945 and 1975 may be roughly designated the high period of decolonization. The first half of this thirty-year period witnessed the Chinese Revolution, the Korean War and the decolonization of [a] great many countries, including India, under the leadership of the national bourgeoisie, both medium and petty. The significant fact about this earlier phase is that neither the Chinese Revolution nor the Independence of India made much impact upon the literary intelligentsia – either in Britain as it recovered from the ravages of World War II, or in the United States as it descended into the most rabid kind of postwar reaction. Rather, it was in France that the successive shocks of the colonial wars in Indochina and North Africa, coming hot on the heels of the Nazi Occupation of France itself, tended to polarize the intelligentsia; the well-known confrontation between Sartre and Camus was the specific expression of a much broader polarization.

In the Anglo-American academy, the radicalizing impact came in the second phase of decolonization – ushered in, schematically speaking, by the Cuban Revolution (1958–59), Algerian independence (1962) and the onset of the Third Indochina War with the introduction of American troops during the Kennedy Administration. The Vietnam War was, of course, the central fact of the whole of this second phase, but the phase had two distinct and principal aspects: revolutionary wars of national liberation, mainly in countries of Indochina and Southern Africa, on the one hand; and, on the other, the consolidation of the national-bourgeois state in the majority of the Asian and African states that had been newly constituted as sovereign nations, where the expanding dynamic of global capitalism was bringing unprecedented growth and wealth to the newly dominant classes. This fundamental distinction between the revolutionary project in the countries under siege and of national-bourgeois consolidation in the rest was often erased from the dissenting ideologies that arose in the Anglo-American academy – except, of course, in those relatively small groups that had Marxist leanings or communist affiliation. In the anti-war movements of this period, the predominant sentiment was that of anti-colonialism, and the bulk of the mobilization, including the main organizers (the role of the Church and pacifist groups is usually understated in accounts from the Left), represented the political traditions essentially of decent liberalism thrown into agony by the scale of savagery and the number of American deaths. What this anti-war sentiment affirmed was the right of national self-determination, and it was in this period of the ascendancy of the national-bourgeois state that cultural nationalism – that is, the characteristic form of the nationalism of the national bourgeoisie – was declared to be the determinate ideological form for progressive cultural production.

This tendency was greatly augmented by the radical sectors of the Afro-American intelligentsia which identified deeply with the emergent groups in newly independent African countries, and by the students from Asia, Africa and the Caribbean who faced various kinds of racism in the Anglo-American academy and resisted that pressure by positing against it the literary documents and cultural practices of the social configurations that were dominant in their own societies but commanded no status in the Western canonical formations. This was a defensive ideology of parochial pride necessitated by the superior power of the metropolitan – predominantly white – academy, with the student coming to represent, in his own eyes as much as in his hosts', the culture of his nation and his newly independent state.[9] Meanwhile, the national-bourgeois state partly basked in the reflected glory of the wars of national liberation, hence in the general valorization of nationalism as such; in part, it was seen as the very expression of the aura of particular leaders – Nasser, Nehru, Nkrumah, Sukarno, Nyerere, Kenyatta, and others – who had led the movements of anti-colonial consolidation. Now, as the stagnation of that type of postcolonial state has become more obvious in more recent years, and as the perception of that stagnation coincided chronologically with the ascendancy of post-structuralism in literary theory, cultural nationalism itself is currently in the process of being discarded as illusion, myth, totalizing narrative.

These monolithic attitudes towards the issue of nationalism – shifting rapidly from unconditional celebration to contemptuous dismissal – are also a *necessary* outcome of a radical theory that is none the less pitched self-consciously against the well-known Marxist premisses and therefore comes to rely, consecutively and at times simultaneously, on the nationalistic versions of the Three Worlds Theory and deconstructionist kinds of post-structuralism. An obvious consequence of repudiating Marxism was that one now sought to make sense of the world of colonies and empires much less in terms of classes, much more in terms of nations and countries and races, and thought of imperialism itself not as a hierarchically structured system of global capitalism but as a *relation*, of governance and occupation, between richer and poorer countries, West and non-West. And whether one said so or not, one inevitably believed that ideas – 'culture' was the collective term in most mystifications, or 'discourse', but it mainly meant books and films – and not the material conditions of life which include the instance of culture itself, determine the fate of peoples and nations. All kinds of visionary hopes were provisionally attached to the ideologies of decolonization. With the colonial relationship broken, the newly independent states were expected to combat imperialism with their nationalist *ideologies*, regardless of what classes were now in power and irrespective of the utter inadequacy of the nationalist ideology as such, even at its best, to protect a backward capitalist country against the countless pressures of advanced capitalism, so long as the confrontation takes place within an imperialist structure – which is to say, on capitalist terms. When the limits of the nationalism of the national bourgeoisie became altogether evident, the hostility toward rigorous kinds of Marxism that had been assimilated from the postmodern avant-garde made it impossible for this literary theory to produce a rationally historicized autocritique of its own prior enthusiasms for that kind of homogenized nationalism. Instead, post-structuralism itself was offered as the determinate answer to nationalism, while – in at least some versions – some discrete elements of Marxism (not to speak of feminism) were reworked into the subordinate clauses of post-structuralism. We thus have a specific conjunction of elements: a radical literary theory in the moment of repudiating the Marxist component of its own past; the rise and fall of the national-bourgeois state in the 'Third World' as the object of this radicalism's passion; capitalism's global offensive and, by the late 1980s, its global triumph; the ascendancy, in the theoretical realm, of post-structuralism. The rise and fall of nationalist ideology in the recent history of this literary theory is thus conjoined with other theoretical developments as well as with more directly political developments in the world. [. . .]

I have presented a very complex history in such telegraphic terms with three purposes in mind. First, I want to emphasize the sheer weight of reactionary positions in the Anglo-American literary formations. Second, I do want to stress the gains which have been made there since the 1960s, despite the havoc caused recently by the more mindless kinds of post-structuralism; for the first time in its history the metropolitan university is being forced, in some of its nooks and niches, to face issues of race and gender and empire in a way it has never done before. One simply has to compare the nature and breadth of today's debates on these issues with the absence of such debates in the 1950s, and even the 1930s, to grasp the degree of change. But, third, I also want to stress that the political vagrancy of much of the radical literary intelligentsia in the United States is such that it has been difficult – so far impossible, in fact – to constitute a properly Marxist political or literary culture, on any appreciable scale. The fundamental and constant danger faced by each radicalism – whether Black, or feminist, or Third-Worldist – is the danger of embourgeoisement. And the triple signs under which radical movements of this kind are at length assimilated into the main currents of bourgeois culture itself are the signs, these days, of Third-Worldist nationalism, essentialism, and the currently fashionable theories of the fragmentation and/or death of the Subject: the politics of discrete exclusivities and localisms on the one hand, or, on the other – as some of the post-structuralisms would have it – the very *end* of the social, the *impossibility* of stable subject positions, hence the *death* of politics as such. In more recent years, of course, we have also witnessed many attempts to reconcile Third-Worldist nationalism with post-structuralism itself.

These possibilities of internal erosion, which exist within the body of the radical discourse as it were, are then greatly augmented, from the outside, by the enormous pressures of the lingering Thatcherite–Reaganite consensus in the metropolitan culture at large. This consensus, especially aggressive now in the moment of imperialism's greatest triumph in its history, is unwilling to grant any considerable space to fundamental dissent of *any* kind, so that demands even for simple decency – that non-Western texts be integrated into the basic syllabuses, that women have the right to abortion or equal pay or the writing of their own history, that normative pressures concede ground to individual sexual choice – are construed as mad attacks on Western civilization and 'family values', and as outright degenerations against which 'the American mind', as Alan Bloom tendentiously calls it, needs to defend itself. I cannot analyse the structure of that pressure here, but a particular consequence is that the individual practitioner of academic radicalism comes to occupy so beleaguered a space that any critical engagement with the limitations of one's own intellectual and political formation becomes difficult. The Right's attack tends, rather, to confirm the sense of one's own achievement. This power of the Right more or less to dictate the terms of engagement, not only in the academy but (even more so) in the culture at large, is surely not a *creation* of the university-based Left – it is, rather, evidence of the Right's power, and sets the objective limits for the Left itself. This pressure on the public space available for dialogues and projects of the Left also has the potential, however, of disorientating further theoretical development inside the restricted space that still does exist.

Those younger literary theorists in Britain and North America who had come out of the student movements of the late 1960s and early 1970s, and started their academic careers more or less after the cooling of America began with Nixon's second Presidential term and as Britain started skidding from the Wilsonian variants of Labourism to outright Thatcherite reaction, found their radicalism caught in a series of contradictions. The *international situation* which had framed much of their radicalism had been intensely revolutionary: the Vietnam War, the Chinese Cultural Revolution, the wars of liberation in the Portuguese colonies, the immensely powerful figures of Fidel and Che Guevara, the victory of *Unidad Popular* in Chile, the student uprisings from Mexico City to Paris to Lahore. Their *academic* training, meanwhile, had been an affair mainly of choosing between 'New Criticism' on the one hand, Frye and Bloom and Paul de Man on the other. Few enough had negotiated, by then, their way through Lukács; Gramsci was then almost entirely unknown in the English-speaking world, and much of the best of Raymond Williams was yet to come. The gap between what moved them politically and what they were doing academically was large enough, but then there was the 'movement' of which they had been, unevenly, a part. Those who were politically the most involved rarely found a coherent organizing centre for their activity once the intensity of the mobilization had peaked; those who found such a centre, for good or ill, disappeared into the anonymity of direct political work; few enough finished their PhDs, and those who did rarely gained the academic sophistication to become theorists. Those who became theorists had been, as a rule, only marginally involved in the *political* movement. Most of them had known the 'movement' mostly in its other kinds of social emphases: certainly the music, the alternative readings of Laing and Marcuse, surely the occasional demonstration – but there had been, through it all, the pressure to write brilliant term papers and equally brilliant dissertations. It was, in other words, mostly the *survivors* of the 'movement' who later became so successful in the profession. Radicalism had been, for most of them, a state of mind, brought about by an intellectual identification with the revolutionary wave that had gripped so much of the world when they were truly young; of the day-to-day drudgeries of, say, a political party or a trade union they had been (and were to remain) largely innocent.

By the time they had secured their teaching positions, the international situation itself had changed. In the metropolises, the Civil Rights Movement had been contained through patronage for segments of the Black petty bourgeoisie, the political content of the anti-war movement frittered away after the retreat of US troops from Vietnam, and Paris itself was normalized soon after the uprising. The cycles of economic recession and stagnation which set in during the early 1970s had the effect, furthermore, of putting the movements for social justice on the defensive. In the imperialized world, meanwhile, Chile was decisively beaten, Cuba contained, China largely incorporated, and the wave of anti-capitalist revolutions was mainly over by the mid 1970s. The revolutionary states which arose at that time were encircled economically and derailed by invasions and insurgencies that were engineered through surrogates; none of them, from Angola to Vietnam, was allowed to become a model of development for postcolonial societies. The revolutionary upheavals which occurred thereafter – in Ethiopia or Afghanistan, for example – had problematic beginnings at best, originating in the radical sectors of the military. Their subsequent development was no better than that of other regimes based on the 'progressive' *coups d'état* elsewhere in Asia and Africa. In other words, for the revolutionary movements and states of the postcolonial world, this was a period of retreat and even outright disorientation.

In a parallel movement, moreover, this was also a period of increasing consolidation of the bourgeois nation-state in much of the rest of the postcolonial world. The international focus shifted accordingly, from revolutionary war ('Two, Three, Many... Vietnams') to such strategies for favourable terms of incorporation within the capitalist world as the Non-Aligned Movement, the North–South Dialogue, UNCTAD, the New Economic Order, the Group 77 at the United Nations, or commodity cartels such as OPEC. If in 1968 the epoch had seemed to belong to the revolutionary vanguard, it seemed to belong now, as the 1980s dawned, to the national bourgeoisie. Radical thought in the universities paid its homage to this new consolidation of the postcolonial national bourgeoisies by shifting its focus, decisively, from socialist revolution to Third-Worldist nationalism – first in political theory, then in its literary reflections.

It was in this moment of retreat for socialism, and resurgence of the nationalism of the national bourgeoisie, that the *theoretical* category of 'Third World Literature' arose, as did the new emphasis on analyses of the 'Colonial Discourse', pushing the focus of thought not into the future but into the past. Since nationalism had been designated during this phase as the determinate source of ideological energy in the Third World by those same critics who had themselves been influenced mainly by post-structuralism, the disillusionment with the (national-bourgeois) state of the said Third World which began to set in towards the later 1980s then led those avant-garde theorists to declare that post-structuralism and deconstruction were the determinate theoretical positions for the critique of nationalism itself. Edward Said is thus quite astute in describing Ranajit Guha, and by extension the Subalternist project as a whole, as 'post-structuralist'.[10] This same tendency can be witnessed in a great many of the more recent literary theorists themselves, as exemplified by Homi K. Bhabha among others. The positioning of post-structuralism as the alternative to nationalism is thus quite evident in his own definition of the project as he has assembled it in *Nation and Narration*:

> My intention was that we should develop, in a nice collaborative tension, a range of readings that engaged the insights of post-structuralist theories of narrative knowledge.... The marginal or 'minority' is not the space of a celebratory, or utopian, self-marginalization. It is a much more substantial intervention into those justifications of modernity – progress, homogeneity, cultural organicism, the deep nation, the long past – that rationalize the authoritarian, 'normalizing' tendencies within cultures in the name of national interest. . . .
>
> (p. 4)

Bhabha, of course, lives in those material conditions of *post*modernity which presume the benefits of modernity as the very ground from which judgements on that past of this *post-* may be delivered. In other words, it takes a very modern, very affluent, very uprooted kind of intellectual to debunk both the idea of 'progress' and the sense of a 'long past', not to speak of 'modernity' itself, as mere 'rationalizations' of 'authoritarian tendencies within cultures' – in a theoretical *mélange* which randomly invokes Lévi-Strauss in one phrase, Foucault in another, Lacan in yet another. Those who live within the consequences of that 'long past', good and bad, and in places where a majority of the population has been denied access to such benefits of 'modernity' as hospitals or better health insurance, or even basic literacy, can hardly afford the terms of such thought. The affinities of class and location then lead Bhabha, logically, to an exorbitant celebration of Salman Rushdie which culminates in pronouncements like the following, itself assembled in the manner of a postmodern pastiche:

> America leads to Africa; the nations of Europe and Asia meet in Australia; the margins of the nation displace the centre; the peoples of the periphery return to write the history and fiction of the metropolis. The island story is told from the eye of the aeroplane which becomes that 'ornament that holds the public and the private

in suspense'. The bastion of Englishness crumbles at the sight of immigrants and factory workers. The great Whitmanesque sensorium of America is exchanged for a Warhol blowup, a Kruger installation, or Mapplethorpe's naked bodies. 'Magical Realism', after the Latin American boom, becomes the literary language of the emergent postcolonial world.

(p. 6)

It is doubtful, of course, that 'magical realism' has become 'the literary language of the emergent postcolonial world', any more than the 'national allegory' is the unitary generic form for all Third World narrativities, as Jameson would contend. Such pronouncements are now routine features of the metropolitan theory's inflationary rhetoric. Not all his collaborators write in accordance with his prescription, but Bhabha's own essay at the end of the volume makes a very considerable effort, albeit in very arcane ways, to pre-empt other kinds of critiques of nationalism by offering such familiar plays on 'post-structuralist theories'.

For these more recent developments in 'theory', especially for those sections of literary theory which surely set the terms for dealing with issues of empire, colony and nation, this general situation had peculiarly disorientating effects. In one kind of pressure, politics as such has undergone remarkable degrees of diminution. Any attempt to *know* the world as a whole, or to hold that it is open to rational comprehension, let alone the desire to change it, was to be dismissed as a contemptible attempt to construct 'grand narratives' and 'totalizing (totalitarian?) knowledges'. The theorist spoke often enough of imperialism and nationalism, sometimes as dialectical opposites but increasingly as twin faces of the same falsity, but the main business of radicalism came to reside in the rejection of rationalism itself (the Enlightenment project, as it came to be called).[11] Only Power was universal and immutable; resistance could only be local; knowledge, even of Power, always partial. Affiliations could only be shifting and multiple; to speak of a stable subject position was to chase the chimera of the 'myth of origins'. In some American dilutions of this theory of the dispersal and fracturing of historical subjects, the idea of 'inquiry', which presumes the possibility of finding some believable truth, was to be replaced with the idea of 'conversation' which is by its nature inconclusive. This idea of theory as 'conversation', may at times pass itself off as Bakhtinian dialogism, but in reality it moves inevitably in one of two possible directions.

The more common one is doubtless that of a peculiarly American kind of pluralism, with no small hint of politeness, accommodation and clubby gentlemanliness, albeit expressed in avant-gardist critical circles in the Barthesian language of 'pleasure of the text', 'free play of the Signifier', etc. The alternative direction, on the other hand, is a more sombre one, for if we accept the more extreme versions of the Foucauldian propositions (a) that whatever claims to be a *fact* is none other than a truth-*effect* produced by the ruse of discourse, and (b) that whatever claims to resist Power is already constituted as Power, then there really is nothing for Theory to *do* except to wander aimlessly through the effects – counting them, consuming them, producing them – and in the process submitting to the interminable whisperings of Discourse, both as Origin and as Fate. This theory-as-conversation also has a remarkably strong levelling effect. One is now free to cite Marxists and anti-Marxists, feminists and anti-feminists, deconstructionists, phenomenologists, or whatever other theorist comes to mind, to validate successive positions within an argument, so long as one has a long list of citations, bibliographies, etc., in the well-behaved academic manner. Theory itself becomes a marketplace of ideas, with massive supplies of theory as usable commodity, guaranteeing consumers' free choice and a rapid rate of obsolescence. If one were to refuse this model of the late-capitalist market economy, and dared instead to *conclude* a conversation or to advocate strict partisanship in the politics of theory, one would then be guilty of rationalism, empiricism, historicism, and all sorts of other ills – the idea of historical agents and/or knowing subjects, for example – perpetrated by the Enlightenment. One major aspect of this particular drift in the theory of the grand masters was summed up succinctly by Lyotard, no small master himself: the age of Marxism is over, 'the age of the enjoyment of goods and services' is here! The world was, in other words, bourgeois.

Much of the avant-garde literary theory of today comes out of such moorings, intellectual and political, with a distinctly consumptionist slant. Quite apart from the remarkable claim that politics resides mainly in radicalizing the practice of one's own academic profession, there has grown, because of equal allegiance to irreconcilable pressures, that same kind of eclecticism among the politically engaged theorists as among the more technicist, conservative ones; it is not uncommon to find, say, Gramsci and Matthew Arnold being cited in favour of the same theoretical position, as if the vastly different political allegiances of these two figures were quite immaterial for the main business of literary criticism. In some of these radicalized versions too, thus, that same market-economy model of theory obtains. [. . .]

Interwoven into [contemporary] patterns of immigration is the ambiguous status of the incoming graduate student who comes from elsewhere, who studies under the full weight of the existing canonicity, who rebels against it, who counterposes other kinds of texts against the so-called canonical text, especially if any are available from his or her own part of the world. These other kinds of texts become, then, the ground, the document, even the counter-canon of her or his national self-assertion. This choice corresponds to the ambiguities of an existential kind, precipitated by the contradictions of the metropolitan, liberal, predominantly white university. It is by nature a site of privilege, and the student comes with the ambition of sharing this privilege. The liberal, pluralistic self-image of the university can always be pressed to make room for diversity, multiculturalism, non-Europe; careers can arise out of such renegotiations of the cultural compact. But this same liberal university is usually, for the non-white student, a place of desolation, even panic; exclusions are sometimes blatant, more often only polite and silent, and the documents of one's culture become little sickles to clear one's way through spirals of refined prejudice. Most such students never quite manage to break through these ambiguities of enticement and blockage; some return, but many get lost in the funhouse of disagreeable habitations and impossible returns. Out of these miseries arises a small academic elite which knows it will not return, joins the faculty of this or that metropolitan university, frequents the circuits of conferences and the university presses, and develops, often with the greatest degree of personal innocence and missionary zeal, quite considerable stakes in overvalorizing what has already been designated as 'Third World Literature' – and, when fashions change, reconciles this category even with post-structuralism. This, too, is by now a fairly familiar pattern.

But there is another kind of individual as well, and here I broach a factor which is very hard for me to discuss against the backdrop of India – I mean the factor of exile! And I do not mean people who live in the metropolitan countries for professional reasons but use words like 'exile' or 'diaspora' – words which have centuries of pain and dispossession inscribed in them – to designate what is, after all, only personal convenience. I mean, rather, people who are prevented, against their own commitment and desire, from living in the country of their birth by the authority of state – *any* state – or by fear of personal annihilation. In other words, I mean not privilege but impossibility, not profession but pain. Naked state terror in India has been directed so rarely at the *dominant* sectors of the literary intelligentsia that it may be difficult for those who have never lived in other zones of underdeveloped capitalism even to imagine the depth, the scope, the persistence of this kind of terror in large parts of the globe. This terror is not directed merely at the communist Left, for the communist Left in most countries of Asia and Africa is very small. Nor is it always rationally calibrated against the actual threat faced by the terrorizing regime; nor is the intensity equal in all parts of the globe where terror is practised. But it is worth remembering that there are entire national configurations, such as the Palestinian, whose intellectuals cannot speak – often cannot even be – inside what are their ancestral boundaries; that there have been whole decades when a Filipino, an Ethiopian, a Kenyan dissident had to choose between death, prison or exile; those who could manage to leave departed under duress. This again is a subject of such vast proportions that I cannot even begin to speak of it with any degree of coherence, but I do want to point out the irony that numerous intellectuals born in the outposts of empire cannot speak – frequently cannot even live – in their own countries, but have arrived, alive and speaking, in what Che Guevara once called 'the belly of the beast' – that is to say, the metropolitan city. Once in the metropolitan city, many have ended up in the metropolitan university, which tends to be more liberal than the kind of regime metropolitan capital prefers in Asia and Africa.

Immigration, in other words, has had its own contradictions: many have been propelled by need, others motivated by ambition, yet others driven away by persecution; for some there really is no longer a home to return to; in many cases need and ambition have become ambiguously and inextricably linked. No firm generalization can be offered for so large and complex a phenomenon, involving so many individual biographies. Nor is a uniform political choice necessarily immanent in the act of immigration as such. What we have witnessed, however, is that the combination of class origin, professional ambition and lack of a prior political grounding in a stable socialist praxis predisposes a great many of the radicalized immigrants located in the metropolitan university towards both an opportunistic kind of Third-Worldism as the appropriate form of oppositional politics and a kind of self-censoring, which in turn impels them towards greater incorporation in modes of politics and discourse already authorized by the prevailing fashion in that university.

Out of these reorganizations of capital, communications and personnel has come the image of 'theorist' as 'traveller', and of literary production itself as a ruse of immigration, of travelling *lightly*. Salman Rushdie's *Shame* [. . .] is only one of the scores of fictions of this period in which a fundamental connection between immigration and the literary imagination is sought or asserted. The fact that some of these intellectuals actually were political exiles has been taken advantage of, in an incredibly inflationary rhetoric, to deploy the word 'exile', first as a metaphor and then as a fully appropriated descriptive label for the existential condition of the immigrant as such; the upper-class Indian who *chooses* to live in the metropolitan country is then called 'the diasporic Indian', and 'exile' itself becomes a condition of the soul, unrelated to facts of material life. Exile, immigration and professional preference become synonymous and, indeed, mutually indistinguishable.

It is significant that although the category of 'Third World Literature posited itself in terms of West and non-West, white and non-white, its reception among the African-American literary intelligentsia, among whom those terms have the most profound resonance, was at best contradictory. Many used it as a *descriptive* category, to signify a coalition of non-white minorities; 'Third World Women', for example, meant non-white women who needed to articulate a feminism different in some key respects from the high-bourgeois feminism of many white professionals, with oppressions of race and class layered together with the issue of gender. In another kind of emphasis, Black Third-Worldism was designed to broaden the perspective beyond the issue of African *origin*, to include more modern dimensions of the experience which was, in turn, shared with other coloured inhabitants of the inner cities, the ghettos, the *barrios*. 'Third World Literature', however, attracted few Black intellectuals. It was among teachers of Black Literature that the perception was immediate, even though it remained largely untheorized, that this category referred to literatures of the *other* minorities, the ones who were constituted not by slavery but by immigration. The commanding representatives of the African–American humanist tradition in this century – Du Bois, Paul Robeson, Richard Wright, among them – had all been deeply moved by the revolutionary and anti-colonial currents on a global scale (virtually the last writing of Du Bois had been a stirring homage to the Chinese Revolution; Wright was ecstatic about Bandung and the Non-Aligned Movement); but they had also known the specificity of African–American enslavement and its unique consequences, hence of the unique tie between this contemporary predicament and its African origin. This dual emphasis on the historical specificity of the African–American experience, on the one hand, and a guarded co-operation with advocates of Third World Literature, on the other, remained in place.

   The Black academic intelligentsia was therefore open to establishing Third World Studies as a separate and adjacent field, but one that was not to encroach upon the distinct identity of Black Studies. This involved no small degree of wariness, partly because it is one of the distinguishing characteristics of the Asian immigrant's middle-class aspiration that even as he/she speaks constantly of non-Western origin, he/she wishes to join, within the United States, not the racially oppressed African–American community, but the privileged white middle class. It is also symptomatic that virtually all the theorizations of Third World Literature in the United States have come either from the immigrant or from that section of the elite white intelligentsia which normally pays scant attention to African–American literature and culture. There are, of course, *some* Black critics who participate in the production of this theory, and there are perhaps even some white critics who come to it from a prior interest in Black Literatures; but they – if and where they exist – are exceptions. In any case, it is in relation to the dominant, canonical tradition that 'Third World Literature' conceptually constitutes itself, even where it inadvertently appropriates the models and aspirations previously specific to the African–American.

That perfectly astute insistence on the specificity of Black experience in America, and on the historic roots of Black America's self-consciousness not in the generality of a 'Third World' but in the particularity of Africa, was, unfortunately, only part of the story. For apart from the almost spontaneously oppositionist positions which *any* Black intellectual, even of the most right-wing persuasion, feels compelled to adopt because of the racist juggernaut in which the whole of the African–American minority is held, this segment of the American intelligentsia has gone through those same processes of initially great radicalization in the 1960s, followed by increasing professionalization and embourgeoisement from the mid 1970s onwards, which has been characteristic of the United States as a whole. The process has been, if anything, more dramatic among the Black intelligentsia, and the irony is worth examining, however briefly.

The most radical phase of the Civil Rights Movement and the Black Nationalist Movements in the 1960s had coincided, paradoxically enough, with the phase of the most dynamic growth and expansion of American capital, thanks to the long wave of the postwar boom, the expansion of the military-industrial complex because of the Vietnam War, high rates of employment and spending, the still-existing US hegemony over its own capitalist partners as well as the world market generally. As a result, the system had at that particular juncture, before the crises came in the 1970s, a historically unprecedented capacity to absorb domestic challenges by incorporating into the margins of its own institutions the more professionally inclined elements of the radical intelligentsia, while the isolation through selective terror of the less compromising individuals and segments was facilitated by their relative isolation caused precisely by the increasing incorporation of the rest. The state-sponsored assassinations of Fred Hampton in his home and of George Jackson in prison, the decimation of the Black Panther Party in Chicago, Oakland, and other major centres, and the methodical disorganization of Black auto workers in Detroit, are all cases in point. It was in the process of this unfolding dynamic of insurrection and containment that the United States witnessed, from the mid 1960s on, a great expansion of educational and professional opportunity for the Black minority – vastly inadequate in terms of what it should have been, but *vast* in comparison with any earlier phase – under pressure of the Black insurrection but made economically feasible by the strength of US capital. By the time capitalist expansion slid into stagnation in the early 1970s, with the effects being felt in educational institutions in subsequent years, the benefits of that first decade had already engendered considerable embourgeoisement among Black campus communities. Retrenchment led, then, not to further radicalization but to a defensive relocation within the existing structures, supervised by faculties which were *socially* predominantly on the Right even though on the question of racial oppression they took, within parameters defined by the institutions, oppositional positions.[12] In outlook and aspiration, Black student bodies had been normalized even before the advent of Reaganism, becoming in their politics, except on the question of race, indistinguishable from the rest.

The twin emphases on professional aspiration and racial oppression produced considerable energy for identitarian politics and for defence of educational facilities, job protection, and so on. But, by the same token, little political energy was left for issues not related to professional advancement and racial identity. These social reorganizations of the Black academic intelligentsia led to a remarkable devolution in its own history. It was common among the Black intellectuals who came of age in the interwar years to have some sort of sympathetic awareness of the Communist Party, while many, of course, started their careers in its publications. By contrast, the Black intelligentsia that came to prominence from the 1960s onwards was marked by its general lack of intellectual moorings in any kind of Marxism or in a politics marked by the communist movement. Figures like Angela Davis stand out in this regard precisely because they are the exceptions in a milieu where Black radicalism, as a distinct social category within American radicalism at large, is even farther removed from Marxism than are several quite distinct groupings in its white component. Feminism was the only progressive ideology which made any substantial new inroads into the Black academic community during this latter phase, as was true in the case of white intellectuals and students as well. The upshot was that with the exception of a very few, Black writers remained curiously disengaged from these larger debates about the contentions between imperialism and the imperialized formations on the global scale, and the consequences of these contentions for culture and literature as such, except from a strictly nationalist standpoint.

Meanwhile, there has been a very considerable shift in the composition of the archive which is to represent the Third World in the metropolitan university, creating new kinds of possibilities for certain kinds of Black critics. In the late 1960s and early 1970s, when the category of Third World Literature first emerged, it was to apply, more or less strictly, to texts that were actually produced *in* the non-Western countries, and it included texts produced in all epochs, including most prominently those from the pre-colonial epochs. The main idea at that time was to construct a counter-canon produced, constitutively, outside Europe and North America; one that displayed some civilizational differences (the word 'difference' was at that time written with a lower-case 'd', as something local and empirically verifiable, not to denote any epistemological category or perennial ontological condition). Documents of the African past were to be the testimonies of African–American heritage in the old continent, as Homer or Shakespeare were the documents of Western civilization; the same applied to Latin American, Caribbean, and Asian literary documents as well. This counter-canon was to be composed, in other words, of documents which referred to that which had been left behind, which had been there before the journey, and which was now to be recouped – by the descendant of the slave, the immigrant, the incoming student – as a resource of both memory and hope. This sense was to survive in very few theorists, and it survived notably in Jameson's treatment of the matter [discussed in Chapter 3, *In Theory, Classes, Nations, Literatures*], which simply would have no theoretical basis if the 'national allegory' were not to come from within the nation which the allegory was to narrate. As the elite immigrant intelligentsia located more or less permanently in the metropolitan countries began appropriating this counter-canonical category as their special preserve and archive, the emphasis kept shifting, from the epochal to the modern, erasing in the process the difference between documents produced within the non-Western countries and those others which were produced by the immigrant at metropolitan locations. With the passage of time, the writings of immigrants were to become greatly privileged and were declared, in some extreme but also very influential formulations, to be the only *authentic* documents of resistance in our time.[13] It was at this point that the singular ascendancy of Salman Rushdie began, and it is notable that apart from Edward Said himself, the critics who have played the key role in redefining literary Third-Worldism in relation mainly to the immigrant, and have also cemented the relationship between this immigrant phenomenon and postmodern ways of reading that archive, have usually been of Asian origin. Once this relationship between the immigrant intellectual, literary Third-Worldism, avant-garde literary theory in general and deconstructionist poststructuralism in particular had been cemented, a different kind of Black critic could then enter this scene of 'Race', Writing and Difference.[14]

In short, there has been a very considerable aggregation of texts and individuals, but mere aggregation of texts and individuals does not give rise to the construction of a counter-canon. For the latter to arise, there has to be the cement of a powerful ideology, however incoherent and loosely defined. This cement eventually came to metropolitan literary theory in the shape of the Three Worlds Theory – especially after the later 1960s, in the global aftermath of the Chinese Cultural Revolution, and more so after the adoption of a certain brand of Maoism by some influential sections of the Parisian avant-garde, from Julia Kristeva to Jean-Luc Godard. Once these pressures of politics, texts, individuals, and certain kinds of radicalisms had opened up this still-expanding field of Third World Literature, it was only natural that a goodly number of other people – European and American, white and non-white – would also start exploring it, from a whole range of diverse political positions, and that some would even want to invest their careers in it. The social collapse of the Comecon countries has, of course, complicated this matter of the 'Three Worlds Theory' a great deal, and it is likely that the category itself may now be abandoned altogether, more out of confusion than anything else, to be replaced simply with eclectic play, thus refurbishing the already hegemonic academic philosophies of 'Difference'.

We shall return to the political origins of the Three Worlds Theory, as well as some alternative ways of theorizing the global structure of imperialism in its current phase, in the concluding chapter of this book. Even in cultural theory as it has developed in the metropolitan countries, an exclusive emphasis on the nation, and on nationalism as the necessary ideology emanating from the national situation, has been a *logical* feature of Third-Worldist perspectives. For once the world is divided into three large unities, each fundamentally coherent and fundamentally external to one another, it is extremely difficult to speak of any fundamental differences within particular national structures – differences, let us say, of class or of gender formation. One is then forced, by the terms of one's own discourse, to minimize those kinds of differences, and to absolutize, on the other hand, the difference between, say, the First and the Third Worlds. The preferred technique among cultural theorists, then, is to look at 'Third World' literary texts in terms always of their determination by the colonial encounter, but rarely in terms of their determination by class and gender formations, or from the standpoint of what the needs of a socialist cultural production, quite beyond the issue of colonial determination, might be. We learn much, in other words, about Lamming and Achebe, García Márquez and Rushdie, as their work negotiates a terrain marked by colonialism, but those same works are never examined from the perspective of socialism as the emancipatory desire of our epoch. The very terms of this discourse repress such alternative starting points, and those terms sit comfortably with the institutions – the university, the literary conference, the professional journal – which are in the business of authorizing such discourses. One would have thought that in any conflict between advanced capitalism and backward capitalism, the latter is bound to lose; socialism, therefore, has to be the third term of the dialectic, without which the antagonism of the other two terms simply cannot be resolved. If, however, socialist political and cultural practices are simply externalized *out* of our struggles, and if those practices are located only in some ideal place designated as the Second World, then a narrow nationalism can be the only insignia under which cultural production within the Third World can take place or be conceptualized.

The cognate subdisciplines of 'Third World Literature' and 'Colonial Discourse Analysis' emerged at a time when radical theory was in the process of distancing itself from the kind of activist culture that had started developing throughout Western Europe and North America during the period of the great anti-imperialist struggles in Indochina and Southern Africa. This distancing on the part of contemporary metropolitan radicalism from its own immediate past has led to other kinds of distancing as well. In terms of historical periodization, there appears to be in both these subdisciplines far greater interest in the colonialism of the past than in the imperialism of the present. In terms of social processes, interest has shifted from the 'facts' of imperialist wars and political economies of exploitation to 'fictions' of representation and cultural artefact. In terms of global spaces, one is hearing, as these subdisciplines now function in the United States, a lot less about the United States itself and a lot more about Britain and France. In terms of academic disciplines, much more prestige attaches now to Literature, Philosophy and radical Anthropology than to Political Economy. In terms of theoretical positions, Marxism is often dismissed as a 'modes-of-production narrative', a 'totalizing system', and so on, while engagements shift more towards Narratology, Discourse Analysis, Deconstruction, or New History of a Foucauldian kind.

To the extent that both 'Third World Literature' and 'Colonial Discourse Analysis' privilege coloniality as the framing term of epochal experience, national identity is logically privileged as the main locus of meaning, analysis and (self-)representation, which is, in turn, particularly attractive to the growing number of 'Third World intellectuals' who are based in the metropolitan university. They can now materially represent the undifferentiated colonized Other – more recently and more fashionably, the *postcolonial* Other – without much examining of their own presence in that institution, except perhaps in the characteristically postmodernist mode of ironic pleasure in observing the duplicities and multiplicities of one's own persona. The East, reborn and greatly expanded now as a 'Third World', seems to have become, yet again, a *career* – even for the 'Oriental' this time, and within the 'Occident' too.

Notes

1. Part of the difficulty in engaging with the post-structuralist philosophical positions, especially as they resurface in Anglo-American literary theory, is that their exaggerated claims of novelty and their propensity to reduce all prior philosophical positions to a mere caricature pre-empt such an engagement. As regards the caricature of Marxism as a 'progressivist modes-of-production narrative', for example, MARX's own critique of the positivist notions of progress begins in his earliest writings and can be traced all the way through his notes on the Russian peasants' commune towards the end of his life. This critique is extended within the Marxist tradition in a great many places, including *History and Class Consciousness* (Cambridge, MA: MIT Press, 1971; original German edition 1923) by Lukács, about whom then, MERLEAU-PONTY makes the following approving remark in his own *Adventures of the Dialectic* (Illinois: Northwestern University Press, 1973): 'He says that the idea of progress is an expedient which consists in placing a contradiction which has already been reduced to a minimum against the backdrop of an unlimited time and in supposing that it will there resolve itself. Progress dissolves the beginning and the end, in the historical sense, into a limitless natural process' (p. 35).

2. For EDWARD SAID's celebration of what he approvingly calls the 'gradual disappearance of narrative history' and his emphasis on irony as the desirable historiographic mode ('Narrative is replaced by irony'), see his essay 'Third World Intellectuals and Metropolitan Culture', *Raritan* IX: 3 (1990): 29–50.

3. For this practice of 'theory' as 'travel', see in particular JAMES CLIFFORD and VIVEK DHARESHWAR (eds), *Traveling Theories, Traveling Theorists, Inscription* 5, an occasional volume brought out by the Group for the Critical Study of Colonial Discourse and the Center for Cultural Studies, Oakes College, University of California at Santa Cruz, 1989.

4. FREDRIC JAMESON is exceptional in this regard in the sense that he does make a limited attempt of this kind, most obviously in 'Periodizing the 60s', his prospectus-essay of 1984, reprinted in *The Ideologies of Theory, Volume Two: Syntax of History* (Minneapolis: University of Minnesota Press, 1988) and in lesser detail wherever he addresses this question. This awareness on his part that periodization is fundamental for anyone who sets out to historicize relations between politics and culture is particularly salutary in a context where literary theorists who address questions of colony and empire are generally given to the broadest assertions, with little regard to the interplay between specificity of periods and multiplicity of determinations.

5. ALTHUSSER's is in some ways a peculiar and even poignant case. He remained a lifelong member of the French Communist Party because he believed in the centrality of the working class in the making of history, yet he advocated the idea of 'history as a human–natural process' which had neither subject nor goal. His highly nuanced essay 'Contradiction and Overdetermination' (*For Marx*, London: New Left Books, 1977) is notable for affirming, against the contemporary radical currents, a final determination by the economic, but his even more influential essay 'Ideology and Ideological State Apparatuses' (*Lenin and Philosophy and Other Essays*, London: New Left Books, 1971) assigns

so vast a space to the state that any methodological distinction between state and not-state as differential sites for ideological production and reproduction becomes difficult to maintain. Inside France, his philosophical positions were forms of intervention in the politics of the Communist Party, with at least a few of them obviously designed to challenge the Stalinist legacies within the party. His chief critic in Britain, E.P. Thompson, denounced him, on the other hand as a Stalinist, while some of his key admirers, Hirst and Hindess among them for some years sifted out the political charge of Althusser's interventions and invoked him, instead, for the worst kind of structuralist constructs, static and anti-historical. If the injection of Althusser's work into Anglo-American debates initially had the salutary effect of forcing greater theoretical rigour, 'theoretical practice' became, in most of the British (and then American) appropriations, an excuse for the worst kind of academic professionalization of Marxism.

6. See Section IV of the essay 'Marxism and Humanism' in ALTHUSSER, *For Marx*, which includes a very peculiar passage on the role of ideology 'in a society in which classes have disappeared':

> If, as Marx said, history is a perpetual transformation of men's conditions of existence, and if this is equally true of socialist society, then men must be ceaselessly transformed so as to adapt them to these conditions: if this 'adaptation' cannot be left to spontaneity but must be constantly assumed, dominated and controlled, it is in ideology that this demand is expressed . . .
>
> (p. 235)

In other words, there is no end to domination and control, even in a classless society; human beings simply cannot be 'left to spontaneity', nor can they *live* the relations of knowledge (which come only through theoretical practice and are not, in any case, *lived*). This entrapment of humankind in ideology, now and for ever, is eerily close to Foucault's notion of the power of discourse.

7. ALTHUSSER, 'Ideology and Ideological State Apparatuses', in *Lenin and Philosophy and Other Essays* (London: New Left Books, 1971).

8. This is not the place to delve into the vexed question of 'humanism', but it is necessary to stress the distinction between the epistemological and the practical (i.e. political and ethical) issues involved. Marx breaks entirely from that humanist epistemology which takes the 'individual' to be the locus of experience and knowledge, and no variant of Marx's writings on ideology and consciousness – on the opacity of experience to itself, and on the social determination (hence the provisional character) of all knowledge – is reconcilable with that bourgeois category of the 'individual'. It is in relation to the constructedness of history (unauthored but humanly made) and the ethical life of the species-being (the struggle from necessity to freedom) that Marxism recoups its humanist energy.

9. Gender specification for non-specific persons in the third person singular is an unfortunate but mandatory aspect of the English language. I tried writing this book with the 'other' gender specification: *she, her*, etc. That exercise turned out to be equally disagreeable – and unnecessarily provocative in an entirely different way.

10. See EDWARD SAID's essay 'Third World Intellectuals and Metropolitan Culture'.

11. These familiar themes of recent French theory were then applied to matters

of colony and empire, in both the literary and the sociological theories, in characteristically subordinate and dependent modes, by a number of the Indian members of this 'post-structuralist' avant-garde, from HOMI BHABHA to PARTHA CHATTERJEE. For the latter's highly derivative debunkings of 'the Enlightenment', 'myths of progress', etc., see *Nationalist Thought and the Colonial World: A Derivative Discourse* (London: Zed Press; Delhi: Oxford University Press, 1986).

12. Anthologies are always interesting barometers of changes in perception, social location and market demand. The increased embourgeoisement of a whole stratum of Black writers from the 1970s onwards is reflected well in the one edited by TERRY McMILLAN, *Breaking Ice: An Anthology of Contemporary African–American Fiction* (New York: Penguin, 1990). In the introduction she cites Trey Ellis, who 'has coined a phrase which he calls "The New Black Aesthetic"' (NBA) and quotes him approvingly:

> For the first time in our history we are producing a critical mass of college graduates who are children of college graduates themselves. Like most artistic movements, the NBA is a post-bourgeois movement; driven by a second generation of [the] middle class. Having scraped their way to relative wealth and, too often, crass materialism, our parents have freed (or compelled) us to bite those hands that fed us and sent us to college. We now feel secure enough to attend art school instead of medical school.
>
> (p. xx)

After some more commentary on this new comfort and opportunity, McMillan goes on to say, in her own words: 'If a writer is trying hard to convince you of something, then he or she should stick to non-fiction. These days, our work is often as entertaining as it is informative, thought-provoking as it is uplifting. Some of us would like to think that the experiences of our characters are "universal"' (p. xxi).

13. For more discussion on this point, see my comments on EDWARD SAID's essay 'Third World Intellectuals and Metropolitan Culture', in Chapter 5, *In Theory: Classes, Nations, Literatures*.

14. See in particular the two statements, editorial and authorial, which bracket the beginning and ending of HENRY LOUIS GATES, JR (ed.), *'Race', Writing and Difference* (Chicago: University of Chicago Press, 1986). Gates, of course, uses the term 'Third World' quite freely, but for him it is not so much a political category as yet another semantic construct in the infinite play of poststructuralist 'Difference' in the articulations of 'minority literature'.

Notes on Authors

(Full publication details are not given where texts also appear in Further Reading.)

CHINUA ACHEBE (1930–) is a distinguished novelist and critic. Born in Ogidi in Eastern Nigeria he studied literature and medicine at the University of Ibadan before going to work for the Nigerian broadcasting company in Lagos. His first novel *Things Fall Apart* was published in 1958. He joined the Biafran Ministry of Information during the Biafran War and subsequently worked as an academic and writer. He has taught and lectured throughout the world.

AIJAZ AHMAD (1942–) is Professorial Fellow at the Centre of Contemporary Studies, Nehru Memorial Museum and Library, New Delhi. He has taught in the United States and India and lectured in many other parts of the world. He is the author of a number of influential articles, the most important of which are collected in *In Theory: Classes, Nations, Literatures* (1992). This is perhaps the most celebrated attack on the concept 'postcolonial' and the forms, politics and institutions of cultural analysis conducted under that rubric.

HOMI K. BHABHA (1949–) is Wayne C. Booth Professor of Rhetoric and English Literature at the University of Chicago. Born to a Bombay Parsee family, Bhabha was educated in India and at Oxford University. Before moving to Chicago, he lectured at Sussex University. He is the author of many influential essays, the most important of which appear in *The Location of Culture* (1994). He has also edited *Nation and Narration* (1990).

DIANA BRYDON (1950–) is based at the University of Guelph. Brought up in Canada, she received her PhD from the Australian National University, she was a guest editor of the special issue of Essays on

Canadian writing, 'Postcolonial Theories and Canadian Literature' (1995). She is the author of numerous articles on postcolonial criticism and is the editor of *World Literature Written in English*.

AIMÉ CÉSAIRE (1913–) was born in Martinique. He studied in Paris where he became active in student politics. An active voice in the early days of the negritude movement his epic poem *Return to My Native Land* was anthologized by Senghor in 1948. In 1955 he published his *Discourse on Colonialism*. Returning to Martinique he became Mayor of Fort de France and a deputy to the French National Assembly.

FRANTZ FANON (1925–1961) was born on the island of Martinique, in the Caribbean. He studied in France, first as a dentist, then as a psychiatrist, where he completed a dissertation in 1951 at Lyon. During this period he wrote three plays and edited a student magazine entitled *Tam Tam*. His first book, *Peau Noire, Masques Blancs* appeared in 1952 (published in English in 1967 as *Black Skin, White Masks*). In 1953 he was appointed head of Blida-Joinville Hospital in Algiers. From 1956 he devoted himself to the Algerian struggle for independence. He wrote *L'An V de la révolution algérienne* in 1959, published initially in Paris, but promptly banned after the first edition, before finally being reissued in English as *A Dying Colonialism* (1965), and again in French as *Sociologie d'une révolution* (1968). *Les Damnés de la terre* appeared in 1961, the year that Fanon died of leukaemia in the United States, in the midst of, in his own words, 'a nation of lynchers'. It was translated as *The Wretched of the Earth* in 1965.

HENRY LOUIS GATES, Jr (1950–) is Professor of English Literature and Chair of Afro-American Studies at Harvard. He is editor of the *Norton Anthology of African–American Literature*. He was born in Piedmont, West Virginia. He enrolled at Potomac State College of West Virginia in 1968, ready to fulfill a childhood ambition to be a doctor of medicine but, influenced by a charismatic teacher, his interests turned to literature. He is the author and editor of a number of crucial works on black writing including *Black Literature and Literary Theory* (1984), *Figures in Black: Words, Signs and the Racial Self* (1987), *The Signifying Monkey: A Theory of African–American Literary Criticism* (1990).

BELL HOOKS (1952–) is Distinguished Professor of English at City College in New York. She was raised in Hopkinsville, Kentucky, one of seven children, within a working-class black Southern Christian culture. She gained her PhD from the University of California at Santa Cruz, and has taught at Yale and at Oberlin College. She is author of many books and articles on race, gender and culture, including *Black Looks: Race and Representation* (1992), and *Feminist Theory: From Margin to Center* (1984).

Her challenging work has been brought to a much wider audience with
the publication of two recent collections of essays on popular culture
and pedagogy – *Outlaw Culture: Resisting Representations* (1994) and
Teaching to Transgress: Education as the Practice of Freedom (1994)
– together with a major text entitled *Killing Rage, Ending Racism* (1995).

ABDUL JANMOHAMED (1945–) is Associate Professor of English at the
University of California, Berkeley. He was born in Kenya, and educated
there and in the United States. He is a founding member and associate
editor of *Cultural Critique*. The author of numerous articles in the
postcolonial field, his major works include *Manichean Aesthetics: The
Politics of Literature in Colonial Africa* (1983), and, with DAVID LLOYD, *The
Nature and Context of Minority Discourse* (1990). He has worked extensively
on the cultural politics of Richard Wright, and on representations of the
intellectual and the colonial subject.

DAVID LLOYD (1955–) is Professor of English at the University of
California at Berkeley. Born in Dublin, he was educated in Dublin and
Belfast, before taking his BA from King's College, Cambridge, in 1977,
and his PhD there in 1982. He was subsequently Assistant and Associate
Professor in the Department of English, University of California at
Berkeley from 1983–93, becoming a full Professor there in 1993. He
is currently Visiting Professor in the Department of Literature at the
University of California at San Diego. He is the author of *Nationalism
and Minor Literature* (Berkeley: University of California Press, 1987),
Anomalous States: Irish Writing and the Post-colonial Moment (Dublin and
North Carolina: Lilliput/Duke University Press, 1993), and coeditor,
with ABDUL JANMOHAMED, of *The Nature and Context of Minority
Discourse* (Oxford: Oxford University Press, 1990). He is currently
working on projects on the Irish body and the training of emotion in
modern Ireland and on aesthetics and politics.

EDWARD W. SAID (1935–) is Old Dominion Foundation Professor in the
Humanities at Columbia University, New York. Born to a Christian Arab
family in Palestine, Said was initially educated in Egypt (to where his
family removed after the 1948 Israeli–Arab war) and the United States,
where he has been consistently active on behalf of the Palestinian cause.
Perhaps the single most influential figure in contemporary postcolonial
studies (and often credited with inaugurating the field), his major books
include *Orientalism* (1978), *The Question of Palestine* (1980), *The World, the
Text, and the Critic* (1983; repr. London: Faber & Faber, 1984), *Covering
Islam* (1981), *After the Last Sky: Palestinian Lives* (1986), *Culture and
Imperialism* (1993) and *Representations of the Intellectual* (London: Vintage,
1994).

275

GAYATRI CHAKRAVORTY SPIVAK (1942–) is Avalon Professor in the Humanities at Columbia University, New York. Born to a Hindu Brahmin family in Bengal, Spivak was educated in India, prior to leaving for the United States for postgraduate study in the early 1960s. The translator of DERRIDA's *Of Grammatology* (1976), she has since become a leading figure in contemporary postcolonial studies and cultural studies more generally. She is the author of *In Other Worlds: Essays in Cultural Politics* (1987), *The Post-Colonial Critic* (1990) and *Outside in the Teaching Machine* (1993). Several of her more important essays, on a wide variety of topics, have recently been collected in *The Spivak Reader* (1996).

HELEN TIFFIN (1947?–) teaches at the University of Queensland, Australia. Along with BILL ASHCROFT and GARETH GRIFFITHS she was the author of the influential study *The Empire Writes Back* (1989). With IAN ADAM she edited *Past the Last Post*. More recently she has edited with ASHCROFT and GRIFFITHS *The Post-Colonial Studies Reader* (1995).

Further Reading

Orientations

Some key essays that deal with problems of definition are KWAME ANTHONY APPIAH, 'Is the Post- in Postmodernism the Post- in Postcolonial?', *Critical Inquiry* 17 (1991): 336–57; VIJAY MISHRA and BOB HODGE, 'What is Post(-)Colonialism?', *Textual Practice* 5: 3 (1991): 399–414; ANNE MCCLINTOCK, 'The Angel of Progress: Pitfalls of the Term "Post-Colonialism"', *Social Text* 31/32 (1992): 1–15; ELLA SHOHAT, 'Notes on the "Post-Colonial"', *Social Text* 31: 2 (1992): 89–113; HELEN TIFFIN, 'Postcolonialism, Postmodernism and the Rehabilitation of Post-Colonial History', *Journal of Commonwealth Literature* 23: 1 (1988): 169–81. A sharp political critique is that of AIJAZ AHMAD in 'The Politics of Literary Postcoloniality', *Race and Class* 36: 3 (1995): 1–20. On periodization and progress see for example HOMI BHABHA, '"Race", Time and the Revision of Modernity', in this Reader. On arguments around theory and language, see the essays by JOYCE A. JOYCE, HENRY LOUIS GATES, Jr and HOUSTON BAKER, in 'A Discussion: The Black Canon: Reconstructing Black American Literary Criticism', *New Literary History* 18: 2 (1987): 333–84. On the uses and abuses of culture in postcolonial criticism, see ARIF DIRLIK, 'Culturalism as Hegemonic Ideology and Liberating Practice', in Abdul JanMohamed and David Lloyd (eds), *The Nature and Context of Minority Discourse* (London and New York: Oxford University Press, 1990), pp. 394–431. On the relationship between postcolonialism and postmodernism, see SIMON DURING, 'Postmodernism or Post-Colonialism Today', in Thomas Docherty (ed.), *Postmodernism: A Reader* (Hemel Hempstead: Harvester Press, 1993), pp. 448–62. Among the many book-length studies available, two important volumes are IAN ADAM and HELEN TIFFIN (eds), *Past the Last Post: Post-Colonialism and Postmodernism* (Hemel Hempstead: Harvester Press, 1991); BILL ASHCROFT, GARETH GRIFFITHS and HELEN TIFFIN, *The Empire Writes Back: Theory and Practice in Post-Colonial Literatures* (London: Routledge, 1989).

Negritude

As a result of its genesis in the world of French colonialism much
of the source material and the critical literature concerning negritude
remains available only in French. Some important works, however,
are to be found in English. Although the French edition was published
in the 1960s, LILYAN KESTELOOT's exhaustive monograph *Black Writers
in French: A Literary History of Negritude* (Washington, DC: Howard
University Press, 1991) remains a broad introduction. Another translated
volume from the French which provides useful background material
for the student is CLAUDE WAUTHIER's *The Literature and Thought of
Modern Africa* 2nd edn (London: Heinemann, 1978). Many works devoted
to more general aspects of African literature are available. Almost all
contain some assessment of negritude. Particularly useful, however, are
ROBERT FRAZER's commentaries in his *West African Poetry: A Critical
Perspective* (Cambridge: Cambridge University Press). JULIO FINN
provides a useful service in his *The Voices of Negritude* (London: Quartet,
1987) in that he attempts to demonstrate the links between the
movement in France and developments elsewhere and in languages
other than French. The reader, however, should be aware of his highly
combative stance on the whole issue.

In some respects the original founders of negritude have not been
particularly well served by translators. As we have seen CÉSAIRE's
Discourse on Colonialism is available in English, but this translation did
not appear until 1972 and is not readily available. His poetry might
be said to have fared better. His epic verse *Return to My Native Land*
(Harmondsworth: Penguin, 1969) appeared in a translation by John
Berger and Anna Bostock. A further translation has appeared in the
United States, *Aimé Césaire: The Collected Poetry* (Berkeley: University of
California Press, 1983; trans. by Clayton Eshelman and Annette Smith).
Of SENGHOR there is far less available, but Sartre's famous preface to
his 1948 collection of poems did appear in an English version translated
by S.W. Allen, *Black Orpheus* (Paris: Presence Africaine, 1975). Much
of FRANTZ FANON's work is engaged in a debate with negritude,
from his early, in terms of its French publication, *Black Skins, White
Masks* (London: Pluto Press, 1986) to *The Wretched of the Earth*
(Harmondsworth: Penguin, 1970). The intellectual climate in Paris over
this period, and beyond, can be read from the pages of the journal that
was published to champion the cause of negritude, *Présence Africaine*.
See V.Y. MUDIMBE *The Surreptitious Speech: Présence Africaine and the
Politics of Otherness 1947–1987* (Chicago: Chicago University Press, 1992).
The response of Anglophone African critics has been more muted. See
EZEKIEL MPHAHLELE *The African Image* (London: Faber & Faber, 1974) or

WOLE SOYINKA *Myth, Literature and the African World* (Cambridge: Cambridge University Press) for typically muted responses.

Very much within the postcolonial frame of critique is CHRISTOPHER MILLER, *Theories of Africans* (Chicago: Chicago University Press). A useful assessment of the movement from a postcolonial perspective has also been provided by BENITA PARRY. See her 'Resistance Theory/ Theorising Resistance or Two Cheers for Nativism', in Francis Barker, Peter Hulme and Margaret Iversen (eds), *Colonial Discourse/Postcolonial Theory* (Manchester: Manchester University Press, 1994).

Frantz Fanon

FANON's major works are, in order of their original appearance, *Black Skin, White Masks*, first published in French in 1952, trans. Charles Lam Markmann with a foreword by Homi Bhabha (London: Pluto Press, 1986), *A Dying Colonialism*, first published in 1959, trans. Haakon Chevalier with an introduction by Adolfo Gilly (New York: Monthly Review Press, 1965; repr. 1970), *The Wretched of the Earth*, first published in 1961, trans. Constance Farrington, with a preface by Jean-Paul Sartre (Harmondsworth: Penguin, 1970), and the volume of essays collected posthumously as *Toward the African Revolution*, first published in English in 1967, trans. Haakon Chevalier (Harmondsworth: Penguin, 1970). A good starting-point is the profile by EMMANUEL HANSEN, 'Frantz Fanon: Portrait of a Revolutionary Intellectual', *Transition* 46 (1974): 25–36.

An important new collection of essays is LEWIS R. GORDON, T. DENEAN SHARPLEY-WHITING, and RENEE T. WHITE (eds), *Fanon: A Critical Reader* (Cambridge, Mass.: Blackwell, 1996). Fanon's humanism is scrutinized in HOMI BHABHA, 'What Does the Black Man Want?', *Remembering Fanon, New Formations* 1 (1987): 121. For other responses, see ROBERT BERNASCONI, 'Casting the Slough: Fanon's New Humanism for a New Humanity', in Gordon et al. (eds), *Fanon: A Critical Reader*, pp. 113–21; LEWIS R. GORDON, *Fanon and the Crisis of European Man: An Essay on Philosophy and the Human Sciences* (New York and London: Routledge, 1995); SIDNEY J. LEMELLE, 'The Politics of Cultural Existence: Pan-Africanism, Historical Materialism and Afrocentricity', *Race and Class* 35: 1 (1993): 93–112. Fanon's new humanist critique of the enlightenment is interrogated in RICHARD C. ONWUANIBE, *A Critique of Revolutionary Humanism: Frantz Fanon* (St Louis, Mo.: Green, 1983), and given a more sympathetic assessment in LEWIS R. GORDON, *Fanon and the Crisis of European Man: An Essay on Philosophy and the Human Sciences* (New York and London: Routledge, 1995).

Fanon the psychologist is treated by HUSSEIN ABDILAHI BULHAN in 'Frantz Fanon: The Revolutionary Psychiatrist', *Race and Class* 21: 3

(1980): 251–71, and in greater depth by JOCK MCCULLOCH, in *Black Soul, White Artifact: Fanon's Clinical Psychology and Social Theory* (Cambridge: Cambridge University Press, 1983). More recent essays include those by STANLEY O. GAINES, Jr, in 'Perspectives of Du Bois and Fanon on the Psychology of Oppression', in GORDON et al. (eds), *Fanon: A Critical Reader*, pp. 24–34, and FRANÇOISE VERGES, 'To Cure and to Free: The Fanonian Project of "Decolonized Psychiatry"', in *Fanon: A Critical Reader*, pp. 85–99.

The problem of the representation of women is raised in an exemplary fashion by GWEN BERGNER in 'Who is that Masked Woman? or, The Role of Gender in Fanon's *Black Skin, White Masks*', *Publications of the Modern Language Association* 110: 1 (1995): 75–88; in NADIA ELIA, 'Violent Women: Surging into Forbidden Quarters', in *Fanon: A Critical Reader*, pp. 163–9; in EDDY SOUFFRANT, 'To Conquer the Veil: Woman as Critique of Liberalism', in *Fanon: A Critical Reader*, pp. 170–8; and more generally, in 'Feminism and Difference: The Perils of Writing as a Woman on Women in Algeria', in MARIANNE HIRSCH and EVELYN FOX KELLER (eds), *Conflicts in Feminism* (New York and London: Routledge, 1990), pp. 326–48. Fanon's position in relation to Pan-Africanism is discussed in SIDNEY J. LEMELLE, 'The Politics of Cultural Existence: Pan-Africanism, Historical Materialism, and Afrocentricity', *Race and Class* 35: 1 (1993): 93–112. The uses of Fanon by a host of contemporary theorists is rehearsed by HENRY LOUIS GATES, Jr, in 'Critical Fanonism', *Critical Inquiry* 17 (1991): 457–70, and treated more critically by CEDRIC ROBINSON in 'The Appropriation of Frantz Fanon', *Race and Class* 35: 1 (1993): 79–91.

Anglophone criticism of Africa and the Caribbean

Many of the Anglophone critics from Africa and the Caribbean combine literary and critical roles in their work. C.L.R. JAMES produced one of the first Anglophone Caribbean novels with his *Minty Alley* (London: Secker & Warburg, 1936) but his autobiographical *Beyond a Boundary* (London: Hutchinson, 1969) provides a useful insight into the role of education in the creation of a critical Caribbean intellectual. His own complex relationship with British imperialism is mirrored by later Caribbean critics such as George Lamming. See LAMMING's *The Pleasures of Exile* (London: Michael Joseph, 1960). Another important voice is that of WILSON HARRIS. His early *Tradition, the Writer and Society* (London: New Beacon Publications, 1967) is a useful prelude to his more mature critical formulations published as *The Womb of Space: The Cross-Cultural Imagination* (Westport/London: Greenwood Press, 1983). A critical evaluation of Harris is provided by A. RIACH and M. WILLIAMS, *The*

Radical Imagination (Liège: University of Liège, 1992). EDWARD
BRATHWAITE's theoretical grapplings with the complexities of Caribbean
societies can be found in his *Contradictory Omens; Cultural Diversity and
Integration in the Caribbean* (Mona: Savacou Publications, 1974) and
*History of the Voice: The Development of Nation Language in Anglophone
Caribbean Poetry* (London: New Beacon Books, 1984).

A great deal of critical work has been generated surrounding
African literature. One starting point is OYEKAN OWOMOYELA, *A History
of Twentieth-Century African Literature* (Lincoln and London: University
of Nebraska Press, 1993). The critical work of CHINUA ACHEBE is best
approached through his *Hopes and Impediments: Selected Essays 1965–1987*
(London: Heinemann, 1988). His fellow Nigerian, WOLE SOYINKA, wrote
the important *Myth, Literature and the African World* (Cambridge:
Cambridge University Press, 1976). SOYINKA's reflections on European
literary theory are contained in 'The Critic and Society: Barthes,
Leftocracy and Other Mythologies', in H.L. Gates (ed.) *Black Literature
and Literary Theory* (London: Methuen, 1984). In the case of Kenyan
NGUGI WA THIONG'O's rejection of colonial education and the use of
English for African literary expression see *Decolonising the Mind: The
Politics of Language in African Literature* (London: James Currey, 1986).
The attacks of the *bolekaja* critics can be found in CHINWEIZU,
ONWUCHEKWA JEMIE and IHECHUKWA MADUBUIKE, *Towards the
Decolonization of African Literature* (Washington DC: Howard University
Press, 1983).

Edward W. Said

SAID's books in the postcolonial field include *Orientalism* (London:
Routledge & Kegan Paul, 1978); *The Question of Palestine* (London:
Routledge & Kegan Paul, 1980); *Covering Islam: How the Media and the
Experts Determine How We See the Rest of the World* (London: Routledge
& Kegan Paul, 1981); *After the Last Sky: Palestinian Lives* (New York:
Pantheon, 1986); and *Culture and Imperialism* (London: Chatto & Windus,
1993) which comprises the more significant essays written in the
preceding decade. Important uncollected essays include 'An Ideology
of Difference' (1985), reprinted in H.L. Gates Jnr (ed.), *'Race', Writing
and Difference* (Chicago: University of Chicago Press, 1986), pp. 38–58
and 'Orientalism Reconsidered' in Francis Barker et al. (eds), *Europe
and Its Others*, vol. 1 (Colchester: University of Essex, 1985), pp. 14–27.

The methodological problems in *Orientalism* are addressed by DENNIS
PORTER's '*Orientalism* and Its Problems' in Francis Barker et al. (eds),
The Politics of Theory (Colchester: University of Essex, 1983), pp. 179–193.
Compare JAMES CLIFFORD, 'On *Orientalism*' in *The Predicament of Culture:*

Twentieth-Century Ethnography, Literature and Art (Cambridge, Mass: Harvard University Press, 1988), pp. 255–76; and ROBERT YOUNG, 'Disorienting Orientalism' in *White Mythologies* (London and New York: Routledge, 1990), pp. 119–40. The problems in applying *Orientalism*'s model of colonial discourse analysis to literary texts is addressed by DENNIS PORTER and by BART MOORE-GILBERT in 'Writing India, Re-orienting Colonial Discourse Analysis' in Bart Moore-Gilbert (ed.), *Writing India: British Representations of India 1757–1990* (Manchester: Manchester University Press, 1996), pp. 1–29. In *Critical Terrains: French and British Orientalisms* (Ithaca and London: Cornell University Press), LISA LOWE (like Dennis Porter) questions whether the European colonizing formations can be homogenized in the way Said assumes in *Orientalism*, and provides important material to show the need for greater attention to issues of gender in colonial discourse analysis. The effects of Said's lack of attention to the issue of gender are also addressed by JANE MILLER in *Seductions: Studies in Reading and Culture* (London: Virago, 1992) and SARA MILLS, *Discourses of Difference: An Analysis of Women's Travel Writing and Colonialism* (London and New York: Routledge, 1993). SARA SULERI's *The Rhetoric of English India* (London and Chicago: Chicago University Press, 1992) questions the assumption of *Orientalism* that the colonizing formation was necessarily secure and confident in its discourses and power (a theme prefigured in Bhabha's early essays). MICHAEL SPRINKER (ed.), *Edward Said: A Critical Reader* (Oxford: Basil Blackwell, 1992) is an important collection of essays covering the range of Said's work. In *Postcolonial Theory: Contexts, Practices, Politics* (London: Verso, 1997), BART MOORE-GILBERT devotes a lengthy chapter to Said's postcolonial work and current debates about it. Said's political affiliations are violently attacked by AIJAZ AHMAD in *In Theory: Classes, Nations, Literatures* (London: Verso, 1992), and from a quite different quarter (though equally violently) by JOHN MACKENZIE in *Orientalism: History, Theory and the Arts* (Manchester: Manchester University Press, 1995).

Gayatri Chakravorty Spivak

SPIVAK is the author of *In Other Worlds: Essays in Cultural Politics* (London and New York: Methuen, 1987), *The Post-Colonial Critic: Interviews, Strategies, Dialogues*, ed. Sarah Harasym (New York and London: Routledge, 1990) and *Outside in the Teaching Machine* (New York and London: Routledge, 1993. Her translations of some stories by Mahasweta Devi are published in *Imaginary Maps* (New York and London: Routledge, 1994). A number of her essays, on a wide variety of topics, have recently been collected in *The Spivak Reader*, ed. Donna

Landry and Gerald MacLean (New York and London: Routledge, 1996). Important uncollected essays include 'Three Women's Texts and a Critique of Imperialism' (1985) in H.L. Gates Jnr (ed.), *'Race', Writing and Difference* (London and Chicago: Chicago University Press, 1986), pp. 262–80; 'The Rani of Sirmur', in Francis Barker et al. (eds), *Europe and Its Others*, vol. 1 (Colchester: University of Essex, 1985), pp. 128–51; 'Imperialism and Sexual Difference' (1986), reprinted in Robert Con Davis and Robert Schleifer (eds), *Contemporary Literary Criticism* (2nd edn; Harlow: Longman, 1989), pp. 517–29; and 'Can the Subaltern Speak?' (1988) reprinted in Patrick Williams and Laura Chrisman (eds), *Colonial Discourse and Post-Colonial Theory: A Reader* (Hemel Hempstead: Harvester/Wheatsheaf, 1993), pp. 66–111.

ROBERT YOUNG's 'Spivak: Decolonization, Deconstruction' in *White Mythologies* (London and New York: Routledge, 1990), pp. 157–213 is perhaps the most enthusiastic account of Spivak's work. In 'Problems with Current Theories of Colonial Discourse', *Oxford Literary Review* 9: 1–2 (1987): 27–58, BENITA PARRY challenges the privileged role ascribed by Spivak to the (female) intellectual in anti-(neo-)colonial struggles. TZVETAN TODOROV's '"Race", Writing and Culture' in H.L. Gates Jnr (ed.), *'Race, Writing and Difference* (London and Chicago: Chicago University Press, 1986), pp. 370–80 provides a critique of Spivak's style, the difficulties of which are defended by IAN SAUNDERS in 'On the Alien: Interpretation After Deconstruction' in Richard Freadman and Lloyd Reinhardt (eds), *On Literary Theory and Philosophy: A Cross-Disciplinary Encounter* (Basingstoke: Macmillan, 1991), pp. 41–58. ROBERT CON DAVIS and DAVID S. GROSS provide a sympathetic analysis of Spivak's conception of political and academic ethics in 'Gayatri Chakravorty Spivak and the *Ethos* of the Subaltern' in J.S. and T.F. Baumlin (eds), *Ethos: New Essays in Rhetorical and Critical Theory* (Dallas: Southern Methodist University Press, 1994), pp. 65–89. For a much more hostile account, see RICHARD FREADMAN and SEAMUS MILLER, 'Deconstruction and Critical Practice: Gayatri Spivak on *The Prelude*' in Freadman and Reinhardt (eds), *On Literary Theory and Philosophy: A Cross-Disciplinary Encounter*, pp. 1–40. For a critique of some problems in Spivak's treatment of radical feminist theory, see SILVIA TANDECIARZ, 'Reading Gayatri Spivak's "French Feminism in an International Frame"': A Problem for Theory', *Genders* 10 (1991): 75–90. In *Postcolonial Theory: Contexts, Practices, Politics* (London: Verso, 1997), BART MOORE-GILBERT devotes a lengthy chapter to Spivak's work and current debates about it.

Homi K. Bhabha

BHABHA is the author of a number of influential essays, the most important of which are collected in *The Location of Culture* (London and

New York: Routledge, 1994). He has also provided an important foreword, entitled 'Remembering Fanon', to Frantz Fanon, *Black Skin, White Masks* (London: Pluto Press, 1986) and edited *Nation and Narration* (London and New York: Routledge, 1990). Uncollected essays which are worth careful consideration include 'The Other Question: Difference, Discrimination and the Discourse of Colonialism' in Francis Barker et al. (eds), *The Politics of Theory* (Colchester: University of Essex, 1983), pp. 148–72; 'Representation and the Colonial Text' in Frank Gloversmith (ed.), *The Theory of Reading* (Brighton: Harvester, 1984), pp. 93–122; and 'The Third Space' in Jonathon Rutherford (ed.), *Identity: Community, Culture, Difference* (London: Lawrence & Wishart, 1990), pp. 207–21. More recent essays include 'Day by Day... with Frantz Fanon' in Alan Read (ed.), *The Fact of Blackness: Frantz Fanon and Visual Representation* (London: ICA, 1996), pp. 186–205; 'Unpacking My Library ... Again' in Iain Chambers and Lidia Curti (eds), *The Post-Colonial Question: Common Skies, Divided Horizons* (London and New York: Routledge, 1996), pp. 199–211; 'Anxious Nations: Nervous States', in Joan Copjec (ed.), *Supposing the Subject* (London: Verso, 1994), pp. 201–17. There is a recent interview with Bhabha by GARY HALL and SIMON WORTHAM, entitled 'Rethinking Authority', in *Angelaki* 2: 2 (1996): 59–64.

The critical response to Bhabha's work has been varied. Perhaps the most positive account comes in ROBERT YOUNG's 'The Ambivalence of Bhabha' in *White Mythologies* (London and New York: Routledge, 1990), pp. 141–56, and there is reference *passim* in YOUNG's more recent *Colonial Desire: Hybridity in Theory, Culture and Race* (London: Routledge, 1995). In 'The Economy of Manichaean Allegory: The Function of Racial Difference in Colonialist Literature', in H.L. Gates Jnr (ed.), *'Race', Writing and Difference* (London and Chicago: Chicago University Press, 1986), pp. 78–106, ABDUL JANMOHAMED accuses Bhabha of a failure to attend sufficiently to the material contexts and realities of colonial oppression and of overlooking critical differences in the psychic economies of colonizer and colonized. Bhabha's failure to attend sufficiently to issues of gender is discussed by ANNE MCCLINTOCK in 'The Return of Female Fetishism and the Fiction of the Phallus', *New Formations* 19 (Spring 1993): 1–22, a theme also of CHRISTINE HOLMLUND, 'Displacing the Limits of Difference: Gender, Race, and Colonialism in Edward Said and Homi Bhabha's Theoretical Models and Marguerite Duras's Experimental Films', *Quarterly Review of Film and Video* 13: 1–3 (1991): 1–22. In 'Problems with Current Theories of Colonial Discourse', *Oxford Literary Review* 9: 1–2 (1987): 27–58, BENITA PARRY challenges Bhabha's focus on discourse as the privileged mode of resistance to (neo-)colonialism, a theme she takes up again in 'Signs of Our Times: Discussion of Homi Bhabha's *Location of Culture*', *Third Text* 28–9 (1994): 1–24. Compare ANIA LOOMBA, 'Overworlding the "Third

World"' (1991), reprinted in Patrick Williams and Laura Chrisman (eds), *Colonial Discourse and Post-Colonial Theory: A Reader* (Hemel Hempstead: Harvester/Wheatsheaf, 1993), pp. 305–23. Bhabha's political vision is violently attacked by AIJAZ AHMAD in *In Theory: Classes, Nations, Literatures* (London: Verso, 1992) and ARIF DIRLIK's 'The Post-Colonial Aura: Third World Criticism in the Age of Global Criticism', *Critical Inquiry* 20 (Winter 1994): 329–56. NEIL LAZARUS has sharp things to say about Bhabha's (mis)reading of Fanon in 'Disavowing Decolonization: Fanon, Nationalism and the Problematic of Representation in Current Theories of Colonial Discourse', *Research in African Literatures*, 24: 2 (1993): 69–98. Compare CEDRIC ROBINSON, 'The Appropriation of Frantz Fanon', *Race and Class* 35: 1 (1993): 79–91. In *Postcolonial Theory: Contexts, Practices, Politics* (London: Verso, 1997), BART MOORE-GILBERT devotes a lengthy chapter to Bhabha's work and current debates about it.

Commonwealth literary studies

The first substantial claim for Commonwealth literary studies as a distinct sub-field is A.L. MCCLEOD's *The Commonwealth Pen: An Introduction to the Literature of the British Commonwealth* (Ithaca: Cornell University Press, 1961). The sub-field developed rapidly in the 1960s; in Britain, for example, courses in Commonwealth literature became available at Leeds and Kent Universities. JOHN PRESS's *Commonwealth Literature: Unity and Diversity in a Common Culture* (London: Heinemann, 1965), the proceedings of a conference at Leeds University, largely established the critical paradigm for the sub-field for the next decade. Its ethos was markedly 'Britocentric', the assumption being that the new literatures of the Commonwealth were tributaries to the great stream of English literature and should be judged by the same (allegedly 'universal') criteria. Later texts such as K.L. GOODWIN's *National Identity* (London: Heinemann, 1970), WILLIAM WALSH's *A Manifold Voice: Studies in Commonwealth Literature* (London: Chatto & Windus, 1970) and *Commonwealth Literature* (Oxford: Oxford University Press, 1973), and WILLIAM NEW's *Among Worlds* (1975) consolidated the field within largely the same terms. By the mid 1970s, however, there was increasing dissent from this paradigm. The focus on Britain as the standard by which to judge the new literatures was increasingly deemed to reinscribe its traditional cultural authority in the neocolonial era. Nationalist critics also objected that the focus on Britain inhibited the development of local national traditions – creative and critical – and inhibited other useful lines of comparison, for example with American literature, or other literatures which were not Anglophone. Many of these objections are registered in HENA MAES-JELINEK (ed.)

Commonwealth Literature and the Modern World (Brussels: Didier, 1975) and DIETER RIEMENSCHNEIDER's *History and Historiography of Commonwealth Literature* (Tübingen: Gunter Narr Verlag, 1983), which also demostrates how Commonwealth literary studies was becoming markedly more theoretical in its formulations. In this volume there is a symptomatic sliding between the terms 'Commonwealth' and 'postcolonial', a transition which is discussed in much more detail in ANNA RUTHERFORD (ed.), *From Commonwealth to Postcolonial* (Mundelstrup: Dangaroo, 1992) – to which Said contributes an important essay. The continuity between Commonwealth literary studies and postcolonial criticism tends to be stressed by critics based in the former 'white Dominions'. BILL ASHCROFT, GARETH GRIFFITHS and HELEN TIFFIN have provided both a foundational text for postcolonial ciriticism in general and provided their own version of the link with Commonwealth literary studies. See notably the section 'The Settler Colonies' in their *The Empire Writes Back* (London: Routledge, 1989). These connections are further developed by DIANA BRYDON and HELEN TIFFIN in *Decolonising Fictions* (Mundelstrup: Dangaroo, 1993).

Other critics have been more sceptical, seeing a distinct break between Commonwealth literary studies and postcolonial criticism. See, for example, HOMI BHABHA's 'Representation and the Colonial Text' in Frank Gloversmith (ed.), *The Theory of Reading* (Brighton: Harvester, 1984) and AIJAZ AHMAD's *In Theory: Classes, Nations, Literatures* (London: Verso, 1992). Compare the hostile comments of SALMAN RUSHDIE's 'Commonwealth Literature Does Not Exist' in *Imaginary Homelands: Essays and Criticisms 1981–1991* (Harmondsworth: Granta, 1992).

Women's and feminist postcolonial criticism

A good starting point is the debate prompted by MICHÈLE BARRETT and MARY MCINTOSH in 'Ethnocentrism and Socialist-Feminist Theory', *Feminist Review* 20 (1985): 23–47, which initially drew four distinct reactions from HAMIDI KAZI, SUE LEES, HEIDI SAFIA MIRZA, and CAROLINE RAMAZANOGLU, grouped under the heading 'Feedback: Feminism and Racism – Responses to Michèle Barrett and Mary McIntosh', *Feminist Review* 22 (1986): 83–105. These critiques were supplemeted and extended by KUM-KUM BHAVNANI and MARGARET COULSON in 'Transforming Socialist-Feminism: The Challenge of Racism', *Feminist Review* 23, (1986): 81–92. Two important interventions come from CHANDRA TALPADE MOHANTY, 'Under Western Eyes: Feminist Scholarship and Colonial Discourses', *Feminist Review* 30 (1988): 61–88, and GAYATRI SPIVAK's 'French Feminism in an International Frame', *Yale French Studies* 62 (1981): 154–84. Recent book-length studies include

LAURA E. DONALDSON, *Decolonizing Feminisms: Race, Gender, and Empire-Building* (Chapel Hill: University of North Carolina Press, 1992); JULIA V. EMBERLEY, *Thresholds of Difference: Feminist Critique, Native Women's Writings, Postcolonial Theory* (Toronto: University of Toronto Press, 1993); KIRSTEN HOLST PETERSEN and ANNA RUTHERFORD (eds), *A Double Colonization: Colonial and Post-colonial Women's Writing* (Mundelstrup: Dangaroo Press, 1986); and RAJESWARI SUNDER RAJAN, *Real and Imagined Women: Gender, Culture and Post-colonialism* (London: Routledge, 1993).

BELL HOOKS has relied for some of her work on radical printing presses, though the publication of two volumes of essays by Routledge in 1994 attests to her growing importance as a cultural critic – *Outlaw Culture: Resisting Representations* (London: Routledge, 1994); *Teaching to Transgress: Education as the Practice of Freedom* (London: Routledge, 1994). Her most important work includes *Ain't I a Woman: Black Women and Feminism* (London: Pluto Press, 1982); *Black Looks: Race and Representation* (London: Turnaround, 1992); *Feminist Theory from Margin to Center* (Boston, Mass.: South End Press, 1984); *Talking Back: Thinking Feminist, Thinking Black* (Boston, Mass.: South End Press, 1989); *Yearning: Race, Gender, and Cultural Politics* (Boston, Mass.: South End Press, 1991). HOOKS is well-known for her dialogues with contemporary thinkers as well as for her own work, and a crucial volume in this respect is the collection co-authored with CORNEL WEST, *Breaking Bread: Insurgent Black Intellectual Life* (Boston, Mass.: South End Press, 1991). Criticism on hooks is sparse, but her work impinges on a whole series of issues central to postcolonial theory, specifically around the complex interaction of race, class and gender. Many of hooks's essays have a strong autobiographical component, and the problem of personal history as both politically enabling and theoretically fraught is raised by SARA SULERI in 'Woman Skin Deep: Feminism and the Postcolonial Condition', in Patrick Williams and Laura Chrisman (eds), *Colonial Discourse and Post-Colonial Theory: A Reader* (Hemel Hempstead: Harvester/Wheatsheaf, 1994), pp. 244–56. HOOKS has been accused of reinforcing the hierarchies that she seeks to expose, and Suleri's essay rehearses that criticism, a difficulty addressed more generally in MARY JOHN, 'Postcolonial Feminists in the Western Intellectual Field: Anthropologists *and* Native Informants', *Inscriptions* 5 (1989): 49–74. Also relevant here is KETU KATRAK's 'Decolonizing Culture: Toward a Theory for Postcolonial Women's Texts', *Modern Fiction Studies* 35: 1 (1989): 157–79. An important exchange, in which the refusal to resolve this 'contradiction' between personal and professional discourse is upheld, is that between HOOKS and MARY CHILDERS, 'A Conversation about Race and Class', in Marianne Hirsch and Evelyn Fox Keller (eds), *Conflicts in Feminism* (London and New York: Routledge, 1990), pp. 60–81. An invaluable document in this debate is JEAN FRANCO's

'Beyond Ethnocentrism: Gender, Power and the Third World Intelligentsia', in Cary Nelson and Lawrence Grossberg (eds), *Marxism and the Interpretation of Culture* (Basingstoke: Macmillan, 1988), pp. 503–15. For a thoughtful engagement with hooks's work, see CLIFFORD L. STAPLES, 'White Male Ways of Knowing', *Postmodern Culture* 2: 2 (1992): 1–33.

Minority discourse and internal colonialism

Two key texts that inform the concepts of 'minority' in the work of JANMOHAMED and LLOYD are GILLES DELEUZE and FELIX GUATTARI, *Kafka: Toward a Minor Literature*, trans. Dana Polan (Minneapolis: University of Minnesota Press, 1986), and LOUIS A. RENZA, *'A White Heron' and the Question of Minor Literature* (Madison: University of Wisconsin Press, 1984). The concept of 'internal colonialism', first elaborated by LENIN in *The Development of Capitalism in Russia*, is expounded most famously in MICHAEL HECHTER, *Internal Colonialism: The Celtic Fringe in British National Development, 1536–1966* (London: Routledge, 1975). The work of JANMOHAMED and LLOYD constitutes a convergence of two approaches to the postcolonial subject. Each had authored individually a number of important texts on Africa and Ireland before they collaborated on *The Nature and Context of Minority Discourse* (Oxford and New York: Oxford University Press, 1990). JANMOHAMED is the author of *Manichean Aesthetics: The Politics of Literature in Colonial Africa* (Amherst, Mass.: University of Massachusetts Press, 1983). He developed this notion of a Manichean division between colonizer and colonized in 'The Economy of Manichean Allegory: The Function of Racial Difference in Colonialist Literature', in Henry Louis Gates, Jr (ed.), *'Race', Writing, and Difference* (Chicago: Chicago University Press, 1986), pp. 79–106. DAVID LLOYD's study of the nineteenth-century Celtic Revival in *Nationalism and Minor Literature: James Clarence Mangan and the Emergence of Irish Cultural Nationalism* (Berkeley: University of California Press, 1987), was followed by a much more wide-reaching analysis of modern Irish identity, and a more explicit engagement with postcolonial theory, in *Anomalous States: Irish Writing and the Postcolonial Moment* (Dublin: Lilliput Press, 1993). The shift was heralded in 'Writing in the Shit: Beckett, Nationalism, and the Colonial Subject', *Modern Fiction Studies* 35: 1 (1989; special issue on *Narratives of Colonial Resistance*, guest editor Timothy Brennan): 71–86. LLOYD and JANMOHAMED, in their own contributions to the *Minority Discourse* collection, pursue their respective and related interests. Both are concerned with exemplary 'minority' figures, European and Afro-American. JANMOHAMED explores the tensions between education and

Further Reading

experience in 'Negating the Negation as a Form of Affirmation in Minority Discourse: The Construction of Richard Wright as Subject', pp. 102–23, while LLOYD investigates the anti-humanism of Jean Genet in 'Genet's Genealogy: European Minorities and the Ends of the Canon', pp. 369–93. Their subsequent work reflects the fusion of their critique of the canonial and their concern with identity construction and the role of the intellectual. Lloyd privileges difference over identity in 'Race under Representation', in Robert Young (ed.), Neocolonialism, Oxford Literary Review 13 (1991): 62–94, and provides a critical appraisal of the notion of 'minority discourse' in 'Ethnic Cultures, Minority Discourse and the State', in Francis Barker, Peter Hulme and Margaret Iversen (eds), Colonial Discourse/Postcolonial Theory (Manchester: Manchester University Press, 1994), pp. 220–38. JANMOHAMED distinguishes between various types of intellectual in 'Worldliness-Without-World, Homelessness-as-Home: Toward a Definition of the Specular Border Intellectual', in Jessica Munns and Gita Rajan (eds), A Cultural Studies Reader: History, Theory, Practice (London and New York: Longman, 1995), pp. 442–62. Three essays in The Nature and Context of Minority Discourse engage with the term in a critical way. ARIF DIRLIK, 'Culturalism as Hegemonic Ideology and Liberating Practice' (pp. 394–431); SYLVIA WYNTER, 'On Disenchanting Discourse: "Minority" Literary Criticism and Beyond' (pp. 432–69); and HENRY LOUIS GATES, JR, 'Authority, (White) Power, and the (Black) Critic: It's All Greek to Me' (pp. 72–101). Arguably the sharpest critique is that of CORNEL WEST, focusing upon the favouring of literature as a cultural form, in 'Minority Discourse and the Pitfalls of Canon Formation', in Munns and Rajan (eds), A Cultural Studies Reader, pp. 413–19.

Towering over the vast area of African–American criticism is the figure of W.E.B. Du Bois. He produced a great diversity of work, but a good introduction to this variety is found in DAVID LAVERING LEWIS (ed.), W.E.B. Du Bois: A Reader (New York: Henry Holt and Co., 1995). Another book which Du Bois himself described as 'epoch-making' in relation to the African–American presence is MELVILLE HERSKOVITS The Myth of the Negro Past (1941; Boston: Beacon Press, 1990). More literary studies pinpoint the Harlem Renaissance. For a general introduction, see NATHAN HUGGINS Harlem Renaissance (Oxford: Oxford University Press). More challenging explorations of the Harlem scene are to be found in HOUSTON A. BAKER JNR, Modernism and the Harlem Renaissance (Chicago: University of Chicago Press, 1987) and JAMES DE JONGH Vicious Modernism: Black Harlem and the Literary Imagination (Cambridge: Cambridge University Press). Slave narratives from an earlier epoch are analysed and introduced in C. DAVIS and H.L. GATES (eds) The Slave's Narrative (Oxford: Oxford University Press, 1985). Some of the insights Gates develops here are expanded in 'The Trope of the Talking Book', in his monograph *The Signifying Monkey: A Theory of African–American Literary Criticism* (New York: Oxford University Press, 1988). This latter work indicates a certain tendency on Gates's part to signify on his own work as this book contains the most developed version of the piece 'The Blackness of Blackness' which is taken from the earlier collection which Gates edited, *Black Literature and Literary Theory* (London: Methuen, 1984). This work on signifying also appears as the final chapter in GATES's *Figures in Black: Words, Signs and the 'Racial' Self* (Oxford: Oxford University Press, 1989). This book also contains an extended discussion of literary theory and the black tradition. It is, however, inevitable that there should be some degree of overlap in Gates's work as his general project has remained constant and his efforts have been geared to elaborating its basic themes. Stepping back from more strictly theoretical concerns he has written the autobiographical *Colored People* (London: Viking, 1994). An intriguing set of questions are asked of the African–American literary tradition by PAUL GILROY, in his *The Black Atlantic: Modernity and Double Consciousness* (London: Verso, 1993).

Dissenting voices

Among the many critiques of postcolonial criticism from within approximately the same discursive field are the following; VIJAY MISHRA and BOB HODGE, 'What is Post(-)Colonialism?', *Textual Practice* 5: 3 (1991): 399–414, which questions the political positionality and meanings of the term; compare AIJAZ AHMAD, 'The Politics of Literary Postcoloniality', *Race and Class* 36: 3 (1995): 1–20 and *In Theory: Classes, Nations, Literatures* (London: Verso, 1992). Both see postcolonial theory in particular as essentially right-wing in its orientations, as does ARIF DIRLIK's 'The Post-Colonial Aura: Third World Criticism in the Age of Global Criticism', *Critical Inquiry* 20 (Winter 1994): 329–56. More measured analyses of such issues, including important arguments about periodization, are provided in ELLA SHOHAT's 'Notes on the "Post-Colonial"', *Social Text* 31/32 (Spring 1992): 99–113 and ANNE McCLINTOCK, 'The Angel of Progress: Pitfalls of the Term "Post-Colonialism"', loc. cit.: 1–15. Periodization is a central issue in DEEPIKA BAHRI, 'Once More With Feeling: What is Postcolonialism?', *Ariel* 26: 1 (January 1995): 51–82, as is the issue of the appropriate grographical remit of the term 'postcolonial'. The latter issue is also discussed in the Introduction to Patrick Williams and Laura Chrisman (eds), *Colonial Discourse and Post-Colonial Theory: A Reader* (Hemel Hempstead: Harvester/Wheatsheaf, 1993), pp. 1–20 and by PETER HULME in 'Including America', *Ariel* 26: 1 (January 1995): 117–23. STUART HALL usefully reviews many of these critiques in 'When was the "Post-

Colonial"? Thinking at the Limit' in Iain Chambers and Lidia Curti (eds), *The Post-Colonial Question: Common Skies, Divided Horizons* (London and New York: Routledge, 1996), pp. 242–60. STEPHEN SLEMON and HELEN TIFFIN (eds), *After Europe: Critical Theory and Post-Colonial Writing* (Mundelstrup: Dangaroo, 1989) questions the Eurocentrism of much of the theory on which figures like Said, Spivak and Bhabha draw. In 'No Direction Home? – Futures for Post-Colonial Studies', PATRICK WILLIAMS assesses the current prospects for postcolonial criticism; see *Wasafiri* 23 (Spring 1996): 3–6.

From outside the discursive field come a number of important critiques of postcolonial theory in particular. In 'Empires of the Senseless', *Observer* (7 February 1993): 55, PETER CONRAD provides a withering account of its politics from the opposite end of the political spectrum to Ahmad and Dirlik. In 'Marginal Returns: The Trouble with Post-Colonial Theory', *Lingua Franca* (September/October 1995): 30–7, RUSSELL JACOBY mounts a similar attack, which also questions the interdisciplinary competence of postcolonial theorists. Perhaps the most substantial such attack in both these respects (by volume at least) is by another historian, JOHN MACKENZIE, in *Orientalism: History, Theory and the Arts* (Manchester: Manchester University Press, 1995). Like Jacoby, MacKenzie also decries the supposedly obfuscatory style of postcolonial theory.

Index

292